A DAILY WALK THROUGH THE PSALMS

A DAILY WALK THROUGH THE PSALMS

Psalm by Psalm for 365 Days

Including Over 250 Teaching
and Preaching Outlines

by

FRANK R. SHIVERS

Unless otherwise noted, Scripture quotations are from
The Holy Bible *King James Version*

Library of Congress Cataloging-in-Publication Data

Shivers, Frank R., 1949-
A Daily Walk Through the Psalms / Frank Shivers

ISBN 978-1-878127-57-0

Library of Congress Control Number:
2025901554

Cover design by
Tim King

For Information:
Frank Shivers Evangelistic Association
2005 Congress Road
Hopkins, South Carolina 29061
www.frankshivers.com

Because

I have found Jesus to be everything He promised to be: my Savior, Friend, Guide, Comforter, Helper, Teacher, Shepherd, Sustainer, and much, much more,

I am excited to present this book to

_____

Date

_____

From

_____

with the prayer

that the reading of its pages will enhance your walk with Jesus and be used by Him to minister to the needs and cares of your life.

To

Rev. V. M. Groover

Martin helped launch my radio broadcast *(The Nugget of Truth)* in the mid-1970s, served on our Board of Directors, taught children and youth at our Bible summer camps, utilized my ministry in revivals in his pastorates, and has been a loyal and supportive friend for fifty years.

Thank you, Martin, for it all. It's been an incredible journey together.

"In these busy days, it would be greatly to the spiritual profit of Christians if they were more familiar with the Book of Psalms, in which they would find a complete armory for life's battles and a perfect supply for life's needs. Here, we have both delight and usefulness, consolation and instruction. For every condition, there is a Psalm that is suitable and elevating."[1]

C. H. Spurgeon.

"There is no one book of Scripture that is more helpful to the devotions of the saints than this, and it has been so in all ages of the church ever since it was written."[2]

Matthew Henry.

"Whatever our mood may be, there is sure to be a psalm which reflects it—whether triumph or defeat, excitement or depression, joy or sorrow, praise or penitence, wonder or anger."[3]

John Stott.

Foreword

The Psalms stand as one of the richest treasures in all of Scripture. Across centuries and cultures, biblical psalms have given voice to the deepest cries of the human heart and lifted countless souls with songs of worship, lament, and praise. Whether in seasons of joy or sorrow, the psalms remind us that God is present, faithful, and near to His people. They have served generation after generation with hope, comfort, and truth that never fades.

In *A Daily Walk Through the Psalms*, Frank Shivers has written a devotional that will bless all believers in their daily walk with the Lord. With scriptural warmth and biblical clarity, Frank invites us to journey through these sacred songs, providing deep insights and comforting truths along the way. This devotional will serve as a lamp to your feet and a light to your path, pointing you back to the God who speaks through His Word.

I can say personally that I have witnessed Frank live out the very truths he shares in these pages. As a young child, I had the privilege of attending his summer camps and hearing him preach from the Psalms. Those lessons in a packed gym at Camp Longridge still reverberate in my soul today. His life and ministry reflect the joy, wisdom, and dependence on God that the psalms call us to embrace.

Today, I have the privilege of being his pastor at Shandon Baptist Church and am honored to commend this work to you. You will be blessed as he brings scriptural insights to your home and heart each day.

Dr. Daniel C. Dickard
Senior Pastor, Shandon Baptist Church
Columbia, SC

Psalm 1:1

The Blessed Man's Separation

"Blessed is the man that walketh not in the counsel of the ungodly, nor standeth in the way of sinners, nor sitteth in the seat of the scornful" (Psalm 1:1).

"Blessed" refers to the heightened happiness and deeply embedded contentment God bestows to those who love Him and live righteously. The psalmist, probably David or Ezra, describes the "Blessed" man as one who avoids associations with the ungodly in three ways. He dismisses their worldly counsel, refuses their corrupt conduct, and avoids their contemptible teaching and mockery of God. Spurgeon says, "His footsteps are ordered by the Word of God, and not by the cunning and wicked devices of carnal men."

Paul echoes the same principle: "Be ye not unequally yoked together with unbelievers: for what fellowship hath righteousness with unrighteousness? and what communion hath light with darkness?" (2 Corinthians 6:14). A yoke is a wooden bar that couples two oxen to each other and a pulling beam so they can plow or pull a wagon. An "unequally yoked" team consisted of two different sorts of oxen (e.g., a strong ox joined to a weak ox). Instead of completing the task, unequally yoked oxen would go around in circles. One can but imagine the frustration that arose between such a team.

The biblical truth is clear. Christians are not to be united (yoked) with unbelievers, for the two share different natures, masters, values, and purposes that would cause inevitable conflict (John 17:16). Solomon says, "Enter not into the path of the wicked, and go not in the way of evil men" (Proverbs 4:14). Simeon advises, "Let not then the rank or talents of men, and still less their gaiety and dissipation, attract your regards; but let the piety of their hearts and the holiness of their lives be their highest recommendation to your friendship."[4]

"We are to have no compromising connection with anything in the world which is alien to God."[5]—J. Denney.

~January 2~

Psalm 1:2
The Blessed Man's Meditation

"But his delight is in the law of the LORD; and in His law doth he meditate day and night" (Psalm 1:2).

What are some benefits of scriptural meditation?

Meditation practice. "In His law doth he meditate day and night." Joshua commanded it (Joshua 1:8), David engaged it (Psalm 119:27; 145:5), Paul encouraged it (Colossians 3:16), and Solomon taught it (Proverbs 2:6; 4:20–23). Scriptural meditation is the contemplation (rumination) and internalization (absorption) of the Word of God[6] and is the duty ("day and night") of the "Blessed" and righteous man.

Matthew Henry wrote, "To meditate in God's Word is to discourse with ourselves concerning the great things contained in it, with a close application of mind, a fixedness of thought, till we are suitably affected with those things and experience the savor and power of them in our hearts."[7] John Owen says, "Meditate on the Word in the Word; that is, in the reading of it, consider the sense in the particular passages, looking to God for help, guidance, and direction."

Meditation profit. Meditation fastens and imprints a scriptural truth to the mind that feeds and fuels the soul. Meditation expunges fear and worry, instilling God's incredible calm and peace. Kempis discovered this, saying, "I have no rest, but in a nook, with *the* Book." Meditation enlightens and clarifies the mind (removes the fogginess, granting understanding); inflames and inspires the soul; instructs and guides the heart (Psalm 39:3); provides consolation, comfort, and confident hope in times of distress and grief; and promotes prayer and praise to God. Meditation increases under-standing, knowledge, holiness, and inner strength. Plumer asserts, "Without meditation, grace never thrives, prayer is languid, praise dull, and religious duties unprofitable."[8]

Meditation pleasure. "But his delight." It's a delightful duty without dread or drudgery when the Scripture and its Author are wholly embraced, loved, and treasured (Psalm 119:103). "Heaven at the end of duty causeth delight in the way of duty."[9] "He is not under the law as a curse and condemnation," wrote Spurgeon, "but he is in it, and he delights to be in it as his rule of life; he delights, moreover, to meditate in it, to read it by day, and think upon it by night."[10]

"Without meditation, the truths of God will not stay with us.... Serious meditation is like the engraving of letters in gold or marble which endures."[11]—Thomas Watson.

~January 3~

Psalm 1:3
The Blessed Man's Stability

"And he shall be like a tree planted by the rivers of water" (Psalm 1:3).

The "Blessed" man is separated from the world, saturated in God's Word, and steadfast in his walk. To be planted depicts the permanency of connection.[12] The stability and security of a transplanted tree depend upon how and where it is planted and by whom. The person who puts faith in Christ for salvation is supernaturally planted in the most favorable location, ensuring he will have the necessary "rivers of water" to bear fruit and never be uprooted. Note the plural of "rivers." If one river should fail, there is another to which he may look for nourishment and stability. Spurgeon says, "The rivers of pardon and the rivers of grace, the rivers of the promise and the rivers of the communion with Christ, are never-failing sources of supply."[13]

No one is born a Christian or grows into one through religious activity. He must be planted by the Holy Spirit's work of regeneration into the family of God (John 3:3). Jesus warns that every tree not planted by God's own hand will be rooted up and cast into outer darkness (Matthew 15:13). The soul "rooted" in Christ (Colossians

3

2:7), however, is immovable even amidst the violent storms that assail (Jeremiah 17:8). That soul may say confidently with David, "I have set the LORD always before me: because he is at my right hand, I shall not be moved" (Psalm 16:8). Where God plants a man (into His wonderful family by grace), He keeps him (Jude 24). "I shall not be, I shall not be moved; I shall not be, I shall not be moved. Like a tree planted by the water, I shall not be moved."

"Our salvation is fastened with God's own hand, and with Christ's own strength, to the strong stake of God's unchangeable nature."— Samuel Rutherford.

~January 4~

Psalm 1:3
The Blessed Man's Fruit

"He...bringeth forth his fruit in his season; his leaf also shall not wither; and whatsoever he doeth shall prosper" (Psalm 1:3).

1. The What of Fruit. "Godliness...is great gain" (1 Timothy 6:6). Fruit and success await a holy and righteous life lived for God (Joshua 1:8).

2. The Kind of Fruit. It is both internal and external.

a. Internally, the believer manifests the fruit of the Spirit, which "is love, joy, peace, forbearance, kindness, goodness, faithfulness, gentleness and self-control" (Galatians 5:22–23 NIV). Additionally, by the power of the Holy Spirit, he crucifies the corrupt flesh to walk in purity and the holiness of life (Galatians 5:24).

b. Externally, the believer bears fruit by fulfilling God's plan for his life (Ephesians 2:10), which includes living a life that glorifies and magnifies God, proclaiming the Gospel to the unsaved to win them to the faith, and enabling the maturity of other believers.

3. The How of Fruit. To be infused with supernatural sap or power to live victoriously, healthily, and productively, the branch (the believer) must abide in the Vine (Christ). It must continuously

draw from the life-empowering sap of the Vine. This is affirmed in Jesus' words: "I am the vine, ye are the branches: He that abideth in me, and I in him, the same bringeth forth much fruit" (John 15:5). MacArthur asserts, "The abiding believer is the only legitimate believer."[14] "No fruit in the life is a proof of no grace in the heart."[15] To bear much fruit, abide or stay put in sweet communion with Christ and feed upon His Word.

4. The When of Fruit. He bears fruit "in his season" (in God's timing). What a promise to claim! Not seeing fruit from your labor yet? It's not "fruit season." Harvest time is coming; you will reap if you faint not (Galatians 6:9). *"His leaf also shall not wither."* A holy man's works and profession will never decay, even in death. "He being dead yet speaketh" (Hebrews 11:4). Spurgeon says, "His faintest word will be everlasting; his little deeds of love will be remembered. Not only will his fruit be preserved, but his leaf also. He will neither lose his beauty nor his fruitfulness."

"The godly are characterized by the success the Lord sends their way."[16]—Willem VanGemeren.

~January 5~

Psalm 1:6

God Knows His Own

"For the LORD knoweth the way of the righteous" (Psalm 1:6).

Paul says, "The Lord knows those who are His" (2 Timothy 2:19 NKJV). Jesus says, "I…know my sheep" (John 10:14). Despite the great mixture in the visible church of wheat and tares, God KNOWS His own and will forever care for and protect them, and when the time comes, take them "Home" safely.

Knowing He knows His own is of priceless worth, benefit, and comfort. But how can a person know if he is in that number?

1. He can know by the promise of Christ to him. "These things have I written unto you that believe on the name of the Son of God;

that ye may know that ye have eternal life" (1 John 5:13). The bottom line about salvation is what God states in Scripture. A man accepts the witness regarding prescription medication and the U.S. Treasury regarding the value of a dollar (a dollar is worth a dollar). John emphatically declares that "the witness [word] of God is greater [more sure, certain, reliable]" than that of man (1 John 5:9).

2. He can know by the presence of the Holy Spirit in him. The Holy Spirit resides in the Christian's heart and bears witness to his transformation by grace (Romans 8:16).

3. He can know by the proof of a changed life through him. Conversion leads to transformation in life (2 Corinthians 5:17). An old African-American saying undergirds this truth: "The day I got saved, my feet got a brand-new walk, and my speech got a brand-new talk." A difference occurs at salvation that continues progressing throughout the Christian's life.

"At present, *wheat and chaff* lie in one floor; *wheat and tares* grow in one field; *good and bad* fishes are comprehended in one net; *good and bad* men are contained in the visible church. Let us wait with patience for God's time of separation."[17]—George Horne.

~January 6~

Psalm 2:1

Why Do the Heathen Rage?

"Why do the heathen rage, and the people devise a vain thing?" (Psalm 2:1 KJ21).

David, as the newly enthroned king, notwithstanding opposition, prepares to battle neighboring heathen nations.[18] The psalm, however, is Messianic, dealing with one greater than David, the Lord Jesus Christ, and the hostile, deep-seated opposition to His redemptive mission (Psalm 2:2; John 1:11; John 5:18).

Why do the heathen rage against Christ? Carnal men see nothing in Christ that they deem worthy of embracing and yielding

6

their allegiance to (Isaiah 53:2). Instead, they see five causes for hatred, antagonism, and rejection of Him.

1. He is the light that exposes their darkness (John 1:9).

2. He is the salt that irritates and disrupts their evil works. "Light is come into the world, and men loved darkness rather than light, because their deeds were evil" (John 3:19). For this reason, man sought to extinguish the light at Calvary, and yet does.

3. He is the Judge who condemns them to temporal and eternal punishment (John 3:18).

4. He is the authoritative ruler over them (Job 24:13). God says, "They will reverence my Son" (Mark 12:6). They reply, "We will not have this man to reign over us" (Luke 19:14).

5. He proclaims salvation is available only on His terms, not theirs (John 10:9; 14:6).

Defying Christ is a "vain thing" (a foolish and futile undertaking). The "Song" that began in Bethlehem's manger 2,000 years ago was heard loudly during Jesus' thirty-three years on earth despite man's resistance and antagonism. It shook the world at His crucifixion, resurrection, and ascension. Despite attempts to silence it, the "Song" lives on. "His truth is marching on. Glory, glory, hallelujah!"

Why do the heathen rage against Christians? Identity with Christ and His cause brings scorn and hatred. Jesus forewarned His disciples: "If the world hates you, you know that it hated Me before it hated you....'A servant is not greater than his master.' If they persecuted Me, they will also persecute you" (John 15:18; 20 NKJV). Spurgeon said, "Dream not that worldlings will admire you, or that the more holy and the more Christ-like you are, the more peaceably people will act towards you. They prized not the polished gem; how should they value the jewel in the rough?"[19]

Following the 'narrow way' (Matthew 7:13–14) taught by Christ and building one's house upon the "Rock" (Matthew 7:24–25) precipitates persecution.[20] However, Jesus promises that when the rains, winds, and floods (in part symbolic of persecution) beat against the "house," it will not crumble or collapse (Matthew 7:24–25).[21]

"Doctrines will be readily believed if they involve in them no precepts, and the church may be tolerated by the world if she will only give up her discipline."[22] – George Horne.

~January 7~

Psalm 2:2
Derision For God

"The kings of the earth form a united front; the rulers collaborate against the LORD and his anointed king" (Psalm 2:2 NET).

God's response is three-fold to the kings and their rulers who rage and revile against Him.

He laughs at them. "He that sitteth in the heavens shall laugh." God's laughter signified that the people's plan to revile Him was ludicrous. One would succeed more in harnessing the wind or controlling the ocean's tide than altering and hampering God's standards and purposes. Wiersbe says, "God is greater than man and need not fear the proud attacks of puny kings."[23]

He speaks to them. "Then shall he speak unto them in his wrath and vex them in his sore displeasure." Man's effort to defy and scoff at God is met with His hot displeasure and holy vengeance. Matthew Henry asserts, "He speaks, and it is done; He speaks in wrath, and sinners are undone. As a word made us so that a word can unmake us again."[24]

He wins over them. "Yet have I set my king upon my holy hill of Zion." They are defeated. All their counsel is for naught. Despite the best efforts of kings like Herod and Agrippa, as well as their provincial rulers, the Jewish Sanhedrin, and the Pharisees, God accomplished what they sought to prevent. Jesus was established as King of Kings and Lord of Lords of all the earth. Hallelujah!

"The moon walks in brightness, though the dogs bark at it."[25]— Matthew Henry.

Psalm 3:2

When All Looks Hopeless
Part 1

"Many there be that say of my soul, "There is no help for him in God" (Psalm 3:2 KJ21).

David's Peril. In confederacy with Ahithophel, Absalom pursued David, his father, with over 12,000 soldiers (2 Samuel 17:1). In contrast, David's army numbered only 600 soldiers in addition to his bodyguard (2 Samuel 15:18). The odds of victory for David were against him. The people mocked him, saying that God had forsaken him. But God gave him the victory.

Note. Expect opposition when employed as God's emissary. It goes with the territory. To help withstand the antagonism, God provides 'companions in tribulation' (Revelation 1:9).

David's Prayer. "'With my voice'—while their voice defies God, my voice shall address God."[26] In adversity, call upon the Lord for rescue. Spurgeon says, "We need not fear a frowning world while we rejoice in a prayer-hearing God."[27] Matthew Henry says of God, "He has the power to save [help], be the danger ever so great; it is His prerogative to save when all other helps and succors fail; it is His pleasure; it is His promise to those that are His."[28]

Note the power of David's prayer. He prayed the battle cry of Israel, "Arise, O LORD, save me"; and God caused the counsel of Ahithophel to Absalom to be replaced with that of Hushai, a secret ally of David, ensuring David's triumph. To pray is to give God a foothold on the battlefield. Plumer wrote, "Perils and frights should drive us to God, not from Him."[29]

"Without the Lord, there is no solution or success; that is, none worth having."[30]—Derek Kidner.

~January 9~

Psalm 3:3
When All Looks Hopeless
Part 2

"But thou, O LORD, art a shield for me; my glory and the lifter up of my head" (Psalm 3:3).

David's Preservation. David's confidence in deliverance from the enemy is cited in three acclamations about God before the battle.

1. A shield to me. A divine canopy of protection encircled David. "What a shield," wrote Spurgeon, "God is for his people! He wards off the fiery darts of Satan from beneath and the storms of trials from above, while at the same instant, he speaks peace to the tempest within."[31]

2. My glory. Even in exile, hiding in the wilderness and caves, God was David's glory, for He was the Champion and Guardian of the royal dignity conferred upon him.[32] David was confident that God would restore him to the throne. "O for grace to see our future glory amid present shame!"[33]

3. The lifter of my head. David confidently believed God would restore him to the throne. God lifts the drooping head to cheer. He rescues the downtrodden and disheartened from the Valley of Baca with renewed hope and peace. Says Matthew Henry, "If, in the worst of times, God's people can lift up their heads with joy, knowing that all shall work for good to them, they will own it is God that is the lifter up of their head, that gives them both cause to rejoice and hearts to rejoice."[34] God lifted up the head of Hezekiah from sickness to health, Mary and Martha's head from sorrow to peace, Peter's head from failure to restoration, David's head from shame to honor, and Samson's head from defeat to victory.

David's Praise. "Salvation belongeth unto the LORD" (Psalm 3:8). Faith praises God for what He will do (David's battle with Absalom was yet in the future), not what He has done. Augustine said, "Faith is to believe what you do not see; the reward of this faith is to see what you believe."

10

David's Pronouncement. "Thy blessing is upon thy people" (Psalm 3:8). God's blessing rests upon His children despite whatever ill or evil befalls them or enemies they confront. Christians are bountifully blessed in Christ with divine favor, comfort, provision, mercy, grace, and strength, but foremost with salvation from their sin. Of the blessing and salvation of the Lord, Luther asserts, "The sense is, it is the Lord alone that saves and blesses, and even though the whole mass of all evils should be gathered together in one against a man, still, it is the Lord who saves; salvation and blessing are in His hands. What then shall I fear?" "If God be for us, who can be against us?" (Romans 8:31).

"We ask no victories that are not Thine."[35]—J. W. Chadwick.

~January 10~

Psalm 3:5
A Good Night's Sleep

"I laid me down and slept; I awaked; for the LORD sustained me" (Psalm 3:5).

Wakeful nights become sleepful when the soul takes refuge in the arms of God. Fear, trouble, sorrow, anxiety, and sinful guilt spur insomnia, but the Lord is its antidote. He "makes sleep possible in an impossible situation."[36] Plumer writes, "The great fountain of peace, tranquility, and security is confidence in God. He will sustain His servants at all times. The preserving care of God over us when asleep is truly wonderful."[37]

Tips for better sleep:

1. Meditate on the Scriptures. Calm the soul by claiming their multitudinous promises (Proverbs 3:24; Psalm 3:3–6; Psalm 27; Psalm 32:7; Psalm 91:5; Philippians 4:7; John 14:27; Romans 8:32–39). Adrian Rogers' habit was to go to sleep meditating (deeply pondering) on a verse of Scripture.

2. Avoid drinking caffeine eight hours before bedtime.

3. Talk to the Lord. "Prayer is a good preparation for sleep."[38] Pray for cleansing of sin, healing of a broken heart, calmness, and control of racing thoughts.

4. Rid the mind of tomorrow's cares. Jesus says, "Don't get worked up about what may or may not happen tomorrow. God will help you deal with whatever hard things come up when the time comes" (Matthew 6:34 MSG).

5. Set your cellphone to receive calls only from people deemed necessary (in an emergency).

6. Be mindful of what is viewed, read, and said at bedtime (Philippians 4:8).

7. Play white noise to drown out potential disruptions to sleep.

8. "Don't let the sun go down on your anger" (Ephesians 4:26 CSB).

9. Don't watch the clock. Worrying about not sleeping impacts sleeping.

10. Watch the food you eat at night. Sugary foods tend to elevate the heart rate and work against sleep. "Sugar has been shown to increase restlessness at night and nighttime awakenings."[39]

"The sleep of the body is the gift of God. He rocks the cradle for us every night; He draws the curtain of darkness; He bids the sun shut up his burning eyes; and then He comes and says, 'Sleep, sleep, my child; I give thee sleep.'"[40]—C. H. Spurgeon.

~January 11~

Psalm 4:3
"Set Apart"

"But know that the LORD hath set apart him that is godly for himself" (Psalm 4:3).

God has "set apart" the godly (the righteous faithful) "for himself" (for His pleasure and to fulfill His divine assignments). Five lessons evolve from the text.

1. To be set apart by God, one must first set oneself apart for God.[41] Paul said, "I beseech you therefore, brethren, by the mercies of God, that ye present your bodies a living sacrifice, holy, acceptable unto God, which is your reasonable service. And be not conformed to this world: but be ye transformed by the renewing of your mind, that ye may prove what is that good, and acceptable, and perfect, will of God" (Romans 12:1–2).

2. Though all believers are set apart to honor and glorify God in life and work (1 Peter 2:9), some are chosen for a specific Christian service (pastor, evangelist, missionary, teacher). Paul said, "It was he who 'gave gifts to people'; he appointed some to be apostles, others to be prophets, others to be evangelists, others to be pastors and teachers" (Ephesians 4:11 GNT).

3. The Holy Spirit confirms the setting apart of a believer through divine impressions, Scripture, and open doors. Sometimes, He uses believers. Samuel notified David that God had set him apart to be king of Israel. Elijah revealed to Elisha his chosen task. Mordecai revealed to Esther God's plan for her to save the Jews from a holocaust at the hands of Haman. The Holy Spirit used a minister at a high school Key Club meeting, indirectly, to inform me of my ministry call as a teenager.

4. No man can set himself apart for ministry; only the Lord commissions. Spurgeon said, "It would have been a fearful thing for me to have occupied the watchman's place without having received the watchman's commission."[42] Without a divine commission or call, the work attempted will be impotent and futile. If one is called, he shouldn't let Satan and all the demons of Hell stop him. But if he isn't, he'd better stop himself.

5. He that opposes the person God has "set apart" opposes God. In addressing his enemies, David reminds them that they are battling a righteous man whom God set apart to be the King of Israel. "The opposition, therefore," Matthew Henry wrote, "which you give to

him [David] and to his advancement is very criminal, for therein you fight against God, and it will be vain and ineffectual."[43]

Moses said, "For Jehovah your God is he that goeth with you, to fight for you against your enemies, to save you" (Deuteronomy 20:4 ASV). John exclaimed, "Greater is He that is in you, than he that is in the world" (1 John 4:4). Edwards exhorts, "Holdfast and preserve that which *you* have. Continue in grace and persist in the ways of virtue, through all opposition. Cleave to the Rock of Ages, and you shall stand immovable; rely on Him, and you shall be upheld; depend on His promises, and you shall never fall."[44]

"When God chooseth a man, He chooseth him for Himself; for Himself to converse with, to communicate Himself unto him as a friend, a companion, and his delight."[45]—Thomas Goodwin.

~January 12~

Psalm 5:1
Audible and Inaudible Praying

"Give ear to my words, O LORD, consider my meditation" (Psalm 5:1).

The text references David's inaudible and audible praying.

1. Inaudible prayer to God is as effective as loud appeals. Spurgeon asserts, "Words are not the essence but the garments of prayer."[46] Sometimes, prayers are unutterable due to distress, weakness, and pain, the inability to articulate clearly what's on the heart (Romans 8:26), vocal impairment, and circumstances that make vocal prayer infeasible, and they must be voiced through the mind, sign language, or written page.

2. The value of auditory prayer. Spurgeon says that vocal prayer "may prevent distraction of mind, assist the powers of the soul, and excite devotion."[47]

3. Utilizing both forms of prayer bears great benefit. Maclaren said, "A cupful of water poured into a hydraulic ram set in motion

power that lifts tons; the prayer of faith [inaudible or audible] brings the dread magnificence of Jehovah into the field."[48]

4. Effectual prayer is based not on its form but on the soul's meditation. Benson says, "He [David] calls his prayer his meditation, to signify that it was not the mere labor of his lips, but that it proceeded from, and was accompanied with, the deepest thoughts and most fervent affections of his soul."[49]

The Bottom Line: Vocal and inarticulate praying enables the Christian to "pray without ceasing" (1 Thessalonians 5:17). Don't judge another's spirituality based upon their ability to pray aloud.

"There may be prevailing intercession where there are no words, and words where there is no true supplication."[50]—C. H. Spurgeon.

~January 13~

Psalm 5:3

Watchtower of Prayer

My voice shalt thou hear in the morning, O LORD; in the morning will I direct my prayer unto thee, and will look up (Psalm 5:3).

Pray to start the day, but then "look up" for its answer. The imagery is taken from a person in the city watchtower who watches for arriving messengers and announces their approach.[51] Habakkuk, like David, used it: "I will stand upon my watch, and set me upon the tower, and will watch to see what he will say unto me" (Habakkuk 2:1). Micah used it: "There I will look [or look out] unto the LORD; I will wait for the God of my salvation; my God will hear me" (Micah 7:7).

It pictures the believer upon making a request of God, looking for its reply expectantly. This looking up and out for an answer demonstrates faith and confidence that God has heard the prayer and will speedily respond. "Many a prayer is offered," says Maclaren, "and no eyes afterward turn to Heaven to watch for the answer, and

15

perhaps some answers sent are like water spilled on the ground, for want [lack] of such observance."[52]

"Prayer lives in a watchtower. The Oratory should be an observatory."[53]—W. S. Plumer.

~January 14~

Psalm 5:7
Qualifications for Right Worship

"But as for me, I will come into thy house in the multitude of thy mercy: and in thy fear will I worship toward thy holy temple" (Psalm 5:7).

Hundreds may stay away from the church, but David said, as for him, "I will come into thy house." Hopefully, he speaks for all who call themselves Christians. David cites four qualifications for proper worship.

1. Experience of God's lovingkindness and mercy. Fellowship with God is not possible by merit but by His love and mercy (Ephesians 2:8–9). Spurgeon said that he would go into God's house, "But I will not come there by my own merits; no, I have a multitude of sins, and therefore I will come in the multitude of Thy mercy. I will approach Thee with confidence because of Thy immeasurable grace."[54]

2. A pure heart. To the question, "Who shall ascend into the hill of the LORD? or who shall stand in his holy place?" the psalmist replies, "He that hath clean hands, and a pure heart" (Psalm 24:3–5). The "dress" of man's soul is all-important in worship, not the "fig leaves." Boice says, "You must be holy, and the secret to being holy is to see sin as God himself sees it and to draw close to him."[55] Matthew Henry said, "It is sin that stops the current of God's favor to us and deprives us of the blessings we used to receive."[56]

3. A righteous fear and holy reverence of God. Plumer said, "All worship, which is destitute of godly fear, is not accepted. Where

16

there is no fear, there is no scriptural piety. The word "worship" might be translated as "bow down." "The posture of worship should be decent and reverent."[57]

4. Earnestness of heart. David's words ring with sincerity and earnestness in heart about worship. Ryle says, "It must not content us to take our bodies to church if we leave our hearts at home."

"They who would grow in grace must love the habitation of God's house. It is those that are planted in the courts of the Lord who shall flourish and not those that are occasionally there."—John Angell James.

~January 15~

Psalm 6:3
The Delays of God

"O LORD, how long?" (Psalm 6:3).

Delays of divine intervention happen to the godliest. Joseph waited three long years in prison to be delivered. Job endured suffering for an untold period before being delivered. The Israelites spent 70 years in Babylonian captivity until they were delivered. Paul battled a "thorn in the flesh" until deliverance came at death. Note five truths about the delays of God.

1. Delays are purposed. In the delays, unknown divine intentions and designs are at play. "For as the heavens are higher than the earth, so are my ways higher than your ways, and my thoughts than your thoughts" (Isaiah 55:9). Delays are always for our good, best end, and God's glory.

2. Delays don't mean God is unconcerned. The unseen hand of God begins to work at the first cry of desperation, only later to be made visibly evident. G. Campbell Morgan said, "He is nigh when He seems absent. He is watching when He seems blind. He is active when He seems idle."[58]

17

3. Delays are not denials. "Delays are not refusals; many a prayer is registered, and underneath it the words: 'My time is not yet come.'"

4. Delays seem to last longer than they do. God's clock differs from ours. "The longest protraction of the fulfillment of a desire will seem but as a winking of an eye when we estimate duration as He estimates it."[59]

5. Don't faint or murmur at the delays. During his last painful illness, Calvin uttered no word of complaint but, looking toward Heaven, would say in Latin, *"Usquequo Domine"* ("LORD, how long?").[60] David Wilkerson wrote, "Commit every prayer to Jesus and go about your business with confidence that He will not be one moment early or late in answering. And, if the answer you seek is not forthcoming, say to your heart, 'He is all I need. If I need more, He will not withhold it. He will do it in His time, in His way; and, if He does not fulfill my request, He must have a perfect reason for not doing so. No matter what happens, I will always have faith in His faithfulness.'"

"God knows that delay will quicken and increase desire, and that if He keeps thee waiting, thou wilt see thy necessity more clearly, and wilt seek more earnestly; and that thou wilt prize the mercy all the more for its long tarrying."[61]—C. H. Spurgeon.

~January 16~

Psalm 7:15–16
The Boomerang Effect of Harming Others

"He made a pit, and digged it, and is fallen into the ditch which he made. His mischief shall return upon his own head, and his violent dealing shall come down upon his own pate" (Psalm 7:15–16).

David says, false charges brought against him (and us) will boomerang to the hurt of their deviser. Solomon says the same: "Those who dig a pit will fall in it; those who roll a stone will have it turn back on them" (Proverbs 26:27 CEB).

People use four shovels to dig pits for the downfall of others.

1. The shovel of slanderous accusations that injure reputation, position, and business. A slanderer is a person who makes a false or malicious statement about another person, either verbally or through innuendoes, gestures, or written communication. Chrysostom speaks of the blindness of malice: "When we supplant the reputation of others, let us consider that we injure ourselves; it is against ourselves that we plot. For perchance with men, we do him harm if we have power, but ourselves in the sight of God, by provoking Him against us."[62]

2. The shovel of allurements to sin. The wicked seek to pull the godly down into the pit of their wanton lifestyle and guilt. Misery loves company (Psalm 141:9).

3. The shovel of corrupt corrupt counsel. Purposeful ill advice has led to the downfall of many, especially the young. Ahaziah "followed the example of Ahab's dynasty because his mother gave him evil counsel" (2 Chronicles 22:3 ISV). Jonadab advised Amnon on how to rape Tamar (2 Samuel 13:3–13). Shemiah counseled Nehemiah to go into hiding cowardly (Nehemiah 6:10–12).

4. The shovel of bad example. "Evil company corrupts good habits" (1 Corinthians 15:33 NKJV). Jehoram followed the example of the evil kings of Israel and became as wicked as King Ahab (2 Chronicles 21:6). This shovel, though perhaps unintentional, digs deep pits of despair and destruction for one's children, and friends.

"His violent dealing shall come down upon his own pate." It's the law of retributive justice. He who sets a snare for another will himself be the victim. "Malice is of the boomerang character, and is apt to turn upon the projector."[63] Haman's gallows for Mordecai claimed him (Esther 7:9). Daniel's bitter rivals' plot against him harmed them (Daniel 6:24). "Their evil will boomerang on them" (2 Peter 2:13 MSG).

"Sin is a kind of boomerang, which goes off into space curiously, but turns again upon its author, and with tenfold force strikes the guilty soul that launched it." – C. H. Spurgeon.

~January 17~

Psalm 8:4
What is Man?

"What is man, that thou art mindful of him?" (Psalm 8:4).

Clarke paraphrases David's question: "What is wretched, miserable man; man in his fallen state, full of infirmity, ignorance, and sin?" Craigie says the question is asked to evoke the resounding answer, "Nothing!" He explains, "In such vastness, it is inconceivable that human beings have significance or meaning; it is inconceivable that God could remember each human being or give attention to each person."[64] Yet He does. Psalm 8:3–6 stands out in the book of Psalms for it underscores God's love and concern for men despite their despicable condition and rebellious attitude toward Him.

What is man? Ask Isaiah, and he answers he is but "grass" (Isaiah 40:6). Ask Jeremiah, and he answers man is "deceitful above all things, and desperately wicked" (Jeremiah 17:9). Ask David, and he answers all classes of men are worthless and deceitful (Psalm 62:9). Ask Job, and he answers, man is a "worm," a mere maggot (Job 25:6). Ask Moses, and he answers, "a living soul" (Genesis 2:7). Ask Spurgeon, "What is man, that thou art mindful of him?" and he answers, "This is an unanswerable question. Infinite condescension can alone account for the Lord stooping to be the friend of man."[65]

Why is God interested in man who spurns His Word and profanes His name? It is because man is stamped with His Divine image, is created with His Divine plan, is the object of His Divine love, and is the crown of His creation ('made a little lower than the angels').

These reasons, in part, explain why God counts man as the apple of His eye and magnifies him above all creation (Job 7:17) and why He "spared not His own Son, but delivered Him up for us all" (Romans 8:32) to provide salvation from the captivity and penalty of sin.

To summarize, Matthew Henry asserts, "Though man is a worm, yet God puts a respect upon him, and shows him an abundance of kindness; man is, above all the creatures in this lower world, the favorite and darling of Providence."[66]

"Oh, the grandeur and littleness, the excellence and the corruption, the majesty and meanness of man!"—Pascal.

~January 18~

Psalm 9:10

They That Know Thy Name

"And they that know thy name will put their trust in thee: for thou, LORD, hast not forsaken them that seek thee" (Psalm 9:10).

Understanding God's name, which reveals His identity, nature, and works, is the grounds for confident trust in Him. Watson says, "Knowledge must carry the torch before faith."[67] To know the Lord is to believe in and trust him (John 17:3). Much is unknowable about God, but that which is needful for trust in Him is clear and perceivable to all who search for it (Job 11:7–8). What do we know about God's name, about Him, revealed in the Scripture and human experience?

1. We know Him as the maker and sustainer of everything (Hebrews 1:3; Colossians 1:17).

2. We know Him to be absolutely holy, just, loving, and righteous (Psalm 89:14; 145:8).

3. We know Him to be the originator and designer of man's salvation from the foundation of the world (Ephesians 1:4).

4. We know He is merciful to forgive all who come to Him in confession and repentance. "The LORD is merciful and gracious, slow to anger and plenteous in mercy" (Psalm 103:8).

5. We know He does not abandon those who trust Him. "For thou, LORD, hast not forsaken them that seek thee" (Psalm 9:10). Thomas a Kempis said, "Love Him, and keep Him for thy Friend, who, when all go away, will not forsake thee, nor suffer thee to perish at the last."

The person who absorbs these truths about God, "taste and see" (Psalm 34:8), will believingly and joyously place trust in Him for pardon, peace, provision, and protection. Note. It is the testimony of those who know His name from knowledge of the Scripture and experience that He is worthy of unconditional and unwavering trust.

"The mother of unbelief is ignorance of God, His faithfulness, mercy, and power."[68]—John Ball.

~January 19~

Psalm 9:13
The Gates of Death

"Have mercy upon me, O LORD; consider my trouble which I suffer of them that hate me, thou that liftest me up from the gates of death" (Psalm 9:13).

The knowledge that God had delivered him from the portal of death gave David confidence and hope to pray for further help.

Have the gates of death been opened to you but closed mercifully by the hand of God? To me, it has happened three times. The experience bears five lessons.

1. We are always near the gates of death, regardless of age or occupation. Billy Graham was right to assert, "All mankind is sitting on death row."[69]

2. We have no power over the gates of death. Their opening and closing reside in the hands of God alone. "It is appointed unto men once to die, but after this the judgment" (Hebrews 9:27). Henry Martyn said, "You are immortal until God's purpose for you is complete."

3. We may enter the gate of death that is least expected. The gates of death are many and varied. The poet Robert Blair states, "Death's thousand doors stand open." The unexpected door is often its entry door. At the time of this writing, an American Airline plane collided with a Black Hawk helicopter over the Potomac River,

tragically killing 67 people. None of them expected to enter death's door on that tragic night in that way.

4. We may enter the gate of death when least expected. All need to say, like David, "There is but a step between me and death" (1 Samuel 20:3 ESV) and pray, like Moses, "So teach us to number our days, that we may apply our hearts unto wisdom" (Psalm 90:12).

5. We cannot change where we go upon entering the gates of death. Spurgeon says, "What I am when death is held before me, that I must be forever. When my spirit departs, if God finds me hymning His praise, I shall hymn it in Heaven; if He finds me breathing out oaths, I shall follow up those oaths in Hell."[70]

"He whose head is in Heaven need not fear to put his feet into the grave."—Matthew Henry.

~January 20~

Psalm 10:1

A Puzzling Question

"Why standest Thou afar off, O LORD?" (Psalm 10:1).

Israel had been delivered from captivity, and their foreign foes, but now, to David, God appears to have lifted His shield of protection, for domestic desperados or bandits plagued the people. Of this, he sought an explanation.

We ask the same question occasionally for a different reason. "Why standest Thou afar off, O LORD?" How might the felt distance between God and us, at times, be explained?

1. Through understanding that it is not God who moves from us but us from Him by sin. The story of the prodigal son unfolds this truth (Luke 15:11–22).

(1. The prodigal left the father, not the father, him. Sin only makes it seem that the reverse is true.

(2. The prodigal found the father where he left Him (Hebrews 13:5; 1 Samuel 12:22; Psalm 37:28). Paul said, "If we are disloyal, he stays faithful" (2 Timothy 2:13 CEB).

(3. The prodigal found the father joyous, not angry, with him. The father runs to him, hugs him, and throws a party for him, reversing what sin had caused him to think would happen.

2. Through understanding that God sometimes withdraws His sweet fellowship from the believer or the conscious sense of His presence and power for unknown purposes for our best.[71]

3. Through understanding, it inflames man's heart with a more profound longing for and pursuit of God. "My soul thirsteth for God, for the living God: when shall I come and appear before God?" (Psalm 42:2).

"We stand afar off from God by our unbelief, and then we complain that God stands afar off from us."[72]—Matthew Henry.

~January 21~

Psalm 11:3
What Can the Righteous Do?

"If the foundations be destroyed, what can the righteous do?" (Psalm 11:3).

The "foundations" are the pillars upon which the fundamental principles of law and justice rest in society (the Word of God, the Bible). They were set in place by our Sovereign God and maintained from the beginning. King Saul's lawless rule eroded these foundations, prompting David's question.

What can the righteous do? "The righteous" refers to those who are upright and godly. It is the duty of the righteous to consider what they ought to do should the foundations of their land be destroyed—undermined by ungodly leadership, anti-Christian legislation, decadent cultural reform, and unchecked lawlessness. What should they do?

1. Like David, they must unflinchingly trust God's sovereign power to safeguard His established foundations and bring judgment to those who seek to undermine them (Psalm 11:4–6).

2. They must resist the pressure of evil to conform fiercely and courageously. Solomon exhorts, "Do not swerve to the right or to the left; turn your foot away from evil" (Proverbs 4:27 ESV).

3. They must refuse to "flee to the mountains" and be vigilant in the battle for all that is right and honorable.

4. They must pray for righteousness to prevail and governance by the godly.

5. They must bear the ungodly rule with holy calmness and levelheadedness.[73]

6. They must remember that certain spiritual foundations can never be shaken or removed (Hebrews 12:28).[74]

7. They are to rest in God, "When all around my soul gives way, He then is all my hope and stay." Hannah Whitall Smith comments, "We will all acknowledge that if our souls are to rest in peace and comfort, it can only be on unshakable foundations. It is no more possible for the soul to be comfortable when it is trying to rest on 'things that can be shaken' than it is for the body. No one can rest comfortably in a shaking bed or sit in comfort on a rickety chair. Foundations, to be reliable, must always be unshakable."

How firm a foundation, O saints of the Lord,
Is laid for your faith in his excellent Word!
~Edward Mote (1834).

Matthew Henry says, "What can the righteous do? Good people would be undone if they had not a God to go to, a God to trust to, and a future bliss to hope for."

"What can the righteous do? They can go on being righteous. And they can stand against the evil of their society."[75]—J. M. Boice.

25

~January 22~

Psalm 12:1

Where Are the Godly?

"Help, LORD; for the godly man ceaseth; for the faithful fail from among the children of men" (Psalm 12:1).

The church faces the same crisis as David: the vanishing of the godly in the pulpit, pew, and public forum. The text suggests four observations in this regard.

1. The influence, example, leadership, faithfulness, and usefulness of spiritual giants now in Heaven are sorely missed.

2. Their kind must be replaced to turn the tide of evil and win the world to Christ.

3. Filling the places vacated by the faithful and godly is challenging.

4. The church's only recourse is to pray for God to furnish more of their kind. This David did, saying, "Help, LORD" (Psalm 12:1). Spurgeon asserted the absence of the godly "should be a trumpet call for more prayer."[76]

We miss the spiritual warriors who once sat in the pew, sang in the choir, ministered from the pulpit, and thundered truth from the radio and television. We tell them what Jonathan told David: "Thou shalt be missed, because thy seat will be empty" (1 Samuel 20:18). These may never be equally replaced, but their kind can and should. "Pray ye therefore the Lord of the harvest, that he will send forth labourers into his harvest" (Matthew 9:38).

Note. How will you be remembered? "Thou mayest choose," said Pilkington, "whether thou wilt be remembered to thy praise or to thy shame.'" Resolve to leave behind the memory of being a righteous man who loved God, obeyed His Word, and served Him faithfully.

"When the Lord has taken home a few more of His faithful, then a storm of persecution will burst forth upon His Church."[77]—Joseph Irons.

~January 23~

Psalm 12:6

The Excellence of God's Word

"The words of the LORD are pure words: as silver tried in a furnace of earth, purified seven times" (Psalm 12:6).

The psalmist describes the Bible in four ways.

1. It is authoritative. The Bible is the Word of God's mouth (2 Timothy 3:16). Kierkegaard said, "The Bible is a letter from God with our personal address on it."

2. It is unflawed. They are "pure words," free from corruption. Plumer remarked, "God's words are pure from all error, all mistakes, all equivocation, all deception, all encouragement to sin, all weakness."[78] It is entirely trustworthy.

3. It is authenticated. The Scripture has been "tried [investigated, tested] in a furnace..., purified seven times" of prophecy, archaeology, history, science, and human experience over two thousand years and has proven true. Matthew Henry summarizes, "The many proofs that have been given of its power and truth; it has been often tried. All the saints in all ages have trusted it and so tried it, and it never deceived them nor frustrated their expectation, but they have all set to their seal that God's word is true."[79]

"Come, search, ye critics," says Spurgeon, "and find a flaw; examine it, from its Genesis to its Revelation, and find an error. This is a vein of pure gold unalloyed by quartz or any earthly substance. This is a star without a speck, a sun without a blot, a light without darkness, a moon without its paleness, a glory without a dimness."[80]

4. It is permanent. David said, "Thou shalt keep them, O LORD, thou shalt preserve them from this generation forever" (Psalm 12:7).

Jesus said, "Heaven and earth shall pass away, but my words shall not pass away" (Matthew 24:35).

Robert Leighton said, "The Scriptures are the golden mines in which alone the abiding treasures of eternity are to be found, and therefore worthy all the digging and pains we can bestow on them."

The bottom line—the Bible:

A Pure Book (Proverbs 30:5)

A Powerful Book (Hebrews 4:12)

A Prized Book (Psalm 19:10)

A Personal Book (Psalm 119:105)

A Profitable Book (Joshua 1:8; 2 Timothy 3:16)

A Permanent Book (Isaiah 40:8)

"God the Father is the giver of Holy Scripture; God the Son is the theme of Holy Scripture; and God the Spirit is the author, authenticator, and interpreter of Holy Scripture."—J. I. Packer.

~January 24~

Psalm 13:2

Wrestling with Dark Thoughts

"How long must I wrestle with my thoughts and day after day have sorrow in my heart?" (Psalm 13:2 NIV).

We, like David, at times, wrestle with negative and dark thoughts—untruths, lies, fears, and doubts—sown in the mind by the enemy. They are only successfully combated by speaking the truths of God's Word to ourselves. Of them, five are pivotal to thwart Satan's attack.

1. God never abandons. "For He hath said, 'I will never leave thee, nor forsake thee'" (Hebrews 13:5).

2. God's love never quits. "For the mountains shall depart, and the hills be removed; but my [loving] kindness shall not depart from thee, neither shall the covenant of my peace be removed, saith the LORD that hath mercy on thee" (Isaiah 54:10). Says Spurgeon, "Christ does not love you today and cast you away tomorrow."[81]

3. God always answers prayer. "Call unto Me, and I will answer thee, and show thee great and mighty things, which thou knowest not" (Jeremiah 33:3). Though the answer to prayer may be long delayed, it doesn't mean God is uncaring and unconcerned, or will not answer.

1. 4. God will deliver. "And call upon me in the day of trouble: I will deliver thee, and thou shalt glorify me" (Psalm 50:15). Whatever the trouble or hardship, God will make a way out.

5. God is for me, not against me. "What then shall we say of these things? If God be for us, who can be against us?" (Romans 8:31 KJ21). Matthew Henry said, "While God is for us, and we keep in His love, we may with a holy boldness defy all the powers of darkness. Let Satan do his worst; he is chained. Let the world do its worst; it is conquered: principalities and powers are spoiled and disarmed and triumphed over in the cross of Christ. Who then dares fight against us while God himself is fighting for us?"[82]

When the negative and untruthful thoughts of the enemy are supplanted with the positive truth of God's Word, then misery, gloom, and despair are dispelled, and the heart is filled with peace.

"All battles are first won or lost, in the mind."—Joan of Arc.

~January 25~
Psalm 14:3
Inborn Depravity

"They are all gone aside, they are all together become filthy: there is none that doeth good, no, not one" (Psalm 14:3).

Man's depravity is manifested in three ways.

1. In his birth. Depravity is inborn. "Behold, I was shapen in iniquity; and in sin did my mother conceive me" (Psalm 51:5). Spurgeon says, "The fountain of my life is polluted as well as its streams."[83] Our sinful nature came with us. Paul states, "For all have sinned, and come short of the glory of God" (Romans 3:23).

2. In his behavior. Man's depravity is displayed in egregious, wanton conduct. Manton states, "There is in man a mint always at work: his mind coining evil thoughts; his heart, evil desires and carnal emotion; and his memory is the closet and storehouse wherein they are kept." Calvin says, "Our nature is not only completely empty of goodness but so full of every kind of wrong that it is always active." Luther said, "Man...does not do evil against his will, under pressure, as though he were taken by the scruff of the neck and dragged into it, like a thief...being dragged off against his will to punishment; but he does it spontaneously and voluntarily."

3. In his belief. A depraved mind leads to a denied God. "There is not one who tries to find God" (Romans 3:11 NLV). Man's adamic nature prevents man from seeing his folly and need for God. Left to himself, he is hopelessly lost (John 6:44). "You would none of you come unto Christ of yourselves," asserts Spurgeon, "unless the Spirit that rested on Christ should draw you. It is true of all men in their natural condition that they will not come unto Christ."[84]

The cure for man's sin is the cleansing power of Christ's blood (1 John 1:7; 1 Peter 1:19).

"As the salt flavors every drop in the Atlantic, so does sin affect every atom of our nature."—C. H. Spurgeon.

~January 26~

Psalm 15:1
The Ideal Worshipper

"LORD, who shall abide in thy tabernacle? Who shall dwell in thy holy hill?" (Psalm 15:1).

David questions God for clarification as to who may enter His Holy presence with assurance of acceptance. Nine characteristics of an acceptable person are indicated.

"Walketh uprightly." They do what is right, just, and holy, ordering their lives by the Word of God. "Speaketh the truth in his heart." They refuse to speak lies to or about man and to God. "Backbiteth not with his tongue." They keep the ninth commandment, refusing to slander others (Exodus 20:16).

"Nor doeth evil to his neighbor." Spurgeon states, "Loving our neighbor as ourselves will make us jealous of his good name, careful not to injure his estate, or by ill example to corrupt his character."[85]

"In whose eyes a vile person is contemned." They do not look with disdain upon others. "He honoreth them that fear the LORD." They esteem highly those who reverence and obey the Lord. "He that sweareth to his own hurt, and changeth not." They keep their word (promises) regardless of the cost.

"He that putteth not out his money to usury." They do not charge exorbitant interest on loans to the poor. "Nor taketh reward against the innocent." They refuse gifts (bribes) offered to close their eyes, to look the other way, or make a favorable decision.

To summarize these traits, Matthew Henry says the man who can ascend the hill of the Lord is "conscientiously honest and just in all his dealings, faithful and fair to all with whom he has to do."[86] Not only does the psalmist state that all who bear these characteristics shall dwell in Jehovah's tent or house, but they will stand unmoved though all the world should shake.[87] Maclaren says, "Righteousness is the one stable thing in the universe."[88] "No storm," says Spurgeon, "shall tear him from his foundations, drag him from his anchorage, or uproot him from his place."[89]

"God welcomes those with clean feet, clean hands, and a clean heart."[90]—Warren Wiersbe.

31

~January 27~

Psalm 16:3

The Prized of Earth

"But to the saints that are in the earth, and to the excellent, in whom is all my delight" (Psalm 16:3).

The saints (the redeemed of the Lord Jesus Christ through His blood), despite their imperfections are *the excellent of the earth* (counted as the magnificent, noble, highly treasured, most honorable ones; the apple of His eye and royalty) for they are Christ's jewels (Malachi 3:17) and the objects of His great love (Ephesians 5:2).

A. W. Pink wrote, "The world's standard of worth is very different from that of God's. Who are the immortals of human history? Caesar, Charlemagne, Napoleon: soldiers and warriors. Among statesmen and politicians, we may mention Gladstone and Lincoln; among dramatists, Goethe and Shakespeare. Those were great in the eyes of Earth, but who were great in the eyes of Heaven? For the most part, they were unknown down here. They were humble and lowly, insignificant in the affairs of the world. Their names were never chronicled among men, but they were written in the Lamb's Book of Life!"[91]

Who are these immortals of history? They are the saints of God. Though saints "are treated as though we are the garbage of the world—the dirt of the earth" (1 Corinthians 4:13 ICB), to Christ, they are *the excellent of the earth* (royalty; aristocrats)! Therefore, saint of the Lord, walk with your head high among the ungodly, despite the status given to you by them.

In whom is my delight. Like David, saints are to delight and take pleasure in each other, not the world's crowd. After all, they have the same Master, share the same love and affection for God, battle the same enemies, strive for the same goals, embrace the same truth, heed the same biblical rules, suffer the same ridicule, share the same allegiance and commitment, and in the end, share the same eternal Home. Matthew Henry says, "It is not enough for us to delight in the saints, but, as there is occasion, our goodness must extend to them;

we must be ready to show them the kindness they need, distribute to their necessities, and abound in the labor of love to them."[92]

Before demeaning a saint, remember Christ counts them as the most honorable on earth.

"The title of 'His Excellency' more properly belongs to the meanest saint than to the greatest governor. The true aristocracy are believers in Jesus. They are the only Right Honorables."[93]—C. H. Spurgeon.

~January 28~

Psalm 16:9
The Christian's Hope

"My flesh also shall rest in hope" (Psalm 16:9).

David possessed an eternal hope of life beyond death with God. Unlike secular hope, biblical hope means certainty, confidence, and assurance of something happening. It's not wishful thinking but undoubtable reality. What is the believer's hope?

1. It consists of the resurrection of the body. Jesus is proof and the preview of the resurrection. He rose bodily and was recognizable, just as will be the case with every believer (Luke 24:39). Paul says, "Just as we have borne the image of the man of dust, we shall also bear the image of the man of heaven" (1 Corinthians 15:49 ESV). Jesus gives the promise of the resurrection: "I am the resurrection and the life. He who believes in Me, though he may die, he shall live" (John 11:25 NKJV). Ryle writes, "The life that we live here in the flesh is not all. The trumpet shall one day sound, and the dead shall be raised incorruptible. Let us cling to it [this hope] firmly and never let it go."

2. It consists of future life in Heaven. Of all the beauty, joys, and riches of Heaven, Jesus will outshine them all.

3. It consists of Christ's return. Paul writes, "Looking for that blessed hope, and the glorious appearing of the great God and our

Saviour Jesus Christ" (Titus 2:13). Fear, anxiety, despair, and misery are dispelled in the hope of Christ's soon return.

4. It consists of reunion with loved ones beyond this life. A grand reunion day of unending fellowship with loved ones and saints awaits the redeemed at death or the Lord's coming (1 Thessalonians 4:17). To know that we will see loved ones and friends again beyond the veil of death grants unspeakable peace and calm amid grave sorrow. What a glorious hope we have in Christ Jesus! "Therefore, my heart is glad, and my glory rejoiceth" (Psalm 16:9a).

"Optimism is a wish without warrant; Christian hope is a certainty, guaranteed by God himself."—J. I. Packer.

~January 29~
Psalm 17:15
David's Resurrection Belief

"As for me, I will behold thy face in righteousness: I shall be satisfied, when I awake, with thy likeness" (Psalm 17:15).

The consummation David anticipated. "When I awake." David expresses confidence in awakening from death to see God's face. Criswell says, "Attempts to argue the silence of the Old Testament regarding life after death and even the resurrection of the righteous pale before verses such as this."[94]

The criterion David met. "I will behold thy face in righteousness." Christ's righteousness, imputed to him, justified him, making everlasting life possible (2 Corinthians 5:21). Upon repentance and faith, Christ provides cleansing and covering for man's unrighteousness (which deserves the wrath of God) with His imputed righteousness, enabling conversion and eternal life.

The confidence David exhibited. "As for me, I will." Note David's certainty: "I will behold thy face." His firm hope should be that of all the redeemed.

The change David expected. "I shall be satisfied...with thy likeness."

1. David believed his body would be made in the likeness of the resurrected body of Christ. The resurrection body of Jesus is the prototype for those whom He has redeemed (1 Corinthians 15:20, 48–49; Philippians 3:21; 1 John 3:2). In the resurrection body, He walked, talked, ate and was recognized (John 21:1–14).

2. He expected to be satisfied and happy in the resurrected state. The earth provides no satisfaction for the saint. But Heaven will. "My happiness," Covill wrote, "will be full in the measure, without the want of anything that can make me happy; all my desires shall be satisfied, and my happiness in respect of duration shall be eternal, without a shadow or fear of a change."[95] Spurgeon says, "My satisfaction is to come; I do not look for it as yet. I shall sleep awhile, but I shall wake at the sound of the trumpet; wake to everlasting joy because I arise in Thy likeness, O my God and King! Glimpses of glory good men have here below to stay their sacred hunger, but the full feast awaits them in the upper skies."[96]

"There is no satisfaction for a soul but in God, and in His face and likeness, His good-will towards us and His good work in us; and even that satisfaction will not be perfect till we come to Heaven."[97]—Matthew Henry.

~January 30~
Psalm 18:1
To Love God Supremely

"I will love thee, O LORD, my strength" (Psalm 18:1).

Spurgeon says, "Our triune God deserves the warmest love of all our hearts. Father, Son, and Spirit have each a claim upon our love."[98]

Consider four aspects of this love.

Its motive. "We love him, because he first loved us" (1 John 4:19). His love for us prompts unfeigned love in return. Matthew Henry asserts, "His love is the incentive, the motive, and moral cause of ours. We cannot but love so good a God, who was first in the act and work of love, who loved us when we were both unloving and unlovely, who loved us at so great a rate, who has been seeking and soliciting our love at the expense of his Son's blood and has condescended to beseech us to be reconciled unto Him."

Its marks. Indicators of love for God are obedience to His Word (John 14:15), abiding in Him (John 15:5–10), and worship (Psalm 63:1–8). Wiersbe said, "Where there is love, there will be service and obedience."[99]

Its mandate. "Thou shalt love the Lord thy God" (Matthew 22:37a). This, Jesus says, is the chief duty of man.

Its measure. "With all thy heart, and with all thy soul, and with all thy mind" (Matthew 22:37b). The expressions denote comprehensiveness, meaning that God is to be loved with all powers and abilities—the heart (the core of one's being), the soul (emotions, affection), the mind (intellect and strength).[100] This love must be exhibited with an undivided heart (Hosea 10:2). There are to be no rivals to His love. Understanding that, David prayed, "Give me an undivided heart, that I may fear your name" (Psalm 86:11 NIV).

"Our love of God must be a sincere love, and not in word and tongue only, as theirs is who say they love Him, but their hearts are not with Him. It must be a strong love; we must love Him in the most intense degree."[101]—Matthew Henry.

~January 31~

Psalm 18:29
The Imprisoning Wall

"By my God have I leaped over a wall" (Psalm 18:29).

David is likely describing the capture of a fortress, perhaps Jebus, later known as "the city of David" or Jerusalem. He gives God all the credit and glory for the feat ("By my God").

Man is captive in the fortress of sin by the power of Satan. His best attempts to escape are futile. He cannot climb over it by religion, tunnel under it by morality, or go through it by good works. He is without hope. But what he cannot do to rescue himself from the miserable and damnable plight, Jesus Christ can and stands ready to do. By His atoning death at Calvary for man's sin and subsequent resurrection, He enables a person to leap over the imprisoning wall to freedom, happiness, meaning, peace, and eternal life.

The song and glory of those who have leaped over the wall to new life is, '*By my God* have I leaped over the wall.' "For there is one God, and one mediator between God and men, the man Christ Jesus" (1 Timothy 2:5). "He is able to deliver thee. He is able to deliver thee. Though by sin oppressed, go to Him for rest. Our God is able to deliver thee."

Whatever wall encloses you, be it adversity, sorrow, sickness, or sin, Christ's hand is outstretched to take your hand and lift you over it to freedom. "If the Son therefore shall make you free, ye shall be free indeed" (John 8:36).

"The greatest enemy to human souls is the self-righteous spirit which makes men look to themselves for salvation."—C. H. Spurgeon.

~February 1~

Psalm 18:33
Hind's Feet and High Places

"He maketh my feet like hinds' feet, and setteth me upon my high places" (Psalm 18:33).

The metaphor of hinds' feet teaches God's provision of strength to meet every trial in three ways.

Hinds' feet are stable. In terrain where a wild goat would have trouble standing and walking, David's feet stood firm while engaged in battle because God had given him "hinds' feet" (the surefootedness and steadiness of a mountain female deer that moves safely along the jagged rocks, slippery rock face, and dangerous cliffs). Habakkuk testifies to the same: "The Sovereign LORD gives me strength. He makes me sure-footed as a deer and keeps me safe on the mountains" (Habakkuk 3:19 GNT). God provides His children with "hobnailed shoes" to prevent them from falling when traversing dangerous and rugged terrain (Ephesians 6:15).

Hinds' feet are swift. David successfully fled Saul, Absalom, and Achish's soldiers by the Lord's strength. In our time of trial, temptation, and trouble, God likewise gives us "hinds'" feet to speedily escape. Matthew Henry states, "We shall be swift for our spiritual race: He will make my feet like hinds' feet, that with enlargement of heart, I may run the way of His commands and outrun my troubles."[102]

Hinds' feet are smart. A mountain deer is clever; ask any deer hunter. They can run with abandonment while "staying on track" and eluding the hunter. God enabled David to outsmart his enemy, though at times it seemed inevitable that he would be captured. God gives His children wisdom to navigate life and battle the foe victoriously (Psalm 18:36). Note. When walking a difficult path, ask the Lord to provide you with "hinds' feet."

And will make me to walk upon mine high places. With God's strength (symbolized by hinds' feet) to enable victorious Christian living, the believer soars to the high places of honor (David was elevated from being a fugitive from Saul to being King), to refuge in times of trouble and temptation, and to happiness, the ability to do spiritual exploits and achievement.

Therefore, will I give thanks unto you (Psalm 18:49). With David, praise God for making your feet "like hinds' feet," giving you strength to stand firm in a trial when otherwise, you would have fallen.

"You can be sure of your footing when you walk close to Jesus."— C. H. Spurgeon.

Psalm 19:1–2
Creation: A Revelation of God

"The heavens declare the glory of God; and the firmament sheweth his handywork. Day unto day uttereth speech, and night unto night sheweth knowledge" (Psalm 19:1–2).

David cites two categories of God's revelation of Himself: creation (Psalm 19:1–6) and the Holy Scripture (Psalm 19:7–11).

Creation.

1. The mighty universe displays the handiwork of God in the heavens and on earth, proclaiming His existence (Psalm 19:1). Packer says, "God's world is not a shield hiding the Creator's power and majesty. From the natural order, it is evident that a mighty and majestic Creator is there."[103]

2. Nonverbally, creation constantly reveals God's existence to man (Psalm 19:2–3). Day and night, nature speaks of God's existence and presence.

3. All see nature's revelation of God regardless of place. This being true, Paul said, "Since earliest times men have seen the earth and sky and all God made, and have known of his existence and great eternal power. So they will have no excuse when they stand before God at Judgment Day" (Romans 1:20 TLB).

4. Nature's revelation of God has no language barrier (Psalm 19:4). It speaks a language in every man's tongue so all may hear its revelation of God. All men equally may say, "You made the skies with your own hands. When I look up, I see the moon and the stars. You have put them all in their right place" (Psalm 8:3 EASY). Job asserts that even the animals—the birds in the sky and the fish in the sea understand they were created by the hand of God (Job 12:7–10).

Addison (1712) wrote: "The spacious firmament on high, with all the blue ethereal sky, and spangled heavens, a shining frame, their great Original proclaim. The unwearied sun, from day to day does his Creator's power display and publishes to every land the work of an almighty hand."

"I love to think of nature as an unlimited broadcasting station, through which God speaks to us every hour if we will only tune in."—George Washington Carver.

~February 3~

Psalm 19:7

The Bible: A Revelation of God

"The law of the LORD is perfect, converting the soul: the testimony of the LORD is sure, making wise the simple" (Psalm 19:7).

God reveals Himself to man not only in creation but also in *the Holy Scriptures (*Psalm 19:7–11).

1. The Scriptures reveal God as compassionate, forgiving, loving, and merciful. "The compassionate and gracious God, slow to anger, abounding in love and faithfulness, maintaining love to thousands, and forgiving wickedness, rebellion and sin" (Exodus 34:6–7 NIV).

2. The Scriptures reveal Him as the creator and sustainer of all that exists. "For by him were all things created, that are in heaven, and that are in earth, visible and invisible, whether they be thrones, or dominions, or principalities, or powers: all things were created by him, and for him: And he is before all things, and by him all things consist" (Colossians 1:16–17).

3. The Scriptures reveal Him as the author and finisher of our salvation. "For God so loved the world, that he gave his only begotten Son, that whosoever believeth in him should not perish, but have everlasting life" (John 3:16).

4. The Scriptures reveal Him as all-powerful. "Our God is in the heavens: he hath done whatsoever he hath pleased" (Psalm 115:3).

5. The Scriptures reveal Him as the holy comforter. "He healeth the broken in heart, and bindeth up their wounds" (Psalm 147:3).

6. The Scriptures reveal Him as our helper in times of need. "The LORD is good, a stronghold in the day of trouble" (Nahum 1:7).

7. The Scriptures reveal Him as being from everlasting to everlasting. "Before the mountains were brought forth, or ever thou hadst formed the earth and the world, even from everlasting to everlasting, thou art God" (Psalm 90:2).

8. The Scriptures reveal Him as holy and righteous. "God is light, and in Him is no darkness at all" (1 John 1:5).

"The Bible is not an end in itself, but a means to bring men to an intimate and satisfying knowledge of God, that they may enter into Him, that they may delight in His Presence, may taste and know the inner sweetness of the very God Himself in the core and center of their hearts."[104]—A. W. Tozer.

~February 4~

Psalm 19:13
Presumptuous Sins

"Keep back thy servant also from presumptuous sins; let them not have dominion over me: then shall I be upright, and I shall be innocent from the great transgression" (Psalm 19:13).

J. A. Alexander states, "As he [David] prays for the forgiveness of his inadvertent sins, so he prays for the prevention of deliberate ones."[105] What is it to sin presumptuously?

1. To sin contrary to spiritual light and knowledge.

2. To sin defiantly of conscience.

3. To sin arrogantly against God's law without fear of punishment. Any form of habitual sin brings divine judgment.

4. To sin willfully in the belief that God is unconcerned about the wrong done.

5. To sin obstinately against the reproof of the Holy Spirit.

6. To sin justifiably, making a fallacious case of it being acceptable. No amount of rationalization can make something wrong right.

7. To sin contemptibly, taking God's mercy and forgiveness for granted (Hebrews 10:29).

How may presumptuous sins be thwarted?

1. By awareness of them and their displeasure to God.

2. By passionate prayer. "Keep back thy servant." Man is so corrupt that only God can keep him from the "dominion or captivity" of presumptuous sin.

3. By fear of committing the great transgression. David seems to refer to "the sin which is unto death," the wrathful judgment of God that takes the believer suddenly to Heaven (1 John 5:16). Immediate confession and cleansing of sin safeguard the believer from this consequence.

4. By restraining from any act that violates the Scripture, the light within the heart, and the impression of the Holy Spirit.

"The whitest robes, unless their purity be preserved by divine grace, will be defiled by the blackest spots."[106]—C. H. Spurgeon.

~February 5~

Psalm 20:7
Worthy of Our Trust

"Some trust in chariots, and some in horses: but we will remember the name of the LORD our God" (Psalm 20:7).

King David had a thousand chariots and seven thousand horsemen captured from the King of Zobah by his foot-soldiers (1 Chronicles 18:4). But says David, he will not trust in them in battle but depend on the Lord for triumph who commanded His kings "not [to] multiply horses" (Deuteronomy 17:16). "They [all that trust in 'chariots and horses'] are brought down and fallen [defeat and collapse]: but we [all that rely upon the Lord] are risen, and stand upright [successful, victorious]" (Psalm 20:8).

Is your foundational trust for help in the hour of adversity, grief, or sickness in physicians, politicians, preachers, personal prowess, or in Sovereign God? David encourages us to "remember the name of the LORD" in times of need and to trust in His power, protection, and provision. Barnes remarks, "We will not forget that our reliance is not on armies, but on God, the living God. Whatever instrumentality we may employ, we will remember always that our hope is in God and that He only can give success."[107]

Spurgeon asserts, "Chariots and horses make an imposing show and with their rattling and dust and fine caparisons make so great a figure that vain man is much taken with them, yet the discerning eye of faith sees more in an invisible God than in all these."[108] The person who trusts in the Lord will be delighted and delivered. This truth is affirmed time and again in Scripture: 2 Chronicles 14:11–12 (Asa); 2 Chronicles 20:12 (Jehoshaphat); 2 Chronicles 32:7–8 (Hezekiah); Psalm 33:17; 34:22; 118:8 (David). Trusting God first and foremost opens the door to Him supplying our needs through miraculous intervention or human agency.

"How apt we are in the hour of stress and trial to turn for help to that which is merely earthly or human and so often fails us. If you once know the blessedness of depending on God, you will find it is a luxury to trust in Him. Your confidence will not be in the natural but in the spiritual."[109]—H. A. Ironside.

~February 6~

Psalm 21:1–2
The King of Kings

"The king shall joy in thy strength, O LORD; and in thy salvation how greatly shall he rejoice! Thou hast given him his heart's desire" (Psalm 21:1–2).

Some view King David in the Psalm, but a greater than David is here—King Jesus. Spurgeon says, "Jesus is not merely *a* King, but *the* King—King over minds and hearts, reigning with a dominion of love, before which all other rule is mere brute force. He was proclaimed King even on the cross, for there, indeed, to the eye of faith, he reigned as on a throne."[110]

1. Observe the king's strength. Jehovah God strengthened Jesus to drink the bitter cup of man's sin at Calvary, making salvation possible (Luke 22:42–43). Matthew Henry says, "Our Lord Jesus, in His great undertaking, relied upon help from Heaven and pleased Himself with the prospect of that great salvation which He was thereby to work out."[111]

2. Observe the king's salvation. David says, "in thy salvation." Jehovah authored, orchestrated, and accomplished it through the death of His only Son on the cross. "Salvation belongs to our God, who is seated on the throne, and to the Lamb!" (Revelation 7:10 CSB).

3. Observe the king's joy. David says the king's rejoicing will be great! Says Spurgeon, "The rejoicing of our risen Lord must, like his agony, be unutterable."[112] Jesus rejoices in the salvation He wrought with singing. The Bible says, "The LORD thy God in the midst of thee is mighty; he will save, he will rejoice over thee with joy; he will rest in his love, he will joy over thee with singing" (Zephaniah 3:17). All the saved ought to joy with Christ in their salvation that brought an eternal transformation to the soul, and broadcast it to the world.

4. Observe the king's favor. "Thou hast given him his heart's desire" (Psalm 21:2). Jehovah answered Jesus' prayers for the salvation of the world (John 17:1–3). Let us pray with our King for the salvation of all people (Psalm 2:8).

King George II attended the premiere performance of Handel's *Messiah* in London in March 1743. The moment the musical began the *Hallelujah Chorus,* he stood up, prompting all to stand. The tradition continues today, acknowledging Jesus Christ as King of Kings and Lord of Lords.

"If you had a thousand crowns, you should put them all on the head of Christ! And if you had a thousand tongues, they should all sing His praise, for He is worthy!"—William Tiptaft.

Psalm 22:1
When God is Silent

"My God, my God, why hast thou forsaken me?" (Psalm 22:1).

Matthew Henry says, "Spiritual desertions are the saints' sorest afflictions; when their evidences are clouded, divine consolations suspended, their communion with God interrupted, and the terrors of God set in array against them, how sad are their spirits, and how sapless all their comforts!"[113]

When the soul feels abandoned by God, do as David.

1. Remember, God is still your God. "My God, my God." Nothing can sever man's union with God.

2. Live by faith, not feeling. "The just shall live by faith." Feelings come and go, but God never will. He is the one constant in a world of change.

3. Make inquiry of God. "Why are you so far away from helping me, so far away from the words of my groaning?" (Psalm 22:1 GW). Vent your burdens and questions to God. "Speech helps to unburden the heart."[114]

4. Never give up on God. "O my God, I cry in the daytime, but thou hearest not; and in the night season, and am not silent" (Psalm 22:2). "When we want the faith of assurance," wrote Matthew Henry, "we must live by a faith of adherence."[115]

5. Speak well of God. "But thou art holy" (Psalm 22:3). Praise God that He is trustworthy, fair, just, and true to His promises and faithful to His people. Says Spurgeon, "However ill things may look, there is no ill in thee, O God!"[116] Stevenson says it is as if David said, "It matters not what I endure. Storms may howl upon me; men

despise; devils tempt; circumstances overpower; and God Himself forsake me. Still, God is holy; there is no unrighteousness in Him."[117]

6. Recall God's trustworthiness to saints in similar trials. "Our fathers trusted in thee: they trusted, and thou didst deliver them" (Psalm 22:4). Spurgeon asserts, "The experience of other saints may be a great consolation to us when in deep waters if faith can be sure that their deliverance will be ours."[118]

"God cannot be far from a man who retains the sense of His holy faithfulness."[119]—S. Conway.

~February 8~

Psalm 22:2
Why Prayers Go Unanswered

"O my God, I cry in the daytime, but Thou hearest not; and in the night season, and am not silent" (Psalm 22:2).

Why are many prayers unanswered?

1. The presence of sin (Isaiah 59:1–2). As Blanchard states, "We cannot expect to live defectively and pray effectively."[120] Matthew Henry states, "The hands must be cleansed by faith, repentance, and reformation, or it will be in vain for us to draw nigh to God in prayer, or in any of the exercises of devotion."[121]

2. The absence of faith (James 1:6–8). Prayer must be delivered in confidence and trust that God hears and will answer. Cowman wrote, "Genuine faith puts its letter in the mailbox and lets go. Distrust, however, holds on to a corner of the envelope and then wonders why the answer never arrives."[122]

3. Praying outside God's will (Luke 22:42). Cymbala says, "The first rule of prayer is not 'faith,' but whether the request is according to God's will." In prayer, always add the proviso, "not my will, but thine, be done." James H. Brooks cautions, "Without submission to the will of God as infinitely right and infinitely wise, prayer is not prayer."[123]

4. Indifference toward the Word of God. Solomon said, "He that turneth away his ear from hearing the law, even his prayer shall be abomination" (Proverbs 28:9). Lawson argues, "When we live in a willful disobedience to any of God's commandments, we cannot impose on the hearer of prayer if we hope that any of our requests will be acceptable to him."[124]

5. An unforgiving spirit. Jesus said, "When you are praying, and you remember that you are angry with another person about something, then forgive him. If you do this, then your Father in heaven will also forgive your sins" (Mark 11:25 ICB).

Answered prayer will come to him who can say, "Nothing between my soul and the Savior."

"God has not placed Himself under obligation to honor the requests of worldly, carnal, or disobedient Christians. He hears and answers the prayers only of those who walk in His way."[125]—A. W. Tozer.

~February 9~

Psalm 23:1–6
The Shepherd Figure of Christ

"The LORD is my shepherd" (Psalm 23:1).

In keeping his father's sheep as a lad, David learned that sheep are dim-witted animals constantly dependent upon the shepherd for survival and guidance. Now much older and wiser, viewing himself as a "dumb" sheep needing constant care and God as the Good Shepherd who supplied it, he pens this psalm to detail how God provided for him (and provides for every believer) throughout life.

1. The salvation of the sheep. "The LORD is *my* shepherd." "By the authority of His redemptive work, His death and resurrection, you can trust Him and call Him your shepherd."[126]

2. The sufficiency of the sheep. "I shall not want." People with Christ as their Good Shepherd will not go lacking, for He banishes want in their lives by His gracious care and provision.

3. The serenity of the sheep. "He maketh me to lie down in green pastures: he leadeth me beside the still waters." Green pastures and still waters are picturesque of tranquility and peace. Under the Good Shepherd's care, the believer finds calm and rest amidst conflict, sickness, and sorrow.

4. The security of the sheep. "I will fear no evil: for thou art with me." The Good Shepherd watches over the flock, ensuring no harm or injury comes to them. David knew this from experience; he once wrestled with a bear and a lion to protect a sheep.

5. The succor of the sheep. "Thy rod and thy staff they comfort me." Whatever "valley of the shadow," that of gloom and sorrow experienced, Christ's presence and care will bring relief, calm, and comfort. To know that He walks with us in and through the valleys of hardship, pain, and death makes them bearable.

6. The sureness of the sheep. "Surely goodness and mercy shall follow me all the days of my life." Simeon states, "All the rest of the world are following after happiness, and it eludes their grasp, but those who believe in Jesus have happiness following after them."[127] And at life's end, the redeemed will dwell in the house of God, with Him, forever.

"In the Lord Jesus, we have sovereignty and sympathy, a king and a shepherd. We have a God who is able and a shepherd who is available, a God in the heavens and a shepherd in our hearts."[128]— Adrian Rogers.

~February 10~

Psalm 23:1–6
The Pearl of the Psalms
Part 1

"The LORD is my shepherd" (Psalm 23:1).

David uses the metaphor of the shepherd and sheep to testify of the Good Shepherd's care and comfort afforded to the sheep in His fold.

The Good Shepherd justifies the sheep (v. 1a). Spurgeon says, "No man has a right to consider himself the Lord's sheep unless his nature has been renewed, for the scriptural description of unconverted men does not picture them as sheep, but as wolves or goats."[129]

The Good Shepherd supplies the sheep (v. 1b–2). Though animals that flock together, sheep receive individualized care from the Shepherd. He ensures no sheep in the fold lacks anything necessary ("shall not want"). Abundant food in green pastures, refreshing water in quiet streams and brooks, and proper shelter to rest are always provided. The Good Shepherd provides His sheep with spiritual nourishment, renewal, rest, and direction through the Holy Scripture.

The Good Shepherd quiets the sheep (v. 2). "He maketh me to lie down." Green pastures and still waters are pictures of tranquility and peace. The Lord's sheep must often be compelled to lie lest they fall. We must "come apart" so we don't "fall apart."

The Good Shepherd revives the sheep (v. 3). "He restoreth my soul." He grants the sheep spiritual and mental rejuvenation. Alexander says, "To restore the soul here is to vivify or quicken the exhausted spirit."

The Good Shepherd guides the sheep (v. 3). He leads the sheep in the right paths, the way of uprightness in heart and faithfulness in duty. He orchestrates the entirety of life to their delight and His glory. Matthew Henry says, "In these paths, we cannot walk unless God both lead us into them and lead us in them."[130]

"Yea, though I walk through the valley of the shadow of death." "Observe," Spurgeon asserts, "that it is not walking *in* the valley but *through* it. We go through the dark tunnel of death and emerge into the light of immortality. We do not die; we do but sleep to wake in glory. Death is not the house but the porch, not the goal but the passage to it."[131]

"If God be as a shepherd to us, we must be as sheep, inoffensive, meek, and quiet, silent before the shearers, nay, and before the butcher too, useful and sociable; we must know the shepherd's voice, and follow him."[132]—Matthew Henry.

~February 11~

Psalm 23:1–6
The Pearl of the Psalms
Part 2

"The LORD is my shepherd" (Psalm 23:1).

Yesterday, five things were noted that the Good Shepherd does for His sheep. Note three more.

The Good Shepherd chides the sheep (v. 2a). Sheep, by nature, are prone to wander, stray from the sheepfold, and, once lost, cannot find their way back. The shepherd's task is to search for and restore them to the sheepfold. Likewise, when a sheep of the flock of the Lord strays into the "far country," He diligently pursues it until it is found. Upon finding it, He rebukes, corrects, and restores it—graciously and mercifully forgives sin when confessed and restores the confessor.

The Good Shepherd abides with the sheep (v. 4b). Parker says, "My hand is locked in Thine; my life is drawn from Thine; my future is involved in Thine; God and the saint are one."[133] Plumer says, "The safety of God's people in this life does not consist in exemption from troubles and perils, but in the care and protection of Him who hides them in His pavilion and in His tabernacle and sets them upon a rock."[134]

The Good Shepherd satisfies the sheep (v. 6). The sheep of the Good Shepherd testify of the bountiful goodness throughout life received from His hand. Barnes observes, "The language is the utterance of a heart overflowing with joy and gratitude in the recollection of the past, and full of glad anticipation (as derived from the experience of the past) regarding the future."[135] "I will dwell in the house of the LORD forever." At last, Christ's sheep will be satisfied with their new home, prepared in Heaven by the Lord.

Maclaren wrote, "God will bring those whom He has fed and guided in journeying and conflict to an unchanging mansion in a home beyond the stars." This He promised (John 14:1–3).

"In special, whatsoever sweet relation the believer standeth in with God, he may assure himself of all the fruits, and good, which that relation can import."[136]—D. Dickson.

~February 12~

Psalm 23:1

Never Wanting

"The LORD is my shepherd; I shall not want" (Psalm 23:1).

The believer's needs God will supply. Things not provided count as contrary to God's will or as unprofitable. Specifically, David cites nine things the sheep of Christ's fold will not go lacking for.

1. I shall not want for tranquility if the Lord is my shepherd, for "He maketh me to lie down in green pastures." Green pastures are places where God feeds the sheep with nourishing truths of manna from His Holy Word and gives them rest, calm, and contentment in the storms of life.

2. I shall not want for restoration, for "He refreshes my soul" (NIV)—not restoration due to wandering astray but from weariness, sorrow, anxiety, and exhaustion caused by care and toil.

3. I shall not want for guidance, for "He leadeth me in the paths of righteousness." Sheep are apt to wander from the safe paths to those of harm. They need the shepherd's guiding hand to order and safeguard their steps so they will not stray. Even doth the sheep of Christ's fold.

4. I shall not want for fearlessness, for "I will fear no evil." Faith and trust expressed in the Good Shepherd to do all promised embolden the sheep in times of danger and trial.

5. I shall not want for a friend, for "thou art with me." His companionship is our support. Friends cannot always be counted upon to help, but we know that no matter how dark the night or fierce the storm is, Christ is a constant friend who sticks closer than a brother.

6. I shall not want for supply, for "thou preparest a table before me." When Christ spreads a table, it's furnished with all that a hungry and thirsty soul desires or needs. "Jesus saith unto them, Come and dine" (John 21:12).

7. I shall not want for happiness, for "my cup runneth over." Christ's sheep know overflowing happiness and satisfaction (John 10:10). He 'anointeth the head with the oil' of gladness and joy (Psalm 45:7).

8. I shall not want for goodness and mercy, for "goodness and mercy shall follow me all the days of my life." The sheep of Christ's fold never have to look for mercy and unfailing love, for they have it forever in Him.

9. I shall not want for an eternal abode, for "I will dwell in the house of the LORD forever" (verse 6 NIV). A home in Heaven is promised to all in Christ's flock (John 14:1–3).

"I shall not want." There are two ways of not lacking a thing in this world. He lacks nothing who has everything. The better way is for a man to look up and bring his desires down to that which God sees fit to give him."[137]—Phillip Brooks.

~February 13~

Psalm 23:5
The Overflowing Cup

"My cup runneth over" (Psalm 23:5).

David exclaimed, "My cup runneth over." The overflowing cup symbolizes the euphoric heart. Nothing is lacking in it of God's superlative care, love, and provision. "He satisfieth the longing soul, and filleth the hungry soul with goodness" (Psalm 107:9). Of it, Augustine said, "Thou hast gladdened my mind with spiritual joy. And Thy inebriating cup, how excellent is it!"[138]

What causes a cup to overflow?

1. Relationship. "I am my beloved's, and my beloved is mine" (Song of Solomon 6:3). "To me, it's so wonderful. To me, it's so wonderful. To me, it's so wonderful to know that Jesus is mine." David said, "We are happy all day because of you" (Psalm 89:16 CEV).

2. Fellowship. An abiding, sweet communion with Christ. "Abide in me, and I in you....These things have I spoken unto you, that my joy might remain in you, and that your joy might be full" (John 15:4, 11). Miles wrote, "And He walks with me, and He talks with me, And He tells me I am His own, And the joy we share as we tarry there, none other has ever known."

3. Worship. Praise, wrapped with remembrance and gratitude for the undeserved goodness of the Lord, brings unspeakable joy (Psalm 63:5). Praise is a spout where 'Heaven comes down, and glory fills my soul' (Psalm 22:3). 'When I mused the fire burned.' Thoughts of Christ's unfailing love and compassion should cause a shouting fit, prompting you to exclaim, "Your unfailing love is better than life itself" (Psalm 63:3 NLT), "My cup runneth over" (Psalm 23:5).

The overflowing cup blesses and refreshes others with its droppings. Trapp said, "Those that have this happiness must carry their cup upright and see that it overflows into their poor brethren's emptier vessels."[139]

"The heart never satisfied, the conscience never at rest, the cup never filled, is the unvarying experience of this world's votaries. Until the heart finds safe anchorage in the love of the Good Shepherd, there never can be an overflowing cup."[140]—J. W. Nichols.

~February 14~

Psalm 24:3–4
How to Meet with God

"Who shall ascend into the hill of the LORD*? or who shall stand in his holy place? He that hath clean hands, and a pure heart; who hath not lifted up his soul unto vanity, nor sworn deceitfully"* (Psalm 24:3–4).

David asks the question upon bringing the Ark of God from the house of Obed-Edom to the Tabernacle prepared for it on Mt. Zion (2 Samuel 6:12).[141]

How is fellowship with the holy and mighty God to be attained? It is with purity and incorruption inside and out. Benson states, "Clean hearts are required in our attendance on the great God."[142] "A man may be clean-handed so far as the eyes of men are concerned and black-hearted to the eyes of God."[143] At Sinai, God told Moses to get the people ready to meet with Him (Exodus 19:10–11). The sanctifying preparation would take two full days; one day wouldn't be enough.

How much earnest time do you spend in preparation to meet with God? Two full days may be unnecessary, but some time certainly is to entertain the audience of a Holy God. God says, "Wash you, make you clean; put away the evil of your doings from before mine eyes; cease to do evil" (Isaiah 1:16). The person who puts away sin and is cleansed not only may ascend "into the hill of the LORD" to fellowship and worship God but "he shall receive the blessing from the LORD, and righteousness from the God of his salvation" (Psalm 24:5).

"The holy God, who is of purer eyes than to behold iniquity, calls here for heart-purity, and to such as are adorned with this jewel, He promises a glorious and beatifical vision of Himself. They shall see God."[144]—Thomas Watson.

Psalm 25:1–2
The Uplifted Soul

"Unto thee, O LORD, do I lift up my soul. O my God, I trust in thee" (Psalm 25:1–2).

Throughout the Psalms, David is found 'lifting up' his soul to the Lord for help, comfort, protection, strength, deliverance, wisdom, and guidance, as in this Psalm. He is seen praying in the morning (Psalm 5:3), at noon and night (Psalm 55:17), seven times throughout the day (Psalm 119:164), and continuously (Psalm 25:15). He delighted in frequent fellowship with the Lord and was elevated by it.

1. Only the soul lifted to God meets with God. Exertion fueled by faith and trust lifts the soul to fixate upon the Lord. David says, "O my God, I trust in thee" (Psalm 25:2). It's one thing to lift up hands and eyes to the Lord and quite another to lift up the soul to Him—the latter results in effective prayer without the former, but never the former without the latter. Spurgeon says, "It is but mockery to uplift the hands and the eyes unless we also bring our souls into our devotions. True prayer may be described as the soul rising from earth to have fellowship with Heaven."[145] A few pounds of soul prayer immeasurably outweigh a ton of heartless prayer.

2. Only the soul lifted *to* God is lifted *by* Him to a higher spiritual ground and receives an answer to prayer.

3. Only he that lifts his soul to God departs touched and changed. His burdens are lifted or become lighter, sorrow is consoled, sin is forgiven, fear abated, deliverance granted, and anxieties calmed. F. W. Brown says the lifted soul is transported with Divine nearness, transformed into Divine likeness, and translated into the Divine presence now and hereafter.[146]

"In worshipping God, we must lift up our souls to him. Prayer is the ascent of the soul to God; God must be eyed and the soul employed."[147]—Matthew Henry.

~February 16~

Psalm 25:11
The Grounds for Pardon

"For thy name's sake, O LORD, pardon mine iniquity; for it is great" (Psalm 25:11).

David details what a person should do with their sin.

1. Own it. "Mine iniquity." Matthew Henry said, "The more we see of the heinousness of our sins, the better qualified we are to find mercy with God."[148] The first step to the cleansing of sin is its admittance.

2. Don't justify it. David did not minimize, excuse, or justify his sin. Forthrightly, he cried, "O LORD, pardon mine iniquity."

3. Go to God with it. The greatness of the sin didn't prevent David from confessing it to the Lord. Great sins don't invalidate the promise of pardon. A sin may be ugly and hideous, but God's forgiveness remains true. The greater the pardon, the greater the glory to the name of the Lord.[149]

4. Claim forgiveness in His name for it. God's name is associated with His mercy, unfailing love, righteousness, faithfulness, and promise to forgive sin (Psalm 25:7). The ground for forgiveness is not personal goodness or merit. It is the lovingkindness of the Lord revealed in His name (Who He Is). Plead forgiveness to the glory and honor of that name. 'For thy name's sake…pardon mine iniquity.'

"Tie a Yellow Ribbon Round the Ole Oak Tree" is a song based on folklore, but its symbolism of love and forgiveness well illustrates God's love for a wayward man. After being released from prison, a son wrote to his parents, informing them that he would be on a train passing their home on a specific day. If he was welcome home, they were to "tie a yellow ribbon round the ole oak tree" in the front yard. The moment arrived when he would know of their decision. As the train neared his house, fearful of not seeing a yellow ribbon, he asked a passenger to look for him. The person looked and didn't see one yellow ribbon but yellow ribbons hanging from every limb of the tree!

All who have wandered far away from God can be assured of a tree full of yellow ribbons awaiting their return. This, the prodigal son attests (Luke 15:20).

"The power of pardon is permanently resident with God; He has forgiveness ready to His hand at this instant."[150]—C. H. Spurgeon.

~February 17~

Psalm 25:17

Persevering Prayer

"The troubles of my heart are enlarged: O bring thou me out of my distresses" (Psalm 25:17).

Ensnared in the net of adversity or affliction, we pray like David: "Bring...me out." How long should we pray for deliverance from an infirmity or adversity? Until it is answered with a yes, no, or not now, or assurance is given that it will be answered. "The most difficult prayer," wrote Ole Hallesby, "and the prayer which, therefore, costs us the most striving, is persevering prayer, the prayer which faints not, but continues steadfastly until the answer comes."[151] "Importunate praying," says E. M. Bounds, "has patience to wait and strength to continue. It never prepares itself to quit praying and declines to rise from its knees until an answer is received."[152]

"The secret of prevailing prayer," writes Duewel, "is simply to pray until the answer comes. The length of time is ultimately immaterial. It is God's answer that counts. The length of time required may often seem perplexing and may prove a test of your faith."[153] Daniel prayed for three weeks before receiving an answer from God (Daniel 10:2). Despite the direction the winds blow, be unshakeable in your confidence that God will answer the prayer based upon His Word and Sovereign will (James 1:6–7). "Will not God make the things that are right come to His chosen people who cry day and night to Him?" (Luke 18:7 NLV).

To underscore the importance of praying with importunity (relentlessly and with fervency), Jesus shared the parable of the importunate widow (Luke 18:1–8). A widow pleaded for help from a judge. Being denied, she pleaded again and again. Finally, the judge said, "'I fear neither God nor man…but this woman bothers me. I'm going to see that she gets justice, for she is wearing me out with her constant coming!' Then the Lord said, 'If even an evil judge can be worn down like that, don't you think that God will surely give justice to his people who plead with him day and night? Yes! He will answer them quickly!'" (Luke 18:5–8 TLB).

The lesson: God wants us to pray and keep praying until His will is granted. "There is always," said Spurgeon, "an open ear if you have an open mouth. There is always a ready hand if you have a ready heart. You have but to cry, and the Lord hears."[154]

"The great fault of the children of God is, they do not continue in prayer; they do not go on praying; they do not persevere. If they desire anything for God's glory, they should pray until they get it."[155]—George Müller.

~February 18~

Psalm 26:2
Divine Scrutiny

"Examine me, O LORD, and prove me; try my reins and my heart" (Psalm 26:2).

David implores God to perform a three-fold examination of his life.

Examine me. Expose the sin in my life. God knows the heart and detects its darkest secrets (Jeremiah 17:9–10). "A man may be clean-handed so far as the eyes of men are concerned and black-hearted to the eyes of God."

Prove me. Test the devotion and commitment of my heart to see if it's strong and unshakeable. Don't overestimate the strength you possess. Peter boasted that he would never deny the Lord, yet he did this three times (Matthew 26:34–35). Spurgeon states, "Trials teach us what we are; they dig up the soil and let us see what we are made of."

Sift me. Purge all impurities in my life. Make me like gold, pure gold free from defect (Job 23:10). Believers should frequently present themselves to God for a scrutinizing examination to see if all is proper in their fellowship with Him and their walk (Psalm 139:23).

Search me, O God, and know my heart today;
Try me, O Savior, know my thoughts, I pray.
See if there be some wicked way in me;
Cleanse me from ev'ry sin and set me free.

—J. Orwin Orr.

"Make up your spiritual accounts daily; see how matters stand between God and your souls. Often, reckonings keep God and conscience friends."[156]—Thomas Watson.

~February 19~

Psalm 26:8
Affection for God's House

"LORD, I have loved the habitation of thy house, and the place where thine honor dwelleth" (Psalm 26:8).

David so loved the house of God that when driven from Zion into exile, it was much missed. He cried, "My soul thirsteth for God, for the living God: when shall I come and appear before God?" (Psalm 42:2). Another time, he said, "The zeal [passion, love, devotion] of Thine house hath eaten me up [consumed me]" (Psalm 69:9) and

"One thing have I desired of the LORD, that will I seek after; that I may dwell in the house of the LORD all the days of my life" (Psalm 27:4). Every saint's heart pounds with that same beat (or should).

Why do Christians love the church?

1. We love its place. We love the church because Christ loves it, was instituted by Him, and is purposed for His corporate worship and adoration, fellowship, and the edification of the saints.

2. We love its preaching. Biblical truth that nourishes the soul and enriches life is proclaimed within its doors.

3. We love its people. Empathy exists with those who profess and proclaim Christ as Lord.

4. We love its purpose. Its main business is to magnify Christ and make Him known (Matthew 28:19–20).

5. We love its provision. We treasure its instruction, support, and sweet fellowship.

6. We love its praise. The saints delight in their adulation to Christ in corporate worship (Psalm 95:3).

7. We love its petition. We love the church because it is "a house of prayer" (Acts 2:42).

8. We love its peace. The church is an oasis of love and tranquility in an ocean of hate and chaos.

9. We love its permanence. The "gates of Hell" are not strong enough to prevent the church's existence or mission (Matthew 16:18).

> I love your church, O Lord!
> Her saints before you stand,
> Dear, as the apple of your eye
> And graven on your hand.
>
> —Timothy Dwight (1800)

"In the sanctuary, prayer and praise and the Word have calmed our minds, raised us to a higher plane, given us a truer sense of the proportion of things, juster views of God and His dealings."[157]—*The Homilist.*

Psalm 27:3
The Basics of Confidence in God

"Yes, though a mighty army marches against me, my heart shall know no fear! I am confident that God will save me" (Psalm 27:3 TLB).

Nothing grants peace and stability in a storm like confidence in God. This confidence is grounded in four things.

1. It is founded on a relationship with God. David exclaimed, "The LORD is *my* light and *my* salvation...the strength of my life" (Psalm 27:1).

2. It is founded on God's willingness and power to help His own. David said, "For thou, LORD, wilt bless the righteous; with favour wilt thou compass him as with a shield" (Psalm 5:12).

3. It is founded on God's past performances. God's past help is a pledge of present help. What He did yesterday for us is an argument for His willingness to do it again. David used the argument (rationale) to fight the giant Goliath. He said to King Saul, "The LORD that delivered me out of the paw of the lion, and out of the paw of the bear, he will deliver me out of the hand of this Philistine" (1 Samuel 17:37). He was calm (virtually fearless) and confident in facing Goliath because of his past victories and deliverances at God's hand. Remembering instills trust in God's faithfulness to be "a very present help in trouble" (Psalm 46:1). Sangster said, "God never gives a blessing just for the hour. Every special blessing is not only for the hour itself but for the future as well. It is a pledge."[158]

4. It is founded on God's promises. David prayed, "Never forget your promises to me, your servant, for they are my only hope. They give me strength in all my troubles; how they refresh and revive me!" (Psalm 119:49 TLB). God's promises are like unseen pillars of rock in deep, troublesome waters that support believers who stand upon them.

"Faith is a living, daring confidence in God's grace, so sure and certain that the believer would stake his life on it a thousand times."—Martin Luther.

~February 21~

Psalm 27:6
Benefits of Confidence in God

"And now shall mine head be lifted up above mine enemies round about me: therefore will I offer in his tabernacle sacrifices of joy; I will sing, yea, I will sing praises unto the LORD" (Psalm 27:6).

David's confidence in God didn't disappoint. He says, "When the wicked, even mine enemies and my foes, came upon me to eat up my flesh, they stumbled and fell" (Psalm 27:2).

1. Confidence in God gives fortitude in battle. To know that the battle is the Lord's grants hope for deliverance. The Bible says, "Do not be afraid or discouraged....For the battle is not yours, but God's" (2 Chronicles 20:15 NIV).

2. Confidence in God grants comfort and calm. David's trust in God displaced worry and stress. Isaiah told the Lord, "Thou wilt keep him in perfect peace, whose mind is stayed on thee: *because he trusteth in thee*" (Isaiah 26:3).

3. Confidence in God dispels worry. Chan wrote, "Worry implies that we don't quite trust that God is big enough, powerful enough, or loving enough to take care of what's happening in our lives."

4. Confidence in God lifts the head up above trials (Psalm 27:6a; Psalm 3:3).

5. Confidence in God births joy, song, and praises unto the Lord (Psalm 27:6b). The psalmist says, "Blessed [happy] are those whose help is the God of Jacob, whose hope is in the LORD their God" (Psalm 146:5 NIV).

"When it actually comes to push of pike, faith's shield will ward off the blow; and if the first brush should be but the beginning of a war, yet faith's banners will wave in spite of the foe."[159]—C. H. Spurgeon.

Psalm 28:2
The Uplifted Hand

"Hear the voice of my supplications, when I cry unto thee, when I lift up my hands toward thy holy oracle" (Psalm 28:2).

Ellicott states that the practice of uplifted hands in prayer seems to have been generally adopted by early Christians.[160] David did it. He lifts his hands toward God from the pit of despair in our text. Not only did he use it, but he advocated it, saying, "Lift up your hands in the sanctuary, and bless the LORD" (Psalm 134:2).

Paul undoubtedly did it, for he encouraged its practice, saying, "I will therefore that men pray everywhere, lifting up holy hands, without wrath and doubting" (1 Timothy 2:8). Solomon engaged it. He "stood before the altar of the LORD in the presence of all the congregation of Israel, and spread forth his hands toward heaven" (1 Kings 8:22).

Ezra and the entire congregation did it. Upon hearing the Law of God read, they "answered, Amen, Amen, with lifting up their hands" (Nehemiah 8:6). Abraham did it. "Abram said to the king of Sodom, 'I have lifted my hand to the LORD, God Most High, Possessor of heaven and earth'" (Genesis 14:22 ESV).

1. The uplifted open palms signify supplication.

2. The uplifted open palms signify utter dependence upon God for help, like that of children who lift up their hands to their mother or father out of need.

3. The uplifted open palms signify the expectation of God's answer. Spurgeon asserts, "Uplifted hands have always been a form of devout posture and are intended to signify a reaching upward

towards God, a readiness, an eagerness to receive the blessing sought after."[161]

4. The uplifted open palms lifted to the Lord signify surrender. Nothing is kept back. A presentation of all that we are is made to Him (Romans 12:1–2).

5. The uplifted open palms to the Lord signify that the heart is not embracing or clutching anything unclean or unholy.

6. The uplifted open palms to the Lord signify praise, adoration, love, and passion for the Lord.

"The lifting up of the hands is a natural symbol of the raising of the heart or the desires to God, and is therefore often mentioned in connection with the act of prayer."[162]—J. A. Alexander.

~February 23~

Psalm 29:2
The Gist of Worship

"Give unto the LORD *the glory due unto his name; worship the* LORD *in the beauty of holiness"* (Psalm 29:2).

David exhorts man and angels to worship God three times in the first two verses of the Psalm.

1. The purpose of worship. It is to glorify and magnify the name of God. Wiersbe states, "Worship is the believer's response of all that he is—mind, emotions, will, and body—to all that God is and says and does." William Temple said, "To worship is to quicken the conscience by the holiness of God, to feed the mind with the truth of God, to purge the imagination by the beauty of God, to open the heart to the love of God, to devote the will to the purpose of God."[163]

2. The priority of worship. Tozer asserts, "We're here to be worshipers first and workers only second."

3. The practice of worship. Worship continuously. An old saint said, as one foot is lifted, let the believer say hallelujah, and then, as it comes down, let him praise the Lord.

4. The preparation for worship. Worship requires an inner garment of holiness and devotion ("beauty of holiness").

5. The posture in worship. It is not a physical posture but a spiritual one that is of supreme importance. Spurgeon says, "Bow before him with devout homage and sacred awe."[164] If the knees bend apart from the heart bowing, the worship is unacceptable unto the Lord.

"Worship is the highest elevation of the spirit, and yet the lowliest prostration of the soul."[165]—C. H. Spurgeon.

~February 24~

Psalm 30:5
Joy Comes in the Morning

"Weeping may endure for a night, but joy cometh in the morning" (Psalm 30:5).

The chastening rod of God to Israel for her rebellious behavior caused weeping and distress "for a night," but upon their repentance, "in the morning," the divine judgment ended and joy was restored.

The promise is an adaptable pledge of God to every sorrowing believer. "Weeping" is pictured as a stranger who lodges with the believer but for the night. The unwanted stranger causes us to toss and turn in unrest, wet our pillow with tears, and become mentally and spiritually strained and drained, miserable and helpless. It appears the night will never end. The "night" (cause of weeping) includes bereavement, which puts the heart in the winepress of perhaps life's deepest woe and sorrow; incurable illness; the frailty of body and mind (dementia); suffering; and various trials and troubles. All *weeping* is relieved by a compassionate and consoling God to whom it is brought. "He heals the brokenhearted and bandages their wounds" (Psalm 147:3 NLT).

Grief is said to last for the night.

1. The night is brief. It will not last for long.

2. The night is under the control of God, as is the day. He that will not suffer thy foot to stumble in the day will not allow you to stumble in the night (Psalm 121:3).

3. The night is compelled to end. It has no power or authority to extend beyond its allotted time. The duration of grief will end by divine decree.

4. The night has glimpses of light. The stars in the heavens sprinkle light in the night. The Holy Spirit doth the same for the saint in the dark nights of sorrow, sickness, and suffering to comfort, sustain, and strengthen. The Bible says, "LORD, you light my lamp; my God illuminates my darkness" (Psalm 18:28 CSB).

5. The night is always followed by morning. The long night of distress and agony seems relentless and unbearable. And well it might be, were it not for the consolation and compassion of Christ. In the morning, the lament of grief gives way to the joy of relief. A. C. Dixon states, "God knows how to make the night produce the morning. Your sorrow shall be transmuted into joy."[166]

"Mourning only lasts till morning; when the night is gone, the gloom shall vanish."[167]—C. H. Spurgeon.

~February 25~

Psalm 31:5
The Saint's Dying Prayer

"Into thine hand I commit my spirit" (Psalm 31:5).

According to Matthew Henry, David meant one of two things by the committal, "Into thine hand I commit my spirit."

1. He was dying and committed himself to God for the heavenly departure.

2. He was in trouble and despair, and placed his trust in God as his hope for help and rescue.

At the threshold of death, the saying is a committal of the soul to God's care and custody for safekeeping through death's dark valley to Heaven. It was the last saying of our Lord on the cross (Luke 23:46), Luther, Polycarp, Melanchthon, Huss, and numerous martyrs. It also resembles Stephen's (Acts 7:59). The saying is one of confidence and certainty in God's promises to give the redeemed everlasting life in Heaven (John 14:1–3). Matthew Henry asserts, "That which encourages us to commit our spirits into the hand of God is that He has not only created but redeemed them."[168]

The saying is not just proper for death, but also for present danger. When his life was threatened, despair overtook him, and trouble surrounded him, David spoke the words (Psalm 31:5). Spurgeon asserts, "So, every day, go to Him with this declaration, 'Into Thine hand, I commit my spirit.' Nay, not only every day but all through the day. Have you to go into a house where there is a fever? I mean, is it your duty to go there? Then go saying, 'Father, into Thine hand I commit my spirit.' I would advise you to do this every time you walk down the street or even while you sit in your own house."[169]

There is no place as certain of safety as is our Lord's "hand." David said, "Even though I walk into the middle of trouble, you guard my life against the anger of my enemies. You stretch out your hand, and your right hand saves me" (Psalm 138:7 GW) and "My soul followeth hard after thee: thy right hand upholdeth me" (Psalm 63:8). Paul declared, "Being confident of this very thing, that he which hath begun a good work in you will perform it until the day of Jesus Christ" (Philippians 1:6).

"Where the spirit is fit for the presence of God, there is no fear of death."[170]—Joseph Parker.

~February 26~

Psalm 31:13
The Slanderous Tongue

"For I have heard the slander of many: fear was on every side" (Psalms 31:13).

Fortify yourself against slander, the lying of others who seek your demise. David faced it. You will. In being defamed, do four things.

1. Pray for the slanderer's poisonous tongue to be silenced. Pray with David, "Let the lying lips be put to silence" (Psalm 31:18). Spurgeon comments: "May God silence them either by leading them to repentance, by putting them too thorough shame, or by placing them in positions where what they may say will stand for nothing."[171]

2. Don't retaliate.

3. Employ the shield of faith. Despite appearances to the contrary, David held fast to the promise of God for deliverance. Plumer said, "Neither the multitude of our foes nor their slanders, nor their counsels, nor their murderous devising, nor anything else can destroy us, or dismay us if God be with us."[172]

4. Remember that God knows the truth. And since He knows of your innocence, He will vindicate you. Spurgeon said, "If a man blows out the candle of a Christian's reputation, God will light it again; if he does not do so in this life, remember that at the resurrection, there will be a resurrection of reputations as well as bodies: 'Then shall the righteous shine forth as the sun in the kingdom of their Father.'"[173]

"Truth is generally the best vindication against slander."—Abraham Lincoln.

~February 27~

Psalm 32:3–5
Confessing Sin
Part 1

"I acknowledge my sin unto thee, and mine iniquity have I not hid. I said, I will confess my transgressions unto the LORD; and thou forgavest the iniquity of my sin. Selah" (Psalm 32:5).

David experienced five stages of the mind and heart to find forgiveness.

The stage of silence (Psalm 32:3a). He sought to hide the sin with Bathsheba from man and God. Adam and Eve attempted to do the same, but to no avail. Augustine said, "In failing to confess, Lord, I would only hide You from myself, not myself from You."

The stage of guilt. David's conscience indicted him day and night with the awfulness of his actions (Psalm 32:4a). He soon discovered the answer to guilt was not an effort to forget or appease it but forgiveness of the sin that birthed it.

A *legend* exists about Pontius Pilate. Tradition says that following the 'washing of his hands' that ultimately led to Jesus' crucifixion, he returned to Rome to report what occurred. From there, it is said that he traveled to Switzerland, where, in anguish of guilt over what he had allowed to happen to Jesus, he committed suicide by jumping off a mountain. Mount Pilatus is allegedly named for him. This is only a legend, but it is no untruth that many people are hounded and chased by guilt over a wrong done, a sin committed.[174] As Adrian Rogers says, "Guilt is eating them alive, and they don't know what to do with it."[175]

The stage of discipline. David was chastised for the unconfessed sin (Psalm 32:4). In the companion text, Psalm 51, he says, "Make me to hear joy and gladness; that the bones which thou hast broken may rejoice" (Psalm 51:8). Gurnall said, "God's wounds cure; sin's kisses kill." A. W. Pink asserted, "Chastisement is designed for our good, to promote our highest interests. Look beyond the rod to the

69

All-wise hand that wields it!" The rod of chastisement may include sickness, sorrow, failure, and even death.

"It does not spoil your happiness to confess your sin. The unhappiness is in not making the confession."[176]—C. H. Spurgeon.

~February 28~

Psalm 32:3–5
Confessing Sin
Part 2

"I acknowledge my sin unto thee, and mine iniquity have I not hid. I said, I will confess my transgressions unto the LORD; and thou forgavest the iniquity of my sin. Selah" (Psalm 32:5).

Yesterday, we noted the first three stages of the mind and heart David experienced regarding his unconfessed sin with Bathsheba and the murder of Uriah. Today, we will note the final two. All but these final two stages might have been avoided had David responded sooner to the tug of God to repent.

The stage of conviction. Conviction, a work of the Holy Spirit, is feeling sullied and defiled over a sin committed and possessing a desire for its forgiveness. It took Nathan's blistering reproof, "Thou art the man" (2 Samuel 12:7), to awaken David's heart to the great sin he had done and the need for forgiveness. The appeal to repent of a sin committed may come but once from a preacher, friend, or colleague.

The stage of confession. David listened to the words of Nathan. "And David said unto Nathan, I have sinned against the LORD. And Nathan said unto David, The LORD also hath put away thy sin; thou shalt not die" (2 Samuel 12:13). In the Psalm before us, he speaks of that moment, saying, "I acknowledge my sin unto thee, and mine iniquity have I not hid. I said, I will confess my transgressions unto the LORD; and thou forgavest the iniquity of my sin" (Psalm 32:5).

70

The result of his heartfelt confession was complete forgiveness, as is the case with all who repent.

Solomon said, "He that covereth his sins shall not prosper: but whoso confesseth and forsaketh them shall have mercy" (Proverbs 28:13). Lutzer says, "Forgiveness is always free. But that doesn't mean that confession is always easy. Sometimes it is hard—incredibly hard. It is painful to admit our sins and entrust ourselves to God's care."[177]

"No sin can be crucified either in heart or life unless it be first pardoned in conscience because there will be want of faith to receive the strength of Jesus, by whom alone it can be crucified. If it be not mortified in its guilt, it cannot be subdued in its power."[178]— William Romaine.

~February 29~

Psalm 32:8
Guidance by God's Eye

"I will guide thee with mine eye" (Psalm 32:8).

As their king, David's servants' eyes were constantly fixed on him, eager to do his bidding. Each knew his duty, and when the eye of their master nodded or turned in a specific direction or way, they rushed to perform the service.[179] God tells David that He will guide or instruct him similarly.

1. 1. Focus on God's eye for guidance through His Word. In Scripture, God gestures, nods, signals, and points the way that we are to go.

2. Focus on God's eye through sensitivity to the promptings and leadership of the Holy Spirit (Acts 16:6). Phillip serves as an example of a person led by the Spirit (Romans 8:14). Phillip's sensitivity to *the directive of the Holy Spirit* ["Arise and go toward the south along the road which goes down from Jerusalem to Gaza" (Acts 8:26–27 NKJV)], sensitivity to *the dictate of the Holy Spirit*

71

["Go near and overtake this chariot" (Acts 8:29–30 NKJV)] and sensitivity to *the desire of the Holy Spirit* ["Then Philip opened his mouth, and beginning at this Scripture, preached Jesus to him" (Acts 8:35 NKJV)] resulted in a sinner's salvation and baptism.[180]

3. Focus on God's eye through the happenings of life (Divine Providence)—like open and shut doors. "Let us keep our eyes fixed on Jesus, on whom our faith depends from beginning to end" (Hebrews 12:2 GNT).

"As servants take their cue from the master's eye, and a nod or a wink is all that they require, so should we obey the slightest hints of our Master, not needing thunderbolts to startle our incorrigible sluggishness but being controlled by whispers and love-touches."[181] —C. H. Spurgeon.

~March 1~

Psalm 32:8

The Guiding Gaze

"I will guide thee with mine eye" (Psalm 32:8).

Strewn throughout the path and duration of life are hidden snares to entrap us; slippery places to hurt us; perils by the heathen, false teachers, and enemies to destroy us; sin to defile us; friends who deceive us; and trouble that crushes us. God promises to guide His children with His eye on this hazardous and treacherous journey.

How does God guide with His eye?

1. He guides with the eye of foresight. He is omniscient. He knows the beginning from the end (Isaiah 46:10). He knows what's best for His children and orders their steps accordingly.

2. He guides with the eye of custodial care. The psalmist said, "The LORD shall preserve thee from all evil: he shall preserve thy soul. The LORD shall preserve thy going out and thy coming in from this time forth, and even for evermore" (Psalm 121:7–8). Never for a moment are we outside His loving care. Let us remind ourselves

of this truth by often repeating the words of Hagar, "Thou God seest me" (Genesis 16:13).

3. He guides with the eye of gentleness. "A look is enough, as opposed to that bit and bridle which the mulish nature requires."[182] "A whip for the horse, a bridle for the ass, and a rod for the fool's back" (Proverbs 26:3), but for us, let it be the eye of the Lord that gently and sympathetically instructs and guides us in the path of righteousness. It was with the eye that Jesus lovingly and tenderly corrected Peter: "And the Lord turned, and looked upon Peter. And Peter remembered the word of the Lord, how he had said unto him, Before the cock crow, thou shalt deny me thrice" (Luke 22:61).

"For His 'eye' to guide us, we must have the power to watch and interpret it."[183]—*The Homilist.*

~March 2~

Psalm 32:8
Divine Direction

"I will instruct thee and teach thee in the way which thou shalt go" (Psalm 32:8).

God is the speaker answering David's prayer for Him to be his hiding place and refuge in times of trouble. The Lord governs and guides the saint's life through five means.

Scripture. "Order my steps in thy word" (Psalm 119:133). The Word of God is a light that shows the path to go (Psalm 119:105).

Saints. "Plans fail with no counsel, but with many counselors they succeed" (Proverbs 15:22 CEB). God uses the godly at times to reveal or clarify His will. The Antioch saints set Paul and Barnabas apart for missionary work (Acts 13:2).

Sanctified senses. A holy mind absorbed with sound biblical truth and values provides governing wisdom and discernment.

Spirit's speaking. "Led by the Spirit" (Romans 8:14). The Holy Spirit guides through promptings, impressions, and nudges. Paul was "constrained by the Spirit" to go to Jerusalem despite the persecution that awaited (Acts 20:22 ESV) and "forbidden of the Holy Ghost to preach the Word in Asia" (Acts 16:6). Simeon was "moved by the Spirit" to go into the temple where Joseph and Mary were dedicating Jesus (Luke 2:27 NIV). The Spirit told Philip to join an Ethiopian in his chariot (Acts 8:29).

Shut doors. Divinely closed doors turn us from the wrong path to the right one. David discovered this lesson when the Philistine commanders rejected him from joining their army. They told King Achish, "'Send him back to the town you've given him!' they demanded. 'He can't go into the battle with us. What if he turns against us in battle and becomes our adversary?'" 1 Samuel 29:4 (NLT). With that closed door, God was up to something. Eventually, Saul would die, and David would become Israel's king. Had the Philistine army's position door not been shut, the latter door would likely never have opened.

"While we are here, in the wilderness of this world, we have need of continual direction from Heaven; for, if at any time we be left to ourselves, we shall certainly miss our way."—Matthew Henry.

~March 3~

Psalm 33:10–11
Unfrustrable Decrees of God

"The LORD bringeth the counsel of the heathen to nought: he maketh the devices of the people of none effect. The counsel of the LORD standeth forever, the thoughts of his heart to all generations" (Psalm 33:10–11).

1. God's plans and decrees are unalterable and unstoppable (Proverbs 21:30). His projects, goals, and purposes "standeth forever." He overmasters the masteries of man. Matthew Henry said, "The execution of it [His counsel, decrees] may be opposed, but cannot in

the least be obstructed by any created power."[184] Spurgeon states, "The cause of God is never in danger; infernal craft is outwitted by infinite wisdom, and Satanic malice held in check by boundless power."[185]

Clarke asserts, "What he has determined shall be done. He determined to make a world, and He made it; to create man, and He created him. He determined that at a certain period, God should be manifested in the flesh, and it was so; that He should taste death for every man, and He did so; that His Gospel should be preached in all the world, and behold it has already nearly overrun the whole earth. All His other counsels and thoughts, which refer to the future, shall be accomplished in their times." Solomon said, "Many are the plans in a person's heart, but it is the LORD'S purpose that prevails" (Proverbs 19:21 NIV).

2. The Lord bringeth the counsel of the heathen to nought (Psalm 33:10). God vetoes and frustrates the counsel of evil men to work against their designed intentions. "He upsets the plans of cunning people, and traps the wise in their own schemes, so that nothing they do succeeds" (Job 5:12 GNT). Haman's counsel to the king about killing Mordecai and slaughtering the Jews was frustrated (Esther 7:1–6); Ahithophel's counsel to Absalom on battling David was seen as foolish (2 Samuel 17:14).

"The counsel of the Lord standeth forever. By which are meant, not the doctrines of the Gospel, nor the ordinances of it; though these will stand firm, and remain to the end of the world; but the purposes and decrees of God, which are wisely formed in Himself, are eternal and unfrustrable."—John Gill.

~March 4~

Psalm 34:1

Perpetual Praise

"I will bless the LORD at all times: his praise shall continually be in my mouth" (Psalm 34:1).

75

David fled Jerusalem upon hearing that Saul wanted him dead, hoping to find refuge in Gath with King Achish, but instead met opposition. He composed this psalm of praise to God with his life in danger and his soul in despair.

Praise God completely. "At all times," in every circumstance and occasion, whether good or bad. Recall that Paul and Silas, despite being whipped and thrown into a dungeon cell, sang praises at midnight to God. Rutherford said, "Praise God for the hammer, the file, and the furnace. The hammer molds us, the file sharpens us, and the fire tempers us." "Praise to God ought to be in all things, for God is in all things." Saith A. C. Dixon, "There is no kind of experience in which a Christian has a right to refuse to praise God, for 'all things work together for good to them that love God.'"

Praise God constantly. Spurgeon says, "Happy is he whose fingers are wedded to his harp."[186] The "garment of praise" (Isaiah 61:3) means to be "wrapped up in praise." Wrap or envelop your soul in continual praise to God.

Praise God compliantly. Peter states, "that ye should shew forth the praises of him who hath called you out of darkness into his marvelous light" (1 Peter 2:9).

Praise God openly. "His praise shall continually be in my mouth." The mouth with the heart should bless the Lord. One person's praise prompts that of another for the rich mercies and blessings God afforded.

Praise God devotedly. Praise must be expressed reverently and thoughtfully. There is no praise without the contemplation and concentration of the soul (Psalm 34:2). At times, as David, we must exhort our soul to praise God with "all that is within me" (Psalm 103:1).

"If we hope to spend our eternity in praising God, it is fit that we should spend as much as may be of our time in this work."[187]— Matthew Henry.

Psalm 34:6

David's Ruse

"This poor man cried, and the LORD heard him, and saved him out of all his troubles" (Psalm 34:6).

The historic occasion of this Psalm is David's ruse as a madman before King Achish to escape prison and perhaps death in Gath (1 Samuel 21:12–15). The question arises whether David sinned in faking his madness and, if so, whether it was right. Did the end justify the means? The answer is an emphatic no.

It's never right to sin. David's conduct was deplorable, degrading, dishonoring, and inexcusable. It was the result of panic and fear, not dependency upon God (1 Samuel 21:12). Matthew Henry says, "This dissimulation of his cannot be justified (it was a mean thing thus to disparage himself, and inconsistent with truth thus to misrepresent himself, and therefore not becoming the honor and sincerity of such a man as David)."[188]

T. De Witt Talmage said, "David, in this case, acted as though there were no God to lift him out of the predicament."[189] The shortest sermon is found on thousands of traffic signs across America: "Keep Right." Though the stars fall from the sky, never compromise truth and right for gain.

"When a company or an individual compromises one time, whether it's on price or principle, the next compromise is right around the corner."—Zig Ziglar.

Psalm 34:8

The Test of Experience

"O taste and see that the LORD is good: blessed is the man that trusteth in him" (Psalm 34:8).

The petition. The invitation is to prove God by experiment. It was when Jonathan tasted the honey that his eyes were enlightened. The truth about God and the spiritual realm awaits the person who refuses to hear without seeing and refuses to hear and see without tasting.

Note that taste precedes seeing here, enabling one's faith to see. "Tasting stands before seeing, for spiritual experience leads to spiritual perception or knowledge, and not vice versa."[190] Taste Christ's comfort in sorrow, mercy in the forgiveness of sin, deliverance from a sin's bondage, the friendship He gives in loneliness and desolation, the hope He offers in despair, and the calm He provides in the storm, and confidence and trust will be placed in Him. Gill says, "Every taste now influences and engages trust in the Lord."[191]

The purpose. Many see but do not taste the Lord's goodness and walk away in disbelief or disdain. It's the tasting that gives illumination to the truth (Romans 2:4). When a person tastes the goodness of the Lord, he discovers Him to be all He claims and more. "Our lack of experience [tasting] constitutes no reason for questioning the reality of this experience or doubting the truth to which it bears witness."[191]

The promise. "Blessed is the man that trusteth in him." "Happy is that people, whose God is the LORD" (Psalm 144:15). The man who trusts in the Lord is saved and the recipient of innumerable blessings, including comfort, hope, peace, security, and joy. "There is no want to them that fear him" (Psalm 34:9b).

The pronouncement. In experiencing God's goodness, a desire wells up to join David in summoning others to "taste and see that the LORD is good." With Brady, we will say, "Oh, make but trial of His love; experience will decide. How bless'd are they—and only they—who in His truth confide." What has been proven true to us will be to others.

"We may reason, argue, resort to logic and marshal Christian evidences, but when all is said and done, a man must taste and see for himself."[192]—William MacDonald.

~March 7~

Psalm 34:11–14
The Path to a Happy Life

"Come, ye children, hearken unto me: I will teach you the fear of the LORD" (Psalm 34:11).

David tells children of learning age four things to do to have a happy and prosperous life. Notably, though a king, he instructed the young about the issues of life.

1. Fear the Lord (Psalm 34:11). The fear of the Lord is recognizing God's character and responding by revering, trusting, worshiping, obeying, and serving Him. Bridges says, *"The fear of the Lord* is at once a bridle to sin and a spur to holiness."[193]

2. Keep the tongue clean (Psalm 34:13). Learn early how to bridle the tongue, for if uncontrolled, it will bitterly wound others and recoil to your hurt. Spurgeon says, "Clean and honest conversation, by keeping the conscience at ease, promotes happiness, but lying and wicked talk stuffs our pillow with thorns and makes life a constant whirl of fear and shame."[194]

3. Depart from evil (Psalm 34:14a). Turn from it. Get off its path. Quit it. Avoid it. And make no provision for it (Romans 13:14).

4. Do good (Psalm 34:14b). On the heels of departure from sin, do what is good and right for yourself and others. To replace evil with good shores up one's stability in purity and holiness (Romans 12:21).

5. Seek peace (Psalm 34:14c). Pursue peace with earnestness; without it, there is no happiness and contentment. Learn the conditions of peace, apply them, and guard them lest they are broken and bring despair and heartache. C. S. Lewis said, "God cannot give us happiness and peace apart from Himself because it is not there. There is no such thing." Says Fenelon, "Resign every forbidden joy; restrain

every wish that is not referred to God's will; banish all eager desires, all anxiety; desire only the will of God; seek him alone and supremely, and you will find peace."

"Life spent in happiness is the desire of all, and he who can give the young a receipt for leading a happy life deserves to be popular among them."[195]—C. H. Spurgeon.

~March 8~

Psalm 34:11
Why Win the Children?

"Come, ye children, hearken unto me: I will teach you the fear of the LORD" (Psalm 34:11).

Note eight pivotal reasons to evangelize children.

1. Salvation is Jesus' priority for all people, including children. "Go out into the highways and hedges, and compel them to come in" (Luke 14:23).

2. Jesus says explicitly that children are not to be hindered in being saved. He said, "Suffer the little children to come unto me, and forbid them not" (Mark 10:14).

3. Children display great interest, openness, and receptivity to the Gospel. Young hearts have not been "hardened" to the Gospel by sin, liberal or false teaching.

4. Children may be a catalyst in winning their parents. It is God's plan to save whole families, and He does it often by first saving one family member and, through that one member, the entire household.

5. Children should be won to Christ in light of the evangelistic 4/14 window of opportunity. Eighty-five percent of people saved are between the ages of 4 and 14. Once a child passes through this window of opportunity, the likelihood of salvation drastically decreases.

6. Children ought to be won to Christ, for they can provide a lifetime of fruitful service to the Lord. Moody was asked how a night's meeting had gone. "We had two and a half conversions," he replied.

"You mean two adults and one child?"

"No," he said, "two children and one adult. The adult has only half his life left."

7. Childhood conversion provides an opportunity for an early call to vocational ministry and its foundational preparation.

8. Christ has a work for us to do at every stage of life, even childhood. Recall that Jesus used a boy's loaves and fishes to feed five thousand, and Josiah, who became king at eight years of age, destroyed the altars of Baal and brought revival to Israel as a teenager.

"Any evangelism after high school isn't evangelism. It's really salvage." —Jay Kelser.

~March 9~

Psalm 34:18

The Sympathizing Jesus

"The Lord is near to those who have a broken heart. And He saves those who are broken in spirit" (Psalm 34:18 NLV).

The occasion of this Psalm is David's ruse as a madman before King Achish to escape prison and perhaps death in Gath (1 Samuel 21:12–15). David's heart was crushed and wounded in the wake of his exile, flight from Saul, the opposition of Achish, and the betrayal of friends. Here, he testifies to God's goodness to comfort and sustain all like him with a broken heart.

"A bruised reed He will not break, and a smoldering wick He will not snuff out" (Isaiah 42:3 NIV). A reed is a plant (cane) with a thin, delicate, hollow stem that is easily bent (bruised) or broken due to its brittleness and frailty. Once bent or broken, it is valueless and useless. This is exemplified with a reed instrument. When the reed is bruised, its beautiful music is spoiled.

Man is a fragile "reed" (feeble, "shaken with the wind"—Matthew 11:7) who, though bruised or broken by sorrow, sickness, adversity, or sin, is sympathetically mended by Christ and restored upon request. In seeing a "bruised reed" (the broken-hearted), Christ says, "I must repair it and restore its beautiful music." He never says, "The flaw in the lute is irreparable; its sweet music impossible to restore, so throw it away."[196] "He healeth the broken in heart, and bindeth up their wounds" (Psalm 147:3).

Christ, "acquainted with grief" (its sorrows and pain), identifies with and feels for *bruised reeds* (Isaiah 53:3–5). Therefore, compassionately, He says, "Come unto me, all ye that labor and are heavy laden, and I will give you rest" (Matthew 11:28). He will prop up and support the broken-hearted and restore their song.

"There is no brokenness of heart which Jesus cannot bind up."[197]— C. H. Spurgeon.

~March 10~

Psalm 34:19
Flawed Reasoning

"Many are the afflictions of the righteous: but the LORD delivereth him out of them all" (Psalm 34:19).

Afflictions plague even the righteous. In seeking an answer for them, adversity-flawed reasoning often overrules reliable faith, intensifying the discomfort and strain.

1. Flawed reasoning for adversity.

a. For example, in sickness, flawed reasoning says, "If God loved me, He would not have allowed my illness and suffering." But reliable faith says, "The fabric of my sickness is sewn in God's love and stitched with nothing but His best for me and is for His glory;

in and through it, He is giving the world a window to see how He compassionately cares for His child."

b. In the bitterest bereavement, flawed reasoning says, "God failed me by taking my loved one or friend; if He truly loved me, He would not have done so. He was wrong. He made a mistake." But reliable faith says, "God never makes a mistake; what He does is always purposed for man's best good. Though bringing misery to me, death was merciful to my loved one, for it spared him from the evil to come in this life; it ushered him into the presence of Christ in Heaven."[198]

c. In the calamities and tribulations of life, flawed reasoning says, "God has abandoned me." Reliable faith says, "In the furnace of affliction, there is always a 'fourth man in the fire' with me, the Lord Jesus Christ (Daniel 3:25). And He, being with me, will give grace to see me through it. Paul found that Christ's presence abided with him in suffering—as a tent spread over him (2 Corinthians 12:9).

2. Reliable faith in adversity.

It says that in trials, Christ spreads a tent of His presence over me to protect and comfort me while accomplishing His plan. Flawed reasoning says about our many afflictions, "Curse God, and die" (Job 2:9). Reliable faith says, "Be strong and brave. Don't be afraid of them. Don't be frightened. The LORD your God will go with you. He will not leave you or forget you" (Deuteronomy 31:6 ICB). Flawed reasoning says, "Give up." Reliable faith says, "Though he slay me, yet will I trust in him" (Job 13:15).

"The book of Job does not set out to answer the problem of suffering, but to proclaim a God so great that no answer is needed."[199]—Billy Graham.

~March 11~

Psalm 34:21
The Weasel and the Rabbit

"Evil shall slay the wicked" (Psalm 34:21).

83

Though extremely slow, the weasel can catch a rabbit. How? Upon getting the scent of a rabbit, the weasel slowly but persistently pursues the rabbit. Though out of sight of the weasel, the rabbit remains in danger and counts itself safe. The weasel never gives up. It stays focused on the one rabbit and refuses to allow other rabbits to deter the pursuit. Eventually, the rabbit grows tired and rests in the meadow; then and there, the weasel seizes it.[200]

This is the way of a sin. Once it has your scent, it will relentlessly pursue until it catches and destroys you. John Owen said, "There is not a day but sin foils or is foiled, prevails or is prevailed on; and it will be so while we live in this world."[201] Therefore, "Be sober, be vigilant; because your adversary the devil, as a roaring lion, walketh about, seeking whom he may devour" (1 Peter 5:8).

"We are too apt to forget that temptation to sin will rarely present itself to us in its true colors, saying, 'I am your deadly enemy, and I want to ruin you forever in hell.' Oh, no! Sin comes to us, like Judas, with a kiss, and like Joab, with an outstretched hand and flattering words."[202]—J. C. Ryle.

~March 12~

Psalm 35:1
The Imprecatory Psalms

"Plead my cause, O LORD, with them that strive with me: fight against them that fight against me" (Psalm 35:1).

The psalm is the first of David's eight imprecatory psalms—prayers for retribution or vengeance on his/God's enemies and was composed while he was fleeing Saul over hill and dale and was the butt of malicious slander.

Several factors are imperative to the understanding of the imprecatory psalms.

1. The psalmist does not pray "in malice or revenge."[203] "Viewing sinners as men," wrote Spurgeon, "we love them and seek their good, but regarding them as enemies of God, we cannot think of them with anything but detestation and a loyal desire for the confusion of their devices. No loyal subject can wish well to rebels."[204]

2. In praying for God's judgment to fall on his enemies, the psalmist leaves it in God's hands.[205] "Not my will, but thine be done." Bullock says, the imprecatory psalms may "remind us that the world is full of injustice and God is just, so we can leave the wrongs that others have delivered to us in His gracious hands."[206]

Note. They do not teach us to bear malice or vengeance. We are to let God fight them (Psalm 35:1). Moses said, "The LORD will fight for you. You just keep still" (Exodus 14:14 CEB). Paul said, "Dearly beloved, avenge not yourselves, but rather give place unto wrath: for it is written, Vengeance is mine; I will repay, saith the Lord" (Romans 12:19) and "Let all bitterness, and heat of passion, and wrath, and clamor, and injurious language, be removed from you, with all malice" (Ephesians 4:31 DARBY). Without our deserving, Christ forgave us "for His name's sake"; let us demonstrate the same lovingkindness.

3. God's retributive judgment ultimately will fall upon the unrepentant and rebellious.[207] It comes suddenly and unexpectedly (Psalm 35:8). "The thunderbolt of judgment," states Spurgeon, "leaps from its hiding-place, and in one crash, the wicked are broken forever."[208] Let us compassionately forewarn them 'that they may flee the wrath of God to come' (Matthew 3:7). "Let the wicked leave their way of life and change their way of thinking. Let them turn to the LORD, our God; he is merciful and quick to forgive" (Isaiah 55:7 GNT).

"Those who are forgiven of God should be of a forgiving spirit and should forgive even as God forgives, sincerely and heartily, readily and cheerfully, universally and forever, upon the sinner's sincere repentance."[209]—Matthew Henry.

~March 13~

Psalm 35:3
Doubt of Salvation

"Say unto my soul, I am thy salvation" (Psalm 35:3).

When a fugitive from King Saul, David pens this psalm seeking the assurance of God's delivering hand upon him in times of trouble. David often played the "fugitive" during his life (1 Samuel 19:1–3, 12; 20:1; 21:1, 10; 22:1, 3; 23:13; 24:1–2; 26:1; 27:1).

The text may be applied to the doubt of the salvation of the soul.

Doubt's subject. The godliest may question their salvation. Spurgeon, the great London preacher, did.

Doubt's source. The cause of doubt regarding salvation is not always known. Is the doubt from God to reveal counterfeit salvation, or is it of Satan to disturb fellowship with God?

Doubt's solution. Stott said, "Clearly, one cannot enjoy a gift unless one knows that one possesses it. Therefore, if God means us to receive and enjoy eternal life, He must mean us to know we possess it." Some say full assurance cannot be known. But God emphatically says it is possible.

David asked God to speak assurance to his soul. "Say unto my soul." A word from God, who cannot lie, dispels doubt and gives assurance of salvation. He speaks this assurance in several ways.

1. Through the Holy Spirit. "The Spirit itself beareth witness with our spirit, that we are the children of God" (Romans 8:16). The Holy Spirit's presence in a believer testifies to their salvation.

2. Through the Holy Scriptures. The Bible is God's speaking to man, assuring salvation to everyone who repents of their sin and places faith in Christ. John states, "These things have I written unto you that believe on the name of the Son of God; that ye may know that ye have eternal life" (1 John 5:13). Therefore, base salvation on Christ's established promises established promises to you (Revelation 3:20;

Romans 10:13), not fleeting feelings, baptism, the Lord's Supper, church membership, or a meritorious life.

3. Through Holy Servants. God uses His ministers to speak words of assurance by unfolding the scripture that addresses the subject.

David's doubt is resolved. He says, "And my soul shall be joyful in the Lord: it shall rejoice in his salvation. All my bones shall say, Lord, who is like unto thee, which deliverest the poor from him that is too strong for him, yea, the poor and the needy from him that spoileth him?" (Psalm 35:9–10). The doubt replaced with blessed assurance was so calming and comforting that all David's bones responded with praise to God. The same is experienced by all when their doubt is dispelled. With Homer Cox, they say:

But it's real, it's real,
Oh, I know it's real;
Praise God, the doubts are settled,
For I know, I know it's real.

"Our ground of trust is not to be found in our experience, but in the person and work of our Lord Jesus."—C. H. Spurgeon.

~March 14~

Psalm 35:27

Magnifying God

"Let them shout for joy, and be glad, that favor my righteous cause: yea, let them say continually, Let the LORD be magnified, which hath pleasure in the prosperity of his servant" (Psalm 35:27).

Upon David's deliverance from Saul and his armies, David praises and magnifies God. "Let the LORD be magnified." Scripture teaches five ways that God may be magnified.

Through service. "Let your light so shine before men, that they may see your good works, and glorify your Father which is in heaven" (Matthew 5:16).

Through suffering. "So now also Christ shall be magnified in my body, whether it be by life, or by death" (Philippians 1:20). Billy Graham said, "When one bears suffering faithfully, God is glorified and honored."

Through Scripture. "For thou hast magnified thy word above all thy name" (Psalm 138:2). The exaltation of the Holy Scripture exalts God.

Through salvation. "And great crowds came to him, bringing with them the lame, the blind, the crippled, the mute, and many others, and they put them at his feet, and he healed them, so that the crowd wondered, when they saw the mute speaking, the crippled healthy, the lame walking, and the blind seeing. And they glorified the God of Israel" (Matthew 15:30–31 ESV). A supernaturally changed life points people to its changer.

Through sanctification. After hearing of the greatness of God, a little girl said, "If God is as big as you say, and He lives in my heart, then He should be poking out." The world ought to see God poking out of the believer's life. When we walk in holiness and purity, the Lord is magnified most (pokes out the most).

Through death. When dying, a saint remarked to his friends, "It was never till today that I got any personal instruction from our Lord's telling Peter by what death he should glorify God. Oh! What a satisfying thought it is that God appoints those means of dissolution (death) by which He gets the most glory for Himself. It was the very thing I needed, for of all the ways of dying, that which I most dreaded is that which I'm experiencing. But oh! My dear Lord, if by this death I can most glorify Thee, I prefer it to all others, and thank Thee that by this means Thou art hastening my fuller enjoyment of Thee in a purer world."

Love of God, so pure and changeless!
Blood of Christ, so rich and free!
Grace of God, so strong and boundless!
Magnify them all in me.

—Elisabeth Codner (1860)

"When David says, 'I will magnify God with thanksgiving,' he does not mean, 'I will make a small God look bigger than He is.' He means, 'I will make a big God look as big as He really is.'"—Tim Keller.

~March 15~

Psalm 36:5–7
The Character of God

"Thy mercy, O LORD, is in the heavens; and thy faithfulness reacheth unto the clouds. Thy righteousness is like the great mountains; thy judgments are a great deep: O LORD, thou preservest man and beast. How excellent is thy lovingkindness" (Psalm 36:5–7a).

1. David praises God's lovingkindness. God's love extends to the heavens and is immeasurable, inexhaustible, unfailing, and limitless (Ephesians 3:18–19).

2. David praises God's faithfulness. God is faithful and true. Augustine said, "God is not a deceiver that He should offer to support us, and then when we lean upon Him, should slip away from us."[210]

3. David praises God's righteousness. God is perfectly right and just in His nature and that which He does. This is unalterable. Abraham said rhetorically, "Shall not the Judge of all the earth do right?" (Genesis 18:25). The answer then and NOW is an unequivocal yes. His righteousness is like the "great mountains" in their stability—immovable and permanent.

4. David praises God's judgment or divine justice. He speaks not of the last judgment (Revelation 20:11–13) but of God's acts in governing the world and affairs of man. It is executed justly and fairly, though sometimes, it is misunderstood and puzzling (Romans 11:33).

God's unfailing love, faithfulness, righteousness, and justice are reasons for calm and peace in the believer's heart. Knowing these unchanging traits of God's character leads us to confidently "trust under the shadow of thy wings" (Psalm 36:7).

"His mercy, faithfulness, righteousness, judgments, preserving providence, are all infinite and perfect, and those who trust in Him live in the holiest, safest shelter—under the shadow of His wings overspreading the 'mercy-seat.'"[211]—*The Pulpit Commentary.*

~March 16~

Psalm 36:7
Under the Shadow of His Wings

"How excellent is thy lovingkindness, O God! Therefore the children of men put their trust under the shadow of thy wings" (Psalm 36:7).

The expression of the wings of God. Chicks run under their mother's wings in times of danger to be kept safe. The wings of God is a fitting metaphor for the enveloping protection from danger God provides for His children who flee to Him in times of trouble.

The expanse of the wings of God. There is more than enough room under the canopy of God's wings for all who seek refuge (shelter and security).

The effect of the wings of God. Under His wings is protection from harm, comfort in grief, strength in weakness, and healing in hurt. Spurgeon states, "Those who commune with God are safe with Him; no evil can reach them, for the outstretched wings of His power and love cover them from all harm. This protection is constant— they abide under it, and it is all-sufficient, for it is the shadow of the Almighty, whose omnipotence will surely screen them from all attack. No shelter can be imagined at all comparable to the protection of Jehovah's own shadow."[212]

The enoughness of the wings of God. Brooks said, "God hath in Himself all power to defend you, all wisdom to direct you, all mercy to pardon you, all grace to enrich you, all righteousness to clothe you, all goodness to supply you, and all happiness to crown you."

The entry to under the wings of God. It is accessed by the believer's trust and confidence in God's faithfulness and unfailing love to care and provide for him (Psalm 61:4). David prayed, "Be merciful unto me, O God, be merciful unto me: for my soul *trusteth in thee*: yea, in the shadow of thy wings will I make my refuge, until these calamities be overpast" (Psalm 57:1). Cushing wrote, "Under His wings, I am safely abiding. Though the night deepens and tempests are wild, still, I can trust Him; I know He will keep me; He has redeemed me, and I am His child."

"There is heat in the world, but there is a great shade under the wings of God."[213]—Augustine.

~March 17~

Psalm 36:8
The Fatness of Thy House

"They shall be abundantly satisfied with the fatness of thy house; and thou shalt make them drink of the river of thy pleasures" (Psalm 36:8).

The Lord's table is fat in substance. It is spread with abundant mercy, forgiveness, grace, love, and peace (Job 36:16). Says Spurgeon, "The riches of nations are as rags and rottenness in comparison with His resources."

The Lord's table is fat in satisfaction. "They shall be abundantly satisfied." Chambers says, "The human heart must have satisfaction, but there is only one Being who can satisfy the last abyss of the human heart, and that is the Lord Jesus Christ." The psalmist said, "For he satisfieth the longing soul, and filleth the hungry soul with goodness" (Psalm 107:9).

The Lord's table is fat in supply. 'The river of pleasure' never stops flowing. Jonathan Edwards says, "There is [in God] an inexhaustible fountain of blessings. Every kind of dainty is in inexhaustible plenty. Therefore, 'tis called rivers of pleasure forevermore. Here, the soul manifests itself abundantly without danger of spending the provision."

To this table often come. "Eat, O friends; drink, yea, drink abundantly, O beloved" (Song of Songs 5:1), and find delight and nourishment for your soul.

"The only bliss attainable or desirable is that which is bestowed by God and resides in him."[214]—J. A. Alexander.

~March 18~

Psalm 36:9
Light in God's Light

"In thy light shall we see light" (Psalm 36:9).

Metaphors teach us much truth about God and the spiritual. In the light of Scripture, we see moral and theological truth. In the light of Calvary, we see man's sinfulness and God's great love to make salvation possible. In the light of the empty tomb, we see what awaits the saint at death. In the light of God's interactions with the hurting, we see God's compassion and care. In the light of the promises, we see God's never-failing pledge to care for His own. In the light of the Holy Spirit, we see God's plan and direction for our lives. In the light of Jesus, we see what God is like and how we ought to live. We see God's miraculous power in the light of a transformed life. In the light of answered prayer, we see God's readiness to respond to the cries of His children. Praise God for the light that He has given to illumine the darkness (John 1:9).

Simeon says, "And to him, all may have access if they will not obstinately immure themselves in impenitence and unbelief. Let us not then 'kindle sparks for ourselves, or walk in the light of our own fires,' but 'come forth to His light,' and 'walk in it' to the latest hour of our lives."[215]

Walk in the light! and you will view
A path, tho' thorny, bright;
For God, by grace, will dwell with you,
And God himself is light!

—Bernard Barton (1826)

"Darkness cannot drive out darkness; only light can do that."—Martin Luther King, Jr.

~March 19~

Psalm 37:1–2
Fret Not at Evil Doers

"Fret not thyself because of evildoers, neither be thou envious against the workers of iniquity. For they shall soon be cut down like the grass, and wither as the green herb" (Psalm 37:1–2).

To prevent fretting and discouragement in the successes of the wicked, David instructs us to remember two things. Their successes and prosperity are short-lived. The fruit of the ungodly will no sooner blossom than they wither. Second, the wicked will come to a horrific end presently and eternally, whereas the righteous will forever bask in the blessings and favor of God (Psalm 37:9–10). Matthew Henry says of the wicked, "Their triumphing is short, but their weeping and wailing will be everlasting."[216]

David states four things that will defeat fretting and enviousness at the ill-gotten gain of evil men.

1. A confident reliance ("trust") in God.

2. A steadiness in doing what is pleasing to God ("do good")

3. A happy and satisfying attitude about God's goodness and blessings ("delight thyself").

4. The submission of self wholly to God ("commit thy way").

"Evil men, instead of being envied, are to be viewed with horror and aversion."[217]—C. H. Spurgeon.

~March 20~

Psalm 37:1
Don't Envy the Ungodly

"Neither be thou envious against the workers of iniquity" (Psalm 37:1).

Instead of envying the ungodly (their possessions, position, prosperity, pleasures, and, yes, their perversion (depraved desires), the righteous should view them with disesteem and displeasure. Why?

1. "The enemies of the LORD" (Psalm 37:20). Foremost, believers should not envy the wicked because they are God's adversaries and opponents.

2. "They shall soon be cut down" (Psalm 37:2). Augustine said, "That which to thee seemeth long, is 'soon' in the sight of God."[218] .

3. "The arms of the wicked shall be broken" (Psalm 37:17). The power of godless men to do wickedly *suddenly* will be crushed, as seen in the collapse of Jezebel and Saul.

4. "The wicked shall perish" (Psalm 37:20). Fuller says, "If the wicked flourish and thou suffer, be not discouraged. They are fated for destruction; thou art dieted for health."[219] The Bible says, "Be not deceived; God is not mocked: for whatsoever a man soweth, that shall he also reap. For he that soweth to his flesh shall of the flesh reap corruption; but he that soweth to the Spirit shall of the Spirit reap life everlasting" (Galatians 6:7–8).

5. "A little that a righteous man hath is better than the riches of many wicked" (Psalm 37:16). Don't envy the ungodly because what you have far exceeds in value and happiness all he possesses. Democritus said, "Happiness resides not in possessions and not in gold; happiness dwells in the soul."

"To envy the evil-doers on account of their prosperity is at once a folly and a danger. Their position is really not enviable."[220]— Rawlinson.

Psalm 37:13
God Gets the Last Laugh

"The LORD shall laugh at him: for he seeth that his day is coming" (Psalm 37:13).

The wicked, with joy and frivolity, engage in wanton conduct, mocking and laughing at the very one who gave them life (Psalm 2:4). But the day is coming (the day of God's wrath) when the laughter will turn to mourning. God will have the final word. However affluent or prosperous, a life of sin and disdain for God always concludes horrifically. "And thou *[shalt]* mourn at the last" (Proverbs 5:11).

Bitter regrets in old age or at the hour of death will occupy the mind of the wicked, eroding peace and hope for the future, prompting sorrow and anxiety. They will wail, "How have I hated instruction, and my heart despised reproof; and have not obeyed the voice of my teachers, nor inclined mine ear to them that instructed me!" (Proverbs 5:12–13). Remorse, remorse, remorse for disregard for God and His Word—what a wrenching end for the wretched on earth! It is a faint shadow of the awfulness of Hell they will experience.

Ironside asserts, "To learn by painful experience if the word of God is not bowed to, is a bitter and solemn thing. God is not mocked; what is sown must be reaped. The unsteady hand, the confused brain, the bleared eye, premature age, and weakened powers, with days and nights of folly to look back on with regret that can never be banished from the memory."[221]

"Remorse is the last witness of the unrepentant to the gospel truth."[222]—Frank Shivers.

~March 22~

Psalm 37:23
The Divinely Orchestrated Life

"The steps of a good man are ordered by the LORD: and he delighteth in his way" (Psalm 37:23).

The Psalm references David's own experience (1 Samuel 25:39).

The life of the godly is divinely established.

1. It is a certainty. There are sovereignly ordered or orchestrated steps for the "good man" (righteous)—he who trusts in the Lord and does good (Psalm 37:3), delights in the Lord (Psalm 37:4), commits (consents) his way unto the Lord (Psalm 37:5), and shuns evil (Psalm 37:8).

2. It is comprehensive. The divine governance is all-inclusive, from when he goes out and comes in to his lying down and rising up. Spurgeon said, "All his course of life is graciously ordained, and in lovingkindness, all is fixed. No fickle chance rules us; every step is the subject of divine decree." Neither joy nor sorrow is known without first passing through the sovereign hand of God. The Lord "orders" each step per His divine plan and pleasure. To get off the track God has established for life is to miss or forfeit the beneficial and blessed plan He intended.

3. It is consensual. Matthew Henry says, "He has all hearts in his hand, but theirs [the righteous] *by their own consent.* By His providence, He overrules the events that concern them to make their way plain before them, both what they should do and what they may expect."

4. It is clear. To the man who wants to be governed by the counsel of God, every step and every stop will be made plain and traversable. Maclaren asserts God is our "Roadmaker, showing us the way and clearing obstacles from it. Calm certitude follows on

willingness to accept God's will, and whoever seeks only to go where God sends him will neither be left doubtful whither he should go nor find his road blocked."[223] God orders man's steps in general, but specifically by the whispers (sometimes shouts) of the Holy Spirit to the soul, Holy Scripture, a sanctified or holy conscience, open and closed doors, interruptions to schedule and plans, the counsel of others, adversity and affliction, and even failure.

The life of the godly is divinely endorsed. "He delighteth in his way." Harman states, "The LORD'S pleasure is shown towards the righteous as they walk in His ways, and He establishes those ways."[224] The text may be taken to mean that the believer who walks in the ordained steps of God finds pleasure.

The life of the godly is divinely ensconced. "Though he fall, he shall not be utterly cast down." Even the godly man will suffer falls on the path. Still, the falls are not permanent, for God is His protector, defender, and helper (Psalm 37:24). Matthew Henry says, "A good man may be in distress, his affairs embarrassed, his spirits sunk, but he shall not be utterly cast down; God will be the strength of his heart when his flesh and heart fail and will uphold him with His comforts so that the spirit He has made shall not fail before him."[225]

"If God has ordained a way for men to walk in, it is the height of folly to walk in any other way."[226]—Marvin R. Vincent.

~March 23~

Psalm 38:4

A Burden Too Heavy to Bear

"I am drowning in the flood of my sins; they are a burden too heavy to bear" (Psalm 38:4 GNT).

David testifies that the consequence of his sin is a "heavy burden," an intolerable burden that he cannot endure. David is a "broken" man (Psalm38:8), a "restless man" (Psalm 38:2), a "troubled man" (Psalm 38: 6a), and an "unhappy man" (Psalm

38:6b) who is about to be a "hopeless man" (Psalm 38:10), when he becomes a "repentant man" (Psalm 38:18). David wrestled through sickness (physical and mental), suffering, sorrow and hostility until repentantly, he says to God, "For I will declare mine iniquity; I will be sorry for my sin" (Psalm 38:18). The Lord quickly forgives and restores him (Psalm 38:22).

Thanks be unto God; forgiveness of sin is available. There is life after failure when the transgression is repentantly confessed. Delayed confession blocks forgiveness's immediate bestowal, allowing sin's bitter poison to work its way into the body, mind, and soul, causing havoc and heartache. The time to confess sin is upon its act. Jesus's blood is sufficient to wash away sin, its sting and stain, but only avails to do so for those who acknowledge and confess it, as did David. The Bible declares, "The blood of Jesus Christ his Son cleanseth us *from all sin*" (1 John 1:7b).

"The voice of sin is loud, but the voice of forgiveness is louder."— D. L. Moody.

~March 24~

Psalm 38:11

A Brother Born for Adversity

"My lovers and my friends stand aloof from my sore" (Psalm 38:11).

Adversity is bearable with a friend's support. Spurgeon said, "Friendship is one of the sweetest joys of life. Many might have failed beneath the bitterness of their trial had they not found a friend."[227] Helen Keller wrote, "I would rather walk with a friend in the dark than alone in the light."

Adversity tests the mettle of friendship. When David needed the comfort and sympathy of friends, they, like the priest and the Levite, passed by on the other side of the road (Luke 10:31).[228] Adversity weeds out the phonies, the unworthy of our trust and love. Spurgeon, from bitter experience, wrote, "It is very hard when those who should be the first to come to the rescue are the first to desert us."

Adversity causes real friends to surface at the top. "Hard times will always reveal true friends!" An authentic friend says, "I may not always be there with you, but I will always be there for you." When Jim Bakker, founder of PTL, was asked about the fall of PTL and the scattering of all the people close to him, including his friends, he commented, "I didn't lose any friends....I just discovered who my true friends are." Solomon says, "A friend loveth [comforts, sympathizes, supports] at all times, and a brother is born for adversity" (Proverbs 17:17). Jonathan was such a friend to David (1 Samuel 23:16).

Adversity bonds friends. Deep friendships are forged among those who walk together in and through life's storms.

"False and hollow as are some professions of friendship, there are others of an opposite kind."[229]—W. S. Plumer.

~March 25~

Psalm 39:4
The Transitoriness of Life

"LORD, make me to know mine end, and the measure of my days, what it is: that I may know how frail I am" (Psalm 39:4).

The five lessons about the transitoriness of life revealed by David should prompt noble and godly resolves in life.

Life is terminal. Death is an inevitability. "There is a time to be born and a time to die" (Ecclesiastes 3:2 NCV). The uncertainty lies in when, where, and how. Death has a thousand doors. Ernest Hemingway said, "All stories, if continued far enough, end in death."

Only God knows life's time frame. God knows "the measure of my days." "It is appointed unto men once to die" (Hebrews 9:27). The time of life at best is but "merely a vapor," a morning mist that quickly is dissolved with the rising sun (James 4:14 AMP). Make each day count.

Man needs to consider life's end. "Make me to know." As the parade roared down the avenue, Caesar's Praetorian Guard whispered, "Remember, Caesar, thou art mortal." Every man needs to hear those words personalized—thou art mortal. You are not indestructible. You will die. Death is no respecter of persons. Your rendezvous with death may be sudden and unexpected. Live in the light of your end.

God is man's best instructor about life's transitoriness. "LORD, make me to know mine end." David knew of life's transitoriness but needed divine insight to understand it fully and apply its reality constantly. We all need that instruction. "No person can be indifferent to death and mortality when God is his teacher."[230] Understanding life's brevity and our frailty prompts better use of time, talent, and treasure for God.

Death instills hope. David's prayer was precipitated by the distress suffered from the wicked's success. As Spurgeon states, he knew that the shorter his life was, the easier he could bear its transient ills. "They who see death through the Lord's glass," says Spurgeon, "see a fair sight, which makes them forget the evil of life in foreseeing the end of life."[231]

"To be prepared to die is to be prepared to live."—C. H. Spurgeon.

~March 26~

Psalm 39:4
Why Men Forget Their End

"LORD, make me to know mine end, and the measure of my days, what it is: that I may know how frail I am" (Psalm 39:4).

David's prayer postulates man's forgetfulness of his end. Why do men forget it?

1. It's not for want of reminders. The cemetery and obituaries bear constant witness to it.

2. It's not because of a lack of knowledge about it. Observation is its perpetual instructor.

3. It's not for the hope of its avoidance. "It is appointed unto men once to die" (Hebrews 9:27).

4. It's not because of its unimportance. Death is an event that requires utmost thought and preparation.[232] "Prepare to meet thy God" (Amos 4:12).

Why do men forget their end? Death is a thing loathed, feared, and dreaded. Second, the stuff and rush of this world choke out its consideration. Third, death brings judgment on sin, something the guilty want to give no thought to.

Why, as David, should man pray to be mindful of their end? To prompt them to redeem the time left by focusing on what matters most—serving God to the fullest, conforming more to His image and plan, witnessing urgently, and preparing to meet God. Matthew Henry says, "When we look upon death as a thing at a distance, we are tempted to adjourn the necessary preparations for it; but, when we consider how short life is, we shall see ourselves concerned to do what our hand finds to do, not only with all our might but with all possible expedition."[233]

"If I do not think of death, yet death will think of me."—C. H. Spurgeon.

~March 27~

Psalm 40:2–3
Out of the Pit

"He brought me up also out of an horrible pit, out of the miry clay, and set my feet upon a rock, and established my goings. And he hath put a new song in my mouth, even praise unto our God: many shall see it, and fear, and shall trust in the LORD" (Psalm 40:2–3).

David's rescue from a "horrible pit" serves as a metaphor for salvation. The horrible pit is man's place of captivity to sin and Satan's domination, where hopelessness, despair, and misery plague.

The "miry clay" pictures the pit's 'deadly quicksand,' which draws sinners downward into deeper moral corruption, despair, and bondage. Adrian Rogers said, "If you're sinking in quicksand, Satan will gladly pat you on the head."

The "cry" or prayer of David pictures the imprisoned sinner's dependence on God for deliverance.

The "rock" symbolizes the new believer's (the rescued) sure, safe, and secure anchor in Christ Jesus (2 Corinthians 1:22). "On Christ the Solid Rock I stand" where there is no chance of loss of salvation.

"Established my goings" pictures the fixed and firm steps of the new convert on solid ground, which Christ enables to prevent them from descending to the pit again (Jude 24).

The "new song" pictures the song of adoration and jubilation birthed in the soul by the Lord at salvation. Sighing is turned to singing. Spurgeon said, "When God sets a man singing, he must sing."[234] Perhaps the new song sung is similar to that of Zelly and Gilmour: "He brought me out of the miry clay; He set my feet on the Rock to stay. He puts a song in my soul today, a song of praise, hallelujah!" Rawlinson says, "Mercy and praise are cause and effect. The deliverance recorded in Psalm 40:2 produces the praise of Psalm 40:3–5."[235]

"The greater the trial, the greater is the deliverance, and the more joyous and loud should be the song which we sing to the praise and glory of God. To praise God for redemption only as we do for a cup of water is shocking."[236]—W. S. Plumer.

~March 28~
Psalm 40:17
Waiting on God's Time

"My God, do not tarry too long!" (Psalm 40:17 ISV).

Believers often experience dire affliction or adversity before God intervenes. As students at the Bible College at Gilgal were eating poisonous pottage, God's power made it whole (2 Kings 4:40). The wine barrel was empty at the wedding feast in Cana before Jesus made more (John 2:3–9). Abraham's knife was lifted to slay his son at Mt. Moriah before the angel stilled his hand (Genesis 22:11–12). The Israelites walked to the edge of the Red Sea before the waters were drawn back (Exodus 14:21–22). David was delivered from death at the hands of Saul's soldiers in mere hours (1 Samuel 19:11). Hezekiah was on his deathbed before God intervened with healing (2 Kings 20:1–5). The night before Peter was to be put on trial (the trial, likely, would have resulted in a death sentence), an angel delivered him from the shackles that bound him in his prison cell (Acts 12:6–11). At midnight, with execution perhaps awaiting at dawn, Paul and Silas were released from the Philippi jail (Acts 16:25–26).

God is never early, never late, always on time. Tozer says, "God never hurries. There are no deadlines against which He must work. Only to know this is to quiet our spirits and relax our nerves." Waiting on God's time to help and deliver builds and strengthens faith and dependence upon Him (Psalm 27:14). The Bible says, "The LORD is good unto them that wait for him, to the soul that seeketh him" (Lamentations 3:25) and "Those who wait for me shall never be ashamed" (Isaiah 49:23 TLB). Matthew Henry asserts, "Those that wait patiently for God, though they may wait long, do not wait in vain."[237]

"Mercy may seem slow, but it is sure. The Lord, in his unfailing wisdom, has appointed a time for the outgoings of His gracious power, and God's time is the best time."—C. H. Spurgeon.

~March 29~

Psalm 40:17

God Thinks About Us

"But I am poor and needy; yet the Lord thinketh upon me" (Psalm 40:17).

David voiced similar words later in the Psalms, saying, "How precious also are thy thoughts unto me, O God! How great is the sum of them!" (Psalm 139:17). Some say God is too busy, far away, holy, or magnificent to think about sinful man. But David states, "The Lord thinketh upon me." Wonder of wonders, God sitting upon Heaven's throne thinks of a worm like me!

> Lord Jesus, think on me,
>   Amid the battle's strife;
> In all my pain and misery,
>   Please be my health and life.
> Lord Jesus, think on me,
>   Nor let me go astray;
> Thru' darkness and perplexity,
>   Point to the heav'nly way.

> —Synesius of Cyrene

God's loving, kind, sympathetic, hopeful, and merciful thoughts are constantly drifting from Him to us (Psalm 40:5). They are innumerable, fixed, and definite. God knows what we are experiencing and has sympathetic thoughts of our estate in His mind— thoughts of our present and eternal well-being. Spurgeon wrote, "Can you realize the wondrous truth that there never is a moment, night or day, in which the great mind of the Eternal ceases to think of you? Then, how safe you are with God always looking upon you! How happy you ought to be with God always thinking of you!"[238]

"Promises are just God's thoughts stored up for men."[239]—Robinson.

104

Psalm 41:3

The Saint's Sickbed Nurse

"The LORD will strengthen him upon the bed of languishing: thou wilt make all his bed in his sickness" (Psalm 41:3).

Merciful saints are assured of the Great Physician's special loving care and support when languishing upon the "sickbed." David says, "The LORD will strengthen him upon the bed of languishing: thou wilt make all his bed in his sickness." The promise is for those who have shown compassion to the needy, hurting, and sick when they were healthy themselves.

Clarke says, "Good, benevolent, and merciful as he is, he must also die. But he shall not die as other men; he shall have peculiar consolations, refreshment, and support while passing through the valley of the shadow of death."[240] The Lord will "strengthen him upon the bed of languishing" (the NEB says, "He nurses him"). He will give him inner strength, relieve his suffering, and make him comfortable on his bed.[241] What a wondrous picture of Christ's care for the sickly of His fold. Says Spurgeon, "How tender and sympathizing is this image; how near it brings our God to our infirmities and sicknesses!"[242]

Hopefully, in life, you have been merciful toward others with your goods, gifts, and time, for such strike at the heart of the Christian faith. But even if not, Christ will "make your sickbed"—similarly, not equally, and just as assuredly. Having the greatest physician in the world at the bedside watching over and caring for you constantly instills comfort, peace, and hope like nothing else.

"A bed soon grows hard when the body is weary with tossing to and fro upon it, but grace gives patience, and God's smile gives peace, and the bed is made soft because the man's heart is content; the pillows are downy because the head is peaceful."[243]—C. H. Spurgeon.

~March 31~

Psalm 41:4

Being Merciful

"I said, LORD, be merciful unto me: heal my soul; for I have sinned against thee" (Psalm 41:4).

The meaning of mercy. Mercy is the desire that a person doesn't get what he deserves for a wrong done. It is the display of undeserved compassion and sympathy.

Its model. God showed mercy by sparing us deserved condemnation. Paul says, "But God is so rich in mercy; he loved us so much that even though we were spiritually dead and doomed by our sins, he gave us back our lives again" (Ephesians 2:4–5 TLB). His mercy is inexhaustible and freely available to every sinner who repents. Spurgeon wrote, "God's mercy is so great that you may sooner drain the sea of its water, or deprive the sun of its light, or make space too narrow, than diminish the great mercy of God."

Its mandate. Recipients of God's mercy are to express mercy to others. James said, "Yes, you must show mercy to others, or God will not show mercy to you when he judges you" (James 2:13 ICB). Barnes says, "Nowhere do we imitate God more than in showing mercy. In nothing does God delight more than in the exercise of mercy."[244]

Its motive. First, demonstrate mercy out of gratitude for the rich mercy received from God and man (Ephesians 2:4–5).

Second, demonstrate mercy out of compliance with its command (James 2:13).

Third, demonstrate mercy out of a need for mercy. Jesus says, "Blessed are the merciful: for they shall obtain mercy" (Matthew 5:7). Philip Henry said, "If the end of one mercy were not the beginning of another, we were undone." Thankfully, His mercies are new every morning (Lamentations 3:23).

Fourth, demonstrate mercy out of empathy with the wounded. In naming types of sins some had committed, Paul said, "And such were some of you: but ye are washed, but ye are sanctified, but ye are justified in the name of the Lord Jesus, and by the Spirit of our God" (1 Corinthians 6:11). Alexander Pope: "Teach me to feel another's woe, to hide the fault I see, that mercy I to others show, that mercy show to me."

"If God should have no more mercy on us than we have charity to one another, what would become of us?"—Thomas Fuller.

~April 1~

Psalm 42:1–2
The Believer's Thirst
Part 1

"As the hart panteth after the water brooks, so panteth my soul after thee, O God. My soul thirsteth for God, for the living God: when shall I come and appear before God?" (Psalm 42:1–2).

Spurgeon says, "A thirst is a lack, a need crying out of its emptiness."[245] The believer should thirst for five things.

The presence of God. Foremost, manifest a thirst for God's presence. Martyn Lloyd-Jones said, "The most vital question to ask about all who claim to be Christian is this: Have they a soul thirst for God?...Is their life centered on Him? Do they press forward more and more that they might know Him?"[246]

The holiness of life. Thirst, as McCheyne put it, to be as holy as a pardoned sinner can be. A grave contradiction exists when one states the fact of personal salvation and yet is content to continue in the old life of sin (2 Corinthians 5:17).

Holy Ghost power. Thirst for supernatural power in walk, witness, and work (Luke 11:13). Spurgeon says, "Without the Spirit of God, we can do nothing. We are as ships without wind or chariots without steeds. Like branches without sap, we are withered. Like coals without fire, we are useless. As an offering without the sacrificial flame, we are unaccepted." Two more thirsts will be discussed in tomorrow's meditation.

107

"One of the greatest foes of the Christian is religious complacency. Orthodox Christianity has fallen to its present low estate from lack of spiritual desire. Among the many who profess the Christian faith, scarcely one in a thousand reveals any passionate thirst for God."— A. W. Tozer.

~April 2~

Psalm 42:2
The Believer's Thirst
Part 2

"My soul thirsteth for God, for the living God." (Psalm 42:2).

The believer should thirst for the presence of God, holiness, and spiritual power, as well as for a deep concern for souls and spiritual progress.

Concern for souls. Indifference toward the unsaved must ever be battled. We must often pray, "Lord help me not get used to boys and girls, men and women dying and going to Hell." From whence comes this concern for the lost?

"Seeing the crowds, He felt compassion for them, because they were distressed and downcast, like sheep without a shepherd" (Matthew 9:36 NASB). A burden for the lost flows from Christ's concern and compassion to all who walk in close fellowship with Him. The disciples observed Jesus' agonies, tears, and passion for the lost and His efforts to win them, "and thus caught His spirit, and so they learned how to be fishers of men."

Spurgeon says, "Your battle-ax and weapons of war must come from the sacred connection with Christ. If you spend much time alone with Jesus, you will catch His spirit and be enflamed by the fire that engulfed His life. The power that stirred men's hearts and consciences in Him will be in your words, even if you cannot speak as eloquently as He did." Pray that the weight of lost immortal souls (burden, concern, interest) that He possesses will be known experientially by you. Pray with Eugene Harrison

108

Lord, give me Thy love for souls,
For lost and wand'ring sheep,
That I may see the multitudes
And weep as Thou didst weep.

Spiritual progress. Don't be satisfied to live in the lowlands while the mountaintops await. Pray, "Lord, lift me up, and let me stand by faith on Canaan's tableland, a higher plane than I have found; Lord, plant my feet on higher ground." Keep longing and craving for higher ground. Maclaren says, "The intention of every Christian life should be a life of increasing luster, uninterrupted, and the natural result of increasing communion with and conformity [continuous growth] to the very fountain itself of heavenly radiance."[247]

"Never did a soul thirst for God, cry out for God, the living God, but God sooner or later, in His own good time, filled that soul with all His fullness, flooded that soul with all the sunshine of His love."[248]—Maclagan.

~April 3~

Psalm 42:2
The Believer's Thirst
Part 3
"My soul thirsteth for God, for the living God." (Psalm 42:2).

Among the things for which we should thirst is righteousness. Jesus said, "Blessed are they which do hunger and thirst after [the whole of] righteousness: for they shall be filled" (Matthew 5:6). Paul writes of the imputed righteousness of Christ whereby the sinner is made right with God (2 Corinthians 5:21). Surely, every sinner should hunger to experience it, for without it, he is left hopeless for time and eternity. Although free to possess, it must be desired and received.

Righteousness used here in the Beatitudes, according to Leon Morris, speaks of an intense pursuit of "upright living"— conformity to God's will, commandments, and expectations, to please and magnify Him. Morris asks a searching question: "How could anyone have a strong desire for a right standing before God without at the same time strongly wanting to do the right?"[249] It just doesn't figure.

What Robert Louis Stevenson called "the malady of not wanting" plagues the masses about the spiritual.[250] They are content with their present spiritual estate, though it is mediocre or worse. If you are in that number, ask the Lord to put the "salt lick" of Heaven on your tongue to make you thirsty for all the spiritual lacks in your life. "It is for the Holy Spirit's help," an old saint says, "that we must pray; it is on His help we must lean; it is He from whom we must ask the power to thirst for God, the living God."[252]

> I hunger and I thirst:
> Jesus, my manna be;
> Ye living waters, burst
> Out of the rock for me.
>
> —John S. B. Monsell (1866)

"Hunger and thirst are appetites that return frequently, and call for fresh satisfactions; so these holy desires rest not in any thing attained, but are carried out toward renewed pardons, and daily fresh supplies of grace."—Matthew Henry.

~April 4~

Psalm 42:5
Battling Melancholy

"Why are you so depressed, O my soul? Why so disturbed within me? Hope in God" (Psalm 42:5 EHV).

The Psalmist, in a state of mental anguish and gloom, arouses himself through self-interrogation not to lose hope but to trust God for consolation. Boice says, "It is a case of the mind speaking to the emotions rather than the emotions dictating to the mind." D. Martyn Lloyd-Jones similarly states, "You have to take yourself in hand; you have to address yourself, preach to yourself, question yourself. You must say to your soul, 'Why art thou cast down'—what business have you to be disquieted? You must turn on yourself, upbraid yourself, condemn yourself, exhort yourself, and say to yourself, 'Hope thou in God'—instead of muttering in this depressed, unhappy way."

The Psalmist had to chide himself three times about hopelessness, fretting, and grieving before victory finally came (Psalm 42:5; Psalm 42:11; Psalm 43:5). In saying the right thing to one's soul, repetition is sometimes needed for the sun to burst out upon its darkness. "Hope thou in God" is healthy to repeat again and again until the soul soars out of its captivity. Thomas Brooks states, "Hope can see Heaven through the thickest clouds."

"A believing confidence in God is a sovereign antidote against prevailing despondency and disquietude of spirit."[251]—Matthew Henry.

~April 5~

Psalm 43:3

Send the Light

"O send out thy light and thy truth: let them lead me; let them bring me unto thy holy hill, and to thy tabernacles" (Psalm 43:3).

The world is shrouded in darkness, with its destructive and damning evil spreading like wildfire. Solomon said, "The way of the wicked is like deep darkness" (Proverbs 4:19 ESV). As believers, we are to battle the darkness, seeking four objectives.

1. Expose the darkness. "And have nothing to do with the unfruitful actions that darkness produces. Instead, expose them for what they are" (Ephesians 5:11 ISV).

2. Engage the darkness. "Our fight is not with people. It is against the leaders and the powers and the spirits of darkness in this world. It is against the demon world that works in the heavens" (Ephesians 6:12 NLV).

3. Emancipate from the darkness. "He has sent me to bind up the brokenhearted, to proclaim freedom for the captives and release from darkness for the prisoners" (Isaiah 61:1 NIV).

4. Extinguish the darkness. "The light shines in the darkness, and the darkness doesn't extinguish the light" (John 1:5 CEB). Darkness is expelled at the sight of light.

God's light (Psalm 119:105) and truth (John 17:17)—the Word of God—must be sent out into the world to obtain these objectives. Ordinary light and fleshly wisdom are futile. Therefore, pray, "O send out thy light and thy truth." Darkness is overcome and consumed by light. "Darkness cannot drive out darkness; only light can do that."[252] "Send the light, the blessed gospel light; let it shine from shore to shore!"

"The more light that is given, the harder the human heart must become to reject it."[253]—Edwin Lutzer.

~April 6~

Psalm 43:4
The Secret to Calm

"Then I will go to the altar of God, to the God of my joyful gladness; with the harp I will give thanks to You, O God, my God" (Psalm 43:4 MEV).

David discovered the cure to his spiritual depression by remembering that God was his mighty deliverer (Psalm 43:1), almighty strength (Psalm 43:2), exceeding joy (Psalm 43:4), eternal hope (Psalm 43:5), exhorting himself not to let fleshly emotions rule his heart (Psalm 43:5) and spending time at the altar in the presence of God (Psalm 43:4).

Four lessons about calm in times of storm may be drawn from David's experience.

1. Calm is found in supplanting panicky emotions with established facts. Maclaren says, "Emotion varies, but God is the same. The facts on which faith feeds abide while faith fluctuates."[254]

2. Calm is found in the secret place of God under the shadow of His wings (Psalm 91:1).

3. Calm is found in the light and truth of God's promises (Psalm 43:3).

4. Calm is found in staying on Jehovah, who is our strength and hope in the raging storm. Spurgeon states, "Hope in God always crests the stormiest billow."[255] "Stayed upon Christ Jesus, hearts are fully blest; finding, as He promised, perfect peace and rest."

"Experience of God's mercies bygone should fasten resolution to use faith hereafter in all troubles. After one trouble, the godly should prepare for another; after one delivery, expect another."[256]—Dickson.

~April 7~

Psalm 44:5
In the Name of Jesus

"Through thee will we push down our enemies: through thy name will we tread them under that rise up against us" (Psalm 44:5).

Spurgeon says, "The Lord's name served instead of weapons and enabled those who used it to leap on their foes and crush them with jubilant valor. In union and communion with God, saints work wonders."[257]

David used the name of the Lord as his weapon of choice (not the armor of Saul) against Goliath. Confronting him, David said, "Thou comest to me with a sword, and with a spear, and with a shield: but I come to thee *in the name of the LORD* of hosts, the God of the armies of Israel, whom thou hast defied" (1 Samuel 17:45). And smallness and weakness won out over bigness and super strength.

The seventy witnesses Jesus dispatched returned and said, "Lord, even the devils are subject unto us *through thy name*" (Luke 10:17). Peter and John prayed following their release from prison for boldness in speaking "that signs and wonders may be done *by the name of thy holy child Jesus*" (Acts 4:30). Paul said to the demon that possessed a woman, "I command thee *in the name of Jesus Christ* to come out of her. And he came out the same hour" (Acts 16:18).

The name of Jesus is the sinner's hope of salvation (1 Corinthians 6:11), the saint's refuge and strong tower in the storm (Proverbs 18:10), and the source of power in prayer (John 14:13–14). "Take the name of Jesus with you, child of sorrow and of woe; it will joy and comfort give you; take it then where'er you go."[258] Those who have experienced the power of that name exclaim, "No one is like you, LORD; you are great, and your name is mighty in power" (Jeremiah 10:6 NIV).

Jesus—It is a Simple Name. The name Jesus is simple enough for the littlest child to say and sing.

Jesus—It is a Sacred Name. The name of Jesus was not humanly selected but supernaturally announced. "Thou shalt call His name JESUS" (Matthew 1:21).

Jesus—It is a Saving Name. The name itself means "Savior."

Jesus—It is a Staying Name. Wiersbe states, "Great names come and go, but the name of Jesus remains. The Devil still hates it, the world still opposes it, but God still blesses it, and we can still claim it!"[445]

Jesus—It is a Soul-Nourishing Name. "The sweet Name of Jesus produces in us holy thoughts, fills the soul with noble sentiments, strengthens virtue, begets good works, and nourishes pure affection," said St. Bernard of Clairvaux.

Jesus—It is a Succoring Name. The name of Jesus "charms our fears and bids our sorrows cease; 'tis music in the sinner's ears; 'tis life and health and peace."

Jesus—It is a Splendorous Name. "Wherefore God also hath highly exalted him, and given him a name which is above every name:

that at the name of Jesus every knee should bow, of things in heaven, and things in earth, and things under the earth" (Philippians 2:9–10).

"To holy people, the very name of Jesus is a name to feed upon, a name to transport. His name can raise the dead and transfigure and beautify the living."—John Henry Newman.

~April 8~

Psalm 44:23

Wakeful and Watchful Eyes

"Awake, why sleepest thou, O Lord?" (Psalm 44:23).

Does God sleep? The Bible answers, "Behold, he that keepeth Israel shall neither slumber nor sleep" (Psalm 121:4). Knowing that God never sleeps is beneficial for five reasons.

1. It wards off the enemy. "The eternal God is thy refuge, and underneath are the everlasting arms: and he shall thrust out the enemy from before thee; and shall say, Destroy them" (Deuteronomy 33:27). A guarded house repels the thief.

2. It engenders rest and calm. "I am the LORD your God. I am holding your hand, so don't be afraid. I am here to help you" (Isaiah 41:13 CEV).

3. It assures unintermittent watchfulness and care. "He holds you firmly in place; He will not let you fall. He who keeps you will never take His eyes off you and never drift off to sleep" (Psalm 121:3 VOICE).

4. It provides constant access to Him. "In whom we have boldness and access with confidence by the faith of him" (Ephesians 3:12).

5. It grants unbroken companionship with Him. "For He Himself has said, 'I will never leave you nor forsake you'" (Hebrews 13:5 NKJV). "And He said, "My presence shall go with thee, and I will give thee rest [peace]" (Exodus 33:14).

"He will be ever watchful and wakeful."[259]—Albert Barnes.

~April 9~

Psalm 45:1b
A Ready Tongue

"My tongue is the pen of a ready writer" (Psalm 45:1b).

Poetically, the psalmist says that as a writer knows what to write and the best way to write it, he is ready to speak of the glories of the King. This he does eloquently, beautifully, and convincingly in the psalm. Our tongue should be equally sharp, informed, and prepared to speak of the deity, incarnation, perfection, miraculous works, atoning death, and resurrection of Christ defensibly (apologetics) and offensively (witnessing). Peter says, "Be ready always to give an answer to every man that asketh you a reason of the hope that is in you with meekness and fear" (1 Peter 3:15).

Solomon says the tongue of a "faithful ambassador is health" (Proverbs 13:17)—not to himself, but to his Master and the people to whom he speaks the Master's Word. That which the faithful messenger says on behalf of the King (he declares all the counsel of God—Acts 20:27) brings the healing cure for the malady of sin, deliverance from the clutches of Satan, peace, and refreshment to the soul. "How beautiful upon the mountains are the feet of him that bringeth good tidings, that publisheth peace" (Isaiah 52:7). "The exclamation," asserts Delitzsch, "does not refer to the pretty sound of their footsteps, but their feet are as if they were winged, because it is a joyful message which they bring."[236]

In contrast, the "wicked messenger" (the believer who fails to tell) betrays the Master's trust, dishonors the Master's name, hinders the Master's plan (Ezekiel 3:17–18), and hurts the Master's heart. Bridges says, "What words can tell the awful mischief of the wicked messenger—ignorant of the worth of his commission, and utterly careless in the discharge of it! Yet the mischief returns upon his head, laden as he is with the guilt of the blood of souls, overwhelmed himself in the eternal damnation of those who have perished through his neglect."[237]

The foremost duty of the redeemed is to keep their tongue as the pen of a ready writer to speak of the King worthily and persuasively when the opportunity arises.

"He who has truth at his heart need never fear the want of persuasion on his tongue."[260]—John Ruskin.

~April 10~

Psalm 45:1–3

The Excellency of Christ

Part 1

"My heart overflows with a goodly theme; I address my psalm to a King. My tongue is like the pen of a ready writer. You are fairer than the children of men; graciousness is poured upon Your lips; therefore God has blessed You forever. Gird Your sword upon Your thigh, O mighty One, in Your glory and Your majesty!" (Psalm 45:1–3 AMPC).

Of this Psalm, Plumer states, "The true and proper divinity of Christ is plainly and beyond all question here asserted."[261] It cites eight distinguishing prophetic traits of the Messiah fulfilled in Christ.

1. Messiah is "fairer than the children of men" (Psalm 45:2a). He is without fault or blemish. Pilate could not find fault in Jesus, nor can any man.

2. Messiah's lips are anointed with grace (Psalm 45:2b). Solomon spoke with great wisdom, but a greater than Solomon is here. Even the officers of the chief priests (enemies) said of Jesus, "Never man spake like this man" (John 7:46). They that heard Jesus speak in the synagogue "bare him witness, and wondered at the gracious words which proceeded out of his mouth. And they said, Is not this Joseph's son?" (Luke 4:22).

Spurgeon observes, "Whoever in personal communion with the Well-beloved has listened to His voice will feel that 'never man spake like this man.' Well did the bride say of Him, 'His lips are like lilies dropping sweet smelling myrrh.' One word from Himself dissolved the heart of Saul of Tarsus and turned him into an apostle; another word raised up John the Divine when fainting on the Isle of Patmos. Often, a sentence from His lips has turned our midnight into morning, our winter into spring."[262] Jesus' words are impregnated with power, comfort, and healing.

3. Messiah's lips are the lips of authority, for all He says is done.

4. Messiah is a 'mighty warrior' (Psalm 45:3). "Gird thy sword upon thy thigh" refers to the Messiah as the conquering King and warrior preparing for battle.[263] He is "O most mighty," "that is Hero; Warrior; Conqueror."[264] Jesus characterizes them each.

"Men are brought to believe in Him because He is true, to learn of Him because He is meek (the gentleness of Christ is of mighty force), and to submit to Him because He is righteous and rules with equity."[265]—Matthew Henry.

~April 11~

Psalm 45:4-7
The Excellency of Christ
Part 2

"And in Your majesty ride on triumphantly for the cause of truth, humility, and righteousness (uprightness and right standing with God); and let Your right hand guide You to tremendous things. Your arrows are sharp; the peoples fall under You; Your darts pierce the hearts of the King's enemies. Your throne, O God, is forever and ever; the scepter of righteousness is the scepter of Your kingdom. You love righteousness, uprightness, and right standing with God and hate wickedness; therefore God, Your God, has anointed You with the oil of gladness above Your fellows." (Psalm 45:1 AMPC).

The psalmist details the prophetic traits of the Messiah, all fulfilled in Jesus Christ. Yesterday, we looked at the first four; today, note the remaining four.

1. Messiah is triumphant in battle (Psalm 45:4). He rides into battle victoriously upon a stallion, crusading for truth, righteousness, and humility. He is the "the way, the truth, and the life" (John 14:6) and builds His kingdom upon the earth on truth and right, which is the direct opposite of what presently exists, erected upon deeds and teachings of darkness. Messiah's kingdom would be founded not upon arrogance, conceit, and pride as that of earthly monarchs but on humility, gentleness, and kindness.[266]

2. Messiah's rule is "forever and ever" (Psalm 45:6a.). Obviously, this did not apply to King Solomon or any other ruler, for they lived, reigned, and died. Messiah's throne would be eternal. Spurgeon says, "No throne can endure forever but that on which God himself sits."[267]

3. Messiah sits upon the throne as Judge to dispense justice (Psalm 45:6b). "Christ himself is the Judge, with the final say on everyone, living and dead" (2 Timothy 4:1 MSG).

4. Messiah is anointed by God (v 7b). Note, 'God anoints God.'[268] The author of Hebrews uses this verse to establish the divinity of Christ. God anointed Jesus as Messiah and Holy Comforter (Luke 4:18).

Jesus fulfilled all eight prophecies, affirming that He is the Messiah, the Savior God sent into the world to save His people from their sins.

"He has assumed our nature and become a man, in order that, by substituting Himself in our place and stead, He might deliver us out of the hands of our great enemy and bring us into an everlasting union with Himself, as 'our Friend and our Beloved.'"[269]—Charles Simeon.

~April 12~

Psalm 45:7

Jesus' Joy in What He Did

"Thou lovest righteousness, and hatest wickedness: therefore God, thy God, hath anointed thee with the oil of gladness above thy fellows" (Psalm 45:7).

The psalmist states that God will anoint the Messiah with a bountiful measure of gladness that exceeds the joy known to others. The prophecy was fulfilled in Jesus. *Jesus was joyous in what He did.* This is known from what He said and what was said of Him.

To God, Christ said, "I delight to do thy will, O my God" (Psalm 40:8). In His sending out the seventy to witness, Luke says, "In that hour Jesus rejoiced in spirit" (Luke 10:21). "Rejoiced in spirit" literally means that He danced with joy. The Hebrews author said, "Looking unto Jesus the author and finisher of our faith; who for the joy that was set before him endured the cross" (Hebrews 12:2). At Jacob's well, Christ told the disciples, "My meat [fullest satisfaction, joy] is to do the will of him that sent me, and to finish his work" (John 4:34). Presently He is seated on Heaven's throne making intercession for the saints (Romans 8:26).

"Think of the gladness of Jesus in His work—its purpose, its objects."[270]—Mark Guy Pierce.

~April 13~

Psalm 45:7

Jesus' Joy from What He Did

"Thou lovest righteousness, and hatest wickedness: therefore God, thy God, hath anointed thee with the oil of gladness above thy fellows" (Psalm 45:7).

Christ not only experienced joy *in* what He did but *from* what He did. He is the good shepherd who rejoiced in finding the one lost sheep (Luke 15:6) and the loving Father who rejoiced greatly at the return of the prodigal (Luke 15:24). It is He who rejoices in Heaven among the angels at the repentance of sinners (Luke 15:10). Christ rejoiced, and rejoices over His people. "For Jehovah enjoys his people" (Psalm 149:4 TLB). He enjoys their praises, worship, prayers, testimonials, witnessing, and service. Zephaniah says, "The LORD thy God in the midst of thee is mighty; he will save, he will rejoice over thee with joy; he will rest in his love, he will joy over thee with singing" (Zephaniah 3:17). What joy it ought to be to us, that He joys over us so much! C. S. Lewis said, "Joy is the serious business of Heaven."

For sure, He was the "man of sorrows, and acquainted with grief" (Isaiah 53:3). He endured suffering and torment to purchase our salvation, but it was always overshadowed by the "oil of gladness." He sowed in tears but always reaped in joy (Psalm 126:5).

Believers are partakers of His joy. Jesus said, "I have told you this so that my joy may be in you and that your joy may be complete" (John 15:11 NIV). No man's joy is complete, full, and satisfying until he partakes of Christ's joy. We may encounter grief and suffering, but it is all enveloped in the joy of the Lord, which is our strength (Nehemiah 8:10). Let us who know the joy of the Lord display and share it.

"The truest, purest joy flows from a discovery of Jesus Christ. He is the hidden treasure that gives such joy to the finder."[271]—Robert Murray McCheyne.

~April 14~

Psalm 46:1

What God is to the Believer

"God is our refuge and strength, a very present help in trouble" (Psalm 46:1).

Psalm 46 was Luther's favorite Psalm. His famous hymn, written on his way to the Diet at Worms, beginning *A strong fortress is our God*, is very much taken from it. In the darkest times [furious opposition], he used to say, "Come, let us sing the 46th Psalm, and let the Devil do his worst." Luther stated, "We sing this Psalm to the praise of God because God is with us, and powerfully and miraculously preserves and defends His church and His word, against all fanatical spirits, against the gates of Hell, against the implacable hatred of the Devil, and all the assaults of the world, the flesh, and sin."[272]

What is God to the believer?

1. A refuge. God is a place of safety, a place where believers hide in times of danger, protected by His almighty hand. The gates to the city of refuge open at the arrival of affliction and adversity. Let the troubled flee into them and be safe from the enemy.

2. A strength. God is the provider of *strength* to thwart the power of sin, cope with grievous sorrow, endure suffering, tear down strongholds to set the captives free from Satan's domain and do His work victoriously. He enables us to bear life's burdens, whatever their difficulty, despair, and distress. Scott says, "If our faith were as strong as our security is good, we need to fear no combination of enemies, no revolutions in kingdoms, and no convulsions in nature; but, in the tremendous dangers, might triumph in the fullest assurance of security and victory."[273]

3. A present help. Immediately when trouble arises, God is there to help just at the right moment. "God shall help her, and that right early" (Psalm 46:5).

4. A certain help. Note the psalmist's emphatic confidence, "God is." Of His help in trouble, no believer should question or doubt.

5. A proven help. God's ableness and willingness to help is well documented in the Scripture. He helped the four Hebrew children in the burning furnace, Daniel in the Lion's Den, Mary and Martha in their grief, Hezekiah in his sickness, and David in his battles. "Hidden in the hollow of His mighty hand, where no harm can

follow, in His strength we stand. We may trust Him fully, all for us to do; those who trust Him wholly find Him wholly true."

"A help found to be very powerful and effectual in straits and difficulties. The words are very emphatic *in the Hebrew*. 'He is found an exceeding or superlative help in difficulties.' We have found Him, and therefore celebrate His praise."[274]—Adam Clarke.

~April 15~

Psalm 46:2
Antidote to Fear

"Therefore will not we fear, though the earth be removed, and though the mountains be carried into the midst of the sea" (Psalm 46:2).

The psalm may refer to the invasion of Israel by Sennacherib and the people's confidence in deliverance by God.

The calamity of the saints. "Though the earth be removed [falls apart]." Fear arises about something dreaded or beyond one's control or comprehension. Fear is the coiled snake ready to strike in the heart of every man about the dying process, terminal disease, death, judgment, and the afterlife. It strikes suddenly and viciously the most ardent saint, imparting venom of terror, horror, and fright, all purposed to torment. Unless checked, it binds the soul (slavish fear), prompting irrational thoughts, actions, decisions, and restlessness.

The calm of the saints. "Will not we fear." Confidence that God is our refuge of safety, strength, and help in trouble, predicated by His unfailing love, care, and power, thrusts fear out the door (1 John 4:18). Leighton said, "When God is in the midst of a kingdom or city, He makes it as firm as Mount Zion, and *that cannot be removed*. When He is in the midst of a soul, though calamities throng about it on all hands and roar like the billows of the sea, yet there is a constant calm within, such a peace as the world can neither give nor take away."[275]

The courage of the saints. "God is in the midst of her." The presence of God on the boat in the storm is a game-changer. It changes cowards into courageous warriors. With God's presence, says the psalmist, he will "not be afraid for the terror by night; nor for the arrow that flieth by day" (Psalm 91:5). Solomon said, "Whoso putteth his trust in the LORD shall be safe" (Proverbs 29:25). "His protective sufficiency. Infinite in its amplitude, impregnable in its resistance, interminable in its duration. We can be involved in no difficulty from which He cannot extricate, exposed to no danger from which He cannot shelter, assailed by no enemies from which He cannot deliver."[276] Why, therefore, should we not be courageous, whatever evil befalls?

"With God on our side, how irrational would fear be! Where He is, all power is, and all love, why should we quail?"[277]—C. H. Spurgeon.

~April 16~

Psalm 46:4

The River of God

"There is a river, the streams whereof shall make glad the city of God, the holy place of the tabernacles of the most High" (Psalm 46:4).

1. The River's Source. Its fountainhead is the immeasurable lake of God's love in Heaven. It flows down to man through the Lord Jesus Christ.

2. The River's Supply. It furnishes innumerable and inexhaustible mercies and blessings of God to all who are thirsty.

3. The River's Streams. Various streams flow from the river to meet diverse needs (1 Corinthians 12:11).[278] "Streams of mercy, never ceasing, call for songs of loudest praise."

4. The River's Security. In olden times, a city surrounded by a river was impregnable. Zion's defense and that of her inhabitants is the river of God that surrounds them.

5. The River's Satisfaction. All who drink of its living waters shall be satisfied and glad.

6. The River's Summon. "If any man thirst, let him come unto me, and drink [and] out of his belly shall flow rivers of living water" (John 7:37–38).

"Happy are they who know from their own experience that there is such a river of God."[279]—C. H. Spurgeon.

~April 17~

Psalm 46:10
Let Go, and Let God

"Be still, and know that I am God" (Psalm 46:10).

Knowing that God is the able deliverer in tumultuous storms, the psalmist instructs, "Be still." Don't be anxious, worried, and panicky; be calm, confiding, and trustful, leaving the matter with God.[280] Wiersbe says, "'Be still' means 'to take your hands off.'"[281] Take your hands off your life, let go, and let God manage its battles, troubles, and healings. Rest and relax in His refuge of strength and safety. "The Lord will fight for you. You just keep still" (Exodus 14:14 CEB).

"And know that I am God" (Psalm 46:10b). We are exhorted to *know* that God is God to remind us of six things in the season of trouble.

1. That God is sovereign and rules all.

2. That His promises are unfailing.

3. That His lovingkindness is unbounded.

4. That His goodness is unending.

5. That His actions are unerring.

6. That His nature and purpose are unchanging.

Knowing these things about God instills trust and confidence in Him to help in times of trouble.

"This sovereign Lord is with us, sides with us, acts with us and has promised He will never leave us."[282]—Matthew Henry.

~April 18~

Psalm 47:5
Christ's Going Up
Part 1

"God is gone up with a shout" (Psalm 47:5).

This is a prophecy of the ascension of Christ.

From where did Christ come down? Christ descended from Heaven to Earth through a virgin birth in Bethlehem's stable (Ephesians 4:8–10).

From where did He go up?[283] From the earth after fulfilling His redemption mission. Through Jesus' descent from Heaven to the Cross, He atoned for man's sins and 'destroyed him that had the power of death, that is, the devil' (Hebrews 2:14). Peter says, "For Christ also hath once suffered for sins, the just for the unjust, that he might bring us to God, being put to death in the flesh, but quickened [made alive again] by the Spirit" (1 Peter 3:18). Paul says, "Wherefore He saith, When He ascended up on high, He led captivity captive, and gave gifts unto men" (Ephesians 4:8). Ironside asserts, "The fact of His having gone up and having been received by the Shekinah—the cloud of divine Majesty—testifies to the perfection of His work in putting away forever the believer's sins."[284]

To where did He go up? To the third heaven, where He now sits on the majestic throne with all authority and power.

With what did He go up?

1. He took up with Him the cancellation of man's sin debt (Colossians 2:14).

2. He took the keys of death and the grave (Revelation 1:18). Matthew Henry says, "He conquered those who had conquered us, such as sin, the Devil, and death. Indeed, He triumphed over these

on the cross, but the triumph was completed at His ascension when He became Lord over all and had the keys of death and Hades put into His hands."[285] MacArthur comments, "The phrase 'when He ascended on high' (Ephesians 4:8) depicts a triumphant Christ returning from battle on earth back into the glory of the heavenly city with the trophies of His great victory."[286]

What was the response TO His going up? He received the shout of gladness and joy (Revelation 19:7), gratitude and praise (Revelation 5:9), victory and triumph from the host of Heaven.

"He is gone up as our glorious Representative to take possession of the inheritance of eternal life, until his fellow-heirs, all believers whom He represents, follow Him."[287]—Erskine.

~April 19~

Psalm 47:5
Christ Going Up
Part 2

"God is gone up with a shout, the LORD with the sound of a trumpet" (Psalm 47:5).

For what purpose did Christ go up?

1. As a Forerunner. Christ's return to Heaven completed the divinely assigned redemptive mission (the final "nail" to be hammered) to make saints ready for Heaven and Heaven ready for them. Before His death and ascension, Jesus told the disciples that He was going away to prepare a place for them (John 14:2). The imagery of Jesus returning to His carpentry skills, pounding nails into boards, and constructing houses for believers in Heaven is spurious.

Arthur Pink unravels the words "I go to prepare a place for you." He said (my paraphrase), 'Jesus has procured the right for every regenerated sinner to enter Heaven by His death on the Cross. He has "prepared" us a place there as our Representative (Forerunner) by planting His royal banner in its soil and procuring it on our behalf. Christ did everything necessary to secure a permanent place in Heaven for His children.'[288]

2. As a Ruler. From Heaven's throne, He governs the affairs of man and the world.

3. As a High Priest. Further, Jesus entered the "holy of holies" on High as our great High Priest, carrying our names in with Him (Hebrews 6:20).

Spurgeon says, "From the hour our Lord left it, this world has lost all charms to us. If He were in it, there were no spot in the universe which would hold us with stronger ties, but since He has gone up, He draws us upward from it. Joseph is no more in Egypt, and it is time for Israel to be gone. No, earth, my treasure is not here with thee, neither shall my heart be detained by thee."[289]

"Christ prepares the place in Heaven for His own, and the Holy Spirit prepares the redeemed on earth for their place in Heaven."[290]—
The Reformation Study Bible.

~April 20~

Psalm 47:6
Let's Praise the Lord

"Sing praises to God, sing praises: sing praises unto our King, sing praises" (Psalm 47:6).

The words may apply to the time when the Ark of God was brought to Mt. Zion, but indeed, also, prophetically to Christ's ascension upon finishing the work of salvation to Heaven.

Four times, saints are called to sing praises. Praises are tributes of honor, appreciation, admiration, and gratitude that are to be expressed to the King of Kings for who He is and what He has wrought. They are purposed to exalt and magnify Him in all the earth.

1. Praise is to be done "with understanding" (Psalm 47:7). If the heathen sang praises with understanding, they wouldn't be worshipping idols of stone but, instead, the true and living God.

2. Praise is to be done all the time. Spurgeon says, "Never let the music pause. He never ceases to be good; let us never cease to be grateful."[291]

3. Praise is to be with all one's being. David said, "Let all that I am praise the LORD; with my whole heart, I will praise his holy name" (Psalm 103:1 NIV). "A conscientious praise of God will keep us back from all false and mean praises, all fulsome and servile flatteries."[292]

4. Praise belongs to only God (Psalm 65:1). Self-praise for accomplishments and successes is arrogant and vain. James reminds us, "Every good present and every perfect gift comes from above, from the Father who made the sun, moon, and stars" (James 1:17 NOG).

In light of all God has done for us, it's grievous that we must be told to praise Him.

"Let our homage be paid not in groans but in songs."[293]—C. H. Spurgeon.

~April 21~

Psalm 47:8
The Holiness of God

"God sitteth upon the throne of his holiness" (Psalm 47:8).

Familiarity with God has led to flippancy in regarding Him. We need a fresh vision or understanding of His holiness (Exodus 3:5).

God's holiness is impeccable. Job 34:10 (NASB19995) says, "Far be it from God to do wickedness...to do wrong." God is holy, ruling on His majestic throne with absolute justice and fairness. He is spotlessly pure, and all His actions are without any tinge of corruption. Clarke says, "He is a holy God; He proclaims holiness. His laws are holy, He requires holiness, and His genuine people are all holy. The throne of His holiness is the Heaven of heavens."[294]

God's holiness is incomparable. First Samuel 2:2 says, "There is none holy as the LORD: for there is none beside thee." None can identify with His perfection. Exodus 15:11 states, "Who is like unto thee, O LORD, among the gods? who is like thee, glorious in holiness?" Heber wrote, "Only Thou art holy; there is none beside Thee."

God's holiness is unapproachable. 1 Timothy 6:16 (ESV) states that God "dwells in unapproachable light, whom no one has ever seen or can see. To him be honor and eternal dominion. Amen." Man's access to the throne of God is only possible through His Son, the Lord Jesus Christ (1 Timothy 2:5). "Now all of us can come to the Father through the same Holy Spirit because of what Christ has done for us" (Ephesians 2:18 NLT).

God's holiness is revelatory. Art Lindsley wrote, "Any vision of God's holiness leads to a sense of our sin and makes us sensitive to the unholiness of the culture around us."[295] This was Isaiah's experience. In being awestruck by what he heard, saw, and felt in his vision of the holiness of God, he cried, "Woe is me! for I am undone; because I am a man of unclean lips, and I dwell in the midst of a people of unclean lips: for mine eyes have seen the King, the LORD of hosts" (Isaiah 6:5). An understanding of God's holiness is a mirror that reveals our sinfulness and need of cleansing, as with Isaiah. "Shallow views of sin are one of the chief dangers of our day, begetting shallow views of atonement and of the relation of Christ's death to our sins."[296]

"The holiness of God is traumatic to unholy people."—R. C. Sproul.

~April 22~

Psalm 47:9

Shields of Protection

"The shields of the earth belong unto God: he is greatly exalted" (Psalm 47:9).

The shields of the earth were created and owned by God for man's protection against the perils of every kind. Note six of them.

1. The shield of government. Paul says, "Rulers are God's servants to help you. But if you do wrong, you have reason to be

afraid. They have the power to punish, and they will use it. They are God's servants to punish those who do wrong" (Romans 13:4 ERV). Righteous laws shield people from wrongdoing and protect them from being wronged or harmed. Without them, chaos would result. Spurgeon says, "Those who are earth's protectors, the shields of the commonwealth, derive their might from Him and are His.'[297]

2. The shield of Scripture. God's Word provides a defensive wall against sin in the heart. David said, "Thy word have I hid in my heart, that I might not sin against [God]" (Psalm 119:11 DARBY).

3. The shield of home. The Christian home, rightly ordered, provides battlements of safety from harm and evil.

4. The shield of faith. The Bible says, "Above all, taking the shield of faith, wherewith ye shall be able to quench all the fiery darts of the wicked" (Ephesians 6:16). Trust in Christ and reliance upon His promises will extinguish the fiery darts of the Devil.

5. The shield of the church. Saints, with locked shields one to another, stand firm against the foe and battle victoriously for righteousness, drawing strength and stamina from one another.

6. The shield of prayer. Bunyan said, "Pray often, for prayer is a shield to the soul, a sacrifice to God, and a scourge for Satan." "Blessed are we," says Spurgeon, "when prayer surrounds us like an atmosphere. Then, we are living in the presence of God; we are continually conversing with Him. May we climb to the top of the mount of communion, and may we never come down from it!"[298]

"You always need divine protection, and, believer in Christ, you shall always have it."[299]—C. H. Spurgeon.

~April 23~

Psalm 48:9
Thoughts of Lovingkindness

"We have thought of thy lovingkindness, O God, in the midst of thy temple" (Psalm 48:9).

131

Kings allied together to attack Israel from the sea, but within eyesight of the shore, they panicked from fear and retreated "hastily" without firing a shot (Psalm 48:4–5).

We have thought. The sons of Korah, the singers in the Tabernacle, took ample time to meditate, reflect, and muse upon the wonder of God's unfailing love in causing the enemy to turn away. To give *thought* equally should be our response to the interventions and works of God. "We think when we analyze, compare, classify."[300] To ponder holy things is to lower your bucket slowly into the well of God's divine nature and wondrous works, only to draw it up when it's overflowing. With such holy musing, 'the fire burns'; memory is rekindled, and the mind enlightened, prompting praise and thanksgiving to the Lord. Hurried devotion or meditation yields little benefit and brings little glory to God. It takes time to be "holy." Such contemplation is "a duty because gratitude demands it, God wills it, and it is honored thereby (Psalm 111:2–4)."[301]

"Holy men are thoughtful men; they do not suffer God's wonders to pass before their eyes and melt into forgetfulness, but they meditate deeply upon them."[302]—C. H. Spurgeon.

~April 24~

Psalm 48:9
A Wondrous Theme for Thought

"We have thought of thy lovingkindness, O God, in the midst of thy temple" (Psalm 48:9).

The sons of Korah, the singers in God's house, first gave thought to the lovingkindness of God before singing of it. Spurgeon asserts, "There are some singers who have not done that, for they have sung solemn words thoughtlessly, caring only for the music, and not for the meaning."

The point of their thoughts. They thought of God's lovingkindness. No theme is more magnificent, wondrous, or beneficial. No subject provides so much matter. Meditate on its cause, cost, and consequence. Think of its impact on you. It intervened in your help-less and hopeless estate in the pit of darkness and dominion of sin, granting undeserved deliverance by the sacrificial and substitutionary death of Jesus at Calvary. Ponder the cleansing He afforded, the change He empowered, and the conversion He enabled. "In loving-kindness, Jesus came, my soul in mercy to reclaim, and from the depths of sin and shame, through grace, He lifted me."

The place of their thoughts. They thought of God's goodness and love "in the...temple." The church's altar, worship, holy atmo-sphere, and one's conversion experience in her gates facilitate thoughts of God's lovingkindness. "One of the richest fruits of the public service of God's house, and the ministry of God's Word, is reaped when we are led to think of God's lovingkindness."[303]

The praise of their thoughts. Heavenly thoughts prompt heart praise. "Great is the LORD, and greatly to be praised."

"It is lovingkindness everywhere, brethren, in the temple of the Lord; turn which way you will, it is all lovingkindness, and nothing else."[304]—C. H. Spurgeon.

~April 25~

Psalm 48:13–14
Benefits of Thoughts about God's Mercy

"Mark ye well her bulwarks, consider her palaces; that ye may tell it to the generation following. For this God is our God forever and ever: he will be our guide even unto death" (Psalm 48:13–14).

While in God's house, the sons of Korah gave deep thought to God's lovingkindness and were richly benefited.

The profit of their thoughts.

1. They witnessed. "That ye may tell it." Their tongues were loosed to speak of God's goodness and love. Thinking of His gracious lovingkindness opens the mouth to proclaim its wondrous

truth to others (Psalm 48:12–13). Spurgeon said, "If you have really tasted of God's lovingkindness, you must tell others about it. You cannot keep the love of God for you a secret. The first instinct of a newborn soul is to tell its joy to somebody else."[305]

2. They rejoiced. Thinking of God's unfailing love and mercy prompted joy and melody in their soul. "Let the people of Zion be glad! You give right judgments; let there be joy in the cities of Judah!" (Psalm 48:11 GNT). "Verily, such a theme lifts the soul heavenward, tunes the lips to song, and speeds the feet to run the race set before us."[306] Upon thoughts of God's goodness, the bells of the heart ring loud and joyously.

3. They affirmed their allegiance to God. "This God is our God forever and ever." Reflections of God's lovingkindness prompt renewed obedience and commitment. Thinking of God's unfailing love gives confidence in salvation and eternal life (Psalm 48:14).

"The lovingkindness of God towards His people in Christ serves greatly to encourage faith and hope, to draw out love to God, and engage to a ready and cheerful obedience to his will."[307]—John Gill.

~April 26~

Psalm 49:6
Riches, a Foolish Confidence

"They…trust in their wealth" (Psalm 49:6).

Why are riches a feeble and corrupt confidence?

1. Riches have no value in illness or terminal disease.

2. Riches bear no value in death. It cannot ward off death.

3. Riches bear no value after death. Its power, at death, to benefit its possessor is forever gone. With Job, all must say, "Naked I came from my mother's womb, and naked shall I return" (Job 1:21). There are no pockets in the shroud of death.

4. Riches bear no value at the Judgment. "Riches profit not in the day of wrath" (Proverbs 11:4). It possesses no power to gain eternal life. God cannot be bribed. The ungodly wealthy will stand as the poorest on earth, stripped naked of earthly possessions, to give an account at the Judgment of their life and relationship with Jesus Christ. Jesus asks, "For what shall it profit a man, if he shall gain the whole world, and lose his own soul?" (Mark 8:36).

"Whoever trusts in his riches will fall" (Proverbs 11:28 ESV). Bridges asserts, "Disappointment will be the certain end of this trust. When we need a staff, we shall find a piercing spear. Or we shall fall, like the withered leaf or blossom before the blast. And how many a lovely blossom has thus fallen! Thus does 'the rich man fade away in his ways!'"308

"Where riches hold the dominion of the heart, God has lost His authority. Covetousness makes us the slaves of the Devil."—John Calvin.

~April 27~

Psalm 49:8

The Preciousness of a Soul's Salvation

"For the redemption of their soul is precious" (Psalm 49:8).

A soul's salvation is precious based on five things.

Based on God's love for it. "For God so loved the world, that he gave his only begotten Son, that whosoever believeth in him should not perish, but have everlasting life" (John 3:16).

Based on what the Bible states about it. "For what shall it profit a man, if he shall gain the whole world, and lose his own soul?' (Mark 8:36).

Based on the price Christ paid to save it. "But God showed his great love for us by sending Christ to die for us while we were still sinners" (Romans 5:8 TLB). "The exceeding value of man's soul is seen in what Jesus has done for it. When we think of Christ leaving

His bright throne in the heavens and becoming a homeless wanderer upon the earth, that He might save lost souls, we can form some estimate of the soul's value."[309]

Based on Heaven's response to it. Jesus said, "In the same way there is more happiness in heaven because of one sinner who turns to God than over 99 good people who don't need to" (Luke 15:7 CEV).

Based on the saint's effort to save it. "I am made all things to all men, that I might by all means save some" (1 Corinthians 9:22).

Don't minimize the preciousness and worth of winning just one soul. R. G. Lee remarked, "One may be many. Andrew brought Simon—just one. But that one won many, for Simon brought 3,000 in one day under God. Jack Stratton, a waiter in a restaurant, brought John Gough to Christ—just one. And Gough brought many to Christ. A Sunday school teacher, Edward Kimball, brought Moody to Christ—just one. But that one won many, for Moody reached two continents for God. But why say more? Just as one digit is valuable in the multiplication table and one letter in the alphabet, far more valuable is just one soul in God's sight."[310] Moody said, "If you win only one soul to Christ, you may set a stream in motion that will flow long after you are dead and gone. So, if you turn one to Christ, that one may turn a hundred; they may turn a thousand, and so the stream, small at first, broadens and deepens as it rolls toward eternity."

"The salvation of one soul is worth more than the framing of a Magna Carta of a thousand worlds."—Keble.

~April 28~

Psalm 49:8
Throw Out a Longer Rope

"For the redemption of their soul is precious" (Psalm 49:8).

Believers are to bear the *precious* gospel seed to *precious* souls (Psalm 126:6; Ezekiel 3:17). They are to sow it fittingly with honor and expectation. Spurgeon says, "Tell it out as those who know it is *precious*, not flippantly. Tell the truth in Jesus, with the firm conviction that there is life in it, and something will come of it. Our estimate of the preciousness of the seed will have much to do with the result of the seed."[311]

A father and son were fishing when the son fell into the water and began to drown. Struggling for life, he cried, "Throw me a rope." The father hurriedly found a rope and threw it at him. But it was too short. The son frantically cried, "Dad, the rope is too short. Throw me a longer rope." Sadly, none other was found. And it was with that cry, "Dad, the rope's too short. Throw me a longer rope," that the son perished.

With evangelistic efforts in decline to rescue the unsaved, Heaven beckons the saints to throw out a longer rope to save them. 'Strengthen the stakes and lengthen the cords.' Expand the rope's reach by increasing its length through the greater distribution of gospel tracts and literature, escalated visitation, witnessing, soul-winning, intercessory prayer, and an upsurge in evangelistic efforts.

"You have one business on Earth—to save souls."—John Wesley.

~April 29~

Psalm 49:15
The Resurrection

"But God will redeem my soul from the power of the grave: for he shall receive me" (Psalm 49:15).

The psalmist reveals four beliefs about the resurrection.

1. The grave imprisons the body, not the soul. Matthew Henry said, "When death breaks the dark lantern, yet it does not extinguish the candle that was pent up in it."[312] Spurgeon remarks, "He will take me out of the tomb, up to Heaven. My spirit God will receive, and my body will sleep in Jesus till being raised in His image, it will also be received into Glory."[313] Paul said, 'To be absent from the body is to be present with the Lord' (2 Corinthians 5:8).

2. The separation of body and soul is only temporary. At the Great Resurrection, soul and body are rejoined. Paul states, "So when this corruptible shall have put on incorruption, and this mortal shall have put on immortality, then shall be brought to pass the saying that is written, Death is swallowed up in victory" (1 Corinthians 15:54).

3. The redeemed soul shall be saved from eternal destruction. "But God will redeem my soul." The Bible says, "There is therefore now no condemnation to them which are in Christ Jesus" (Romans 8:1).

4. The Lord Jesus Christ shall receive the ransomed at death. "For he shall receive me." He will receive them with favor and acceptance into the mansion prepared in Heaven for them (John 14:2–3). "As God 'took Enoch,' when he 'was not' (Gen. 5:24)—took him to be with Himself—so He will 'receive' every righteous soul, and take it home, and give it rest and peace in His own dwelling-place."[314] No saint crosses the chilly waters of Jordan alone. Christ walks each step with him.

"Wherefore comfort one another with these words" (1 Thessalonians 4:18).

"I shall have a resurrection from the dead and an entrance into His glory, and death shall have no dominion over me."[315]—Adam Clarke.

~April 30~

Psalm 50:14

Pay Your Vows

"Pay thy vows unto the most High" (Psalm 50:14).

God rebukes Israel not for their consistency in offering burnt sacrifices (Psalm 50:8) but for the motive with which it was done (Psalm 50:11–12). They viewed Him as a weak and hungry God, anxiously awaiting the next sacrifice to be fed.[316] God instructs them to worship rightly with proper motives by exhibiting thanksgiving, praise, and payment of vows.

Pay thy vows.

1. Vows are not a religious duty but a voluntary promise to God or man to do or abstain from a particular thing, sometimes for the return of a specific benefit (Genesis 28:20–22).

2. Vows are not wrong when made thoughtfully and appropriately, within the ability or means to keep, not about any wicked thing, and kept speedily (Ecclesiastes 5:4–7).

3. Vows are to be kept. Don't forget or break in the calm vows made in a crisis (Matthew 5:33). The chief butler forgot his vow to Joseph in Potiphar's prison for two long years (Genesis 40:23; 41:1). Solomon wisely states, 'It is better not to make a vow than to make a vow and not fulfill it' (Ecclesiastes 5:5).

4. Vows never expire. When broken vows are recalled, pay them. Unpaid vows remain on the debit account. "Pay to God," Spurgeon says, "the love you promised, the service you covenanted to render, the loyalty of heart you have vowed to maintain."[317] Pay to man that which was pledged, agreed to, and promised.

"Pay that which thou hast vowed; pay it in full and keep not back any part of the price; pay it in kind, do not alter it or change it."[318]— Matthew Henry.

~May 1~

Psalm 50:15
The Day of Trouble

"And call upon me in the day of trouble: I will deliver thee, and thou shalt glorify me" (Psalm 50:15).

Asaph accuses the people of hypocritical worship in the psalm—they worship God with their lips, but their hearts oppose

Him. The text is an invitation to troubled souls from a loving and caring God to seek Him in times of need.

The problem denoted. The day of trouble is a time of distress and despair from which none are exempt. On such a day, God summons us to rely upon Him for our deliverance. Matthew Henry states, "We must thus acknowledge Him in all our ways, depend upon His wisdom, power, and goodness, and refer [trust] ourselves entirely to Him."[319]

The promise declared. "I will deliver thee." The promise, conditional upon believing, confident prayer, is extensive and includes both temporal and eternal deliverance.[320] Spurgeon says a promise from God is like a check payable to a person to bestow upon him something good. The person, he says, is to endorse the check personally with his name, believing it to be true. With that done, he is to present the promise to the Lord for payment as a person presents a check at the bank counter. A failure to endorse the check in faith voids it.[321] The text is such a promise check payable to the believer. Take it, and make its withdrawal at the throne of God. He will answer by giving deliverance in trouble or from trouble. Ironside said, "When we cry to the Lord in hours of distress, He does not remove the cause of our trouble in every case, but always gives the needed grace to bear whatever we are called upon to endure."[322]

The praise displayed. "Thou shalt glorify me." Response to deliverance is to be expressed with gratitude, renewed consecration and holiness, and a widespread declaration to others of what He did. "We will 'glorify' God for being with us in trouble, as delivering us from trouble, as making trouble work for our good."[323]

"Back of all our troubles is God; back of all our sorrows, all our sins, is God—God wanting to bring comfort in sorrow, God anxious to forgive and deliver us out of all our troubles and distresses. God is not feeding His children on false hopes."[324]—R. G. Lee.

~May 2~

Psalm 50:22

Forgetfulness of God

"Now consider this, ye that forget God, lest I tear you in pieces, and there be none to deliver" (Psalm 50:22).

Forgetfulness of God.

1. Its comprehensiveness. Forgetfulness of God is widespread. Amazing, with reminders of God in the rolling thunder, purple mountains' majesty, stars twinkling in the night sky, vast deep oceans, birds singing in the trees, and in their conscience, man forgets their maker and sustainer (Mark 4:19). What is shocking is that among the forgetful of God are the religious. It's the religious crowd, those snatched as a brand from the burning and blessed richly, that often forget God! They forget Him, not as utterly as the infidels and atheists, but grievously enough for God's rebuke.

2. Its cause. The forgetfulness among the wicked and righteous occurs when affluence, successes, pleasures, pursuits, and busyness cause soul neglect. "Therefore have they forgotten me" (Hosea 13:6).

3. Its consequence. Forgetfulness of God results in chastisement for the saved. It results in terrible and painful punishment for the wicked (Psalm 50:22b). David says, "The wicked shall be turned into hell, and all the nations that forget God" (Psalm 9:17). Matthew Henry says, "Those that will not consider the warnings of God's word will certainly be torn in pieces by the executions of his wrath. When God comes to tear sinners in pieces, there is no delivering them out of his hand."[325]

4. Its conquest. Turn from it at once. Remember God. Time and again, exhortation is given in Scripture not to forget but to "Remember the LORD thy God" (Deuteronomy 8:18; see also Ecclesiastes 12:1). Watch against it. Stay close to the Cross to prevent it. Keep thy heart with all diligence lest it overtake you (Proverbs 4:23).

5. Its confidence. Even though man may forget God, God will never forget man. "For the LORD your God is a merciful God. He will not leave you or destroy you or forget the covenant with your fathers that he swore to them" (Deuteronomy 4:31 ESV). With summons and warning, He says, "Repent, all of you who forget me" (Psalm 50:22a NLT).

"Satan does not here fill us with hatred of God, but with forgetfulness of God."[326]—Dietrich Bonhoeffer.

~May 3~

Psalm 50:23

Glorifying God

"Whoso offereth praise glorifieth me: and to him that ordereth his conversation aright will I shew the salvation of God" (Psalm 50:23).

We praise and glorify God in eight ways.

1. By the display of gratitude. "My mouth is filled with Your praise, and with Your glory all the day" (Psalm 71:8 ESV). "My lips will glorify you" (Psalm 63:3 NIV).

2. By holy conduct. "Therefore glorify God in your body" (1 Corinthians 6:20). A life lived in righteousness and purity, free from defilement. God disdains pretentious and formalistic praise and praise dressed in dirty garments.

3. By good works. Jesus said, "Let your light so shine before men, that they may see your good works, and glorify your Father which is in Heaven" (Matthew 5:16). "Herein is My Father glorified, that ye bear much fruit" (John 15:8).

4. By how troubles are handled. Thomas Watson asserts, "We glorify God by walking cheerfully. It is a glory to God when the world sees a Christian hath that within him that can make him cheerful in the worst times; he can, with the nightingale, sing with a thorn at his breast."[327]

5. By generosity to God's cause. "As a result of your ministry, they [the poor believers in the Jerusalem church] will give glory to God. For your generosity to them and to all believers will prove that you are obedient to the Good News of Christ" (2 Corinthians 9:13 NLT).

6. By the endurance of persecution. "Yet if any man suffer as a Christian, let him not be ashamed; but let him glorify God on this behalf" (1 Peter 4:16).

7. By how we die. Paul said, "Christ shall be magnified in my body, whether it be by life, or by death" (Philippians 1:20).

8. By answered prayer. "And whatsoever ye shall ask in My name, that will I do, that the Father may be glorified in the Son" (John 14:13).

Note. The chief end of our being, giving, and doing is to glorify and magnify the Lord. For sincere praise with lips and life, God promises reward. "If you keep to my path, I will reveal to you the salvation of God" (Psalm 50:23b NLT).

"The Chief end of man is to glorify God and to enjoy Him forever."— *The Westminster Shorter Catechism.*

~May 4~

Psalm 51:1
David's Spiral Downward

"Generous in love—God, give grace! Huge in mercy—wipe out my bad record. Scrub away my guilt, soak out my sins in your laundry. I know how bad I've been; my sins are staring me down" (Psalm 51:1–3 MSG).

The saddest words in David's biography are, "Then it happened" (2 Samuel 11:1 AMP). King David, a spiritual giant who penned many Psalms and pursued God's very heart, in a weak moment, dropped his guard and committed adultery. Observe the downward spiral of David's fall.

1. David laxed. Laxing his guard, He walked onto the king's balcony unclothed with the armor of God, unexpectant of temptation.

143

Matthew Henry says, "Idleness gives great advantage to the tempter. Standing waters gather filth."[328]

2. David looked. Seeing Bathsheba bathing, he should have returned to his room immediately, but he tarried. Temptation is not a sin, but giving it place is.

3. David lusted. David's inquiry about Bathsheba and sending servants to get her was lust in action.

4. David loved. Then, the evil deed was done. "She came in unto him, and he lay with her" (2 Samuel 11:4).

5. David's loss. The wanton pleasure brought David pain. The child conceived in the act died. His reputation and testimony were damaged, and piercing guilt ravaged his soul.

6. David lamented. In brokenness and tears, he cried, "My sin is ever before me....Make me to hear joy and gladness; that the bones which thou hast broken may rejoice" (verses 3, 8). Happily, David was forgiven for this grievous sin, for he states, "Blessed is he whose transgression is forgiven, whose sin is covered" (Psalm 32:1).

7. David's lessons. Learn from David's sin. Clothe yourself in the armor of God (Ephesians 6:10–18). Don't give place to sin. Flee temptation when it springs up. Root yourself deeply in the Word of God. Hide it in your heart that you might not sin against God (Psalm 119:11). Walk in the Spirit that you might not fulfill the desire of the flesh (Galatians 5:16). Upon moral failure, don't delay its repentance.

"Weak dallying with forbidden desires is sure to end in wicked clutching at them."—Alexander Maclaren.

~May 5~

Psalm 51:2
An Overview of Psalm 51

"Wash me thoroughly from mine iniquity, and cleanse me from my sin" (Psalm 51:2).

What resulted from David's cry for mercy and forgiveness? It is revealed in Psalm 32. David exuberantly says, "I acknowledge my sin unto thee, and mine iniquity have I not hid. I said, I will confess my transgressions unto the LORD; and thou forgavest the iniquity of my sin" (Psalm 32:5). David proves there is forgiveness and a future after the most heinous sin.

Man's basis for forgiveness of sin, revealed in Psalm 51, is the following:

1. Consciousness of it (awareness of sin is the first step to repentance and restoration),

2. Contrition over it (brokenness and sorrow for it), and

3. Confession and petition about it (acknowledgment to God of the sin couched in pleas for His undeserved and unmerited mercy, pity, and grace for its forgiveness provided through the blood of Jesus Christ).

In praying, exhibit trust in the Lord as David did, that He will blot out your sins and make you clean. "Christ receiveth sinful men, even me with all my sin." Hallelujah! Says Jeremy Taylor, "It is the greatest and dearest blessing that ever God gave to men, that they may repent; and therefore, to deny or to delay it is to refuse health when brought by the skill of the physician—to refuse liberty offered to us by our gracious Lord."

"Many mourn for their sins that do not truly repent of them; they weep bitterly for them, and yet continue in love and league with them."[329]—Matthew Henry.

~May 6~

Psalm 51:1

Blueprint for Repentance

"Have mercy upon me, O God, according to thy lovingkindness: according unto the multitude of thy tender mercies blot out my transgressions" (Psalm 51:1).

A year after David's sins of adultery and murder, Nathan confronts him regarding them. Crushed beneath their weight, he acknowledges the sins and pleads to God for cleansing, forgiveness, and restoration. David uses three words to depict his wicked behavior. *Transgressions* depict rebellious disobedience. *Iniquity* is wrongdoing. *Sin* is the failure to do that which is right. The three cover every form of evil, and united implies the deepest guilt.[330]

The Psalm sets forth a blueprint for repentance.

1. Sin must be acknowledged as transgression, iniquity, and sin against God. "Against thee, thee only, have I sinned" (verse 4). David knew his sin was against Bathsheba and Uriah, but even more grievous against God.

2. Sin must be personally owned. "My sin is ever before me" (verse 3). He did not cast blame upon another (Bathsheba) but took full responsibility for his actions.

3. Sin must be confessed and repented. He asks God to *blot out* his sin (as a debt in a ledger book that is erased or marked "paid in full"). And, "Wash me thoroughly from mine iniquity, and cleanse me from my sin." It's a picture of a woman at the riverbank beating a soiled garment against the rocks until every stain is gone and it's clean. David wants God to wash him so that no trace of sin is left and that he may be pronounced clean.

Augustine says, "He that imploreth great mercy, confesseth great misery."[331] Note. David based his repentance not on his merit but upon God's lovingkindness and multitude of tender mercies. Swindoll says, "He settled his case with God as he rested in the truth of God's Word."[332] Each time a great sinner is forgiven and restored, it gives evidence of Christ's forgiveness when we sin and repent.

"Without mercy, I am totally, finally ruined and undone."[333]—Adam Clarke.

Psalm 51:4

Sin is Against God

"Against thee, thee only, have I sinned, and done this evil in thy sight" (Psalm 51:4).

David was remorseful that his notorious sinful conduct was against Bathsheba and Uriah. Still, he realized that it specifically was against the Holy God, the supreme maker and ruler of the world (2 Samuel 11:27). Says Barnes, "His crime against Uriah and his family was of the deepest and most aggravated character, but still the offense derived its chief heinousness from the fact that it was a violation of the law of God."[334] Plumer said, "All sin is against God in this sense that it is His law that is broken, His authority that is despised, His government that is set at naught."[335]

To know that the sin we commit, big or small, is hated by and detestable to God will help deter it. Chambers said, "The conviction of sin by the Holy Spirit blots out every relationship on earth and makes us aware of only one—'Against You, You only, have I sinned.'"[336]

Many Christians say theologically, as David, that all sin is against God. Practically, however, they live otherwise concerning specific sins. To sincerely believe that every evil and sinful act is against God would crush our hearts and bring tears of repentance to the soul. We would cry with David, saying, "You are really the one I have sinned against; I have disobeyed you and have done wrong. So it is right and fair for you to correct and punish me" (Psalm 51:4 CEV). "Wash me thoroughly from mine iniquity, and cleanse me from my sin" (Psalm 51:2).

"Take the very smallest sin and see its guilt in the fact that it has been committed against God."[337]—Magee.

~May 8~

Psalm 51:7–15
The Consequences of Sin
Part 1

"Purge me with hyssop, and I shall be clean: wash me, and I shall be whiter than snow" (Psalm 51:7).

David's sin with Bathsheba had bitter consequences for both her and him.

1. It cost him a soiled heart. David prays, "Wash me thoroughly from mine iniquity, and cleanse me from my sin" (Psalm 51:2). It is impossible to violate God's commandments without dirtying the heart with the filthiness of its abomination.

2. It cost him a stinging conscience. "My sin is ever before me" (Psalm 51:3). Upon the conscience being awakened to the sin committed by a "Nathan" or sermon, it is set on fire with burning guilt and remorse. Barnes says, "The memory of David's guilt followed him; it pressed upon him; it haunted him. It was no wonder that this was so. Everything reminds the soul of it, and nothing will drive away its recollection. In such a state, the sinner has no refuge—no hope of permanent peace—but in the mercy of God."[338]

3. It cost him a sickened body. "Make me to hear joy and gladness; that the bones which thou hast broken may *rejoice"* (Psalm 51:8). The crushing weight of sin upon the soul causes mental anguish and stress. It affects the whole body.

"Men are greatly terrified at the multitude of their sins, but here is a comfort—our God hath multitude of mercies."[339]— Archibald Symson.

~May 9~

Psalm 51:7

The Consequences of Sin
Part 2

"Purge me with hyssop, and I shall be clean: wash me, and I shall be whiter than snow" (Psalm 51:7).

David's two-fold sin cost him sorely. Yesterday, we saw that it cost him a soiled heart, a stinging conscience, and a sickened body. Note four more consequences of his sin.

1. It cost him a spoiled testimony. Nathan told David, "Because by this deed thou hast given great occasion to the enemies of the LORD to blaspheme" (2 Samuel 12:14). Sin undoes in a moment a godly reputation that takes years to restore. Note.

Reputation is to be prized. "A good reputation is more valuable than costly perfume" (Ecclesiastes 7:1 NLT). Socrates said, "Regard your good name as the richest jewel you can possibly be possessed of."

Reputation is to be pursued. Paul said, "Have a good reputation with those who are outsiders" (1 Timothy 3:7 KJ21). Resolve to be like Demetrius, who had "good report [reputation of godliness] of all men, and of the truth itself" (3 John 12).

Reputation is to be pruned. All that sullies and stains the reputation must be purged from life through confession and repentance. It's not a man's faith that causes others to speak ill of him, but his inconsistencies in living that faith.

Reputation is to be protected. Peter says, "Always let others see you behaving properly" (1 Peter 2:12 CEV). Billy Graham said, "When wealth is lost, nothing is lost; when health is lost, something is lost; when character is lost, all is lost." Moody said, "If I take care of my character, my reputation will take care of itself."

2. It cost him a gloomy disposition. "Make me to hear joy and gladness" (Psalm 51:8a). Spurgeon says, "No voice could revive his

149

dead joys but that which quickeneth the dead."[340] The backslider is the unhappiest person on earth.

3. It cost him a shut mouth. "O Lord, open thou my lips" (Psalm 51:15). Sin smothers and stifles testimony and praise. No man can open a mouth shut by sin except God. Spurgeon asserts that David feared "to speak till the Lord unstops his shame-silenced mouth."

4. It cost him severed fellowship. "Renew a right spirit within me" (Psalm 51:10). David's fellowship, not relationship with God, was interrupted. Barnes says, "The language is that of one who had done right formerly, but who had fallen into sin, and who desired that he might be brought back into his former condition."[341]

What sin ultimately cost David costs every man. There's a payday for sin. "Be sure your sin will find you out" (Numbers 32:23).

"God does not allow his people to sin successfully."—C. H. Spurgeon.

~May 10~
Psalm 51:12
The Loss of Joy

"Restore unto me the joy of thy salvation" (Psalm 51:12).

David's prayer for the renewal of the joy of salvation indicates four truths.

1. Joy accompanies salvation. Joy restored is first possessed. Matthew Henry states, "A child of God knows no true nor solid joy but the joy of God's salvation, joy in God his Savior and in the hope of eternal life."[342] Isaiah says, "As fresh water brings joy to the thirsty, so God's people rejoice when he saves them" (Isaiah 12:3 GNT). "Salvation is the most profound miracle a person can experience, and the joy that comes with it is inexpressible."

2. Sin is a thief of the joy of salvation. "Make me to hear joy and gladness" (Psalm 51:8a). Under the weight of sin and its

condemnation, joy is absent. David's joy was extinguished in his two-fold sin, adultery and murder.

3. The joy of salvation is restored upon repentance. David knew that cleansing pardon of sin preceded joy. In any other order, "it is vain presumption or idiotic delirium."[343] The believer who has lost the joy of salvation pants and longs for its return. He says, like Job, "Oh that I were as in months past" (Job 29:2). God gave the joy at the first. It is He who must revive and return it.[344] And this He will do for every "David" who expresses deep sorrow and repentance over their sin.

4. Happiness is impossible without the joy of salvation. Nothing can satisfy the absence of Christ's joy and peace, not pleasures, pursuits, or possessions. C. S. Lewis said, "God cannot give us happiness and peace apart from Himself because it is not there. There is no such thing."[345] Matthew Henry says, "What peace [and joy] can they have who are not at peace with God?"

"The most miserable man on Earth is not an unsaved man. The most miserable man on Earth is a saved man out of fellowship with Jesus Christ."—Adrian Rogers.

~May 11~

Psalm 51:13
Witnessing Insights
Part 1

"Then will I teach transgressors thy ways; and sinners shall be converted unto thee" (Psalm 51:13).

"Teach transgressors thy ways." Upon restoration, David promises to instruct rebellious sinners in God's ways. The term "ways of God" may mean God's path (Psalm 1:1), the conduct God requires relating to His will and commandments (Deuteronomy 5:33), or that conduct approved by God (Isaiah 53:6).[346] The most integral meaning of "thy ways" is instructions in the ways God forgives and restores the sinful (Acts 20:21; John 3:3).[347] Observe six takeaways suggested from David's fall and recovery about witnessing.

Sin closes the lips of vibrant and compelling testimony. "Then will I." David's tongue failed to tell of the ways of God following his fall. Condoned and unrepentant sin seals the mouth in wanting to witness or to do so effectively. The prophet long ago thundered, "Be ye clean, that bear the vessels of the LORD" (Isaiah 52:11).

All the bad done, though forgiven, may take time to be forgotten by others. David's hypocritical conduct followed him throughout his life and to this day. Forgiven sins may leave nail holes in life. Paul faced a similar problem. His past as a persecutor of Christians was an obstacle at the start to some believers' acceptance (Acts 9:26). Though he started preaching the Gospel immediately in Damascus (Acts 9:20), it took Barnabas' intercession for the church to accept him (Acts 9:27–28).

"Penitents should be preachers."[348]—Matthew Henry.

~May 12~

Psalm 51:13
Witnessing Insights
Part 2

"Then will I teach transgressors thy ways; and sinners shall be converted unto thee" (Psalm 51:13).

Don't let yesterday's forgiven sins impede today's witnessing efforts. Neither David nor Paul refused to allow former sins to hamper their effort to win sinners to the Lord. Always looking over your shoulder at forgiven and cleansed sins weighs the soul down and interferes with witnessing. Don't let the past define your future.

Chambers states, "Never let the sense of past failure defeat your next step." Satan attacked Martin Luther in a dream with a scroll listing his sins. On reaching its end, Luther asked the Devil, "Is that all?"

The reply came back, "No." The Devil unfolded a second scroll with more sins and, after that, a third scroll, yet with more sins. With all the sins of Luther cited, the Devil was silent.

"You've forgotten something," Luther exclaimed triumphantly. "Quickly write on each of them, 'The blood of Jesus Christ, God's son, cleanses us from all sins.'" When Satan seeks to hinder witnessing with the recall of former sins that have been forgiven, tell him to do the same and push full steam ahead.

Spurgeon said, "If you have found life, proclaim it to the dead; if you have found liberty, publish it to the captives; if you have found Christ, tell of Him to others."[349] Make the motto of your witnessing that of the prophet Ezekiel: "And they, whether they will hear, or whether they will forbear, (for they are a rebellious house,) yet shall know that there hath been a prophet among them" (Ezekiel 2:5).

"Go for souls. Go for souls, and go for the worst."—General William Booth.

~May 13~

Psalm 51:13
Witnessing Insights
Part 3

"Then will I teach transgressors thy ways; and sinners shall be converted unto thee" (Psalm 51:13).

Note three more witnessing insights drawn from the text.

Despite a shameful past, witness with the expectation of success. "And sinners shall be converted unto thee." Notwithstanding his sordid past, David was confident that God would use him to win souls (Psalm 126:5–6). Paul was sure of the same: "I am made all things to all men, that I might by all means save some" (1 Corinthians 9:22). Spurgeon said to the Lord, "Thou wilt bless my pathetic testimony to the recovery of many who, like myself, have turned aside unto crooked ways."[350] Make yourself useful and available, and God will use you to impact souls.

Restored or converted sinners are effective evangelists to the wicked. They speak from experience and are sympathetic to sinners confronted with the gospel message. They can tell the sinner, 'I sat where you sat' (Ezekiel 3:15) and found the way to forgiveness and happiness, and here's how.

Witness with the Holy Spirit's power. The Holy Spirit's presence and power must rest upon us and uphold us to win souls (John 6:63). David prayed, "Take not thy Holy Spirit from me" (Psalm 51:11) and "uphold me with thy free Spirit" (Psalm 51:12b). All witnessing apart from His enablement is futile (Acts 1:8).

"A proper theology of evangelism…will result in a profound zeal to win the lost."[351]—Lewis Drummond.

~May 14~

Psalm 51:17

A Broken-Heart

"The sacrifices of God are a broken spirit: a broken and a contrite heart, O God, thou wilt not despise" (Psalm 51:17).

1. Broken hearts grieve for sin and the pain it caused to God. We should never feel casual or unconcerned about the sins committed, even petty ones. All sin is against God, and that should break our hearts.

2. Broken hearts are moldable, pliable, and mendable. It's the broken-up clay that the potter can fashion into something beautiful and valuable. God specializes in healing broken hearts and damaged lives. Peter marred his life, and God mended him. He found Jonah marred and mended him. He found David marred and mended him. Despite our failures, sins, and mistakes, God will mend us upon confessing our sins and repentance. "Pick up the broken pieces and bring them to the Lord."

3. Broken hearts over sin originate with God. David attests that it was God who 'broke his bones' (Psalm 51:8). The Holy Spirit smites the conscience (heart) of him who sins with weighty conviction, which brings deep grief and crushing sorrow. Note. A broken heart cannot be manipulated into being. It must come by God's touch of conviction.

4. Broken hearts are not shunned or snubbed by God. Spurgeon states, "Never yet has God spurned a lowly, weeping penitent, and never will he while God is love and while Jesus is called the man who receiveth sinners."[352]

"A heart crushed is a fragrant heart."[353]—C. H. Spurgeon.

~May 15~

Psalm 51:6
"They Are Without Excuse"

"Behold, thou desirest truth in the inward parts: and in the hidden part thou shalt make me to know wisdom" (Psalm 51:6).

He makes me to know wisdom. Matthew Henry states, "The power and Godhead of God are invisible things, and yet are clearly seen in their products."[354] The Bible argues that God holds man accountable for repentance and faith in Him for three reasons.

1. The natural revelation of His existence (Romans 1:20). God's fingerprints are visible in creation and nature.

2. The internal revelation of His existence. God writes His law upon the heart, enlightening man's path to Him (Hebrews 8:10).

3. The divine revelation of His existence. God reveals Himself through His Son (Hebrews 1:1–4). "No man is able to stand before God and say that he turned away from God because God did not give any light. All men have had the revelation of God; therefore, all men are accountable to Him."[355]

Imagine being hopelessly lost in the deep forest at midnight when a light appears. Acting upon the light, you discover its source—the burning headlamps of a jeep. A detailed map showing the way out of the forest is on the jeep's hood. Immediately, you tear the map into small pieces and demolish the headlamps of the jeep. Sounds absurd. In this scenario, who would be responsible for your remaining lost? Certainly not the one who provided the jeep, headlamps, or map![356] Sadly, this is often man's response to the light God provides.

"He who denies the existence of God has some reason for wishing that God did not exist."—Augustine.

~May 16~

Psalm 52:2–4
The Malicious Tongue

"The tongue deviseth mischiefs; like a sharp razor, working deceitfully. Thou lovest evil more than good; and lying rather than to speak righteousness. Selah. Thou lovest all devouring words, O thou deceitful tongue" (Psalm 52:2–4).

Doeg, Saul's chiefest herdsman (1 Samuel 21:7), inferred to Saul that David was his enemy and that Ahimelech, who gave him bread and Goliath's sword, was a traitor. Ahimelech did as Doeg indicated, but not for the reason he told Saul; he helped him because David said he was on an errand for Saul. David rebuked Doeg, stating he loved lying lips more than speaking the truth and evil more than that which was good.

Note. *A falsehood, by implication, is still a slanderous lie.* Doeg told the truth, but not all of it.[357] Matthew Henry remarks, "It will not save us from the guilt of lying, to be able to say there was some truth in what we said if we make it appear otherwise than it was."[358] To insinuate an untruth or tell a half-truth about another is still slanderous lying, which God promises to punish severely (Psalm 52:5).

Lying tongues are destructive. Doeg's lying tongue led to the execution of Ahimelech, eighty-four priests, and the destruction of the whole city of Nob (1 Samuel 22:19). Spurgeon asserts, "There are words that, like boa constrictors, swallow men whole, or like lions, rend men to pieces; these words evil minds are fond of. Their oratory is evermore furious and bloody."[359] Be named among those as Ahimelech, who speak honorably and truthfully of others rather than the Doegs who talk of them viciously and maliciously.

"Tongue sins are great sins; like sparks of fire, ill words spread and do great damage."[360]—C. H. Spurgeon.

~May 17~

Psalm 52:4
The Lying Tongue

"Thou lovest all devouring words, O thou deceitful tongue" (Psalm 52:4).

1. Slanderous lying is the Devil's work. Newton states, "Lying is Satan's work. And when we engage in lying, we let our hearts become Satan's workshop."[361]

2. Slanderous lying is like opening the cage of a venomous snake upon another. Its poisonous fangs destroy life. "One lie has the power to tarnish a thousand truths."[362]

3. Slanderous lying is like throwing a lit match onto a keg of dynamite. The explosion is far more devastating than perhaps intended or imagined.

4. Slanderous lying is like gutting a feather pillow in the face of hurricane-force winds. The "feathers" can never be retrieved. "Tongues," says Spurgeon, "are more terrible instruments than can be made with hammers and anvils, and the evil which they inflict cuts deeper and spreads wider."[363]

5. Slanderous lying is like playing dominoes. The words keep impacting lives. Mark Twain said, "One of the most striking differences between a cat and a lie is that a cat has only nine lives."

"A false witness will not go unpunished, and he who breathes out lies will not escape" (Proverbs 19:5 ESV). Wiersbe states, "All liars will be punished (Proverbs 19:5, 9); and when they "eat their own words," it will be like gravel (Proverbs 20:17). Hell is waiting for the one who "loves and practices a lie" (Revelation 22:15 NKJV)."[364] Matthew Henry remarked, "They set God at a distance from them, but from afar, His arrows can reach them."[365]

"One of the things that should characterize a child of God is his truthfulness."[366]—J. Vernon McGee.

~May 18~

Psalm 52:5
The End of Malicious Men

"God shall likewise destroy thee forever, he shall take thee away, and pluck thee out of thy dwelling place, and root thee out of the land of the living" (Psalm 52:5).

Doeg's malicious acts would be punished. He would be plucked up and flung away. He would be uprooted and destroyed. He would be banished to that land where he could no longer trouble the righteous. Doeg thought he ruined David, but he perished.

Spurgeon says, "God will turn the tables on malicious men and mete to them a portion with their own measure."[367] David said, "The righteous also shall see…and shall laugh at him" (Psalm 52:6). The righteous will get the last laugh—a laugh that is aroused from consideration of God's retributive judgment, justice, and righteousness.[368] The psalmist states, "Liars, do you know what the Lord has for you? Do you know what you will get?" (Psalm 120:3 ERV). Let Doeg serve as an example of the end of him who has a poisonous, injurious, falsifying, and destructive tongue.

How do we respond to liars? Just like Paul and Spurgeon. Paul testifies, "When we are slandered [reputation attacked], we try to be conciliatory and answer softly" (1 Corinthians 4:13 AMP).

Spurgeon said, "We would say of the general gossip of the village and of the unadvised words of angry friends—do not hear them, or if you must hear them, do not lay them to heart. If we are compelled to hear the hasty language, we must endeavor to obliterate it from the memory and say with David, 'But I, as a deaf man, heard not; and I was as a dumb man that openeth not his mouth' (Psalm 38:13)."[369] When slandered, to know that God knows the truth and, in time, will vindicate us is an unparalleled source of strength, stamina, and comfort.

"Let not thy peace depend on the tongues of men."—Thomas á Kempis.

~May 19~

Psalm 52:7

The Crumbled Life

"Lo, this is the man that made not God his strength; but trusted in the abundance of his riches, and strengthened himself in his wickedness" (Psalm 52:7).

A crumbled life that ends in severe judgment results from any of four things that characterized Doeg.

1. "Made not God his strength." Doeg's life crumbled because he lived alienated from God and His Word. Great will be the fall of the house not built on the Rock, despite its outward appearance of stability (Matthew 7:27).

2. "Trusted in the abundance of his riches." Doeg's life crumbled because of his arrogant dependence on money instead of God. Clarke said, "He had got much, he hoped to get more, and expected that his happiness would multiply as his riches multiplied. And this is the case with most rich men." Solomon warns, "He that trusteth

in his riches shall fall" (Proverbs 11:28). Note. To be blessed with riches is to be tempted to trust in them. The Bible warns: "If riches increase, set not your heart upon them" (Psalm 62:10).

3. "Lovest evil more than good." Doeg's life crumbled because His heart was bent continually toward unfathomable, ruinous evil (Psalm 52:3). Horne says, "As the Christian spirit delighteth itself in goodness, truth, and love, so the antichristian spirit is here characterized by its offending, not out of ignorance or inadvertence, but mere love of wickedness, falsehood, and malice."[370]

4. "Strengthened himself in his wickedness." Doeg's life crumbled because of his stubborn refusal to hearken to God's rebuffs and calls to repentance, insisting that he live by his own rules. Solomon says, "He, that being often reproved hardeneth his neck, shall suddenly be destroyed, and that without remedy" (Proverbs 29:1). Lawson comments, "But woe to that man who is stubborn and obstinate after many reproofs. He despises a merciful appointment of God for his recovery and tramples upon precious pearls. He refuses to bow before the Lord—and he shall be dashed in pieces like a potter's vessel! He perhaps designs to reform at some other time—but he is hardened in sin and puts off his intended repentance until judgment comes upon him unexpectedly, and he is ruined forever! The reproofs which he received will then be like hot thunderbolts to him, and the remembrance of them will feed the worm that never dies."[371]

"Wealth and wickedness are dreadful companions; when combined, they make a monster."[372]—C. H. Spurgeon.

~May 20~

Psalm 52:8
David, Like an Olive Tree

"But I am like a green olive tree in the house of God: I trust in the mercy of God forever and ever" (Psalm 52:8).

Doeg turned away from God, lived wickedly, trusted in riches for his strength, and was cursed (uprooted from it all to destruction). In contrast, David was like a green olive tree in the house of God, a man who continually trusted in God's lovingkindness and was blessed.

1. David is like a green olive tree in his soul's rootage. He is planted deep in God's edifying and nourishing soil. Unlike Doeg, David depended on the Lord for nourishment, fellowship, and help.

2. David is like a green olive tree in terms of fruitfulness. Filled with the sap of the Holy Spirit, David bears much fruit for the Lord. Jowett says, "When we are 'rooted' in Him, every branch of the life is pervaded by rivers of sap, and every faculty is urged by Divine energy into manifold fruitfulness."[373]

3. David is like a green olive tree that prospers. To the extent that he abided in the vine (John 15:4–5) and the love and mercy of God (Psalm 52:8), David prospered (Psalm 1:3).

4. David is like a green olive tree's perpetuity. It is an evergreen that has a life of 500 years. David's spiritual leaf would never wither but last forever (Psalm 1:3).

5. David is like a green olive tree in stature. An olive tree can grow to a height of 50 feet with a limb span of 30 feet. He that walks with God is tall and mighty in stature.

Essentially, a green olive tree represents the godly who abide in Christ and draw life-nourishing sap from Him, the Vine, enabling them to be blessed richly and bear much kingdom fruit.

"When we are rooted in God, everything is sappy."[374]—J. H. Jowett.

~May 21~

Psalm 52:8–9
Christians Like Olive Trees

"But I am like a green olive tree in the house of God: I trust in the mercy of God forever and ever. I will praise thee forever, because thou hast done it: and I will wait on thy name; for it is good before thy saints" (Psalm 52:8–9).

What must a person do to become like a green olive tree?

1. He must trust in God. "I trust in the mercy of God forever." David doesn't trust (depend on and take refuge) in the world, like Doeg, but in God's mercy (lovingkindness, pity). It is unchangeable and interminable in its rich supply of the support needed.

2. He must be thankful. "I will praise thee forever." David extolled God and thanked Him for the rich mercy and blessings bestowed. A thankful heart has praising lips.

3. He must wait on the Lord. "I will wait on thy name." David's hope and confidence in the future would be as it was in the present, in the name of the Lord, to supply every need. "My soul, wait thou only upon God; for my expectation is from him" (Psalm 62:5). Matthew Henry says, "That it is very good for us to wait on that name, that there is nothing better to calm and quiet our spirits when they are ruffled and disturbed, and to keep us in the way of duty when we are tempted to use any indirect courses for our own relief than to hope and quietly wait for the salvation of the Lord."[375]

"While others trust in the riches of their own righteousness and services, and make not Christ their strength, do thou renounce all, and trust in the mercy of God in Christ, and thou shalt be like a green olive when they fade and wither."[376]—William Gurnall.

~May 22~

Psalm 53:1
The Fool

"The fool hath said in his heart, There is no God. Corrupt are they, and have done abominable iniquity: there is none that doeth good" (Psalm 53:1).

In Proverbs, Solomon identifies five kinds of fools.

1. The ignorant fool (Proverbs 1:22a). The naïve.

2. The mocking fool (Proverbs 1:22b). The scornful and scoffer.

3. The opinionated fool (Proverbs 1:7). The egotistical, unreasonable person.

4. The wicked fool (Proverbs 12:15). The stubborn-headed to instruction and correction.

5. The atheistic or practical atheistic fool (Proverbs 23:9). The close-minded to the truth.

The text addresses the atheistic or practical atheistic fool. This fool's wicked and profane conduct and warped mind corrupt or decimate the knowledge of God he possesses. "Have the workers of iniquity no knowledge" (Psalm 53:4). It also prevents knowledge of God necessary for belief and conversion.

Buzzell explains, "One cannot gain knowledge of spiritual things if he begins at the wrong point, refusing to fear the Lord (i.e., to recognize God's character and respond by revering, trusting, worshiping, obeying, and serving Him)."[377] Solomon says, "The fear of the LORD is the beginning of knowledge: but *fools despise* wisdom and instruction" (Proverbs 1:7). "A man is evil in his actions because he has cast off the fear of God, and such wickedness is a proof that he has lost all reverence for God and care to please him."[378]

This fool's denial of God doesn't make Him any less existent. Spurgeon says, "Doubting the existence of God will not stop the Judge of all the earth from destroying the rebel who breaks His laws; nay, this atheism is a crime which much provokes Heaven and will bring down terrible vengeance on the fool who indulges it." At the outset of a gospel presentation or that of a moral issue, make sure that you are not casting pearls before swine. Only those open-minded to truth will receive, not "despise," your words (Proverbs 23:9).

"The fear of the Lord is at once a bridle to sin and a spur to holiness."[379]—Charles Bridges.

~May 23~

Psalm 53:1
The Way of the Atheistic Fool
Part 1

"The fool hath said in his heart, There is no God. Corrupt are they, and have done abominable iniquity: there is none that doeth good" (Psalm 53:1).

The psalmist states eight marks of the atheistic fool.

He denies that God exists. E. Y. Mullins said, "He said it in his heart; his head knew better." [380]

He rules his own life. The reason for man's denial of God's existence is the freedom they gain to govern their behavior (Psalm 53:1). Wiersbe states, "The fool not only says there is no God; he also says no to God." [381]

He is corrupt and depraved. "Corrupt are they, and have done abominable iniquity" (Psalm 53:1). Spurgeon asserts, "They are rotten. It is idle to compliment them as sincere doubters and amiable thinkers—they are putrid." [382] There is no filthiness like the filthiness of sin, and the fool's life overflows with it.

He does not understand. "To see if there were any that did understand" (Psalm 53:2). Paul says, "A person who isn't spiritual doesn't accept the things of God's Spirit, for they are nonsense to him. He can't understand them because they are spiritually evaluated" (1 Corinthians 2:14 ISV).

He does not seek God. The fool is closed-minded to the reality of God. "No knowledge" (Psalm 53:4). If he sought the truth about God sincerely, he would find it. The Lord says, "And ye shall seek me, and find me, when ye shall search for me with all your heart" (Jeremiah 29:13). The atheistic fool is one by choice.

"There are none so blind as those who will not see. The most deluded people are those who choose to ignore what they already know."—John Heyward.

~May 24~

Psalm 53:1
The Way of the Atheistic Fool
Part 2

"The fool hath said in his heart, There is no God" (Psalm 53:1).

Yesterday, five traits of the atheistic fool were cited, as outlined in Psalm 53. Note three more.

He does not call on God. "They have not called upon God" (Psalm 53:4). The man that calls upon the name of the Lord shall be saved (Romans 10:13). Fools, acting insanely, won't. Instead, they mock those who do.

He does not fear the Lord. "Where no fear was" (Psalm 53:5). The fear of the Lord is the starting point to knowledge of spiritual truths (Proverbs 9:10). It is twofold in its nature. The fear is a deep-seated reverence for the thrice-holy God (Isaiah 6:3), the creator and sustainer of all that exists. "The LORD of Hosts, him you shall regard as holy; let him be your fear, and let him be your dread" (Isaiah 8:13 RSV). Secondly, it is the heart manifestation of love, honor, trust, and loyalty to His person, coupled with obedience to His law and counsel. "How blessed is everyone who fears the LORD, Who walks in His ways" (Psalm 128:1 NASB 1995).

He will be brought to shame. "Thou hast put them to shame" (Psalm 53:5). Spurgeon says, "They are the objects of divine contempt."[383] The Bible says, "For that they hated knowledge, and did not choose the fear of the LORD: they would none of my counsel: they despised all my reproof. Therefore shall they eat of the fruit of their own way, and be filled with their own devices" (Proverbs 1:29–31).

"We truly fear God just in proportion as we truly love Him."[384]—
Wardlaw.

~May 25~

Psalm 53:3
The Fact of Sin

"Every one of them is gone back: they are altogether become filthy; there is none that doeth good, no, not one" (Psalm 53:3).

Sin is a fact. Having looked down from Heaven on humanity, God testifies there is "none that doeth good" and "corrupt are they." Similarly, Paul states, "For all have sinned, and come short of the glory of God" (Romans 3:23). Sin is an evil, abominable act against God. Carson said, "Sin defies God, utterly corrupts each individual, corrodes all social relationships, and issues in death." Chambers says, "We have to recognize that sin is a fact, not a defect; sin is red-handed mutiny against God."

Sin is a fountain. Sin originated in the garden when Adam obeyed Satan instead of God. Paul said, "When Adam sinned, sin entered the entire human race. His sin spread death throughout all the world, so everything began to grow old and die, for all sinned" (Romans 5:12 TLB). Every person's heart is diseased with the filthiness and corruption of sin, and from it flows the fruit of sin.

Sin is a force. Sin enslaves and dominates people, causing their perpetual corruption and spiritual death (Romans 6:12). Spurgeon said, "The fallen race of man, left to its own energy, has not produced a single lover of God or doer of holiness, nor will it ever do so."[385]

Though no man has the strength to overcome sin, he can do so through the power of Christ. Paul says, "Sin shall not have dominion over you: for ye are not under the law, but under grace" (Romans 6:14). John says, "greater is he that is in you, than he that is in the world" (1 John 4:4). At salvation man no longer is a slave to sin. He possesses the power of the Holy Spirit to be an overcomer, and he shall be as long as he relies upon that power (Romans 7:24–25).

"Sin is no little thing. It girded the Redeemer's head with thorns, and pierced his heart....Look upon all sin as that which crucified the Savior, and you will see it to be 'exceeding sinful.'"—C. H. Spurgeon.

~May 26~

Psalm 54:1
Pray In Jesus' Name

"Save me, O God, by thy name, and judge me by thy strength" (Psalm 54:1).

David cries, "Save me, O God, by thy name" (Psalm 54:1). God's name is equated with His character, nature, and strength. David pleaded that name for rescue and refuge from King Saul's massive army and friends who betrayed him. God answered speedily, sparing his life.

Christians close their prayer by saying, "In Jesus' name" because man's sinful nature prohibits access to a holy God through any other means: "For there is one God, and one mediator [bridge] between God and men, the man Christ Jesus" (1 Timothy 2:5). It is the means of receiving that for which we ask (John 14:13) and is praying (asking) in agreement with the desire and will of Jesus.

Timothy Keller asserts, "To pray in Jesus' name means to acknowledge that we only have access to the Father's attention and grace through the mediation and work of our Savior." To pray in Jesus' name is to pray based on His authorization to make our petitions known (as is John 14:14, "If ye shall ask anything in *My name*, I will do it.").

Hallesby wrote, "Nothing means so much to our daily prayer life as to pray in the name of Jesus. If we fail to do this, our prayer life will either die from discouragement and despair or become simply a duty which we feel we must perform."[386] Join Spurgeon in praying, "Lord Jesus, cause me to know in my daily experience the glory and sweetness of Thy name, and then teach me how to use it in my prayer, so that I may be even like Jacob, a prince prevailing with God. Thy name is my passport, and secures me access; Thy name is my plea, and secures me answer; Thy name is my honor, and secures me glory."[387] In Jesus' name, Amen.

"When asking in Jesus' name, first consider His Approval—Does Jesus approve this thing? His Authorization—Is it something He has authorized? His Acclaim—Is it for His glory?"[388]—Adrian Rogers.

~May 27~

Psalm 54:2
A Powerful Recourse in Trouble

"Hear my prayer, O God; give ear to the words of my mouth" (Psalm 54:2).

Doeg's betrayal was expected (1 Samuel 22:22), but not the disloyalty by the Ziphites, who were of the same tribe as David. They revealed the location of David's hiding place to Saul, who immediately took three thousand soldiers to seek him in the wilderness of Ziph (1 Samuel 26:2). With King Saul's massive army pursuing, friends betraying, and ruthless people assaulting, David prays for divine intervention and deliverance, the only recourse. Matthew Henry says, "David has no other plea to depend upon than God's name, no other power to depend upon than God's strength, and these he makes his refuge and confidence."[389]

The prayer of David was heard. Just as Saul's men were about to close a net in on David (1 Samuel 23:26), a messenger informed Saul that the Philistines had invaded the land (1 Samuel 23:27), forcing an end to the pursuit. David safely escaped to En-Gedi (1 Samuel 23:29).

Jesus said, "Men ought always to pray, and not to faint" (Luke 18:1). Believers live in an evil, polluted society. The only escape from its toxic fumes, which promote spiritual fainting (drifting, backsliding, worldliness), is the intake of "pure air" from the atmosphere of Heaven, which occurs in prayer. Prayer is to the believer what an oxygen mask is to those who work in hazardous waste facilities, an essential to survival. This oxygen mask for believers should be worn continuously ("always to pray"). The apostle Paul states, "Pray without ceasing" (1 Thessalonians 5:17). Whatever the need and trouble, take it to Him who says, "Call upon me in the day of trouble: I will deliver thee, and thou shalt glorify me" (Psalm 50:15).

"We should learn from the example of David that even in the greatest danger, we should resort to no forbidden means, nor grow faint, but should call upon the name of God, and commit to Him all our concerns as to the Supreme Judge."[390]—*The Berleberg Bible.*

~May 28~

Psalm 54:7
Power of Prayer

"For you have rescued me from my troubles and helped me to triumph over my enemies" (Psalm 54:7 NLT).

David attests to the power of prayer. Deliverance from the massive army of Saul, betrayers, and other enemies resulted from prayer. Prayer works. "The proof," saith Chadwick, "that God answers prayer is in praying."[391] Prayers in Jesus' name, based upon Scripture and God's will, are accompanied by answers. S. D. Gordon writes, "True prayer never fails. It cannot because it depends on God and His pledged Word."[392]

"It is not a matter of doubt," saith Spurgeon, "as to whether God hears and answers prayer—if there is any fact in the world that is proved by the testimony of honest men, this is that fact!"[393] He certainly proved prayer's power. It was said of him that his prayers raised up more of the sick than the treatments of any doctor in London.[394] Susannah (his wife) and William Harrald in *From the Pulpit to the Palm-Branch* wrote, "He had many answers to prayer. The record of his answered prayers would, of itself, fill a volume."[395]

Multiplied testimonies verify that diseases are cured, monetary needs are supplied, marriages are restored, lives are transformed, accidents are averted, jobs are provided, protection is granted, ministry doors are opened, great works are done, and revival fires are ignited through the efficacy of prayer. Miracle after miracle is recorded all through the sacred pages of the Bible in response to the prayer of faith. E. M. Bounds says, "Miracles and faith went hand in hand. They were companions. The one was the cause; the other was the effect. The miracle was the proof that God heard and answered prayer."[396]

"Pray on for the impossible, and dare. Upon thy banner this brave motto bear: 'My Father answers prayer.'"—Author Unknown.

~May 29~

Psalm 55:6
A Wrong Longing

"And I said, Oh that I had wings like a dove! for then would I fly away, and be at rest" (Psalm 55:6).

David had much to make him want to take the wings like a dove and fly away from it all. King Saul tried to kill him. His people and a close friend betrayed him. He could only find rest and be happy if he could escape these troubles, hurts, and cares, so he mistakenly thought.

When sicknesses and troubles beset us, we tend to wish to be taken away from them. But such longing is ill-advised for five reasons.

1. It would be futile. Flight from trouble cannot escape it. "No wings of doves or eagles could bear us away from the sorrows of a trembling heart. Inward grief knows nothing of the place."[397]

2. It would be detrimental to the soul's health. We are placed in the storm or battle to be made perfect through suffering (2 Corinthians 12:9). Paul further states, "For our light affliction...worketh for us a far more exceeding and eternal weight of glory" (2 Corinthians 4:17). Suffering and hardship mature the saint in faith, godliness, and holiness. Later, David said, *"Before* I was afflicted I went astray: but now have I kept thy word" (Psalm 119:67).

170

3. It would be a display of distrust. To flee what God ordained expresses doubt in His ability and willingness to sustain in it and deliver from it. Recall He said, "I will be with him in trouble; I will deliver him, and honor him" (Psalm 91:15).

4. It would be a display of cowardice. Spurgeon wrote, "It is cowardly to shun the battle which God would have us fight."[398]

5. It would make matters worse. Amos said, "You will run from a lion, only to meet a bear. You will escape to your house, rest your hand on the wall, and be bitten by a snake" (Amos 5:19 CEV).

The bottom line. It's far better to take rest and shelter beneath the shadow of His wings against slander, betrayal, and wickedness than to flee them on the pinions of a dove. Trusting in the shadow of His wings is the safest and most secure refuge in times of trouble. It is there that rest, peace, and happiness, despite overwhelming hardship and grief, are found. "He shall cover thee with his feathers, and under his wings shalt thou trust: his truth shall be thy shield and buckler" (Psalm 91:4).

"O Lord our God, under the shadow of Your wings, let us hope in Your custody."[399]—Augustine.

~May 30~

Psalm 55:12–14
A Friend's Betrayal

"For it was not an enemy that reproached me; then I could have borne it: neither was it he that hated me that did magnify himself against me; then I would have hid myself from him" (Psalm 55:12).

David was the victim of betrayal by a servant of King Saul, Doeg the Edomite (Psalm 52), the Ziphites (Psalm 54), and now, in Psalm 55, by an intimate friend named Ahithophel (2 Samuel 15:31). The latter betrayal cut his heart to pieces. All betrayal brings anguish to the soul. But there is no anguish, hurt, or sorrow comparable to the betrayal of one who is counted the dearest of friends. The Psalm is David's voice of a wounded heart.

Maclaren remarks on David's experience: "The psalmist feels that the defection of his false friend is the worst blow of all. He could have braced himself to bear an enemy's reviling; he could have found weapons to repel or a shelter in which to escape from open foes, but the baseness which forgets all former sweet companionship in secret and all association in public and in worship, is more than he can bear up against."[400] Saith Spurgeon, "We can bear from Shimei what we cannot endure from Ahithophel."[401]

When a friend violates our trust, turns against us, or abandons us in trouble or crisis, it is a crushing blow, a sharp dagger to the heart. Its comfort and healing only come at the hand of the Lord, and that over time. "He healeth the broken in heart, and bindeth up their wounds" (Psalm 147:3). Thomas Moore says, "Here bring your wounded hearts, here tell your anguish; Earth has no sorrow that Heaven cannot heal."

"Against a known foe, we are on our watch, but the unsuspected stroke of a friend takes us by surprise."[402]—John Calvin.

~May 31~

Psalm 55:22
Burdens Are Lifted at Calvary
Part 1

"Cast thy burden upon the LORD, and he shall sustain thee" (Psalm 55:22).

"Burdens" are the hardships of life that weigh us down with anxiety, worry, fear, despair, hurt, suffering, and dread, filling our hearts with pain and eyes with tears.

The problem with life's burdens ("thy burden"). Burdens are part and parcel of every man's life, regardless of status or saintliness. The Bible says, "For every man shall bear his own burden"

(Galatians 6:5). Shakespeare says it's not hard to bear the toothache of another, but when one's own jaw is throbbing, that's a different story. Sometimes, the burden that must be borne is beyond our ability. Paul says, "For we do not want you to be unaware, brethren, of our affliction…that we were burdened excessively, beyond our strength, so that we despaired even of life" (2 Corinthians 1:8 NASB1995). Paul counted his situation as virtually hopeless. Sooner or later, all God's children embrace a desperate situation where neither they nor anyone else can grant deliverance from its clutches.

The provision for life's burdens ("cast thy burden upon the LORD"). The Hebrew word for "cast" means "to throw down, to hurl away forcefully, to dispose of and to reject." Relief is possible and available for life's burdens, but it requires trusting God with them by vigorously casting them at His feet. The more faith one exhibits in the Lord to completely manage the burden, the greater the relief.

Spurgeon wrote, "If you tell your troubles to God, you put them into the grave; they will never rise again when you have committed them to Him. If you roll your burden anywhere else, it will roll back again like the stone of Sisyphus." In Greek mythology, Sisyphus' punishment by Zeus was to roll a boulder up a mountain for eternity. Each time it neared the top, it would roll back to the bottom.

"Many servants set out to serve God with great courage and with the right motives. But with no intimate fellowship with Jesus Christ, they are soon defeated. They do not know what to do with their burden, and it produces weariness in their lives."—Oswald Chambers.

~June 1~

Psalm 55:22
Burdens Are Lifted at Calvary
Part 2

"Cast thy burden upon the LORD, and he shall sustain thee" (Psalm 55:22).

The promise for life's burdens ("And he shall sustain thee"). The Hebrew word for "sustain" means "support, clasp, contain, and manage." It pictures a vessel that contains cargo. The Lord is man's "vessel" where life's burdens (heavy cargo) are carried and managed. Note that the promise is not that God will remove the burden (though He may) but that He will grant increased strength and stamina to equal its weight. Paul's burden, "the thorn in the flesh" (unknown as to its nature), was cast upon the Lord three times. Though it was not removed, he was given sufficient grace to bear it (2 Corinthians 12:9).

The premise for the promise. Peter says, "Casting the whole of your care [all your anxieties, all your worries, all your concerns, once and for all] on Him, for He cares for you affectionately and cares about you watchfully" (1 Peter 5:7 AMPC). Charles Weigle (1932) poetically illustrates the text, saying, "No one ever cared for me like Jesus; there's no other friend so kind as He." God willingly bears our burdens out of compassionate concern.

A minister in study asked his young son to retrieve a large book upstairs. Soon, the father heard sobbing on the staircase and went to investigate. He found his son on the top of the stairway, crying bitterly with the large book he had tried to lift and carry lying at his feet. "Oh, Daddy," he cried, "I can't carry it. It's too heavy for me." In an instant, the father was upstairs. Stooping down, he picked up the book and the child and carried them to the room below. *And that,* he found himself thinking later, *is how God deals with His children.*[403] He carries both our "burdens" and us.

"As a camel kneels before his master to have him remove his burden at the end of the day, so kneel each night and let the Master take your burden."—Corrie Ten Boom.

~June 2~

Psalm 56:3
When Afraid, What to Do
Part 1

"What time I am afraid, I will trust in thee" (Psalm 56:3).

In times of fear, do six things.

1. Focus on Christ, not the subject of the fear. G. Campbell Morgan says, "The man who measures things by the circumstances of the hour is filled with fear; the man who sees Jehovah enthroned and governing has no panic."[404] Adrian Rogers states, "Fear caused Timothy to forget (2 Timothy 1:7). Focusing on what you fear takes your eyes off the Lord—His blessings, what He has done in the past, and what He will do in the future."[405] What is put in God's control by faith is always under His control.

2. Tap hold of the power God has given to conquer fear. The Holy Spirit's power is operative in us and assuages fear. It instills courage in the face of the howling and frightening winds that assail (2 Timothy 1:7). Maclaren said, "Only he who can say, 'The LORD is the strength of my life' can say, 'Of whom shall I be afraid?'"

3. Trust God and His promises. Hope and confidence in thwarting fear are found in the reliability and assurances of God. "He hath said, I will never leave thee, nor forsake thee" (Hebrews 13:5). Fear is conquered and replaced with calm and peace when the heart says, "Yea, though I walk through the valley of the shadow of death, I will fear no evil: for thou art with me; thy rod and thy staff they comfort me" (Psalm 23:4). The presence of Jesus aboard the "ship" gives calm and rest to its passengers when all about it is tumultuous.

"Christ liveth in me. And how great the difference—instead of bondage, liberty; instead of failure, quiet victories within; instead of fear and weakness, a restful sense of sufficiency in Another."[406]— Hudson Taylor.

~June 3~

Psalm 56:3
When Afraid, What to Do
Part 2

"What time I am afraid, I will trust in thee" (Psalm 56:3).

In addition to the three things shared yesterday to cope with fear, note three more.

1. Hold fast to the sovereignty of God. Spurgeon said, "When you go through a trial, the sovereignty of God is the pillow upon which you lay your head."

2. Don't doubt God's love for you. Perfect love drives away all fear. The Bible states, "Where God's love is, there is no fear, because God's perfect love drives out fear" (1 John 4:18 NCV). Fear has no place in love. Understanding God's love banishes fear. Adrian Rogers comments, "When you see God's mighty power on one hand and His mighty love on the other, fear melts away. Rest in that love. Say, 'Lord, no matter what happens to me, I know You love me.'"[407] Gurnall says, "The chains of love are stronger than the chains of fear."[408] Tozer wrote, "Love casts out fear, for when we know we are loved, we are not afraid. Whoever has God's perfect love, fear is gone out of the universe for him."[409]

3. Fear is not the judge of your spirituality; how you respond to it is. Let it press you to trust fully in the Lord.

Believers ask, "Whom shall I fear?" It's a question that answers itself. Spurgeon asserts, "The powers of darkness are not to be feared, for the Lord, our light, destroys them; and the damnation of Hell is not to be dreaded by us, for the Lord is our salvation."[410]

"If the Lord be with us, we have no cause of fear. His eye is upon us, His arm over us, His ear open to our prayer—His grace sufficient, His promise unchangeable."[411]—John Newton.

~June 4~

Psalm 56:8
Tears in a Bottle

"Thou tellest my wanderings: put thou my tears into thy bottle: are they not in thy book?" (Psalm 56:8).

David states that God records life's tribulations (trials, trouble, and sorrow) in the book of remembrance and treasures up tears they induce *in His* "bottle." Spurgeon says the text "implies that they are caught as they flow."[412]

1. Every teardrop is a treasured jewel to the Lord.

2. No tear flows down the cheek unnoticed, unremembered, or uncollected.

3. God storing our tears in a bottle reminds us of His constant awareness and compassionate concern regarding life's hurts and troubles.

4. The same tears that a believer bitterly weeps will presently or in time be converted into tears of joy, peace, and comfort by the same power that turned water into wine.

5. God ensures tears are not wasted but will work for our good.

6. Our tears will be changed into songs of praise (Psalm 56:10).

7. The fears that brought the tears will be banished through trust in God (Psalm 56:11).

8. A future day is coming when the last tear ever to be shed will be wiped from the eye (Revelation 21:4).

"God has a bottle and a book for his people's tears, both those for their sins and those for their afflictions."[413]—Matthew Henry.

~June 5~

Psalm 56:9–13
Praises to God

"In God will I praise his word: in the LORD will I praise his word" (Psalm 56:10).

In concluding the Psalm, David praises God for five things.

1. David praises God for His Word. "Will I praise his word." He expresses gratitude for the promises of God, which he trusted

and that sustained him. Give glory to God for honoring and keeping His Word to you.

2. David praises God for His protection. "I will not fear what flesh can do unto me." He expresses gratitude for the restraining hand of God upon his enemies. Give glory to God for preserving your life from evil and the wicked. "If it had not been the LORD who was on our side" (Psalm 124:1), where might we be?

3. David praises God for his surefootedness in the trial. "Wilt not thou deliver my feet from falling?" He expresses gratitude for the strong hand of God upon him that enables him to stand in the fiercest of storms. Give glory to God for His strong hand that tightly grips your hand, preventing a stumble and fall (Jude 24).

4. David praises God for being for him. "This I know; for God is for me." He expresses gratitude for God being on his side to safeguard and deliver him from harm. Give glory to God because He is for you and ever is a friend that sticketh closer than a brother seeking your best good. Paul asks a rhetorical question: 'And if God be for me, who shall stand successfully against me?'

"This I know." Spurgeon says this is "one of the believer's certainties, his axioms, his infallible, indisputable verities. "For God is for me." This we know, and we know, therefore, that none can be against us who are worth a moment's fear. "If God be for us, who can be against us?"

Matthew Henry said, "The saints have God for them; they may know it; and to Him they must cry when they are surrounded with enemies." For this, we should give unending praise!

5. David praises God for sparing his life from death. "Thou hast delivered my soul from death." He expresses gratitude for the number of times God spared his life from the sword of his enemies. Give glory to God because He has quickened you from spiritual death to newness of life in Christ Jesus. "And you hath he quickened, who were dead in trespasses and sins; Wherein in time past ye walked according to the course of this world, according to

the prince of the power of the air, the spirit that now worketh in the children of disobedience" (Ephesians 2:1–2).

"O give thanks unto the LORD; for he is good: for his mercy endureth forever!" (Psalm 106:1).

"If a man just stops to think what he has to praise God for, he will find there is enough to keep him singing praises for a week."— Dwight L. Moody.

~June 6~

Psalm 56:12
Remember Your Vows

"Thy vows are upon me, O God" (Psalm 56:12).

The vows David references and pledges to keep probably pertain to those made in times of trouble and sorrow (Psalm 66:13–14). Perhaps you have made similar vows in the hour of crisis. Consider their biblical requirements.

1. Vows must be legitimate in principle. Some vows should not be made, especially those that violate the Scripture and moral law. For example, to vow to commit a sinful or wrong act or to get even with someone who offended you is insensible, foolish, and unacceptable.

2. Vows must be doable in practice. Don't make a vow until you are confident that what you have committed to can be done. It is ludicrous to rashly vow to do a task beyond your ability, time, location, or health.

3. Vows must be thoughtful in pledge. Serious deliberation is crucial regarding the cost of keeping a vow and the consequences of not keeping it. It's a severe blunder to fail to do what you have vowed for three reasons: it offends God, injures the soul, and brings judgment. Once a vow is made, it's irretrievable. It must not be evaded, denounced, or excused.

4. Vows must be timely in performance. "Defer not to pay it; for he hath no pleasure in fools" (Ecclesiastes 5:4). The longer the obligation is postponed, the less likely its fulfillment.

"Vows made in storms are forgotten in calm."—Thomas Fuller.

~June 7~

Psalm 57:1
A Mighty Refuge

"Be merciful unto me, O God, be merciful unto me: for my soul trusteth in thee: yea, in the shadow of thy wings will I make my refuge, until these calamities be overpast" (Psalm 57:1).

Says Spurgeon, "The figure is very beautiful. The Lord overshadows His people as a hen protects her brood or as an eagle covers its young, and we, as the little ones, run under the blessed shelter and feel at rest."[414] The word for *shadow* means protection and defense; underneath God's shadow is safety from danger. In the covert of His wings, saints find a strong and loving refuge as the body grows frail, feeble, and fatigued.

Make my refuge means to flee for protective shelter. It reminds us of the six cities of refuge allocated to the Levite tribe that provided asylum for those guilty of manslaughter from the Avenger of Blood until they received a fair trial (Numbers 35:11–28). Note the comparison between these cities and Christ, the soul's eternal Refuge.

1. The cities of refuge were easily accessible. The cities of refuge were Kadesh, Shechem, Hebron (located in the West Bank), and Bezer, Ramoth, and Golan (located in the East Bank). Christ, the soul's refuge from the penalty of sin (eternal death), trouble, and sorrow, is easily reachable from any place on earth.

2. The gates of the cities were always open. The gates into the presence of Christ remain open day and night.

3. None were restricted from entry. Jews and non-Jews alike were welcome to flee to these cities of refuge (Galatians 3:28).

Regardless of nationality or degree of sin committed, all are invited to escape to the refuge provided by Jesus Christ. None are turned away. Jesus says, "I won't send away anyone who comes to me" (John 6:37 CEB).

4. The refuge seeker had to make a case for his innocence; otherwise, he would have to leave the city to meet death at the hands of the Avenger of Blood. In Christ Jesus, thankfully, the sinner fleeing to Him for refuge finds immediate pardon and mercy upon his saying, "God, give mercy. Forgive me, a sinner" (Luke 18:13 MSG), and the troubled saint finds consolation and help.

5. The innocent would have to remain within the city walls until the death of the present high priest. (Otherwise, the avenger of blood could slay him without punishment.) The forgiven must abide in Christ or risk peril at the hand of Satan.

In times of trouble, saints quickly flee to their safety zone, their mighty Refuge, under 'the shadow of His wings.' Ortberg says, "Finding *ultimate refuge* in God means you become so immersed in His presence, so convinced of His goodness, so devoted to His lordship that you find even the cave is a perfectly safe place to be because He is there with you."[415] Knowing He is there with us, wherever the "there" is, gives peace and lionlike courage to face the trial or trouble triumphantly. "Thus far the LORD has helped us" (1 Samuel 7:12 NIV). Knowing that God helped us yesterday gives confident assurance of His help today and tomorrow.

"What a blessed truth to understand that, in the middle of all of our difficulties and calamities, we have a refuge."—A. W. Tozer.

~June 8~

Psalm 57:6
Snares
Part 1

"They have prepared a net for my steps; my soul is bowed down: they have digged a pit before me, into the midst whereof they are fallen themselves. Selah" (Psalm 57:6).

When in a cave hiding from King Saul and his soldiers, David composed the Psalm.

Satan has prepared snares or entrapments in the believer's path.

1. The snares are secretive (Proverbs 1:17). Calvin states, "Satan, who is a wonderful contriver of delusions, is constantly laying snares to entrap ignorant and heedless people."

2. The snares are personalized. They are based on a person's most susceptible temptation and weakest point. Ambrose said, "The devil's snare does not catch you unless you are first caught by the devil's bait."

3. The snares are destructive. Scripture cautions —by admonition and by example—not to underestimate the enemy's power to bring a Christian down. If the adversary can destroy a Samson, a David, and a Demas, any one of us is vulnerable (Judges 16:18–21; 2 Samuel 11:3–5; 2 Timothy 4:10). Paul cautions, "Let him that thinketh he standeth take heed lest he fall" (1 Corinthians 10:12).

4. The snares are imprisoning. No animal caught in a snare can escape without help. Upon falling into a pit of Satan, a person's only hope of escape is in the power of the Lord. 'The arm of flesh will fail you; you dare not trust your own.' Deliverance comes at the hand of the Lord. "God is unto us a God of deliverances, and unto Jehovah, the Lord belongeth escape from death" (Psalm 68:20 ASV). "He breaks the power of canceled sin; He sets the prisoner free."

"Life hath quicksands. Life hath snares!"—Henry Wadsworth Longfellow.

~June 9~

Psalm 57:6

Snares

Part 2

"They have prepared a net for my steps" (Psalm 57:6).

Four characteristics of a snare were shared yesterday. Today, three more are considered.

1. The snares are unpredictable. Satan is sly and will repeatedly reset the same trap or devise one entirely off the radar.

2. The snares are to be feared. Horace said, "The cautious wolf fears the pit, the hawk regards with suspicion the snare laid for her, and the fish the hook in its concealment."

3. The snares may be thwarted or escaped. "Surely he shall deliver thee from the snare of the fowler" (Psalm 91:3). Spurgeon wrote, "God delivers His people from the snare of the fowler in two senses. *From, and out of.* First, He delivers them from the snare— does not let them enter it; and secondly, if they should be caught therein, He delivers them out of it. The first promise is the most precious to some; the second is the best to others."[416] But the former is always the better. Why? Blake said, "Better to shun the bait than struggle in the snare." To that, we say amen.

How might snares be shunned? Test the spirits. It is impossible to see the traps until it's too late. Still, the believer may discern their "location" and avoid captivity (Hosea 14:9). "Test the spirits whether they are of God" (1 John 4:1 KJ21).

Let experience help. Learn from past places of vulnerability.

Pray specifically for the detection and awareness of snares. With David, pray, "Keep me from the snares which they have laid for me, and the traps of the workers of iniquity" (Psalm 141:9 KJ21).

Comply wholly with God's Word. Tozer says, "To be entirely safe from the Devil's snares, the man of God must be completely obedient to the Word of the Lord. The driver on the highway is safe, not when he reads the signs but when he obeys them."

Then will I say, "My God, Thy power
Shall be my fortress and my tower;
I, that am formed of feeble dust,
Make Thine almighty arm my trust."

Thrice happy man! Thy Maker's care
Shall keep thee from the fowler's snare;
Satan, the Fowler, who betrays
Unguarded souls a thousand ways.

—Issac Watts

"The Devil's snare does not catch you unless you are first caught by the Devil's bait."—Ambrose.

~June 10~

Psalm 57:7
A Fixed Heart

"My heart is fixed, O God, my heart is fixed: I will sing and give praise" (Psalm 57:7).

Upon what was David's heart fixed?

On God Himself. No house can stand in the storm without a firm or fixed foundation. It is only as secure as the foundation upon which it rests. Man's foundation is the Lord Jesus Christ (Matthew 7:24–27). Fixate the heart on the person of Christ.

On prayer. "I will pray morning, noon, and night, pleading aloud with God; and he will hear and answer" (Psalm 55:17 TLB). Fixate the heart on communion and fellowship with Christ.

On the Holy Scripture. "I am your servant. Help me understand so that I may come to know your written instructions" (Psalm

119:125 GW). Fixate the heart on understanding the teaching and instruction of the Scriptures.

On Christian duty. "I delight to do thy will" (Psalm 40:8). David served God's purpose for his generation (Acts 13:36). Fixate the heart on fulfilling the will of the Lord for your life.

On God's house. "One thing have I desired of the LORD, that will I seek after; that I may dwell in the house of the LORD all the days of my life, to behold the beauty of the LORD, and to enquire in his temple" (Psalm 27:4). David loved God's house and the people who gathered there. Fixate the heart on faithfulness to God's house.

On praise. "I will sing and give praise." Fixate the heart on the worship and praise of God.

On unrelenting trust. "The LORD is my strength and my shield; my heart trusted in him, and I am helped" (Psalm 28:7). Fixate the heart on the dependence of Christ.

"The heart must be fixed, fixed for the duty, fitted and put in the frame for it, fixed in the duty by a close application, attending on the Lord without distraction."[417]—Matthew Henry.

~June 11~

Psalm 58:1–6
Judiciary Corruption

"Do ye indeed speak righteousness, O congregation? Do ye judge uprightly, O ye sons of men?" (Psalm 58:1).

The text reveals that King Saul called a council to judge David in absentia for treason against the throne. The judges, desiring to gain the King's favor, pronounced David unjustly guilty. The Psalm is David's response to the miscarriage of justice.

He calls the judges dumb, "wicked," "sons of men" (they were, as he, mere man), poisoners (like the poison of a deadly viper, their words were venomous), and unjust (they tipped the scales of justice in favor of Saul). The wicked judges were *deaf* to the proof of David's innocence. David declares their judgment by the righteous Judge of Heaven (Psalm 58:6–9). Corruption extended beyond King Saul to the judicial court, causing a miscarriage of justice for David.

It is a sad day for any country when the judiciary acts unjustly, criminally, and prejudicially toward the accused. When corruption arises in any government, immediate measures must be taken to purge it. Every person deserves *fairness* from the bench of justice.

Note. "Judges have often been false to their trust. They have prostituted their power to selfish ends."[418] Some are like Agesilaus, who, in a short letter to Hydreius the Carian, said: "If Nicias is innocent, acquit him; if he is not innocent, acquit him on my account; however, be sure to acquit him."[419] Solomon was sorely vexed over the corruption in the judicial system. He said, "I also noticed that under the sun there is evil in the courtroom. Yes, even the courts of law are corrupt!" (Ecclesiastes 3:16 NLT).

"Now more than ever, the people are responsible for the character of their Congress. If that body be ignorant, reckless, and corrupt, it is because the people tolerate ignorance, recklessness, and corruption."[420]—James Garfield (July 1877).

~June 12~

Psalm 58:1–6
Righteous Judiciaries

"Do ye indeed speak righteousness, O congregation? Do ye judge uprightly, O ye sons of men?" (Psalm 58:1).

In contrast to corrupt judges and judiciaries, the righteous judge with truth, honor, and integrity. "Open thy mouth, judge righteously" (Proverbs 31:9). "Mercy and truth preserve the king: and his throne is upholden by mercy" (Proverbs 20:28).

1. The righteous judiciaries reject bribes to alter decisions or the law. "A wicked man taketh a gift out of the bosom to pervert the ways of judgment" (Proverbs 17:23).

2. They expose and punish the wicked. "Partiality in judging is not good. Whoever says to the wicked, "You are in the right," will be cursed by peoples, abhorred by nations, but those who rebuke the wicked will have delight, and a good blessing will come upon them" (Proverbs 24:23–25 ESV).

3. The righteous judiciaries restrain from appetites and activities that interfere with judging honorably. "It is not for kings, O Lemuel, it is not for kings to drink wine; nor for princes strong drink: Lest they drink, and forget the law, and pervert the judgment of any of the afflicted" (Proverbs 31:4–5).

4. The righteous judiciaries will be honored by the Lord. "How blessed are those who maintain justice, Who practice righteousness at all times!" (Psalm 106:3 NASB). The corrupt will be severely judged (Psalm 57:6–9).

"Every institution, including the judiciary, has its share of black sheep and corrupt judges."—Prashant Bhushan.

~June 13~

Psalm 59:1–2
The Open Window

"Deliver me from mine enemies, O my God: defend me from them that rise up against me. Deliver me from the workers of iniquity, and save me from bloody men" (Psalm 59:1–2).

David recounts God's deliverance from Saul's men, who sought to kill him. The soldiers watched him by night at his house to make sure he didn't escape and plotted his murder for the next day.

David's wife, Michal, learned of the plot and warned him, saying, "If thou save not thy life tonight, tomorrow thou shalt be slain" (1 Samuel 19:11). David convinced himself that God had a way to deliver him. And that way, he discovered, would be through Michal's counsel of escape through a window (1 Samuel 19:12).

The application.

1. God delivers us from the mightest of enemies. "The LORD on high is mightier than the noise of many waters, yea, than the mighty waves of the sea" (Psalm 93:4). Whatever or whoever is the enemy, God is mightier.

2. Faith expects God to work and waits confidently, trusting He will. "Because of his strength will I wait upon thee: for God is my defense" (Psalm 59:9).

3. Pray, "deliver me," and immediately look for the "open window" of escape that God will provide. Spurgeon says, "Unbelief would have suggested that prayer was a waste of breath, but not so thought the good man, for he makes it his sole resort. He cries for deliverance and leaves ways and means with his God."[421]

"Trust [God] as what He is, and trust Him because of what He is, and see to it that your faith lays hold on the living God Himself and on nothing besides."[422]—Alexander Maclaren.

~June 14~

Psalm 59:16
Sing Praises

"But I will sing of thy power; yea, I will sing aloud of thy mercy in the morning: for thou hast been my defense and refuge in the day of my trouble" (Psalm 59:16).

David would praise God, when? "In the morning." Morning—with its fresh energy, quiet bliss, serenity, and undisturbed moments—is my treasured time to meet with the Lord. "O LORD, in the morning you hear my voice; in the morning I plead my case to you and watch" (Psalm 5:3 NRSVUE). Ralph Cushman wrote, "I met God in the morning when my day was at its best. And His presence came like sunrise, like a glory in my breast." Matthew Henry said, "God's compassions are new every morning, and therefore, it is fit to begin the day with his praises."[423] Spurgeon said,

"The early morning hour should be dedicated to praise: do not the birds set us the example?"

David would praise God, how? "I will sing aloud." Unashamedly, David would render praise. The goodness of the Lord deserves the loudest praise. Don't be shy. Don't hold back. Give God the praise to which He is most worthy. Says Spurgeon, "The greater our present trials, the louder will our future songs be, and the more intense our joyful gratitude."[424]

David would praise God, why? "Thou hast been my defense and refuge." He thanks God for His protection, defense, strength, and shelter in trouble. He praises God for His mercy. "The God of *my* mercy." What beautiful words they are to repeat, "The God of *my* mercy." David praised God for His personalized mercy. Begin prayer and praise by saying, "O thou God of *my* mercy."

"There is no kind of experience in which a Christian has a right to refuse to praise God, for 'all things work together for good to them that love God.'"—A. C. Dixon.

~June 15~

Psalm 60:8
What the Ungodly Teach Us

"Moab is my washpot" (Psalm 60:8).

The Moabites defiled Israel by seducing them to worship Baal (Numbers 25:3). They were now David's "washpot," a mere pot to hold dirty water. The metaphor meant that Moab's sinfulness and punishment unintentionally helped Israel's purification (washing clean of defilement).[425]

The ungodly may serve the good of the saint (be their "washpot") in several ways.

1. They display the ravages of sin, showing its danger and destructive force and warning us not to follow.

2. They display sin's punishment of horrific pain and suffering, teaching us that sin is not worth its cost.

3. They display hopelessness in crisis, proving that man's only hope is not found in the stuff of the world but in Christ alone.

4. They display meaninglessness, as did Solomon, substantiating that a life without Christ is empty and vain.

5. They display unrest and fear at death's door, revealing the hopelessness of future life with loved ones and God.

6. They display guilt for the sin done (though hidden), proving that sins' marks are inerasable apart from the cleansing blood of Christ.

7. They display a lack of peace, indicating that serenity and happiness only come in knowing Christ.

8. They display the damnable end of the wicked, confirming Jesus is the way to a happy end in Heaven.

"Faith finds honey in the lion and a washpot in filthy Moab."[426]— C. H. Spurgeon.

~June 16~

Psalm 61:1–8
The Benefits of Prayer

"Hear my cry, O God" (Psalm 61:1).

David outlines the benefits of prayer based on his own experience.

Prayer helps you to reach further (Psalm 61:2). Prayer transcends time and space to accomplish God's purposes.

Prayer helps you to soar higher (Psalm 61:2). "Prayer lifts the soul into the heavens where it hugs God in an indescribable embrace."

Prayer helps you to go deeper (Psalm 61:4). Talking to God forges one's relationship with Him. The Bible says, "Draw nigh to God, and He will draw nigh to you" (James 4:8). Bounds said, "Prayer makes a godly man, and puts within him the mind of Christ, the mind of humility, of self-surrender, of service, of pity, and of prayer. If we pray, we will become more like God or quit praying."

Prayer helps you to joy greater (Psalm 61:8a). Piper says, "Prayer is God's appointed way to fullness of joy because it is the vent of the inward burnings of our heart for Christ."

Prayer helps you to obey fuller (Psalm 61:8b). The power and strength of God are needed to follow Him regardless of cost and consequence. Bounds said, "Prayer puts into those who sincerely pray a spirit of obedience, for the spirit of disobedience is not of God and belongs not to God's praying hosts."[427] Chambers asserts, "One great effect of prayer is that it enables the soul to command the body."[428]

"Every new victory which the soul gains is the effect of a new prayer."—John Wesley.

~June 17~

Psalm 61:2–3
"A Rock Higher Than I"

"From the end of the earth will I cry unto thee, when my heart is overwhelmed: lead me to the rock that is higher than I. For thou hast been a shelter for me, and a strong tower from the enemy" (Psalm 61:2–3).

The Psalm is written during the time of David's exile.

David's Removal. Absalom forced David into exile from his homeland and throne beyond the Jordan River. The Psalm was written during David's time of exile.

David's Relapse. "My heart is overwhelmed." David's heart was broken and crushed by his forced exile and Absalom's betrayal, and there, in that faraway land from friends, bitter loneliness and despair enveloped him.

David's Recourse. "I cry unto thee." David's only recourse for help was with God. One may be out of reach of friends for their help, but never God. He is a constant companion, ready to help in times of need. To pray when overwhelmed with troublesome waters, when the heart is drowning, is hard, "yet gracious men plead best at such times."[429] David knows who the high Rock of Refuge is that can heal his brokenness, grant comfort, and secure him from harm. But grief and hurt blind the path to Him. "I see Thee to be my refuge, sure and strong, but alas! I am confused and cannot find Thee; I am weak and cannot climb Thee."[430] Guidance is needed, and he prays, "Lead me," take my hand, dear Lord, and lead me to thy blessed haven of rest. Note. Matthew Henry says, "That which separates us from our other comforts should drive us so much the nearer to God, the fountain of all comfort."[431]

David's Relief. The Psalm begins with tears and sorrow and ends with praise and peace. David is preserved, abiding with God, and praising God's name (Psalm 61:7–8). All laden with a load of care ripping their heart asunder, may, like David, find the same relief in the *Rock that is higher than I.*

"**Tribulation brings us to God, and brings God to us.**"[432]— C. H. Spurgeon.

~June 18~

Psalm 61:1
Lead Me to the Rock

"Lead me to the rock that is higher than I" (Psalm 61:2).

David, "overwhelmed" by trouble, asked that he might be *led to God's Rock* of Refuge. In Spurgeon's day, it was not unusual for ships to wreck off the northern coast of England, causing the loss of many lives because the rocks were inaccessible. He tells of a man who resided atop one such cliff and chiseled steps into it from the beach upward to a place of safety. Drowning mariners using the steps could reach a higher rock that was otherwise too high to climb, saving their lives. A time came when the storms wore away the steps, and a chain-railing was erected to help the drowning to be rescued.

The Holy Spirit is to man what the chiseled steps and chain railing were to the drowning mariners. He leads the spiritually blind to eternal safety from the penalty of sin by convicting them of sin, revealing Christ, and illuminating the gospel truth (John 16:8). Note. We will never get to Christ without being "led" to Him.

"A Savior would have been of no use to us if the Holy Spirit had not gently led us to Him and enabled us to rest upon Him."[433]— C. H. Spurgeon.

~June 19~

Psalm 62:5
When You Don't Know What to Do

"My soul, wait thou only upon God; for my expectation is from him" (Psalm 62:5).

The word David uses for "expectation" in Hebrew means "to rescue, save, deliver from illness, physical peril, enemies, or death— anything that threatens the well-being or life of the one who prays."[434] Hope is a good synonym for *expectation*; "my hope" is from God. In times of adversity and infirmity, God alone was the foundation for David's hope and confidence, his Refuge and Strong Tower in time of need.

What to do when you don't know what to do.

1. Exhort your soul to be still ("My soul, wait thou only upon God"). Restrain impulsive reactions while waiting for divine

interaction. Don't panic. Remain calm. Let God speak, instruct, and console.

2. Trust God explicitly ("only upon God"). To place one foot on the rock and the other in quicksand doth not avail. "Put not your trust in princes, nor in the son of man, in whom there is no help" (Psalm 146:3)." Maclaren said, "If God sends us on stony paths, He will provide us with strong shoes."[435]

3. Place hope ("my expectation") in God. Says Spurgeon, "Happy is the person who feels that all he has, wants, and expects are to be found in his God."[436] Statham says, "There is nothing that fills life with such joy and rest as expectation!"[437] Don't stagger at His promises, readiness, and eagerness to help. Simeon states, "We must trust Him no less when we see no way for our deliverance than when the promised relief is visibly at hand."[438]

"One of the greatest strains in life is the strain of waiting for God."—Oswald Chambers.

~June 20~

Psalm 63:8

Pursuit of God

"My soul followeth hard after thee: thy right hand upholdeth me" (Psalm 63:8).

It's not the "creature comforts" for which David sighs but the manifested presence of the Lord. All about him seemed to be a spiritual desert, a land where the *living water* that alone satisfies thirst was absent. His lips are parched, his soul famished for lack of it, and he cries out in desperation, "My soul thirsteth for thee, my flesh longeth for thee in a dry and thirsty land, where no water is" (Psalm 63:1b).

David uses a similar metaphor in Psalm 42:1–2. In the wildernesses of spiritual drought, resolve to do as David and follow hard after God until He is found. Don't be docile. Pursue God diligently. 'Follow hard after Him.' To follow hard after God is to cleave to Him, to be glued and adhered to Him.

Matthew Henry wrote, "To press hard after God is to follow Him closely, as those that are afraid of losing the sight of Him, and to follow Him swiftly, as those that long to be with Him. This David did."[439] F. F. Bruce stated, "The soul's deepest thirst is for God Himself, who has made us so that we can never be satisfied without Him."[440]

"You satisfy my soul." (Psalm 63:5 GW). "Satisfaction. A rare word!" says Spurgeon, "The richest man in England [or elsewhere] has not found it. The greatest conqueror has never won it. The proudest emperor cannot command it. It is a spiritual blessing, a divine grace that comes from *the great satisfying God—the God who is Himself all sufficient to fill the human heart.*"[441]

"I want deliberately to encourage this mighty longing after God. The lack of it has brought us to our present low estate."—A. W. Tozer.

~June 21~

Psalm 64:1–4
Preservation from Enemies

"Hear my voice, O God, in my prayer: preserve my life from fear of the enemy" (Psalm 64:1).

David's enemies sought his downfall.

1. They planned what words to say that would pierce David the deepest. "When words are made as sharp as possible by wit and malice, they have a frightful keenness of penetration."[442] Poisonous arrows (lies, slander, defamatory remarks) *"leave a slur, even if it be wholly disproved"*[443] (2 Samuel 15:2–6; 16:5–13).

2. They schemed in secret an insurrection strategy. Ahithophel and Absalom devised a plan to kill David and take control of the kingdom (2 Samuel 17:1–14).

3. They didn't fear Jehovah, who stood with David. "And David said unto him, How wast thou not afraid to stretch forth thine hand to destroy the LORD's anointed?" (2 Samuel 1:14). The prophet's warning, "Touch not mine anointed," went unheeded.

4. They "shoot at him" when least expected. Therefore, "Be alert, be on watch! Your enemy, the Devil, roams around like a roaring lion, looking for someone to devour" (1 Peter 5:8 GNT).

5. They sought to destroy a righteous man. "They...shoot in secret at the perfect." Says Spurgeon, "Sincere and upright conduct will not secure us from the assaults of slander. The Devil shot at our Lord himself, and we may rest assured he has a fiery dart in reserve for us."[444] Jonathan Swift said, "The worthiest people are the most injured by slander, as is the best fruit which the birds have been pecking at."

With David, pray to be protected from lying and slanderous tongues. It's better to escape it than to battle it.

"It is easy to splash mud, but I would rather help a man to keep his coat clean."[445]—Peter the Great.

~June 22~

Psalm 64:5–10
Vindication of the Righteous

"They encourage themselves in an evil matter: they commune of laying snares privily; they say, Who shall see them?" (Psalm 64:5).

What results when God intervenes on behalf of the believer over the slanderer?

With the slanderer (Psalm 64:7–9)

1. They understand God stands firm with the righteous. To oppose one of the least of His children is to battle Him.

2. They learn that God punishes those who harm His own. Their arrows are turned back against them, wounding them with injuries none can heal.

3. They fear the Lord. Fear of the Lord quickly develops when experiencing His mighty power in judgment.

4. They "declare the work of God" far and wide. They make known that to slander and lie against a believer is to have to reckon with their God.

With the righteous (Psalm 64:10).

1. They "shall be glad in the LORD." Delivered from the danger, the believer rejoices. "A thrill of joy passes through the whole of God's people, whether they were involved in the danger escaped or not."[446]

2. They "shall trust in him." Every deliverance experienced or witnessed instills deeper faith and trust in the Lord.

3. They "shall glory" in God's strength, His triumph, and the downfall of their enemy.

"Have patience awhile; slanders are not long-lived. Truth is the child of time; ere long she shall appear to vindicate thee."— Immanuel Kant.

~June 23~

Psalm 65:2
God Hears Prayer

"O thou that hearest prayer" (Psalm 65:2).

God has a reputation for hearing prayer. "O thou that hearest prayer." It "is His inalienable attribute, His 'nature and property,' to hear and answer prayer."[447] Spurgeon states, "God not only has heard, but is now hearing prayer, and always must hear prayer, since He is an immutable being, and never changes in His attributes. Every right and sincere prayer is as surely heard as offered."[448]

Prayer is heard and answered based on the purging of sin. "Thou shalt purge them away." By what means shall it be purged away? Not by works of righteousness or religious duty and affiliation but by "The blood of Jesus Christ his Son [who] cleanseth us from all sin" (1 John 1:7).

Micah said, "Who is a God like unto thee, that pardoneth iniquity...He will turn again, he will have compassion upon us; he will subdue our iniquities; and thou wilt cast all their sins into the depths of the sea" (Micah 7:18–19). "First comes forgiveness by expiation, for such is the meaning of 'covering' [purge away]. Then the cleansed soul has 'access with confidence'; then approaching, it happily dwells a guest in the house and is supplied with that which satisfies all desires."[449]

By terrible things in righteousness wilt thou answer us. God hears prayer and answers it in wondrous, surprising ways (Isaiah 64:3).

Thou...art the confidence of all the ends of the earth. God is a person's only trustworthy source of confidence or reliance. There is no one else on whom they can safely rely for their care and needs.

Praise waiteth for thee. Spurgeon says, "Shall not our praises balance our prayers? If the Lord gives goodness, shall not we give gratitude?" The more prayer is heard and answered, the more we have to sing the praises of God.

"Thou canst answer every prayer, for Thou art able to do for us more than we are able to ask or think, and Thou wilt answer every prayer of faith, either in kind or kindness."[450]—Matthew Henry.

~June 24~

Psalm 66:16
What God Did for My Soul

"Come and hear, all ye that fear God, and I will declare what he hath done for my soul." (Psalm 66:16).

L. R. Scarborough said, "Every Christian is called in the hour of salvation to witness a winning testimony for Jesus Christ. Nothing in Heaven or Earth can excuse him from it." A winning testimony includes four statements.

1. My life before meeting Christ. Share what was missing in your life or its emptiness, meaninglessness, or deception before salvation. What futile efforts were taken to meet these needs? Speak of past sins or bad habits briefly, if warranted, but without specificity. Around what things did your life revolve?

2. How I realized my need for Christ. What influenced you to become a Christian (search for meaning, purpose, peace, etc.)? Share the circumstances that surrounded your decision to follow Christ. Was it a sermon, a chapel talk at camp, a relationship, an addiction, an accident, an illness, or an encounter with a soulwinner?

3. What I did to become a Christian. Share how you became a Christian. "At that point, my heart was crushed with the weight of my sins and the need of Jesus. I walked down the aisle to the altar, where I knelt and asked Jesus to forgive and save me." Make clear the exact *how* of your salvation experience.

4. My life since I became a Christian. Share how Jesus has supplied your needs and blessed you beyond measure. Share what you count to be the most beautiful part of your relationship with Jesus. Share the changes Jesus made to your life (2 Corinthians 5:17). Tell of the wondrous peace and joy and eternal hope of Heaven you now possess.

Look for opportunities to share it—over coffee with an unsaved friend, classmate, or fellow worker, during church visitation, or at a church service. Share it while waiting in a grocery store line, getting a haircut, at a social outing with a friend, or traveling on public transportation.

"It is experience, not logic, which grips the heart of a seeking sinner. To tell one's spiritual experience is more convincing than a thousand theories."[451]—Roland Q. Leavell.

~June 25~

Psalm 66:18
Sin Hinders Prayer

"If I regard iniquity in my heart, the Lord will not hear me" (Psalm 66:18).

There is much praying without effect due to unconfessed sin in the heart.

If I regard iniquity in my heart. Spurgeon writes, "Nothing hinders prayer like iniquity harbored in the heart; as with Cain, so with us, sin lies at the door and blocks the passage. If you refuse to hear God's commands, He will surely refuse to hear your prayers."[452] To regard iniquity in the heart is to give it place, cherish it, delight in it, and not loathe and forsake it. Prayers are mere words in the wind when cold, formal, heartless, voiced for the admiration of men, or from an unclean heart. Isaiah declared, "It's your sins that have cut you off from God. Because of your sins, he has turned away and will not listen anymore" (Isaiah 59:2 NLT).

But verily, God has heard me. God heard David's prayer, indicating that he had confessed sin and was cleansed. Note. Horne asserts, "The prayer which is 'heard,' is the prayer of the penitent, heartily grieved and wearied with sin, hating, and longing to be delivered from it. For God heareth not hypocrites, who, while they outwardly disavow, yet inwardly 'regard' and cherish iniquity."[453] Unheard and unanswered prayers happen when sin is willingly harbored.

An employee who worked for a city located in a valley was fired. He angrily plugged the primary pipe that supplied water to the city from the reservoir high in the mountain. Not until he confessed the deed and the pipe was unplugged did the flow of water resume. The riches of God's grace will flow abundantly and swiftly into the heart that unplugs the pipe of its hindrance. Have you inadvertently blocked the pipe, thereby preventing God's blessings? While unconfessed sin plugs the pipe of blessing (Jeremiah 5:25), the heart swept clean of sin allows it to flow unimpeded (1 John 1:9).

"It is no use praying unless we are living as children of God. Then, Jesus says, 'Everyone that asketh receiveth.'"[454]—Oswald Chambers.

~June 26~

Psalm 67:1–2

Missionary Praying

"God be merciful unto us, and bless us; and cause his face to shine upon us; Selah. That thy way may be known upon earth, thy saving health among all nations" (Psalm 67:1–2).

David's prayer for the heathen, our prayer for them, is three-fold.

1. That the gospel message may be sent to all the earth. 'Among all nations.' "The psalmist's prayer, while beginning with himself, expands till he embraces the whole earth."[455] David prays for Israel and then immediately prays for the every nation. He overleaps all boundaries, bringing all people to God on his knees.[456] D. James Kennedy said, "So often we pray narrowly, attending only to our needs. Instead, we should pray broadly for everyone. We should pray for the lost that they might be saved and for the saved that they might win the lost."[457] Ryle urges, "We should try to bear in our hearts the whole world, the heathen."[458]

2. That the heathen may receive the Gospel and be saved. The words "saving health" are better translated as "salvation." Therefore, the central focus of missionary praying is for the salvation of the heathen. We must agonize at God's footstool for all men to come to the knowledge of the truth.

3. That the heathen would worship God. "Let the people praise thee." When nations and people bow their knees to God, they will "be glad and…praise…God."

"Prayer is the mighty engine that is to move the missionary work."[459]—A. B. Simpson.

~June 27~

Psalm 68:5
Care For the Orphan and Widow

"A father of the fatherless, and a judge of the widows" (Psalm 68:5).

"A father of the fatherless." God cares for the orphans and opposes all who deal with them mischievously. He is their defender against injustice. He is their protector, watching over them lest they be taken advantage of in some way or mistreated. Matthew Henry says, "His omnipotence is engaged and employed for their protection, and their proudest and most powerful oppressors will not only find themselves an unequal match for this but will find that it is at their peril to contend with it."[460] Pray for the orphans' welfare. Intervene on their behalf when abused, neglected, or in need. Adopt an orphan if God prompts.

"A judge of the widows." He draws a circle of fire about the widow, keeping injurious intruders out. He will be her avenger, defender, and provider (Jeremiah 49:11). Those who take advantage of a defenseless widow will not escape God's fury; they will be brought to ruin (Exodus 22:22–24). "God has an ear open to all their complaints and a hand open to all their wants."[461]

Spurgeon says, "When the husband of earth is removed, the godly widow casts herself upon the care of her Maker."[462] We must embrace widows in our hearts, adopt them in our churches, support them with our gifts, and envelop them in our prayers. To do more is warranted; to do less is unconscionable. It is this that Christ expects, solicits, requires, and judges. Let us, therefore, hearken passionately and caringly to the task. "Take care of widows who are truly needy" (1 Timothy 5:3 CEB). In so doing, we will be like Job, who said, "I caused the widow's heart to sing for joy" (Job 29:13).

"Great potentates in the world respect the noblest and the richest in the land, the men who may adorn their court and strengthen their authority. But the highest glory of God is to be compassionate to the miserable [orphans and widows]."[463]—Arnd.

~June 28~

Psalm 68:1–2
Smoke and Melted Wax

"Let God arise, let his enemies be scattered: let them also that hate him flee before him. As smoke is driven away, so drive them away: as wax melteth before the fire, so let the wicked perish at the presence of God" (Psalm 68:1–2).

Smoke represents the enemy of God and His people. Note.

1. Smoke is a weak vapor that has no resistance. The faintest breath of air drives it away.

2. Smoke can suffocate, but with the fresh air of the Spirit, it's harmless. With the same ease as a mere breath drives away smoke, the mightest of armies of opposition are driven away by the power of God. No army can stand against Jehovah. Defeating them is a breeze.

Melted wax also represents the saint's enemy. "As wax melteth before the fire."

1. Hardened wax softens in the fire. "Wicked men are haughty till they come into contact with the Lord."[464]

2. Wax in the fire dissipates; it melts away (Psalm 97:5). The enemy will vanish and disappear at the hand of God's might and judgment.

Application.

1. Don't fear the enemy because they are as smoke and wax.

2. Pray against their evil advances in the world and their enmity with God and the saints. "Let God arise, let his enemies be scattered." "Selfishness in all its forms, tyranny, hate, worldliness,

and unbelief, must be scattered by God's power."[465] Matthew Henry says, "Though we are to pray for our enemies as such, yet we are to pray against God's enemies as such, against their enmity to him and all their attempts upon his kingdom."[466]

3. Rejoice in the victory that God has given over the enemy. "But let the righteous be glad; let them rejoice before God: yea, let them exceedingly rejoice."

4. Magnify the name of the Lord. Extol the name of the Lord for what He has done (Psalm 68:4).

"God's holy wrath is poured out on what He hates because it damages and destroys what He loves."—Sinclair Ferguson.

~June 29~

Psalm 69:7
Christ in Psalm Sixty-nine

"Because for thy sake I have borne reproach; shame hath covered my face" (Psalm 69:7).

David shares seven traits that would identify the Messiah. Jesus fulfilled them each.

1. People would hate the Messiah without cause (Psalm 69:4). The Jews and Gentiles were opposed to Christ without cause.

2. They who oppose the Messiah would be among the mighty (Psalm 69:4). Mighty men of power like Pilate and Herod stood against Christ.

3. The Messiah would be rejected by His own people (Psalm 69:8). Jesus "came unto his own, and his own received him not" (John 1:11).

4. Messiah would be jealous of God's glory (Psalm 69:9). "The zeal of thine house hath eaten me up." Jesus quoted the prophecy during the cleansing of the Temple.

5. Man's antagonism toward God would fall on the Messiah (Psalm 69:9). Paul related these words to Christ (Romans 15:3).

6. On the Cross, they would give Messiah vinegar (Psalm 69:21). The soldiers gave Christ vinegar to drink as He hung on the Cross (John 19:29–30).

7. A price would be paid in exchange for the Messiah (Psalm 69:22). Judas sold Jesus for thirty pieces of silver to the Roman soldiers.

8. Messiah's enemies would be crushed (Psalm 69:25). Specifically, the prophecy refers to Messiah's betrayer (Judas), but at large, to those who assisted in the act, the chief priests, and elders.[467] Judas' betrayal of Jesus fulfilled the prophecy.

Only the true Messiah would fulfill divine prophecies made hundreds of years before His coming about His life, works, family, rejection, miracles, death, resurrection, and second advent, and this Jesus did to the letter.

"Suffice it to believe that Jesus Christ our Lord, the Messiah, came exactly as it was prophesied."[468]—C. H. Spurgeon.

~June 30~

Psalm 70:1
Help Me Fast, God!

"Make haste, O God, to deliver me; make haste to help me, O LORD" (Psalm 70:1).

It is always proper to bring pressing troubles to God's remembrance, asking for speedy assistance as David did

. Four times in five verses, he begs God to act quickly on his behalf. Why the urgency? David's immediate peril required it. He was "poor and needy." His enemies sought to kill him ("they that seek after my soul"), took delight in his hurt ("that desire my hurt"), and sarcastically made fun of his calamity ("that say, Aha, aha").

In difficult straits, when not days but hours may be too late for help, it is appropriate to pray concisely (David's prayer was short), pleading with God for swift answers. Says Spurgeon, "It is not forbidden us, in hours of dire distress, to ask for speed on God's part in His coming to rescue us."[469]

> Make haste, O God, my soul to bless!
>   My help and my deliv'rer thou;
> Make haste, for I'm in deep distress,
>   My case is urgent; help me now.
>
> ~C. H. Spurgeon (1866).

"'Make no tarrying'—my wants are many, my danger great, my time short. O God, delay not!"—Adam Clarke.

~July 1~

Psalm 71:9
Resolutions for Old Age
Part 1

"Cast me not off in the time of old age; forsake me not when my strength faileth" (Psalm 71:9).

Spurgeon says, "This psalm, written by an old man, is especially suitable for an old man. It is numbered seventy-one, and it may suit those who have reached that age, but it is also appropriate to us all in prospect of the days of feebleness that will come to us, sooner or later, if we are spared to grow old."[470]

The psalmist suggests ten resolutions for growing old with God.

1. Ditch the talk about aches and pains and speak of God's greatness and goodness. God and man alike hate a grumbler, whiner, and complainer. "My lips shall greatly rejoice when I sing unto thee; and my soul, which thou hast redeemed" (v. 23). *Avoid a grumbling tongue.* "And when the people complained, it displeased the LORD: and the LORD heard it" (Numbers 11:1). To God's displeasure, the Israelites complained and grumbled in the wilderness about His

206

manner of provision for their needs. Few things are worse than hearing the elderly grumble and complain in light of all God's blessings.

2. Reminisce about God's goodness continuously. "My tongue also shall talk of thy righteousness all the day long" (v. 24). "Christians have many treasures," says Spurgeon, "to lock up in the cabinet of memory."[471] And in old age, open the cabinet, recalling God's manifold goodness throughout life.

"Age is opportunity no less than youth itself."—Henry Wadsworth Longfellow.

~July 2~

Psalm 71:9
Resolutions for Old Age
Part 2

"Cast me not off in the time of old age; forsake me not when my strength faileth" (Psalm 71:9).

David shares ten resolutions for old age in this Psalm, two of which were shared yesterday.

1. Exhibit hope and trust in God as you did in youth, stubbornly refusing to yield to despair or depression despite frailty or infirmity or abode in a nursing home or hospital. "For thou art my hope, O Lord GOD: thou art my trust from my youth" (v. 5).

2. Look to God, not man, as a refuge in adversity and infirmity. "Be thou my strong habitation, whereunto I may continually resort:...for thou art my rock and my fortress [and] my strong refuge" (vv. 3, 7). Solomon states that God's name is like "a strong tower" that keeps us safe and secure from the enemy (Proverbs 18:10).

3. Pray more. "Incline thine ear unto me, and save me" (v. 2). Prayer is the never-failing means whereby the believer is sustained physically, strengthened spiritually, and renewed mentally. Thomas Watson said, "Prayer delights God's ear; it melts His heart; and

opens His hand. God cannot deny a praying soul."[472] There is more time to pray in old age and more for which to pray. With Andrew Murray, make "the place of secret prayer to become the most beloved spot on earth."[473]

"I would suppose God's greatest gift to a man, [is] that in his last days he have strength to serve the Lord God."[474]—W. A. Criswell.

~July 3~

Psalm 71:9
Resolutions for Old Age
Part 3

"Cast me not off in the time of old age; forsake me not when my strength faileth" (Psalm 71:9).

In the Psalm, the psalmist suggests ten resolutions for old age. Today, we consider the final five.

1. Never compromise the biblical convictions of youth, but fully adhere to them. "O God, thou hast taught me from my youth" (v. 17). Old age is not the time to backpedal on biblical principles and beliefs taught and embraced in younger years.

2. Resolve to press on passionately and perseveringly to finish well. "O God, be not far from me: O my God, make haste for my help" (v. 12).

3. Tell of the Lord. "My mouth shall shew forth thy righteousness and thy salvation all the day" (v. 15). Use opportunities to witness in every circumstance and arena, claiming the promise of fruitfulness in old age. "Even in old age they will still produce fruit; they will remain vital and green" (Psalm 92:14 NLT).

4. Watch for the silver lining of blessings in life's woes and render praise. "Thou, which hast showed me great and sore troubles, shalt quicken me again" (v. 20). Display faith in the fire, trusting God to be in its midst, bringing glory to His name and using it for good (Romans 8:28).

5. Resist evolving into the *stereotypes* of older people (critical, complaining, negative, cantankerous, unproductive, self-centered, or overly demanding). "Thou shalt increase my greatness, and comfort me on every side. I will also praise thee with the psaltery, even thy truth, O my God: unto thee will I sing with the harp, O thou Holy One of Israel. My lips shall greatly rejoice when I sing unto thee; and my soul, which thou hast redeemed" (v. 21–23).

Let your countenance and conduct reflect His presence in old age. Join the Psalmist as a singer in old age, praising God for manifold blessings, comfort, and salvation. Sometimes joy births singing; sometimes singing births joy. Therefore, whatever state sing unto the Lord. It is medicine to the soul.

"Old age is just as important and meaningful a part of God's perfect will as is youth. God is every bit as interested in the old as the young."[475]—J. O. Sanders.

~July 4~

Psalm 72:17
The Everlasting Name

"His name shall endure forever: his name shall be continued as long as the sun: and men shall be blessed in him: all nations shall call him blessed" (Psalm 72:17).

The psalmist speaks of the name of Christ in three ways.

It's prophetical. "His name." Jesus was born in obscurity over 2,000 years ago and was crucified. Yet His name lives on and is the most renowned among men. Spurgeon states, "God's name is eternal and will never be changed. His character is immutable; His fame and honor also will remain for all eternity."[476]

It's perpetual. "There will always be life in the name of Jesus, and sweetness and consolation."[477] Like the ringing of a bell, Christ's name sends out its chimes through the ages, assuring His people that He will keep His promises (to exhibit mercy and grace, forgiveness, salvation, and deliverance from sin's cruel bondage) and give them entrance at last into Heaven. While the names of the great men of history have perished, Christ's name remains unchanged in its fame, glory, power, and permanence.

It's permanent. To destroy the memory of the name of Jesus, you would have to silence every saint; demolish every church; obliterate millions of gravestones scattered throughout the earth; burn every Bible, piece of literature, and art that bespeaks it; shut down tens of thousands of funeral homes; and mutilate every gospel song written and recorded.

Take hope. The name on which you called for rescue from sin, comfort in sorrow, healing in sickness, and deliverance in trouble will never be demolished. It will endure forever on earth as your defender and sustainer and be your praise forever in Heaven. Confidently, you may say, "Thy name, O LORD, endureth for ever; and thy memorial, O LORD, throughout all generations" (Psalm 135:13). Embrace, praise, reverence, extol, and declare that wonderful name.

"Great names come and go, but the name of Jesus remains. The Devil still hates it, the world still opposes it, but God still blesses it, and we can still claim it!"[445]—Warren Wiersbe.

~July 5~

Psalm 72:17–20
How to Pray for Jesus

"Prayer also shall be made for him continually; and daily shall he be praised" (Psalm 72:15).

Seventeen psalms are ascribed to David beyond this one, but this is his final. In his dying breath, he prays for and pronounces a blessing upon Solomon and his rule of Israel. But a greater than Solomon is visible; the Messiah's kingdom is prophetically declared and prayed for.

"Prayer also shall be made for him continually." How? Prayer is made to Jesus, in part, when offered on behalf of His cause.

1. The dimension of its supply. Pray for the Lord's work to have sufficient resources to fulfill their mandate and mission, as stated in Matthew 28:18–20.

2. The diffusion of its message. Pray for the widespread distribution of the Gospel and its receptivity all over the world.

3. The dispatch of its workers. "Pray ye therefore the Lord of the harvest, that he will send forth labourers into his harvest" (Matthew 9:38). Pray for the necessary workers to be thrust out into the harvest and their preservation from harm.

4. The defeat of its enemies. "He delivereth me from mine enemies: yea, thou liftest me up above those that rise up against me: thou hast delivered me from the violent man" (Psalm 18:48). Pray for the binding of the strong man, the tearing down of strongholds, and every impedance to the Gospel's advancement to be thwarted (2 Corinthians 10:3–5). "Break the arms of those who are wicked and evil. Seek out their wickedness until there's no more to find" (Psalm 10:15 CEB).

5. The development of its kingdom. Pray for its growth and global expansion and for its glory or fame to increase throughout the earth.

The prayer closes with a double amen: "Amen, and Amen," signifying an earnest desire that what is requested will happen. May it be the ending to our prayers.

"May all blessings be upon His head; all His people desire that His cause may prosper; therefore, they hourly cry, 'Thy kingdom come.' Prayer for Jesus is a very sweet idea, and one which should be forevermore lovingly carried out; for the church is Christ's body, and the truth is His scepter; therefore, we pray for Him when we plead for these."[478]—C. H. Spurgeon.

~July 6~

Psalm 73:2
Narrow Escapes

"But as for me, my feet were almost gone; my steps had well nigh slipped" (Psalm 73:2).

Looming danger of shipwreck awaits us from three directions.

Slippery places of theological doubt. Asaph doubted God's justness in witnessing the prosperity and success of the wicked. Trials can challenge faith and question God's love and care. Matthew Henry states, "There are storms that will try the firmest anchors."[479] When men doubt the trustworthiness of God to do right, their faith wavers, and their feet wobble. C. S. Lewis said, "Faith is the art of holding on to things your reason has once accepted, in spite of your changing moods."[480] Don't doubt in the night what you believed in the light.

Slippery places of worldliness. The preoccupation with the allurements and attractions of the world provides an unsure footing, causing many to stumble and fall, like Demas (2 Timothy 4:10). Drummond said, "So long as the regenerate man is kept in this world, he must find the old environment at many points a severe temptation."[481] John Wesley cautions, "If, after having renounced all, we do not watch incessantly and beseech God to accompany our vigilance with His, we shall be again entangled and overcome." Guard against being entangled with the affairs and things of the world (2 Timothy 2:4).

Slippery places of sin. The most slippery of places, which can cause a fall, is a favorite sin. That's why Paul cautioned, "Neither give place [a foothold or beachhead] to the devil" (Ephesians 4:27). To steer the ship near the rocks is to court a shipwreck. In an employment interview, three chauffeurs were asked the same question: "If you were my driver, how close to the mountain's edge could you drive my car?"

"Within inches," the first replied.

212

The second said, "Within several feet."

The third chauffeur said, "If I were your driver, I would keep your car as far away from the edge as possible." He got the job. With sin, don't flirt with it. Stay far away from its edge.

"It may be observed that good men are liable to slips and falls, to fall into sin, snares, and temptations, and from their steadfastness in the faith, but not totally and finally; for God is able to keep them, and does keep them, from a total and final falling away."[482]—John Gill.

~July 7~

Psalm 73:2

Lessons From Slippery Places

"But as for me, my feet were almost gone; my steps had well nigh slipped" (Psalm 73:2).

Asaph narrowly escaped the slippery place of envy over the success of the wicked (Psalm 73:2). He says, "My steps had well nigh slipped."

We have all experienced narrow escapes from the slippery paths of sinful temptation.

What might be learned from them?

1. Narrow escapes should engender gratitude to God for their gracious deliverance. "You have grazed rocks on which others were broken; slipped on precipices on which others have fallen; singed your wings in flames by which others have perished. Oh, how you ought to contemplate your narrow escapes and shudder in fear for what may have occurred and thank God that it did not!"

2. They should engender sympathy for those who didn't escape the same fall. With compassion, we should join Bradford in saying about them, "There but for the grace of God go I."

3. They ought to engender greater discipline or restraint. Narrow escapes reveal the saint's need to abstain from playing near

or on the Devil's playground. The Bible says, "Do not give the devil a way to defeat you." (Ephesians 4:27 ICB). It's been said that we don't fall into sin; we walk into sin.

4. They should engender the probability of a fall. Narrow escapes forewarn of a coming fall unless the behavior is changed. A narrow escape today doesn't preclude one tomorrow.

5. They should engender heightened consecration to the Lord. Slippery places and narrow escapes indicate a spiritual imbalance, flaw, defect, or weakness. Its remedy is renewed dedication and surrender to the Lord (Romans 12:1–2).

"'But my feet were almost moved.' When were the feet moved, except when the heart was not right?"[483]—Augustine.

~July 8~

Psalm 74:2
Grounds For Eternal Security

"Remember thy congregation, which thou hast purchased" (Psalm 74:2).

With the holy city, its sanctuaries and sacred vessels desecrated and consumed in fire to the roaring cheer of the Chaldees, Asaph begs God to "remember" (think upon thy people that you have so wondrously redeemed from the hand of Pharaoh's tyranny) and vindicate thy holy name (Psalm 74:10–11).

Asaph argues that the high cost that God paid for Israel's deliverance from Egyptian bondage is grounds to believe in His faithfulness to them now. Paul presents the same argument for God's faithfulness to His children: "He that spared not his own Son, but delivered him up for us all, how shall he not with him also freely give us all things?' (Romans 8:32). Spurgeon says, "What a mighty plea is redemption. From before the world's foundation, the chosen were regarded as redeemed by the Lamb slain; shall ancient love die out, and the eternal purpose be frustrated? Can election fail and eternal love cease to flow? Impossible. The woes of Calvary, and the covenant of which they are the seal, are the security of the saints."[484]

The divine purchase or transaction at Calvary, "which thou hast purchased of old" (2000 years ago), shall ever be enduring proof of God's everlasting love for His children despite troubles and trials at the hand of the "Chaldees." Hear Paul convincingly say, "Who shall separate us from the love of Christ? Shall tribulation, or distress, or persecution, or famine, or nakedness, or peril, or sword?...Nay, in all these things we are more than conquerors through him that loved us" (Romans 8:35, 37). God's merciful and gracious purchase of sinners from the power and penalty of sin through Christ is sure grounds for their eternal assurance in salvation and help in their time of need.

"The woes of Calvary, and the covenant of which they are the seal, are the security of the saints."[485]—C. H. Spurgeon.

~July 9~

Psalm 74:11–23
Grounds to Plead God's Help

"Why withdrawest thou thy hand, even thy right hand? pluck it out of thy bosom" (Psalm 74:11).

Asaph witnessed the Babylonians' ravage, pollution, and destruction of Jerusalem and the captivity of its inhabitants and besought God for explanation and deliverance. When your world is caving in and the outlook is extremely bleak, do as Asaph. Spurgeon asserts, "When God seems to fold His arms, we must not fold ours, but rather renew our entreaties that He would again put His hand to the work."[486]

Asaph's prayer is inquisitive. He did no wrong to ask God why the wicked triumphed over the righteous. When all is in turmoil and hope is lost, ask God for an understanding of His mysterious ways in your life. Note. Israel was allowed to be overthrown because her priests and leaders had led her to practice idolatry.

Asaph's prayer is argumentative.

1. He pleaded God's deliverance of Israel from captivity based on His ransom of them from the hands of Pharaoh in Egypt (Psalm 74:2). The believer's redemption from Satan's hand at Calvary gives certainty of God's everlasting abiding care and protection (Romans 8:32).

2. He pleaded divine interposition based on the imminent danger (Psalm 74:9). "There is no more any prophet." Spiritual crises and emergencies provide a key to Heaven's door.

3. He pleaded deliverance based on the past works of God (Psalm 74:13–17). Spurgeon says, "Each past miracle of grace assures us that He who has begun to deliver will continue to redeem us from all evil."[487]

4. He pleaded deliverance based on the vindication of God's name from the reproach and insult of the wicked (Psalm 74:18; 22–23). Joshua similarly used the plea to invoke God's help (Joshua 7:9).

5. He pleaded deliverance based on God's word (Psalm 74:20). God is eternally bound to all He has said and promised. Boldly but humbly, hold God to what He said. He delights in His people's firm stance on His word and their trust in claiming His promises.

"When the power of enemies is most threatening, it is comfortable to flee to the power of God by earnest prayer."[488]—Matthew Henry.

~July 10~

Psalm 75:1
Praise to the Uplifting God

"Unto thee, O God, do we give thanks" (Psalm 75:1).

The Psalm expresses praise and gratitude to the uplifting God. "For not from the east or from the west and not from the wilderness *comes lifting up*, but it is God who executes judgment, putting down one and lifting up another" (Psalm 75:6–7 ESV). "All the horns of the wicked I will cut off, but the horns of the righteous shall be lifted up" (Psalm 75:10 ESV).

The circumstances of the Psalm are unknown. It may have been the romping, *uplifting* victory of God over Sennacherib during Hezekiah's reign (2 Kings 19:35), the continuation of the Babylonian captivity (Psalm 74), David's *uplifting* (restoration to the throne) following Absalom's treasonous revolt (2 Samuel 19:9–11) or another historical event in which God *uplifted* Israel to victory in battle.

David's *uplifting* in Psalm 40 comes to mind, wherein he says, "I waited patiently for the LORD. He turned to me and heard my cry. He *lifted me out* of the pit of destruction, out of the sticky mud. He stood me on a rock and made my feet steady" (Psalm 40:1–2 NCV). Every Christian has reason to praise God unceasingly for their *uplifting* from the miry clay of sin's degradation and defilement to the Solid Rock of salvation.

The believer must also praise the Lord for the many *upliftings since conversion*—from a favorite sin, sickness, failure, defeat, and despair. Spurgeon says, "Never let us neglect Thanksgiving. We should praise God again and again. Stunted gratitude is ingratitude. For infinite goodness, there should be measureless thanks."[489]

"The more we meditate upon the astonishing love, His amazing sacrifice, the more we feel that if we had a thousand minds, hearts, souls, we would crown him Lord of all."[490]—Fuller.

~July 11~

Psalm 76:3
The Mighty Warrior

"There he breaks the weapons of our enemies" (Psalm 76:3 TLB).

Asaph (a different man from the earlier cited Asaph) composes the Psalm to celebrate God's defeat of the Assyrian general Sennacherib in 701 B.C. (2 Kings 19:35). It serves as a staunch reminder that God is the Mighty Warrior who forever defends His people from the hand of the enemy. It takes only a word from His mouth to romp the strongest and fiercest of armies (Psalm 76:6). It is true that if God be for us, none can stand against us (Romans 8:31).

Note several spiritual contrasts.

The saint's enemy is not Sennacherib but one mightier. Peter describes him as "your adversary the devil, as a roaring lion, walketh about, seeking whom he may devour" (1 Peter 5:8).

The battleground is not near Jerusalem but in our hearts. The heart is the arena of spiritual warfare. God made His *home* in Jerusalem near His people to assure them of His presence and protection (Psalm 76:2). He abides in the believer to ensure the same and to enable them to conquer the Devil.

The battle weaponry is not flesh and blood (chariots and horses and flaming arrows and sharp swords) *but the strength of God.* Though "stouthearted," brave, confident, and arrogant, Satan and his demons shall be "spoiled" (rendered powerless, impotent by having their weapons stripped) by the mighty hand of God (Colossians 2:15). "At thy rebuke, O God of Jacob, both the chariot and horse are cast into a dead sleep" (Psalm 76:6). It is God's rebuke of Satan that grants triumph o'er him and his devices. Morison comments, "Before God, no enemy can possibly stand, when once His wrath is kindled. Beneath His shadow, the most inveterate and formidable foes cannot injure the objects of His unchanging love."[491]

"The best-appointed armies, the most magnificent warlike preparations under God's rebuke soon come to nought."[492]—W. S. Plumer.

~July 12~

Psalm 77:2–3
The Dark Night of the Soul

"In the day of my trouble I sought the Lord: my sore ran in the night, and ceased not: my soul refused to be comforted. I remembered God, and was troubled: I complained, and my spirit was overwhelmed. Selah" (Psalm 77:2–3).

Boice says the Dark Night of the Soul "is a state of intense spiritual anguish in which the struggling, despairing believer feels God abandons him."[493] In experiencing the dark night of the soul, the saint should do six things with the psalmist.

1. Seek the Lord as the only source or means for help and rescue (Psalm 77:2). He should say, "I will lift up mine eyes unto the hills, from whence cometh my help. My help cometh from the Lord, which made heaven and earth" (Psalm 121:1–2). It is futile to rely upon the arm of flesh for deliverance.

2. Cry unto the Lord for deliverance (Psalm 77:1). The Lord hears audible and mental prayer. Still, the former is sometimes immensely therapeutic, enabling one to vent pent-up agony, anger, and pain. Audible praying helps one retain focus.

3. Pray with incessant importunity (Psalm 77:2). Keep knocking on Heaven's door until it opens (Luke 11:8). Spurgeon says, "Importunity prevailed. The gate opened to the steady knock. It will be so with us in our hour of trial; the God of grace will hear us in due season."[494]

4. Remember God's goodness in the past (Psalm 77:11). Remember God's former mercies unto you (Psalm 77:10–15). Matthew Henry remarks, "The remembrance of the works of God will be a powerful remedy against distrust of His promise and goodness, for He is God and changes not."[495]

5. Maintain hope. "There ariseth light in the darkness" (Psalm 112:4). The word *ariseth* refers to the sunrise. "For the good man, the darkest night of trouble and sorrow will have a dawn of hope."[496]

6. But unlike the psalmist, the distraught saint should not refuse to be comforted with the comfort provided (Psalm 77:2). Up and be done with such refusal and avail yourself at once of the consolation afforded by Christ through the Holy Spirit in sundry ways (ministers, Bible promises, hymns and songs, fellow saints, etc.).

"At times, even the most dedicated Christian feels 'in the dark' and wonders why God seems so far away."[497]—Warren Wiersbe.

~July 13~

Psalm 77:19
The Unknown Footsteps of God

"Thy way is in the sea, and thy path in the great waters, and thy footsteps are not known" (Psalm 77:19).

God does much of which He gives no accounting (His "footsteps are not known"). Samuel Slater says, "He often goeth so much out of our sight, that we are unable to give an account of what He doeth, or what He is about to do."[498] "Although the works of God," states Calvin, "are in part manifest to us, yet all our knowledge of them comes far short of their immeasurable height. [They] far surpass the limited powers of our understanding."[499]

His "footsteps are not known." Spurgeon says, "None can follow Thy tracks by foot or eye. Thou art alone in Thy glory, and Thy ways are hidden from mortal ken. Thy purposes Thou wilt accomplish, but the means are often concealed; indeed, they are in themselves too vast and mysterious for human understanding."[500] The actions of God defy human comprehension and will remain in part a mystery until He chooses to interpret them.

That which is known is that God promises to take the sorrows of life (the unexplainable, senseless, unfair) and supernaturally use them for good in the lives of His children and to benefit His kingdom on earth (Romans 8:28). Let us trust God, when we cannot trace Him. Jerry Bridges says, "Confidence in the sovereignty of God in all that affects us is crucial to our trusting Him."[501]

"How often has there been a footstep of God where we have not discerned it! We had an illness, or a bereavement, or a disappointment, or a loss. The world said, "How unfortunate!" but God passed our way; the world could not see His footprint—blessed were we if we could."[502]—P. B. Power.

~July 14~
Psalm 78:4
Parental Instruction

"We will not hide them from their children, shewing to the generation to come the praises of the LORD, and his strength, and his wonderful works that he hath done" (Psalm 78:4).

The Psalm instructs Israel to remember and pass down to their children the history of God's wondrous works and unfailing compassion among their forefathers, primarily in the Exodus deliverance and wilderness wandering. Likewise, they were to teach them about the unfaithfulness and murmuring that occurred during that time, which sorely grieved and displeased the Lord. Every generation has the innate obligation and responsibility assigned to it by the Lord to pass on to the next His teaching and mighty acts among His people ("His wonderful works"). The church is ever only one generation away from becoming extinct.

The Bible states that if children are in the home, there must be a school for their spiritual instruction and training (Deuteronomy 6:7). Timothy's house had a schoolhouse. Paul said of him, "And that from a child thou hast known the holy scriptures, which are able to make thee wise unto salvation through faith which is in Christ Jesus" (2 Timothy 3:15). Timothy's mother, Eunice, and grandmother, Lois, taught him to know and love the Lord. Samuel's house was a schoolhouse. Hannah's faith and godliness were instilled in young Samuel. John and Charles Wesley's house was a schoolhouse. Their mother, Susannah, devoted several hours a week to spiritual things with each of them (alone). Someone has said, "The Methodist Church began at Susannah Wesley's knee when she rocked Charles in a cradle and held John on her lap while she patiently taught him to read, 'In the beginning God created the heaven and the earth.'"

Homes like Timothy's, Samuel's, and John and Charles Wesley's produce godly men and women who enhance the kingdom of God. Hutchins said, "Secular education is only partial education; it omits to train the moral and spiritual, the higher elements of our being."[503]

221

"Take all occasions to discourse with those about thee of divine things; not of unrevealed mysteries, or matters of doubtful disputation, but of the plain truths and laws of God, and the things that belong to our peace."[504]—Matthew Henry.

~July 15~

Psalm 78:4

The Home School Curriculum

"We will not hide them from their children, shewing to the generation to come the praises of the LORD, and his strength, and his wonderful works that he hath done" (Psalm 78:4).

What curriculum should the homeschool embrace? Expound the Word (teach doctrines, attributes of God, commandments). Teach sound biblical principles to govern all of life. Teach them right from wrong. Clarify Christian beliefs and values. Instruct them on the importance of faithfulness to the church. Instill good, noble, and honorable habits. Teach them the importance of prayer, daily devotions, and Scripture memory. Warn them about the dangers of wrong companions, dishonesty, disobedience to God, and immorality. Encourage them to witness to their friends and serve the Lord, regardless of the cost or the consequences. Teach them to love, magnify the Lord, and depend upon His mighty strength. Rehearse to them the work of God in their redemption.

Why should parents instruct their children? "That they might set their hope in God, and not forget the works of God, but keep his commandments" (Psalm 78:7). The hearing of the Word instills faith and allegiance to God and the gospel (Romans 10:17). In the absence of light, the darkness prevails (2 Corinthians 4:3–4). Note. John Locke states, "Parents wonder why the streams are bitter when they have poisoned the fountain." Spurgeon said, "When fathers are tongue-tied religiously with their offspring, need they wonder if their children's hearts remain sin-tied?"[505]

"The highest privilege and purpose as a parent is to lead the child in the way of Christ."—Max Lucado.

~July 16~

Psalm 78:9–10
Things Not to Forget

"The children of Ephraim, being armed, and carrying bows, turned back in the day of battle. They kept not the covenant of God, and refused to walk in his law" (Psalm 78:9–10).

Ephraim serves as a parable, a teachable lesson of four truths.

1. That we are prone to forgetfulness of God's works. Ephraim "forgot his works, and his wonders that he had shewed them" (Psalm 78:11)—the dividing of the Red Sea when pursued by Pharaoh's army enabling them to pass on dry land (Psalm 78:13); the pillar of fire by night and the cloud by day by which God guided their safe travel (Psalm 78:14); the water from the rocks that quenched their thirst (Psalm 78:15–16) and the manna and quail provided for their food (Psalm 78:25–29). Asaph says, "For all this they sinned still, and believed not for his wondrous works" (Psalm 78:32). They murmured, complained, and doubted God's ability to care for them despite His mighty works (Psalm 78:17, 18, 22). Note. A rich past provides a treasure of strengthening memories of God's faithfulness and trustworthiness.

2. That there are consequences for sin (Psalm 78:31). Sin is intolerable, even among the choicest of God's people. God winks at no man's sin, not even that of ministers (Psalm 78:64). Be sure your sin will find you out. God gives man space to repent before executing judgment (Psalm 78:38).

3. That hypocritical repentance is impotent (Psalm 78:36–38). The Lord hates momentary repentance, lying repentance, manipulative repentance, and heartless repentance. Acceptable repentance stems from "a broken spirit: a broken and a contrite heart" (Psalm 51:17).

223

4. That God detests hollow worship. The Lord despises outwardly observant worship that is inwardly hollow and polluted (Isaiah 1:15). Much worship is not worship.

"Sin brings judgment, and unbelief has consequences."[506]—J. M. Boice.

~July 17~

Psalm 78:14
By Day and Night

"In the daytime also he led them with a cloud, and all the night with a light of fire" (Psalm 78:14).

God led the Israelites when there was light all around and when everything was enveloped in deep darkness. They were never out of His protective custody and care for a moment. In the nighttime, when there is deep darkness and despair (whatever their cause), clutch five eternal certainties for calm and comfort.

1. God's care is undoubting. Doubt not, deny not, question not God's care for you, for it hath been documented in Scripture: "He cares for you" (1 Peter 5:7 ESV), and substantiated experientially by untold millions innumerable times.

2. God's care is unchanging. The God of the mountain (daytime when all is well) is the God of the valley (night when all is dreadful). As God cares for and maintains our cause in the day tenderly and lovingly, so does He in the night.

3. God's care is unceasing. "God's watch is an undivided one."[499] It is comprehensive, complete, and continuous. God isn't on "shift duty"; He doesn't rotate on and off, providing the custodial care summoned.

4. God's care is untiring. Unwearyingly and patiently, God manifests loving care. Friends and family wearied by our nighttime episodes gradually faint and fade away—but not God. Unrelentingly ("shall neither slumber nor sleep"—Psalm 121:4), He holds our

hand, cools our fevered brow, and calms our disturbed soul throughout the night.

5. God's care is unfailing. It is efficacious. The Bible says, "The LORD *shall* preserve thee from all evil: he *shall* preserve thy soul" (Psalm 121:7). God's lovingkindness and tender mercies always provide the medication (grace) necessary to enable us to make it through the night. "We never can enjoy any real repose of soul unless it is in the consciousness that God is near us, above us, manifesting Himself for us. A watchful and a watching God is the believer's warrant for repose (rest, peace); we repose beneath when we are sure that He watches above."[507]

"Can you trust Him for your soul and not for your body? He has never refused to bear your burdens; He has never fainted under their weight. Come, then, soul! have done with fretful care and leave all thy concerns in the hand of a gracious God."[508]—C. H. Spurgeon.

~July 18~

Psalm 78:19
A Can-Do God

"They said, Can God furnish a table in the wilderness?" (Psalm 78:19).

Amidst hardships, the Israelites in the wilderness murmured, asking a foolish question: "Can God?" Ludicrous, I say, because God had already proven that He could during the Exodus. He had delivered them from the plagues, Pharaoh and his army, the mighty waters of the Red Sea, thirst (water from the rock and pure water at Marah), hunger (manna and quail), and led them by the cloud by day and pillar of fire by night (Psalm 78:12–16). Yet despite these miraculous deeds, unbelief in God's ability to provide "a table in the wilderness" (Psalm 78:19) was expressed.

The saint who trusts God need not question the ability and readiness of God to intervene in times of trouble or sorrow.

Spurgeon states, "To question the ability of one who is manifestly Almighty is to speak against Him."[293] To the question, "Can God?" the saint readily responds, "Yes, God can!"

The curious servants of Hezekiah perhaps asked about the possibility of his recovery, "Can God?" Before Isaiah was hardly out the door, it was thundered, "God can" (2 Kings 20:1–5). When the three Hebrew children were cast into the fiery furnace, Nebuchadnezzar and soldiers alike asked, "Can God?" When they witnessed the fourth man in the fire and all walking around unharmed, they answered, "God can" (Daniel 3:25). When Daniel was put into a den of lions, Darius asked, "Can God?" Early the following day, he learned, "God can." When the widow of Zarephath and her son were famished with hunger, she asked, "Can God?" Long afterward, the miraculous jar of oil and flour continued to meet the need. She discovered "God can" (1 Kings 17:7–16). Our God is a God who *can!*

"Those that set bounds to God's power speak against him."[294]— Matthew Henry.

~July 19~

Psalm 78:25
Angel's Food

"Man did eat angels' food: he sent them meat to the full" (Psalm 78:25).

Manna tasted like wafers made with honey (Exodus 16:31) and was provided to the Israelites during their forty years in the wilderness. It serves as a fitting emblem of Christ, the bread of life.

1. The manna was divinely given. It was supernatural. Jesus, the bread of life, was sent by God to save man from his sins.

2. The manna was saving and sustaining. It prevented their perishing in the wilderness. Jesus, the bread of life, prevents man's eternal perishing in Hell.

3. The manna was freely given. Every day except the sabbath, manna freely covered the land like a morning frost until the people entered Canaan. Jesus freely gave himself to the death at Calvary to save sinners (John 10:18).

4. The manna was equally accessible. The young and old alike found the manna easy to get. The manna (salvation) God affords in Jesus is available and reachable to the worst of sinners.

5. The manna was suitable for all. None benefited more than another from it. Christ promises eternal life and abundant life to all who trust Him without exception (John 10:10). Spurgeon said, "The multiplicity of His elect does not divide the loaf of His affection. He has an infinite affection for each one, and He will take care of the details of each chosen life."[509]

6. The manna had to be partaken. Its benefit was in its consumption, not admiration. Christ is sufficient for salvation to all, but only to those who partake of the salvation He provides. Jesus says to many, "And ye will not come to me, that ye might have life" (John 5:40). Note. The manna had to be gathered early in the morning. Christ should be sought early in life.[510]

"Christ is given for the life of the world; none are excluded from the benefit of this bread, but such as exclude themselves."[511]— Matthew Henry.

~July 20~

Psalm 78:36
Flattering God

"Nevertheless they did flatter him with their mouth, and they lied unto him with their tongues" (Psalm 78:36).

Israel, when judged for their sin, sought to flatter God with hollow words to win back His favor. It was all pretentious and deplored by God. How do we flatter God?

1. With praise without heart. To sing songs and lift the hands in worship without sincerity of heart. "This people draweth nigh unto me with their mouth, and honoureth me with their lips; but their heart is far from me" (Matthew 15:8).

2. With promise without honesty. To promise God that which is never intended to be done like Israel (Psalm 78:36).

3. With prayer without humility. To repent without truthfulness and brokenness of heart is a mere show and manipulative ploy hoping to avert God's judgment (Psalm 78:34–37).

"Hypocrites are those that only make a lip-labor of religion and religious worship. In word and tongue, the worst hypocrites may do as well as the best saints, and speak as fair with Jacob's voice."[512]—Matthew Henry.

~July 21~

Psalm 78:41
Limiting God

"Yea, they turned back and tempted God, and limited the Holy One of Israel" (Psalm 78:41).

To limit God is to impede, interfere with, or confine His work and purposes.

1. The Holy One of Israel is limited by distrust. "Yea, they spake against God; they said, Can God furnish a table in the wilderness?" (Psalm 78:19). To doubt God's ability to forgive your darkest sin, deliver from the sorest trial, and grant guidance in the blinding storm is to judge His might as finite, and insufficient limiting His help. "And because of their unbelief, he couldn't do any miracles among them except to place his hands on a few sick people and heal them. And he was amazed at their unbelief" (Mark 6:5–6 NLT).

2. The Holy One of Israel is limited by disobedience. "They… refused to walk in His law" (Psalm 78:10). Sin blocks blessing. God sought to bless the Israelites, but their stubbornness to sin interfered.

The church at Laodicea limited the Lord's work in her midst (Revelation 3:20).

3. The Holy One of Israel is limited by demands. "They murmured and complained, demanding other food than God was giving them" (Psalm 78:18 TLB). Israel's insistence on their want subverted God's purpose for their best good. Spurgeon said, "Shall mortal dare to dictate to his Creator? Shall it be possible that man shall lay down his commands and expect the King of Heaven to pay homage to his arrogance?"[513] It is always in man's best interest to say to God, "Not my will, but Thine be done."

4. The Holy One of Israel is limited by dissent. "But turned back, and dealt unfaithfully like their fathers: they were turned aside like a deceitful bow" (Psalm 78:57). We limit God by frowning at the manna and demanding the quail—dissatisfaction with the manner of His blessing and its measure.

"Beware in your prayers, above everything else, of limiting God, not only by unbelief but by fancying that you know what He can do. Expect unexpected things."—Andrew Murray.

~July 22~

Psalm 79:8
Nail Holes

"O remember not against us former iniquities: let thy tender mercies speedily prevent us: for we are brought very low" (Psalm 79:8).

Asaph asks God not to punish Israel for the Pre-exilic sins of their ancestors (Exodus 20:5). The text suggests a personal application.

Though it is proper to ask God not to remember our sins, their memory is invaluable. A father who took his son into the garage and drove a nail into the wall dramatized this truth. He said, "Son, pull the nail out with this hammer." Using the claw end of the hammer, the boy extracted the nail. The father said, "Now, pull out the nail hole."

1. Nail holes are reminders of what we would have become if it were not for grace. Paul, upon cataloging several forms of sin, stated, "And such were some of you: but ye are washed, but ye are sanctified, but ye are justified in the name of the Lord Jesus, and by the Spirit of our God" (1 Corinthians 6:11). With Bradford, every redeemed soul may say upon looking at the wicked, "There but for the grace of God go I."

2. Nail holes reveal weaknesses and vulnerabilities in the wall. Susceptibility to the sin that made the hole forever exists. The emancipated drunk, drug addict, gambler, pornographer, etc., have their former sin ever couched at their door. Once a sin pierces the armor, the occasion for it intensifies.

3. Nail holes serve as a preventative against sin. The memory of old sins and their consequence is humbling and self-abasing, prompting cautionary conduct lest they be committed again.

4. Nail holes are not intended to be taunting. Though buried in the grave, old sins can taunt and bring despair. Make sure they have been placed under the covering of the blood of Christ for pardon (1 John 1:7) and then declare them forever erased. Refuse to allow skeletons of yesterday to harm and wreak havoc on life.

"Sin leaves a permanently weak place in the wall, and we will forevermore have to fight a particularly difficult battle at that point."[514]—Ray Steadman.

~July 23~

Psalm 79:10
A Theological Error

"Wherefore should the heathen say, Where is their God?" (Psalm 79:10).

Jerusalem had been conquered by the Babylonians. The Temple and city were savagely destroyed (Psalm 79:1), bodies were strewn in the streets left unburied (Psalm 79:2–3), and the sacred city had been defiled by heathens with their sacrilegious acts (Psalm 79:1). Psalm 137 depicts the people's woeful and despondent estate. Asaph, on behalf of the people, cries out to God for rescue, restoration (Psalm 79:8–9; 11), and vindication (Psalm 79:6–7; 12) based in part on the flawed theology of the wicked who thought God would not allow His people to suffer oppression and persecution at the hands of another (Psalm 79:10).[515]

God does allow bad things to happen to His people (Matthew 5:45). Why does He do this? To put their faith and allegiance to Him to the test. To prove their unwavering trust in and love to God. To mature the saint, develop their spiritual muscles, and purify their heart more toward the Lord. Sometimes, bad things happen to God's children for the advancement of His cause and the expansion of His kingdom. Sometimes, bad things happen to them to put on display God's loving care and power to sustain His own in the darkest of nights and deepest of trials. And, sometimes, God says of the bad and sad that occurs, "Will disclose the reason later." Until then, we trust His heart and live by His promise that "all things work together for good to them that love God, to them who are the called according to his purpose" (Romans 8:28).

"It is in cleaving by faith [to Christ] in the deep waters, and in climbing the difficult ascent, we reach the firmest footing, and the highest, brightest, holiest elevation in our Christianity—the complete absorption of our will in God's will."[516]—Octavius Winslow.

~July 24~

Psalm 80:1
Shepherd, Savior, and Vine

"Give ear, O Shepherd of Israel, thou that leadest Joseph like a flock; thou that dwellest between the cherubims, shine forth." (Psalm 80:1).

Asaph prays using three titles of God—Shepherd, Savior, and Vine which bolster confidence that God will hear and answer.

As sheep of His pasture (Psalm 80:1), heirs of His salvation (Psalm 80:3), and branches in His Vine (Psalm 80:14–15), the child of God is promised and assured of help in the hour of need.

As Shepherd, He is our constant guide and companion, granting safety and security from all harm. As Savior, He is our rescuer, deliverer, and restorer from the power and penalty of sin. As the True Vine, He is the source of our spiritual vitality, strength, victory over sin, nourishment, and fruitfulness.

"This testimony doth confess both Christ and the vineyard; that is, Head and Body, King and people, Shepherd and flock, and the entire mystery of all Scriptures, Christ and the Church."[517]—Augustine.

~July 25~

Psalm 80:18
The Quickening to Salvation

"Quicken us, and we will call upon thy name" (Psalm 80:18).

The rebellious turn from God to sin. The Adamic nature's bent is toward sin, not God. The Bible states, "As it is written: 'There is no one righteous, not even one; there is no one who understands; there is no one who seeks God'" (Romans 3:10–11 NIV).

The rebellious must turn to God from sin. It was said about the Thessalonians that they "turned to God from idols to serve the living and true God" (1 Thessalonians 1:9). Salvation hinges on the sinner's turnabout from sin, a miraculous change that God brings about. The Lord can turn the sinner's heart to Him when it is turned to sin. Scarborough says, "God holds the reins that guide souls to Him." Thus, Asaph prays, "Turn us again, O God, and cause thy face to shine; and we shall be saved" (Psalm 80:3).

A person turns to God when struck with His holy, majestic, and powerful presence and is crushed with a sense of spiritual need. Both of these are quickened by the Holy Spirit through various channels (John 16:8). If the Holy Spirit does not persuade a man to turn to God because of the gospel's truthfulness, the biblical record, spiritual need, and future judgment, nothing else can. Jesus said, "No man can come to me, except the Father which hath sent me draw him" (John 6:44).

"No conversion to God but by His grace."[518]—Matthew Henry.

~July 26~

Psalm 81:10
Open Thy Mouth Wide

"Open thy mouth wide, and I will fill it" (Psalm 81:10).

To open thy mouth wide in prayer is to ask great things of God fearlessly and confidently. Just ask God, "Open thy mouth wide," thrust open thy widows toward Heaven, and He will do more than requested or thought possible. Solomon asked for wisdom. But God gave him more. He not only made him the wisest of all men but also gave him "riches, and honor" (1 Kings 3:13). The prodigal son asked to be treated as a hired servant (Luke 15:19), but God gave him more. He was treated as royalty (Luke 15:22). Jacob prayed for food, clothing, and safety at home in Bethel. But God gave him more. Not only did God do as he asked, but He profoundly blessed him (Genesis 33:5–11).

Whatever the need or care, ask God. He can do above all that we ask or think (Ephesians 3:20). Packages of all sizes of answered prayers await delivery at your asking. And though asking is a simple thing to do, it must be done to receive ("For everyone that asketh receiveth"—Matthew 7:8). Ravenhill shares, "The law of prayer is the law of the harvest: sow sparingly in prayer, reap sparingly; sow bountifully in prayer, reap bountifully."[519] The storehouse of Heaven is filled with inexhaustible treasures. Open thy mouth wide and hesitate not to ask for them.

"The hound [saint] that hath a sure trail [numerous answered prayers] runs with confidence, while his doubting companion stands baying aloft in disappointed perplexity."[520]—James McConkey.

~July 27~

Psalm 81:13–16
The What Might Have Been

"Oh that my people had hearkened unto me, and Israel had walked in my ways! I should soon have subdued their enemies, and turned my hand against their adversaries. The haters of the LORD *should have submitted themselves unto him: but their time should have endured for ever. He should have fed them also with the finest of the wheat: and with honey out of the rock should I have satisfied thee"* (Psalm 81:13–16).

God reminisces over what might have been for Israel had they only hearkened unto His voice. In obeying God, Israel would have experienced victory rather than defeat (Psalm 81:14), plenty instead of little (Psalm 81:16), and the best instead of the worst (Psalm 81:16). The lesson. Rebellion against God causes the forfeiture of blessings that were intended but withdrawn. A holy walk will prevent the sadness and sorrow of *what might have been.*

"For of all sad words of tongue or pen, the saddest are these: 'It might have been.'"[521]—John Greenleaf Whittier.

~July 28~

Psalm 82:1–2
The Judge's Prayer

"God standeth in the congregation of the mighty; he judgeth among the gods. How long will ye judge unjustly, and accept the persons of the wicked? Selah" (Psalm 82:1–2).

Judges serve as God's representatives to govern without partiality or favoritism in full consideration of all the facts with judicial prudence (Psalm 82:3). The august title of "gods" is applied to them. Namely because, to them, "the word of God came."[522] And by that Word, they are discharging their duties honorably and legally. Such judgeship ensures equality and fairness for all verdicts rendered and deters societal corruption.

Asaph reminds corrupt judges that though in a position of honor and prestige, they are not "the untouchables," God will strike them with swift and severe punishment (Psalm 82:7). Judges must remember, above all else that theirs is a sacred office that is to be governed by the Holy and Just God. They must honorably fulfill their divine charge: "Take heed what ye do: for ye judge not for man, but for the LORD, who is with you in the judgment" (2 Chronicles 19:6).

A judge who besmirches his office and duty will have his "robe plucked off his shoulders."[523] Calvin says, "The dignity, with which judges are invested, can form no excuse or plea, why they should escape the punishment which their wickedness deserves."[524]

"May the Almighty grant that the cause of truth, justice, and humanity shall in no wise suffer at my hands."[525]—Abraham Lincoln (The Judge's Prayer).

~July 29~
Psalm 83:1
The Silences of God

"Keep not thou silence, O God: hold not thy peace, and be not still, O God" (Psalm 83:1).

Threatened with extermination by a mighty coalition of armies, Asaph, on behalf of Israel, begs God not to remain silent but intervene victoriously in their behalf. Note seven truths about the silences of God.

1. In the silence of God, there are unknown divine intentions and designs at play.

2. God's silence doesn't mean He is unconcerned or is failing to answer our cries for help. Spurgeon says, "Thy prayers are all filed in Heaven, and if not immediately answered, they are certainly not forgotten, but in a little while shall be fulfilled to thy delight and satisfaction."[526]

3. Others often misunderstand the silence of God to us. Job's friends shared several reasons for his great adversity and sorrow. But they were all wrong.

4. The reason for the silences of God will be manifest, so patiently wait. Good always comes when Christ delays to intervene. When Jesus called Lazarus to "come forth" out of the tomb, the reason for His silence to Mary and Martha became manifest.

5. The silences of God seem to last longer than they do. Heaven's clock differs from ours. A thousand years with Christ are as a day and a day as a thousand years. Matthew Henry states, "Cast not away your confidence because God defers His performances. That which does not come in your time will be hastened in His time, which is always the more convenient season. God will work when He pleases, how He pleases, and by what means He pleases. He is not bound to keep our time, but He will perform His word, honor our faith, and reward them that diligently seek Him."[527]

6. The silences of God, at times, happen to test the measure of man's faith.

7. The silences of God in our life may be for a witness of sustaining grace to onlookers.

"He may delay because it would not be safe to give us at once what we ask: we are not ready for it."—George McDonald.

~July 30~

Psalm 83:1

Response to the Silences of God

"Keep not thou silence, O God: hold not thy peace, and be not still, O God" (Psalm 83:1).

David prayed, "Unto thee will I cry, O LORD my rock; be not silent to me: lest, if thou be silent to me, I become like them that go down into the pit" (Psalm 28:1). How do you respond to the silences of God? You keep trusting Him as your rock of refuge and salvation.

1. You don't doubt in the night what you believe in the light.

2. You keep praying. Pray for a breakthrough. Spurgeon says, "When God seems to close His ear, we must not, therefore, close our mouths, but rather cry with more earnestness; for when our note grows shrill with eagerness and grief, He will not long deny us a hearing."[528]

3. You keep patiently waiting. Chambers says, "One of the greatest strains in life is the strain of waiting for God." God will speak at the right time.

4. You remove the earplugs. Randy Alcorn remarks, "What we call God's silence may actually be our inability, or in some cases (certainly not all) our unwillingness, to hear him."[529]

"Believers who are maturing not only respect God's silence, they model it as well. So we must wait patiently, in the silence, for the Lord to step in...in His time and way."[530]—Chuck Swindoll.

~July 31~

Psalm 84:2

To Envy the Birds

"My soul longeth, yea, even fainteth for the courts of the LORD: my heart and my flesh crieth out for the living God" (Psalm 84:2).

Although unknown, the writer may be David, as the text describes his longing for the house of God in Jerusalem, which he was forced to abandon due to being pursued by King Saul, or during Absalom's rebellion.

The psalmist envied the sparrows and swallows nested in God's house for four reasons.

1. Their access to God's house. David longed to come and go freely to God's house as they did.

2. Their accommodation in God's house. They could nest in palaces but chose to do so near the altars of God. Of all places David could be, He longed to abide with the birds in the presence of God in His house.

3. Their association with God's house. The birds dwelt near the worshippers and priests and fed on crumbs they dropped in the court of the Lord. David longed for the same. The saint loves the courts of the Lord and longs for each opportunity to enter her gates. Why? There, sweet fellowship is experienced, biblical truth is expounded, wickedness is exposed, the soul is fed, but most importantly, Christ is present and worshipped. To David, spending a day in God's house was "better than a thousand" elsewhere. Barnes says, "I should find more happiness, more true joy, in one day spent in the house of God, in His worship, in the exercises of true religion than I could in a thousand days spent in any other manner."[531]

4. Their aegis in God's house. David longed to know the peace, calm, and security of the birds sheltered and nestled in God's house despite the storms that assailed.

David envied the doorkeeper, also. He said, "I had rather be a doorkeeper in the house of my God" (Psalm 84:10). A doorkeeper managed entry to God's house. They opened and closed its doors, governed its entrance (prevented unlawful entry by the unclean disrupters and attackers), and informed the people where to go and what to do in worship.[532] Church greeters perform a similar essential duty. Here's David's point: Whatever else I might do, the most menial job in God's house exceeds its splendor, happiness, and honor. The least afforded in God's house always exceeds the more provided elsewhere.

"David says not, 'Oh how I long for my palace, my crown, my scepter, my kingdom'; but, 'Oh how I long to return to the house of God!'"[533]—C. H. Spurgeon.

~August 1~

Psalm 84:5–7
Weakness Changed to Strength

"Blessed is the man whose strength is in thee; in whose heart are the ways of them. Who passing through the valley of Baca make it a well....They go from strength to strength, every one of them in Zion appeareth before God" (Psalm 84:5–7).

The valley of Baca, the dry, parched, arid, sun-burnt terrain on the route to Jerusalem (Zion), demanded divine help for the Israelites to endure and survive. Much there is on the highway to heavenly Zion that draws tears from the believer's eyes, requiring divine strength to navigate and sustain. The believer who trusts the arm of flesh to uphold him will falter in despair and misery—a lesson many learn the hard way.

By what means do believers discover their frailty and feebleness to find all-sufficient strength in God? The psalmist said, "He weakened my strength in the way" (Psalm 102:23). Ultimately, it is seen through defeat and despair in battling temptation, coping with trials, hardships, and persecution, and overcoming sorrow and grief. Our impotence and inability to conquer these afflictions and adversities reveal the utter weakness of the flesh and the need for supernatural strength and power.

Weakness to resolve life's trials and troubles is a tool in and of itself that God uses to crush dependence on self to compel trust in Him alone. Billy Graham said, "When we come to the end of ourselves, we come to the beginning of God."[534] "Blessed is the man whose strength is in THEE" (Psalm 84:5). In Him is found "Comfort under trial, blessing through trial, hope beyond trial."[535]

"So far from being wearied, believers gather strength as they proceed. Each individual becomes happier; each holy song, more sweet and full."[536]—C. H. Spurgeon.

~August 2~

Psalm 85:6-7
Heart-cry for Revival

"Wilt thou not revive us again: that thy people may rejoice in thee? Shew us thy mercy, O LORD, and grant us thy salvation" (Psalm 85:6–7).

The psalmist prays for a heartfelt revival for Israel.

Revival's cause. Israel was backslidden. Spiritual declension brings the need for revival. Packer says, "Revival is the visitation of God, which brings to life Christians who have been sleeping and restores a deep sense of God's near presence and holiness." While praying, John Wesley, Whitfield, and some friends experienced such an awakening on New Year's Eve, 1739. Wesley wrote: "About three in the morning, as we were continuing instant in prayer, the power of God came mightily upon us, insomuch that many cried out for exceeding joy, and many fell to the ground. As soon as we recovered a little from the awe and amazement at the presence of His Majesty, we broke out with one voice, 'We praise Thee, O God, we acknowledge Thee to be the Lord.'"[537]

Revival's conditions.

1. Contrition. Israel was remorseful. Godly sorrow and brokenness over sin prompt the heart-cry for revival. "Wilt thou not revive us again?"

2. Confession and repentance. Israel prayed, "Show us thy mercy....Turn us, O God." Revival is conditional upon the saint confessing and repenting of sin (2 Chronicles 7:14).

Revival's consequence. Israel was healed and restored (Psalm 85:8). All who return to God in brokenness over sin with repentance will be revived with rekindled love for God, His Word, work, the unsaved, and the church (Luke 15:22–24).

In the Ulster Revival (Ireland), 1859, a minister wrote: "The difficulty used to be to get the people into the church, but the difficulty now is to get them out."[538] Everything, including the theatre, in the Ulster Revival was eclipsed with the words, "What's the News?" W. Hind Smith, upon visiting Ulster at the time, recalled those words' extraordinary popularity: "Wherever I went, I heard 'What's the News?' Everybody, it seemed, sang it. If you purchased a railway ticket, you would hear the booking clerk singing, 'The Savior died on Calvary, That's the news, that's the news.' Or if you asked a policeman the way, you would hear him commence, after he had directed you, as he continued upon his beat, 'His work's reviving all around; that's the news!'" The revival spread throughout the United Kingdom, resulting in 100,000 conversions. Send such a revival again, dear Lord, and let it begin in me.

"Revival is a divinely initiated work in which God's people pray, repent of their sin, and return to a holy, Spirit-filled, obedient, love relationship with God."—Henry Blackaby.

~August 3~

Psalm 86:5

Forgiveness

"For thou, Lord, art good, and ready to forgive; and plenteous in mercy unto all them that call upon thee" (Psalm 86:5).

"For thou, Lord, art good." As Spurgeon wrote, the thrust of this Psalm of David is that God is "good at giving and forgiving, supplying us with His good, and removing our evil."[539] That incomprehensible goodness is the motivation to look to Him for forgiveness.

"Unto all them." Faber (1862) wrote, "There's a wideness in God's mercy, like the wideness of the sea." And that wideness includes you and me.

"Plenteous in mercy." The lovingkindness of God is inexhaustible. Spurgeon says, "God does not dispense His mercy from a store so impoverished as to give out altogether, but His goodness flows abundantly."[540]

"Ready to forgive." God's mercy to forgive is immediately available and not difficult to receive. Simeon says, "He is far more 'ready to forgive,' than they are to ask forgiveness; and will multiply His pardons beyond all the multitude of their offenses."[541]

"That call upon thee." Forgiveness, though plenteous, available, and free, must be requested. "If we confess our sins, he is faithful and just to forgive us our sins, and to cleanse us from all unrighteousness" (1 John 1:9). The only sin God will not forgive is the one unconfessed.

"He is a sin-pardoning God; not only He can forgive, but He is ready to forgive, more ready to forgive than we are to repent."[542]—Matthew Henry.

~August 4~

Psalm 86:7
What to Do in Time of Trouble

"In the day of my trouble I will call upon thee: for thou wilt answer me....Because thou, LORD, hast holpen me, and comforted me" (Psalm 86:7, 17).

The specific "trouble" to which David refers is not directly stated. He faced multiplied troubles before and after becoming King of Israel.

Trouble is a part of life that all experience. R. G. Lee said, "Trouble is one word in every man's dictionary. No bars or bolts or doors can keep trouble out or away. But let us thank God for the balm He gives to troubled hearts, for the comfort and gladness He brings to those who are in grief."[543] What are we to do in the time of trouble?

Call on the Lord. "I will call upon thee." Prayer should be the first recourse in a crisis. Spurgeon says, "There is an end to a man when he makes an end to prayer. It is hard to pray when the very heart is drowning, yet gracious men plead best at such times."[544]

For thou wilt answer me. Confidently, we bring our troubles to God, knowing He will hear and speedily answer. "A prayer," writes Spurgeon, "should be the presentation of God's promise endorsed by your personal faith. We expect our God to answer our prayer all the more surely when we are in trouble. David so expected."[545]

For You, O Lord, have helped me and comforted me. David's plea (argument) for help and comfort was based on God's help in the past. Boice says, "David buttresses his prayers with sound arguments."[546] In prayer, argue for the help of God based on His promises, lovingkindness and mercy, the help provided in former days of trouble, and the glory it will bring to His name (Psalm 115:1).

"Show me evidence of Your favor. Then those who hate me will see it and be ashamed" (Psalm 86:17 NET). David asks God to answer his prayer in a manner that will cause the ungodly to know that His hand helped him. May answers to our prayers magnify the goodness of God unto the lost, bringing them to salvation

"Prayer is not flight; prayer is power. Prayer does not deliver a man from some terrible situation; prayer enables a man to face and to master the situation."—William Barclay.

~August 5~

Psalm 87:3
The City of God
Part 1

"Glorious things are spoken of thee, O city of God" (Psalm 87:3).

What is said of the magnificent city of God in the Scripture?

1. It's a place of purity. Scripture states, "Nothing unclean shall enter [heaven], nor anyone who practices abomination or falsehood, but only those who are written in the Lamb's book of life" (Revelation 21:27 RSV). Heaven is a holy city. Its inhabitants wear white robes to symbolize their faultlessness through Christ Jesus (Revelation 6:11; Jude 24). "They…have washed their robes, and made them white in the blood of the Lamb" (Revelation 7:14).

Note. Heaven is the throne room of God and glistens with perfection. Man's adamic nature (sinful) is wholly destroyed upon entering Heaven, giving place to the dominion of the new nature (righteousness, holiness, purity) in Christ Jesus. Thus, Heaven is void of any trace of sin, temptation, or inclination to sin. God will not judge sin anymore since it does not exist in His holy house. [547] "No wish, no desire, no hunger towards that which is unclean shall ever be found in the perfect city of God. Nor even thought of evil can be conceived there, much less a sinful act performed." [548]

2. It's a place of peace. "What Heaven holds is no more a reason for rejoicing than what it lacks." [549] Saints in Heaven are healthy and happy, free from the grip of pain, sorrow, sickness, suffering, and the hostility known on earth (Revelation 21:4). The unpleasant and painful things of this life are vanquished (Revelation 22:3). They know rest and possess tranquility. "The voice of weeping shall no longer be heard in her" (Isaiah 65:19 MEV).

Though the text is prophetic regarding the Millennial reign of Christ, it certainly pictures Heaven, where all tears shall be wiped away (Revelation 21:4). Joy floods the city of God. David said, "In Your presence is fullness of joy; At Your right hand are pleasures forevermore" (Psalm 16:11 NKJV).

3. It's a place of plenty. In Heaven, saints drink from the inexhaustible fountain of the riches of God's bountiful blessings. Whatever the need, sufficient is its provision.

"There is no panic in Heaven! God has no problems, only plans."— Corrie Ten Boom.

~August 6~
Psalm 87:3
The City of God
Part 2

"Glorious things are spoken of thee, O city of God" (Psalm 87:3).

What is said of the magnificent city of God in the Scripture? Yesterday, three characteristics of the City of God were shared. Today, two more are considered.

1. It's a place of privilege. So, what will we do in Heaven? Criswell says, "We shall not be passive spectators, just observing, but an active, vital part of the whole recreated kingdom of God."[550]

Saints will serve in Heaven (Revelation 7:15). "There'll be no idleness in Heaven. We will serve Him with perfect joy and happiness."[551] This service implies judging and ruling the world with God (Luke 19:17–19). Here, we serve Him with frailty, there without limitation or imperfection.

Saints will sing in Heaven (Revelation 5:9). The song of the redeemed in Heaven is: "Worthy is the Lamb that was slain to receive power, and riches, and wisdom, and strength, and honor, and glory, and blessing" (Revelation 5:12). Heaven is a place of endless adoration (worship) of the Lord. The unending praise is fueled by the bountiful mercy of God that makes Heaven possible for the saint.

Saints will shout in Heaven. In his vision of Heaven, John said, "Then I heard again what sounded like the shouting of a huge crowd, or like the waves of a hundred oceans crashing on the shore, or like the mighty rolling of great thunder, 'Praise the Lord. For the Lord our God, the Almighty, reigns'" (Revelation 19:6 TLB).

Saints will socialize in Heaven. Friends of the Earth will be friends in Heaven. But also think of the fellowship afforded to all the saints of all ages, including the disciples, evangelists, missionaries, and pastors.

2. It's a place of permanence. Heaven is eternally durable and permanent. Heaven is "a building of God, an house not made with

hands, eternal in the heavens" (2 Corinthians 5:1); "an inheritance incorruptible, and undefiled, and that fadeth not away" (1 Peter 1:4). "We don't have a permanent city here, but rather we are looking for the city that is still to come" (Hebrews 13:14 CEB).

"We talk about Heaven being so far away. It is within speaking distance of those who belong there. Heaven is a prepared place for a prepared people."—D. L. Moody.

~August 7~

Psalm 88:6
The Gloomiest Psalm

"Thou hast laid me in the lowest pit, in darkness, in the deeps" (Psalm 88:6).

Heman's prayer, the gloomiest and saddest of the Psalms, expresses what it is to experience the dark night of the soul without resolution. The cause of the melancholy, perhaps, was a loathsome illness. As with Paul's thorn in the flesh, its identity is probably concealed, so all who are in difficulty may parallel it to their own.[552] Whatever the trouble, its severity caused him to feel that

1. God had abandoned him, and His anger, like ocean "waves," beat upon him continuously (Psalm 88:5; 7).

2. Friends and acquaintances had deserted him (Psalm 88:8).

3. That he was hopelessly entrapped without a way out ("I am shut up, and I cannot come forth"—Psalm 88:8).

Several lessons emerge.

1. None are exempt from severe trials. Heman, though righteous (1 Chronicles 25:5), suffered severely. Troubles come to all, regardless of spiritual estate.

2. Some trouble may be traced to the wrath of God (Hebrews 12:6). Says Pink, "Chastisement is designed for our good, to promote

our highest interests. Look beyond the rod to the All-wise hand that wields it!" Gurnall said, "God's wounds cure; sin's kisses kill."

3. Keep the right theological view in hardship. Heman was wrong to think God abandoned him (Psalm 88:5). He was mistaken to believe that death was a state of hopelessness, that it was a pit out of which no man escapes (Psalm 88:5). He was wrong to think God shut His ear to his prayers for help (Psalm 88:2). Errant belief misinterprets circumstances and increases the distress.

4. Don't give up on prayer (Psalm 88:9). Spurgeon says, "His distress had not blown out the sparks of his prayer, but quickened them till they burned perpetually like a furnace at full blast."[553]

5. Unrelieved suffering may have to be borne. The psalmist's prayer ends like it began, in gloom and despair. Kidner said, "It's witness to the possibility of unrelieved suffering as a believer's lot. The happy ending of most Psalms of this kind is seen to be a bonus, not a due."[554]

"Instead of complaining at his lot, a contented man is thankful that his condition and circumstances are no worse than they are. Instead of greedily desiring something more than the supply of his present need, he rejoices that God still cares for him. Such a one is 'content' with such as he has."—A. W. Pink.

~August 8~

Psalm 89:21
Precious Lord, Hold My Hand

"I will steady him with my hand; with my powerful arm I will make him strong" (Psalm 89:21 NLT).

The Sovereign God of all creation says to His children, 'I will hold thy hand.' The grasp of His hand conveys His loving care, willingness, and ableness to help. Knowing that Jesus clutches your hand imparts several benefits.

1. It brings calm in calamity. A little boy, about to undergo surgery, was asked if he could bear it. The boy replied, "Yes, if my father will hold my hand." Saints can bear up to and endure more than imagined with the Heavenly Father holding their hand.

2. It brings strength and courage in conflict. Matthew Henry says, "No good work can miscarry in the hand of those whom God Himself undertakes to strengthen."[555]

3. It brings direction in distress. We don't have to know the next step if our hand is clasped in God's hand; He is in control, guiding every footstep (Psalm 37:23).

4. It brings perseverance in pain. His hand clutching our hand infuses new grace to endure the severest trial. Tim Keller said, "Suffering is unbearable if you aren't certain that God is for you and with you."

5. It brings comfort in grief. "He healeth the broken in heart, and bindeth up their wounds" (Psalm 147:3).

6. It brings calm in death. The clasped hand of God will be our comfort, peace, and courage in crossing chilly Jordan into sweet Canaan Land. "I won't have to cross Jordan alone."

"Storms may be howling and blowing, but Jesus is holding my hand."—Alfred Barrett.

~August 9~

Psalm 89:15–16
We Have Heard the Joyful Sound

"Blessed is the people that know the joyful sound: they shall walk, O LORD, in the light of thy countenance. In thy name shall they rejoice all the day: and in thy righteousness shall they be exalted" (Psalm 89:15–16).

Ethan, the Ezrahite, pens the psalm probably during the Exile. Six things are stated about people who hear the joyful sound, the word of deliverance of the Lord.

1. They receive the message of salvation by faith and repentance. "The people that know."

2. They govern their life by God's Word and counsel. "They shall walk."

3. They are happy people. "In Thy name shall they rejoice all the day." Matthew Henry asserts, "Those that rejoice in Christ Jesus, and make God their exceeding joy, have enough to counterbalance their grievances and silence their griefs; therefore, their joy is full and constant; it is their duty to rejoice evermore."[556]

4. They are an exalted people. "In Thy righteousness shall they be exalted." They become sons of God. "Behold, what manner of love the Father hath bestowed upon us, that we should be called the sons of God" (1 John 3:1). Their garments are changed from rags to riches and filthiness to righteousness (2 Corinthians 5:17). They are lifted from eternal doom and torment to everlasting life and delight (John 10:28).

5. They are divinely favored. "In thy favor [which through Christ we hope for] our horn shall be exalted." Chambers said, "Grace is the overflowing favor of God, and you can always count on it being available to draw upon as needed."

6. They are shielded from harm. "The LORD is our defense." He will be our refuge and strong tower in times of trouble.

"They [the redeemed] not only enjoy His benefits but also confiding in His favor, they pass the whole course of their life in mental peace and tranquility."[557]—John Calvin.

~August 10~

Psalm 89:48

The Step of Death

"What man is he that liveth, and shall not see death? Shall he deliver his soul from the hand of the grave?" (Psalm 89:48).

The psalm details the promise made to David of the perpetuity of his throne. With calamities and even death threatening the promise's fulfillment, the psalmist pleads for the promise to be soon fulfilled.

Death is a sure step. "It is appointed unto men once to die." Yet, Young says, "All men think all men are mortal but themselves." Does not knowing how you live indicate the truth of the statement? An end is coming. Billy Graham states, "All mankind is sitting on Death Row."[558]

Life, the Bible states, is like a mere "handbreadth" in duration (Psalm 39:5), the measurement of four fingers, "one of the smallest measures in the Hebrew system of measuring." It passes as quickly "as a tale that is told" (Psalm 90:9). The hands on the wall clock or the watch, the display on the cell phone, the passing of one day to the next, the throb of the heart, the sudden death of others, and the growing decay of the body all are testament to life's frailty and brevity.

Death is a separating step. At death, the wheat is separated from the tare (Matthew 13:30), the sheep from the goat (Matthew 25:31–33), and the twain shall never meet again. The rich man in Hell was separated from Lazarus and the redeemed in Heaven by a great, uncrossable divide (Luke 16:26).

Death is a sudden step. "There is but a step between me and death" (1 Samuel 20:3). A step is taken in mere seconds, and death is said to be a step. The life of the strongest and healthiest may snap at any moment, just like that of the weakest and sickest. Unknown to us, the words may be surprisingly said to us as to the rich fool, "this night thy soul shall be required of thee" (Luke 12:20).

Death is a sentencing step. Saith Spurgeon, "What I am when death is held before me, that I must be forever. When my spirit departs, if God finds me hymning His praise, I shall hymn it in Heaven; if He finds me breathing out oaths, I shall follow up those oaths in Hell."[226]

Death is a shunned step. Man is prone to skirt the subject of death; it's the last thing desired to be discussed or considered. That reluctance should prompt the prayer: "So teach us to number our days, that we may apply our hearts unto wisdom" (Psalm 90:12). Why? Realizing the frailty of life is imperative for prioritizing life's affairs, pruning away life's possessions, planning for life's closure, and preparing for life's departure. "What will ye do in the end?" (Jeremiah 5:31).

"Death is the beaten road of all mankind; it is the way of all flesh."— J. Edwards.

~August 11~

Psalm 89:48
The Benefit of Anticipation of Death

"What man is he that liveth, and shall not see death?" (Psalm 89:48).

Death spares no man. It visits the young and old, the good and the bad alike. Philip, King of Macedon, had a servant who told him daily, "Remember, sir, that you are a mortal man." Like him, we forget that we face a death day and need reminders of it. Anticipating death is advantageous for seven reasons.

1. Coming death prompts diligence in duty. "I must work the works of him that sent me, while it is day: the night cometh, when no man can work" (John 9:4).

2. Coming death evokes the best use of time. There is no time to trifle (Ephesians 5:16).

3. Coming death motivates its readiness. Isaiah said, "Set thine house in order; for thou shalt die, and not live" (2 Kings 20:1). How is one to set his "house in order" for death?

a. Trust Christ as Lord and Savior.

b. Square things with Him through confession and repentance (1 John 1:9).

c. Discharge religious duties to God and obligations to man (settle debts, fulfill promises, etc.).

251

d. Prepare a last will.

4. Coming death incites holiness. When a Christian believes death is coming, he wants to be clean (undefiled with sin) to face it.

5. Coming death instills comfort. Death is joy because it ends suffering, battles, sorrow, and sin, uniting us with Christ and loved ones in Heaven (2 Corinthians 5:1).

6. Coming death imparts wisdom. Moses said, "Teach us how short our lives really are so that we may be wise" (Psalm 90:12 ICB). Spurgeon asserts, "To be prepared to die is to be prepared to live." Awareness of death prompts consideration of salvation and holiness.

7. Coming death prompts detachment from the world. The world and flesh lose their grip on those who know death is nigh (1 Corinthians 7:31).

"Fit or not fit, we must all die, and we know not how soon. As death leaves us, the judgment must find us."—William Tiptaft.

~August 12~

Psalm 90:12

Living with the End in View

"Teach us to number our days" (Psalm 90:12).

Moses likens man's lifetime to seven things: to a speck of the day (Psalm 90:4), to a small portion of a night (Psalm 90:4), to a dream that quickly disappears (Psalm 90:5), to a blade of grass that blossoms in the morning only to wither and die in the evening (Psalm 90:6), to a mere passing thought (Psalm 90:9), to a mighty gale force wind that blows it away quickly like a piece of straw (Psalm 90:9), to a bird that swiftly flies away (Psalm 90:10). They all are intended to awaken man to the brevity and frailty of life, to its sudden, unexpected end, so that he may make every day count for God.

Why are we slow to number our days? We don't like how they add up. We don't see the paramount need. We think old age is the time to ponder death, not the springtime of youth and middle age. Therefore, we must do as Moses instructs and beg God to help us number them; if He doesn't, we will not.

"He whose head is in Heaven need not fear to put his feet into the grave."—Matthew Henry.

~August 13~
Psalm 90:12
Hearts Unto Wisdom

"That we may apply our hearts unto wisdom" (Psalm 90:12).

Moses instructs us to order life by divine wisdom. Wisdom is "the ability to apply God-given knowledge to the practical affairs of life."[559] Wisdom's only source is God, who, through the Holy Scriptures, instills in the heart knowledge of the core governing principles of life and gives insight into their application so that one may live pleasing to Him and have happiness and success in the spiritual and physical realm.

This is why Solomon states that possession of it is better than gold (Proverbs 3:14; 16:16) and is to be desired above that of rubies (Proverbs 8:11), and conversely, that he who refuses to walk in it "wrongeth his own soul: all they that hate me [wisdom] love death" (Proverbs 8:36). Additionally, he said, "He who gets wisdom loves himself" (Proverbs 19:8 RSV), and "Happy is the man that findeth wisdom" (Proverbs 3:13).

Wisdom is vital to gain, for it clarifies right from wrong, truth from falsities, better from best, the pleasing in God's sight from the woeful, and the expedient from the less important. Wisdom benefits life with happiness, success, safety, confidence, peace, contentment, and added days (Proverbs 3:16–26).

"Wisdom is the right use of knowledge. To know is not to be wise. Many men know a great deal and are all the greater fools for it. There is no fool so great a fool as a knowing fool. But to know how to use knowledge is to have wisdom."—C. H. Spurgeon.

~August 14~

Psalm 91:14-15a
The "I Will's" of God
Part 1

"Because he hath set his love upon me, therefore will I deliver him: I will set him on high, because he hath known my name. He shall call upon me, and I will answer him: I will be with him in trouble" (Psalm 91:14–15a).

Spurgeon said, "All Heaven lies before the grasp of the asking man; all the promises of God are rich and inexhaustible, and their fulfillment is to be had by prayer."[560]

The psalmist extends seven promises to the person who cleaves to the Lord with deep, robust affection, devotion, and trust.

1. I will deliver him. God affirms His promise twice in the psalm to provide a means of escape or rescue to His children in their calamity or crisis. "From the snare of the fowler" (Psalm 91:3). Spurgeon says they are delivered from either entering it or from it should they fall into it. He says, "The first promise is the most precious to some; the second is the best to others."[561]

2. I will set him on high. God promises to put him in a place inaccessible to the enemy, enabling his protection, joy, and peace (Proverbs 18:10).

3. I will answer him. They will possess power in prayer. "The effectual fervent prayer *of a righteous man* availeth much" (James 5:16). Spurgeon says, "Prayer…wins answers from God. God does put forth power in answer to prayer."[562]

4. I will be with him in trouble. "Trouble" refers to times of distress, especially those caused by emotional pain or anxiety.

254

Watson asserts, "God will hold our head and heart when we are fainting!"[563] Spurgeon says, "Heirs of Heaven are conscious of a unique divine presence in times of severe trial. God is always near in sympathy and in power to help His tried ones."[564] God will be with us in trouble to prevent our sinking under its burden.[565]

"The inviolable faithfulness of the Promiser is good security for the accomplishment of the promise."[566]—John Jardine.

~August 15~

Psalm 91:15b-16
The "I Will's" of God
Part 2

"I will deliver him, and honor him. With long life will I satisfy him, and shew him my salvation" (Psalm 91:15b–16).

The psalmist extends seven promises to the person who cleaves to the Lord with devotion and trust. Yesterday, four were cited. Today, we consider the final three.

1. I will honor him. *Honor* bears the meaning of something weighted down, as one might be with riches of gold and silver. God has weighed down His children with a great honor far exceeding the weight and value of silver and gold. Gill remarked, "The Lord will honor such that know Him, and love Him. All His saints are honored by Him, by taking them into His family and giving them a name better than that of sons and daughters of the greatest potentate, by clothing them with the righteousness of His Son, by adorning them with the graces of His Spirit, by granting them communion and fellowship with Himself, and by bringing them to His kingdom and glory."[567]

2. I will satisfy him with a long life. The righteous will be rewarded or blessed with a happy and full life. Spurgeon remarks, "The man described in this Psalm fills out the measure of his days, and whether he dies young or old, he is quite satisfied with life and is content to leave it."[568] Bonar says, "He liveth long who liveth

255

well! All other life is short and vain. He liveth longest who can tell, of living most for heavenly gain. He liveth long who liveth well! All else is being flung away. He liveth longest who can tell, of true things truly done each day."

3. I will show him My salvation. The promise extends beyond this life and the grave, assuring our eternal Home in Heaven with the Lord.

"Every promise is built upon four pillars: God's justice or holiness, which will not suffer him to deceive; his grace or goodness, which will not suffer him to forget; his truth, which will not suffer him to change; and his power, which makes him able to accomplish."[569]—Salter.

~August 16~

Psalm 91:11
The Help of Angels

"For he shall give his angels charge over thee, to keep thee in all thy ways" (Psalm 91:11).

Angels perform various services on behalf of the Lord to the saints (Hebrews 1:14).

They escort saints from Earth to Heaven at death. Lazarus, at his death, "was carried by the angels into Abraham's bosom [Heaven]" (Luke 16:22). David Jeremiah says, "For every Christian, the time is coming when we will move into our Heavenly homes, assisted by the Lord's real estate agents—called angels....they take believers home to Heaven when we die and help us move into our new houses."

They protect saints. God dispatched angels, especially in emergencies, to warn, help, and protect the saints (Daniel 6:22). Graham states, "Angels guide, comfort, and provide for people in the midst of suffering and persecution."

They observe saints. It is uncertain if glorified saints can see saints on earth, but angels can and serve as their encouragers and helpers (1 Corinthians 4:9).

They comfort saints. An angel comforted and strengthened Daniel (Daniel 10:19).

They show saints how to worship. Angels constantly worship God night and day in an exemplary fashion. "And let all the angels of God worship Him" (Hebrews 1:6).

"Not one guardian angel, as some fondly dream, but all the angels are here alluded to. They are the bodyguard of the princes of the blood imperial of Heaven, and they have received a commission from their Lord and ours to watch carefully over all the interests of the faithful."[570]—C. H. Spurgeon.

~August 17~

Psalm 92:10
Fresh Wind, Fresh Fire

"I shall be anointed with fresh oil" (Psalm 92:10).

The psalmist, perhaps David, needed an anointing of "fresh oil," the power, guidance, illumination, and joy that the Holy Spirit provides.

Departure of the "fresh oil." What causes the believer to lose the fresh oil of the Spirit?

1. Restraint of the Holy Spirit. "Quench not the Spirit" (1 Thessalonians 5:19). Resistance to the Spirit's presence, plan, and work quenches His power.

2. Neglect of soul. Failure to abide in Christ through the intake of the Word, worship, prayer, obedience, and fellowship causes staleness and dryness to abound in the soul.

3. Sinful indulgence. "And grieve not the holy Spirit of God" (Ephesians 4:30). Impurity halts the flow of the Spirit's might and

blessings. Of the anointing oil, the Bible says, "Upon man's flesh shall it not be poured" (Exodus 30:32).

4. Physical relapse. Strenuous mental and physical taxation or trial can result in spiritual emptiness.

Return of the "fresh oil." David was confident of the Spirit's fresh anointing. "I shall be anointed." All who meet the prescribed requirements may. The anointing or infilling of the Holy Spirit is acquired by confession and denunciation of sin, surrender of self to the Holy Spirit's control, and request of God (Luke 11:11–13).

"It is the signature of the Holy Ghost upon our work and witness that makes all the difference."—Duncan Campbell.

~August 18~

Psalm 92:12
Palm Tree Christians
Part 1

"The righteous shall flourish like the palm tree" (Psalm 92:12).

The psalmist uses the palm tree metaphor to picture the righteous. Eight traits of the palm tree symbolically characterize the Christian.

1. Palm trees grow straight. The Christian remains straight, unbending in faith and practice despite battling the storms of conflict, calamity, and persecution. He exhibits a life of separation from the world and is not twisted or warped theologically or morally.

2. Palm trees bear fruit in old age. "They shall still bring forth fruit in old age; they shall be fat and flourishing" (Psalm 92:14). Matthew Henry says, "It is promised that they shall bring forth fruit in old age. When they are old, other trees leave off bearing, but in God's trees, the strength of grace does not fail with the strength of nature. The last days of the saints are sometimes their best days, and their last work is their best work."[571]

3. Palm trees symbolize victory. The Romans customarily gave victors in games and wars a palm branch to symbolize triumph. The Christian life is one of victory over the world, sin, and death in Christ Jesus.

4. Palm trees provide shade—cooling, refreshing shade from the sun's intense heat. This is especially true in third-world countries where air conditioning is unknown or scarce. Likewise, the Christian provides cooling and refreshing shade for the world's weary, worn, and wounded.

"It is a friendly lighthouse, guiding the traveler to the spot where water is to be found."[572]—Unknown.

~August 19~

Psalm 92:12
Palm Tree Christians
Part 2

"The righteous shall flourish like the palm tree: he shall grow like a cedar in Lebanon" (Psalm 92:12).

Yesterday, four of the eight traits of the palm tree that characterize the Christian were shared. Note the remaining four.

1. Palm trees grow tall. The tallest palm tree grows in Colombia and is 197 feet tall. It grows slowly but steadily. Christians grow tall spiritually if they regularly nourish their souls through God's Word, prayer, and worship.

2. Palm trees are exceptionally durable. They are hurricane-resistant and remain upright in the fiercest of storms. The "Palm tree Christian" anchored to the solid Rock remains steadfast and immovable and always abounds in the work of Christ in the most ferocious storm. In contrast, the wicked are counted as mere grass that soon fades away.

3. Palm trees are evergreen. Regardless of the season, the palm tree supplied with life-giving sap remains perennially green, unaffected by external conditions. The Christian, fed with the sap of the Spirit, bears fruit in every season of life.

4. Palm trees are productive. They bear much fruit. The godly abound in fruitfulness by their abiding in the Vine. J. C. Ryle says, "The Spirit never lies dormant and idle within the soul; He always makes His presence known by the fruit He causes to be borne in heart, character, and life."[573]

"What an emblem of the righteous in the desert of a guilty world!"[574]—Joseph Angus.

~August 20~

Psalm 92:14
The Golden Years

"They shall still bring forth fruit in old age; they shall be fat and flourishing" (Psalm 92:14).

Every season of life has its divine purpose, including the golden years. Retiring to a rocking chair is not an option. Spurgeon suggests a four-fold work for old people.

1. They should bear testimony to God's faithfulness.

2. They should instill peace in the troubled and fearful about the future. "When the young Christian comes to them, they say, 'Do not fear; I have gone through the waters, and they have not overflown me; and through the fire, and have not been burned. Trust in God; down to old age, He is the same, and to hoary hairs, He will carry you.'"

3. They should warn of the dangers that lie ahead. "The warnings of the old have a great effect, and it is their peculiar work to guide the imprudent and warn the unwary."

4. They should convert the young.[575] To the list, include the fact that they should also mentor the young. "Wise counsel to the younger is the duty of the aged."

The Bible is full of elderly men and women who served God effectively. Moses (80) and Aaron (83) were chosen to lead the Israelites out of Egyptian bondage. Joshua was selected to direct the conquest of Canaan during the last thirty years of his life. He died at age 110. Caleb was involved in the conquest of Canaan with Joshua while in his eighties (Joshua 14:10). Daniel served the Lord for over 70 years and was well over 80 when serving as one of the three governors over the kingdom of Babylon. Zacharias and Elizabeth, John the Baptist's parents, were 'both well advanced in years' while he was still serving in the Temple.

In Philemon 9, Paul refers to himself as "the aged" (KJV), "old man" (NLT), and "an elderly man" (Holman), yet he had not slowed down in ministry. While in prison, he was writing epistles and, upon release, resumed ministry among the saints.

Resolve to submit joyfully and willingly to what God wants you to do. There is no discharge or retirement in serving the Lord, only promotion to Heaven or desertion.

"God sends His servants to bed when they have done their work."[576]—Thomas Fuller.

~August 21~

Psalm 93:1–2
The Supreme Ruler of All

"The LORD reigneth, he is clothed with majesty; the LORD is clothed with strength, wherewith he hath girded himself: the world also is stablished, that it cannot be moved. Thy throne is established of old: thou art from everlasting" (Psalm 93:1–2).

Though an anticipatory psalm of Christ's kingdom rule on earth, it depicts that rule presently from Heaven's throne.

Christ reigns personally. "The LORD reigneth." King Jesus rules, not world leaders, nature, and evil. All is under His sovereign control. Comfort, hope, and strength are found in the words, "The LORD reigneth." Voice them to the captive, troubled and hurting. Speak them when walking through sorrow and the valley of the shadow of death.

Christ reigns majestically. "He is clothed with majesty." Christ is clothed with all the regalia and splendor of a supreme and sovereign king. John Owen says, "On Christ's glory I would fix my thoughts and desires, and the more I see of the glory of Christ, the more the painted beauties of this world will wither in my eyes, and I will be more and more crucified to this world."[577] Kempis said, "Those who attempt to search into the majesty of God will be overwhelmed with His Glory!"

Christ reigns mightily. "He...is clothed with strength." His power is incomparable and unconquerable. From Heaven's throne, He thus reigns, thwarting evil, saving sinners, vindicating His name, and protecting saints.

Christ reigns permanently. "Thy throne is established of old." His kingdom is everlasting, and "of the increase of His govern-ment...there shall be no end" (Isaiah 9:7). Matthew Henry says, "God's right to rule the world is founded in His making it; He that gave being to it, no doubt, may give law to it, and so His title to the government is incontestable."[578]

Christ reigns triumphantly. "The LORD on high is mightier than the noise of many waters." His enemies may make a lot of noise, but are impotent to thwart His works. It is all empty boasts, lies, and threats. When Christ returns, the clamorous noise will be forever silenced.

"The sovereignty of God is that golden scepter in His hand by which He will make all bow, either by His word or by His works, by His mercies or by His judgments."—Thomas Brooks.

~August 22~
Psalm 94:19
Troubling Thoughts

"Within me thy comforts delight my soul" (Psalm 94:19).

The Psalmist was weighed down with troubling and anxious thoughts of doubt and confusion regarding God's failure to execute swift judgment upon the wicked. He couldn't understand why God allowed the wicked to boast of their evil conduct (Psalm 94:4, 7), engage in hideous conduct (Psalm 94:5–6), and afflict His people (Psalm 94:5) without immediate punishment (Psalm 94:3).

What are the comforts of the Lord to anxious and troublesome thoughts?

1. The precious promises. God's promises should be fastened to the mind so that in times of worrisome thoughts, they may be recalled to put the detrimental ones to flight.

2. The divine attributes. Troubling thoughts find solace and comfort in God's omnipotence, omniscience, omnipresence, and unfailing love. He is the mighty defender and deliverer who promises good to His children.

3. The remembrance of God's past works. "Hitherto, the Lord has helped me."

4. The saturation of the Holy Scripture. Wanton thoughts are expelled through the intake and meditation of the Word. Darkness cannot cohabitate with light.

5. The Holy Spirit's rule. Upon request, the Holy Spirit will bring every thought captive to the obedience of Christ (2 Corinthians 10:5). He demolishes Satan's stronghold of destructive reasoning, speculation, and thoughts.

"Internal comfort is given by God Himself to the perplexed and troubled in spirit, whereby they are 'delighted,' or, rather, 'soothed and solaced.'"[579]—G. Rawlinson.

~August 23~

Psalm 94:19

The Comfort That Calms

"Within me thy comforts delight my soul" (Psalm 94:19)

Thy comforts delight my soul. Medicine for troublesome and haunting thoughts is not found in alcohol, drugs, or suicide. Matthew Henry says, "The world's comforts give but little delight to the soul when it is hurried with melancholy thoughts; they are songs to a heavy heart. But God's comforts will reach the soul and will bring with them that peace and that pleasure which the smiles of the world cannot give and which the frowns of the world cannot take away."[580]

The comforts of the Lord will cheer, satisfy, and encourage the weary soul. They will bring peace and sing consoling songs in the night. "The heart's agitation is calmed. The shock is allayed. The troubled mind finds peace. Its darkness is turned into day, and its motions are no more those of fear but the ecstasies of pure delight."[581]

What are God's comforts?

1. The truths He taught. "He shall cover thee with his feathers, and under his wings shalt thou trust: his truth shall be thy shield and buckler" (Psalm 91:4).

2. The promises He made. "This is my comfort in my affliction: For thy word hath quickened me" (Psalm 119:50).

3. The Holy Spirit He sent. "Likewise the Spirit also helpeth our infirmities" (Romans 8:26).

4. The saints He consoled. "He comforts us in all our affliction, so that we may be able to comfort those who are in any kind of affliction, through the comfort we ourselves receive from God" (2 Corinthians 1:4 CSB).

"From my sinful thoughts, my vain thoughts, my sorrowful thoughts, my griefs, my cares, my conflicts, I will hasten to the Lord; he has divine comforts, and these will not only console but actually delight me."[582]—C. H. Spurgeon.

~August 24~

Psalm 95:8
The Hardened Heart

"Harden not your heart, as in the provocation, and as in the day of temptation in the wilderness" (Psalm 95:8).

Israel, despite the work of God in their exodus from Egyptian bondage, refused to trust God for provision in the wilderness wanderings. Stubbornly rebellious, they murmured and disobeyed His counsel, which provoked the wrath of God. They were excluded from entering the promised rest in Canaan (Numbers 14:22–23).

Hardness of heart is the state of persistent rejection and spurning of God's appeal to be Lord and Savior. The Bible says, "He, that being often reproved hardeneth his neck, shall suddenly be destroyed, and that without remedy" (Proverbs 29:1). Note.

1. The hardness of the heart develops over time by obstinacy to God's frequent rebukes and summons to repent. Over forty years, Israel repetitively ignored God's rebukes. Persistent sin sears the conscience and deafens it to God's summons and reproofs. Note. Sixty-three percent of individuals who become Christians do so between the ages of 4 and 14.[583]

2. The unremitting refusal to respond repentantly to God's rebuke results in sudden judgment. The Israelites were excluded from entering Canaan. To ignore the divine summons to turn from sin is to court danger. For the unsaved, "Every particular repeated act of sin sets us one advance nearer to Hell."[584] For the believer, continued obstinacy leads to loss of blessings, rewards, and, perhaps, life (1 John 5:16). To Job's question, "Who hath hardened himself against him, and hath prospered?" (Job 9:4), the Bible and experience answer, no man.

3. Today is the time to repent and get right with God (Hebrews 3:8). Adrian Rogers says, "Tomorrow, you will have more sin to repent of. And tomorrow, you will have a harder heart to repent with."

"Many now harden themselves against the word preached by the ministers of Christ. They 'puff at' all the judgments denounced against them."[585]—Charles Simeon.

~August 25~

Psalm 96:13
The Judgment of God

"Before the LORD: *for he cometh, for he cometh to judge the earth: he shall judge the world with righteousness, and the people with his truth"* (Psalm 96:13).

David prophetically speaks of Christ's second coming and judgment. *He shall judge the world*—the characteristics of Christ's judgment.

1. The judgment will include all people. "He cometh to judge the earth." Gill says Christ will "judge the earth; the inhabitants of it, when all works, words, and thoughts, good and bad, will be brought to account; and every man will be judged, as those shall be, with or without the grace of God."[586]

2. The judgment will be just. "With righteousness shall he judge" (Isaiah 11:4). The judgment will be without error. Man will get his rightful due. Jefferson said, "My heart trembles when I reflect that God is just." Says Winslow, "Throughout eternity, the lost soul will be testifying to this truth: 'God is holy; I was a sinner; I rejected His salvation, I turned my back upon His Gospel, I despised His Son, I hated God Himself, I lived in my sins, I loved my sins, I died in my sins, and now I am lost to all eternity! And God is righteous in my condemnation!'"[587]

3. The judgment will be fair. 'With his truth shall he judge.' His judgment will be impartial. Says Spurgeon, "Honesty, veracity,

266

integrity, will rule upon his judgment-seat."[588] None will be favored above another.

4. The judgment will be irrevocable. The verdict is unappealable, inescapable, and eternal. "Prepare to meet thy God" (Amos 4:12).

"Since God is a just Judge, we must love and laud His justice and thus rejoice in God even when He miserably destroys the wicked in body and soul; for in all this, His high and inexpressible justice shines forth."—Martin Luther.

~August 26~

Psalm 97:10
The Hate of Evil

"Ye that love the LORD, hate evil" (Psalm 97:10).

The Christian may condone evil, promote it, defend it, engage in it, or hate it. Few believers actually hate evil as God commands.

1. To hate evil is to abhor it bitterly. It is to count all forms of it as an enemy and to 'hate the very garments spotted by it' (Jude 23).

2. To hate evil is to avoid it tenaciously. It is to never give place to it. "Enter not into the path of the wicked, and go not in the way of evil men. Avoid it, pass not by it, turn from it, and pass away" (Proverbs 4:14–15).

3. To hate evil is to assail it prudently. "And have no fellowship with the unfruitful works of darkness, but rather reprove them" (Ephesians 5:11). It is to protest and condemn evil openly. "The only thing necessary for the triumph of evil is for good men to do nothing."

"We cannot love God without hating that which He hates."[589]— C. H. Spurgeon.

~August 27~

Psalm 97:11
A Light Sown for the Righteous

"Light is sown for the righteous, and gladness for the upright in heart" (Psalm 97:11).

The light that is sown for the righteous is Jesus. He is the divine seed sown in death and raised, producing abundant and eternal life (John 12:24). As the sun rises to rid the blackness of night, Christ has risen from the dead to extinguish the darkness of sin and its consequences upon the righteous, scattering rays of joy, peace, happiness, comfort, forgiveness, hope, and contentment upon their path.

Its full harvest awaits in Heaven. Until that glorious day, let them that love the Lord "hate evil" (despise sin of all kind in self and others universally), "rejoice in the LORD" (in gratitude for the "light" sown and its showers of benefits) and give thanks in "remembrance of his holiness" (Christ's flawlessness and perfection).

"The Gospel of Jesus, wherever it goes, sows the whole earth with joy for believers, for these are the people who are righteous before the Lord."[590]—C. H. Spurgeon.

~August 28~

Psalm 98:1
Why Christians Sing

"O sing unto the LORD a new song; for he hath done marvelous things: his right hand, and his holy arm, hath gotten him the victory" (Psalm 98:1).

The psalm is a joy and praise psalm about Israel's deliverance and restoration from Exile by the hand of God. Christian people have always been singing people. Their churches and meeting places vibrate with joyful songs, whether in catacombs, cruel huts, soundproof hidden chambers, or exquisitely constructed sanctuaries. Tyndale said the Gospel "signifies good, merry, glad, and joyful tidings, that makes a man's heart glad and makes him sing, dance, and leap for joy."

Christians sing primarily for four reasons.

1. They sing to magnify. Singing praises God's character and mighty works. Spurgeon says, "God is to be praised with the voice, and the heart should go therewith in holy exultation."

2. They sing to testify. Singing spiritual songs bears witness to biblical truth. It tells the Gospel. The Israelites shared their faith with the ungodly in numerous psalms (hymns). Paul and Silas witnessed in jail by song. Martyrs of the faith sang while being killed, planting seeds of the Gospel in the hearts of their persecutors. Luther said, "The gift of language combined with the gift of song was given to man so that he could proclaim the Word of God through music." Sing everywhere. The songs sung have gospel wings.

3. They sing to edify. Christians encourage, comfort, and build up one another in song. The Bible says, "Talk with each other much about the Lord, quoting psalms and hymns and singing sacred songs, making music in your hearts to the Lord" (Ephesians 5:19 TLB). This is why what is sung should impart theological truth, not just feel-good emotions. Note. They sing, likewise, to nourish and strengthen their souls with biblical truth. Chrysostom said of singing, "Nothing so lifteth up the soul, so looseth it from the chains of the body, and giveth it a contempt for all earthly things."[591]

4. They sing to jollify. Christians sing to express marvelous joy over their miraculous salvation wrought by Jesus' death and resurrection. Their happiness in salvation is uncontainable and bursts forth in an unstoppable song.

"Have an eye to God in every word you sing."—John Wesley.

~August 29~

Psalm 99:6-8

Intercessors

"Moses and Aaron among his priests, and Samuel among them that call upon his name; they called upon the LORD, *and he answered them"* (Psalm 99:6).

Moses, Aaron, and Samuel engaged in intercessory prayer, a duty that befalls all the saved.

The practice of it. "I exhort therefore, that, first of all, supplications, prayers, intercessions, and giving of thanks, be made for all men" (1 Timothy 2:1). To be an intercessor for others, to bear their sorrows, heartaches, burdens, cares, and needs to the Lord, is the most incredible kindness we can do for them. Be an intercessor as Moses, who stood in the gap between Israel and God in prayer for their forgiveness (Psalm 106:23); As Aaron, who "stood between the dead and the living," praying for the plague in the land to be stayed (Numbers 16:48); and as Samuel, who in Israel's distress cried out to God for their relief (1 Samuel 7:9). Spurgeon said, "They made it their life's business to call upon Him in prayer, and by so doing brought down innumerable blessings upon themselves and others."[592]

Paul exhorts, "Pray much for others" (1 Timothy 2:1 TLB). Prayer (intercession) for others is to be continuous. Not doing so is more than carelessness; it is a sin (1 Samuel 12:23). Note. Abraham pleaded for Sodom and Gomorrah, Jeremiah for apostate Israel, Samuel for Saul, David for the Jewish people, Daniel for the Israelites in Babylonian captivity, Paul for the saints at Philippi and elsewhere, Epaphras for the Colossian believers, and Christ for Peter and the disciples. It is commendable to have it said of a believer that "he prayed for his friends" (Job 42:10).

The Power of it. Matthew Henry wrote of Moses, Aaron, and Samuel's intercession: "He answered them and granted them the things which they called upon Him for. They all wonderfully prevailed with God in prayer; miracles were wrought at their special instance and request; nay, He not only condescended to do that for them which they desired, as a prince for a petitioner, but He communed with them as one friend familiarly converses with another."[593] Hallesby said, "Prayer is the conduit through which power from Heaven is brought to earth."[594] Saith Spurgeon, "It is a very great privilege to be permitted to pray for our fellowmen. Such prayers are often of unspeakable value to those for whom they are offered."[595]

The Periphery of it. Halverson says, "No place is closed to intercessory prayer: no continent, no nation, no city, no organization, no office. No power on earth can keep intercession out."[596]

"So often, we pray narrowly, attending only to our own needs. Instead, we should pray broadly for everyone."[597]—D. James Kennedy.

~August 30~

Psalm 99:6
Ways God Answers Prayer
Part 1

"They called upon the LORD, *and he answered them"* (Psalm 99:6).

We don't know how God will answer prayer, but we know it will be answered.

1. The answer to prayer may be delayed.[598] Gurnall said, "Some prayers have a longer voyage than others, but then they return with richer lading at last, so that the praying soul is a gainer by waiting for an answer."[599] Let's not hurry the Lord in response to prayer.

2. The answer to prayer may be unrecognized. The prayer is answered, but the answer is missed because of the unexpected way in which it was (Acts 12:15–16).

3. The answer to prayer may yet have conditions to be met to be fulfilled.

4. The answer to prayer may not be that which was requested. Sometimes, we receive exactly what is asked; other times, something far better (though we may not think so).

"I think we shall find a great many of our prayers that we thought unanswered answered when we get to Heaven."[600]—D. L. Moody.

~August 31~

Psalm 99:6
Ways God Answers Prayer
Part 2

"They called upon the LORD, and he answered them" (Psalm 99:6).

Yesterday's entry shared four ways God answers prayer. There are three more to be considered.

1. Its answer may be found in the silence of God, not in that which is visible and tangible. Chambers advises, "You say, 'But He has not answered.' He has; He is so near to you that His silence is the answer. His silence is big and has a terrific meaning that you cannot understand yet, but presently you will."[601]

2. The answer to prayer may be a denial. Sometimes, we do not know what we ask for; thankfully, it's not granted. Matthew Henry writes, "Though God accepts the prayer of faith, yet He does not always give what is asked for. When God does not take away our troubles and temptations, yet if He gives grace enough for us, we have no reason to complain."[602]

3. God does not hear some prayers, so they go unanswered. Isaiah declared, "It's your sins that have cut you off from God. Because of your sins, he has turned away and will not listen anymore" (Isaiah 59:2 NLT). Unheard and unanswered prayer happens when we willingly harbor sin in our lives.

"God will either give us what we ask or give us what we would have asked if we knew everything He knows."[603]—Timothy Keller.

Psalm 100:1–2
Sing Praises to God

"Make a joyful noise unto the LORD, all ye lands. Serve the LORD with gladness: come before his presence with singing" (Psalm 100:1–2).

The psalm summons people everywhere to praise God.

1. The subject of praise. "Unto the LORD." The object of praise is God and His bountiful goodness and mercy in salvation, caring supervision, and provision. He alone is worthy of praise and adoration.

2. The scope of praise. "All ye lands." All countries and people have experienced God's goodness and should praise Him. Says Spurgeon, "Never will the world be in its proper condition till with one unanimous shout it adores the only God."[604]

3. The shape of praise. "Make a joyful noise." Praise and thanksgiving to God include loud cheering, great delight and joy, and jubilant singing. Plumer states, "The singing required must be with joyful lips, with a joyful voice, with triumphing. Nothing is more offensive to God than that we bow the head like a bulrush and give way to sadness and gloom when we are called to joyful thanksgiving."[605]

4. The spread of praise. "Declare His glory among the heathen, His wonders among all people" (Psalm 96:3). Every people group in every land is to be told the miracles and acts of God in creation and redemption with the intent of evangelizing them. "Preach the gospel to every creature" (Mark 16:15). Watts says, "Let those refuse to sing, who never knew our God, but favorites of the heavenly king, may speak their joys abroad."

"Perhaps it takes a purer faith to praise God for unrealized blessings than for those we once enjoyed or those we enjoy now."—A. W. Tozer.

~September 2~

Psalm 100:3–5
Thankfulness to God

"Enter into his gates with thanksgiving, and into his courts with praise: be thankful unto him, and bless his name" (Psalm 100:4).

Commonly referred to as "the Old Hundredth," the psalm voices seven reasons to express thanksgiving to God.

1. *"The LORD...is God."* Jehovah is the true and self-existent God worthy of man's adoration and worship.

2. *"It is he that hath made us."* God is the creator, sustainer, and owner of man and all that exists. Apart from Him, we and the world would have no being.

3. *"We are his people."* He authored redemption's plan, making reconciliation with Him possible. "For you were once darkness, but now you are light in the Lord" (Ephesians 5:8 CSB). We are brands plucked from the fire. "We bless the Lord with the most fervent gratitude as we realize that he has healed our disease and redeemed our life from destruction."[606]

4. *"The sheep of his pasture."* God is the Good Shepherd who provides for and protects the flock. His pastures are green and luxurious.

5. *"For the LORD is good."* Praise God for who He is. He is holy and righteous in character, incapable of wrong, and forever just in His dealings with man. Praise Him for His commandments and plan for man, which are good, as is His rule.

6. *"His mercy is everlasting."* God's lovingkindness is unfailing and unchangeable from generation to generation.

7. *"His truth endureth to all generations."* God has been, is, and forever will be faithful to His Word and promises. All that He promised will come to pass. Matthew Henry says, "No word of His shall fall to the ground as antiquated or revoked."[607] Says Spurgeon, "Our heart leaps for joy as we bow before One who has never broken His word or changed His purpose."[608]

"Beloved Friends, we may well continue to praise God, for our God continues to give us causes for praise!"—C. H. Spurgeon.

~September 3~

Psalm 101:3
Watch What You Watch

"I will set no wicked thing before mine eyes" (Psalm 101:3).

As king, David purposed not to look at any corrupt or evil thing. Why? The eyes are the inlet into the mind, and 'what a man thinketh that he is' (Proverbs 23:7). "What fascinates the eye," says Spurgeon, "is very apt to gain admission into the heart."[609] Jesus said, "The eye is the lamp of the body. If your eyes are healthy, your whole body will be full of light. But if your eyes are unhealthy, your whole body will be full of darkness" (Matthew 6:22–23 NIV).

In keeping the eyes healthy, the whole body (one's life) will be healthy (full of light). Jesus said, "Let's not pretend this is easier than it really is. If you want to live a morally pure life, here's what you have to do: You have to blind your right eye the moment you catch it in a lustful leer. You have to choose to live one-eyed or else be dumped on a moral trash pile" (Matthew 5:29–30 MSG).

"In all our worldly business, we must see that what we set our eyes upon is right and good and not any forbidden fruit, and we never seek that which we cannot have without sin"[610]—Matthew Henry.

~September 4~

Psalm 101:1–8
Counsel For a Ruler

"I will not know a wicked person" (Psalm 101:4).

As king, David resolved to rule by a five-fold criterion.

1. As king, he would walk uprightly. "I will walk within my house with a perfect heart." David pledged, as king, not to engage in wanton indulgences as an Eastern ruler might but to behave right and honorably based on the precepts of the Lord. "I will behave myself wisely." Matthew Henry says, "When we make the word of God our rule and are ruled by it, the glory of God our end and aim at it, then we walk in a perfect way with a perfect heart."[611] The Bible says, "Mercy and truth preserve the king: and his throne is upholden by mercy" (Proverbs 20:28).

2. As king, he would depend on God. Understanding his weakness to govern the nation, David prays, "O when wilt thou come unto me?" He says, like Moses, "If thy presence go not with me, carry us not up hence" (Exodus 33:15).

3. As king, he would root out corruption. Only those vetted as incorruptible, reliable, and trustworthy would be in his administration. "No one who acts deceitfully will live in my palace; the one who tells lies will not be retained here to guide me" (Psalm 101:7 CSB). David would choose the godly to govern. "Mine eyes shall be upon the faithful." Spurgeon says, "He would seek them out, engage their services, take care of them, and promote them to honor." Those who are not faithful to God are not likely to be loyal to men. Paul states, "Do not be deceived: 'Bad company corrupts good morals'" (1 Corinthians 15:33 CSB).

4. As king, he would not condone wickedness. He said, "My goal each day will be to destroy the wicked living in our land. I will force all who do evil to leave the city of the LORD" (Psalm 101:8 ERV). David pledged to overthrow the wicked and hold them accountable at the outset of his rule. There would be no safe havens or sanctuary cities for criminals and instigators of evil. Says Spurgeon, "To favor

sin is to discourage virtue; undue leniency to the bad is unkindness to the good."[612]

5. As king, he would worship God. "I will sing of mercy and judgment: unto thee, O LORD, will I sing." Whatever the position and demands, time must be made to sit at God's table and footstool.

"In the measure that the principles of the New Testament control the minds of the men who administer the civil government, peace, and prosperity prevail; as none know better than the openly skeptical."[613]—H. A. Ironside.

~September 5~

Psalm 101:8

How to Support a Godly Ruler

"My goal each day will be to destroy the wicked living in our land. I will force all who do evil to leave the city of the LORD" (Psalm 101:8 ERV).

King David pledged to rule Israel justly in keeping with Judeo-Christian values, but the help of God's people was needed.

Christians, likewise, must assist their godly ruler (king, president, prime minister, etc.).

1. By ensuring their safety in executing duties at home and abroad.

2. By replacing the ungodly who author or support anti-god legislation and laws. Solomon says, "Take away the wicked from before the king, and his throne shall be established in righteousness" (Proverbs 25:5). A primary way to do this is at the polls.

3. By influencing the governing officials of the opposition party for support. "Righteous lips are the delight of kings; and they love him that speaketh right" (Proverbs 16:13).

4. By praying for them. "Pray in that way for kings and for all rulers and people who have authority. Pray for God to help them, so that we may live our lives without trouble or danger. Then we can live

in a good way that respects God and other people" (1 Timothy 2:2 EASY). "The king's heart is in the hand of the LORD, as the rivers of water: he turneth it whithersoever he will" (Proverbs 21:1).

"A king brings stability to a land by justice."—Solomon (Proverbs 29:4 EHV).

~September 6~

Psalm 102:16
How to Build Up the Church

"When the LORD shall build up Zion, He shall appear in His glory" (Psalm 102:16).

How may Zion, the church, be said to be built up?

1. Through evangelism. There is no substitute for personal soulwinning and evangelistic events for church growth. Ed Stetzer said, "Don't let your church be a *cul-de-sac* on the Great Commission highway." The church can either evangelize or fossilize.

2. Through edification. The training and discipleship of believers through preaching, instruction, and example are essential to the church's spiritual and numerical success (Ephesians 4:11–12).

3. Through church planting. A multiplicity of churches provides numerical growth of the body at large. Plant churches in virgin soil. Spurgeon asserts, "The building up of an empire must often be by coloniza-tion, and it is the same with the Church."[614]

4. Through the agency of the Holy Spirit. "When the LORD shall build up Zion." It is God who must "build up Zion." He must give the increase (1 Corinthians 3:6–7). Evangelism, edification, and church planting without the power and blessing of the Holy Spirit are futile since He is the cause of church success and growth. No undertaking should occur apart from His authority and anointing. "All is vain unless the Spirit of the Holy One comes down; Brethren, pray, and holy manna will be showered all around."

5. Through prayer. Prayer builds up and fortifies the church. "Cause thy face to shine upon thy sanctuary" (Daniel 9:17). Pray for God's face to shine on the church. Spurgeon says, "Wherever God's face shines upon his Church, note what happens. First, her walls are rebuilt. Desolations, when God shines upon them, glow into perfection; we shall soon see our church-members multiplied and all things in proper order if the Lord will but shine upon us. Then shall you see each one of the Lord's servants in his right place, ministering before the Lord. The Church of God needs a thousand things, but you can put them all into one if you say, 'The Church of God needs her God.'"[615]

"Let us all cherish an ardent desire of seeing the Church of God in a more prosperous state and manifest that desire by our utmost exertions in its favor."[616]—N. Hill.

~September 7~

Psalm 102:6–7
The Pelican, Owl, and Sparrow
Part 1

"I am like a pelican of the wilderness: I am like an owl of the desert. I watch, and am as a sparrow alone upon the house top" (Psalm 102:6–7).

The psalmist uses three birds to describe his soul's estate. He identifies with the gloomy pelican, which can sit for hours and days with its bill resting on its breast. He identifies with the desert owl, which lives in desolation and loneliness. The psalmist identifies with the sparrow that incessantly mourns the loss of its mate on a house rooftop alone.

Do you relate to the birds' metaphorical meaning? Do melancholy, loneliness, and sadness overtake you? If so, as with the psalmist, comfort is found in five things.

1. Comfort is drawn in the eternality of God. "But thou, O LORD, shall endure forever." Horne says, "Amidst the changes and chances of this mortal life, one topic of consolation will ever remain, namely, the eternity and immutability of God. Kingdoms and empires may rise and fall; nay…but Jehovah is ever the same; His years have no end, nor can His promise fail, any more than Himself."[617]

2. Comfort is drawn in the help God will provide. "Thou shalt arise, and have mercy upon Zion. "He [the psalmist] firmly believed and boldly prophesied that apparent inaction on God's part would turn to effective working. Others might remain sluggish in the matter, but the Lord would most surely bestir Himself."[618]

3. Comfort is drawn in God's ready response to prayer. "He will regard the prayer of the destitute, and not despise their prayer." Brooks said, "Prayer crowns God with the honor and glory that are due His name, and God crowns prayer with assurance and comfort. Usually, the most praying souls are the most assured souls." "Trouble and perplexity," says Melanchthon, "drive me to prayer, and prayer drives away perplexity and trouble."[619]

"If the Lord be with us, we have no cause of fear. His eye is upon us, His arm over us, His ear open to our prayer—His grace sufficient, His promise unchangeable."—John Newton.

~September 8~

Psalm 102:6–7

The Pelican, Owl, and Sparrow
Part 2

"I am like a pelican of the wilderness: I am like an owl of the desert. I watch, and am as a sparrow alone upon the house top" (Psalm 102:6–7).

Comfort in distress and depression is gained in five things, three of which were shared yesterday.

1. Comfort is drawn in the goodness of God. "For he hath looked down from the height of his sanctuary; from heaven did the LORD behold the earth; To hear the groaning of the prisoner; to loose those that are appointed to death [doom]." Matthew Henry said, "The hope of deliverance is built upon the goodness of God."[620]

2. Comfort is drawn in the sovereignty of God. "Of old hast thou laid the foundation of the earth: and the heavens are the work of thy hands." Says Spurgeon, "The sovereignty of God in all things is an unfailing ground for consolation; He rules and reigns whatever happens, and therefore all is well."[621]

"God is of an eternal duration. The eternity of God is the foundation of the stability of the covenant, the great comfort of a Christian."—Stephen Charnock.

~September 9~

Psalm 103:3a

Subjects of Praise
Part 1

"Who forgiveth all thine iniquities" (Psalm 103:3a).

In the recital of God's benefits to man, the first David records is the forgiveness of sins. John R. Rice said, "Forgiveness is the highest aim of God."[622] To have experienced it is man's foundational reason for praise. Not only does God forgive the initial sin of disobedience that results in a reconciled relationship (salvation), but the "sins" committed afterward.

In the aftermath of the fire that destroyed the Metropolitan Tabernacle, London Jowett observed that every pillar was wrenched or twisted. Later, he said, "When the fire of sin breaks out in my body, every pillar of my life gets a wrench." This wrenching (effects) of sin in man requires God's healing—purification, and sanctification, which He graciously provides. Simeon well states, "To be forgiven one sin is a mercy of inconceivable magnitude; but

281

to be forgiven all, all that we have ever committed, this is a mercy which neither the tongues of men nor of angels can ever adequately declare."[623] Other benefits, in contrast, are incomparable. Spurgeon says, "First, we are blessed with the pardon of sin, and then we bless God for the pardon of sin."[624]

"Who healeth all thy diseases" (Psalm 103:3b). One of God's compound names declares He heals: *Jehovah-Rapha* ("I am the LORD that healeth"—Exodus 15:26), as does the Bible (James 5:14–16). "Among the greatest blessings which we receive of God is recovery from sickness."

Praise Him for renewing physical health, enabling strength to abound again. The miraculous restoration gives a new lease on life.[625]

"Before you go out into the world, wash your face in the clear crystal of praise. Bury each yesterday in the fine linen and spices of thankfulness."—C. H. Spurgeon.

~September 10~

Psalm 103:4–5
Subjects of Praise
Part 2

"Who redeemeth thy life from destruction" (Psalm 103:4a).

Praise God for rescue from Hell. Gill states, "The people of God are redeemed from sin, the cause of it; and from the curse of the law, in the execution of which it lies; and from Satan, the executor of it; and all this by Christ, through which the saints are secure from going down to the pit of destruction."[626]

"Who crowneth thee with lovingkindness and tender mercies" (Psalm 103:4b). Two of the foremost blessings of God, which encircle His people and deserve much praise, are His steadfast love and rich mercy. His love is past understanding, and His mercies are new each morning.

"Who satisfieth thy mouth with good things" (Psalm 103:5a). Praise God for a satisfying life filled with good things. Matthew Henry states, "It is only the favor and grace of God that can give satisfaction to a soul, can suit its capacities, supply its needs, and answer to its desires."[627] Says Spurgeon, "No man is ever filled to satisfaction but a believer, and only God Himself can satisfy even him."[628]

"One of the saddest proofs of our fallen condition is our propensity to forget God's benefits, especially his unspeakable gift, Jesus Christ. Nothing but the basest ingratitude could chill our hearts or shut our lips."[629]—W. S. Plumer.

~September 11~
Psalm 103:12
Promised Pardon

"As far as the east is from the west, so far hath he removed our transgressions from us" (Psalm 103:12).[630]

The peculiarity of the pardon. What David states is not true for all men; it is only for those who confess and repent of their sins to the Lord.

The positivity of the pardon. David was confident of forgiveness based on God's promises. Don't allow Satan to browbeat you with doubt that the sin confessed has not been forgiven and forgotten by God. "If our heart condemn us, God is greater than our heart" (1 John 3:20). Take God's word over that of the Devil. The Bible says, "If we confess our sins, he is faithful and just to forgive us our sins, and to cleanse us from all unrighteousness" (1 John 1:9) and "He will put away our iniquities: and he will cast all our sins into the bottom of the sea" (Micah 7:19 DRA).

The perfection of the pardon. Instead of enumerating the transgressions, David says, "our transgressions." Naming every variance of sin would have resulted in the omission of one or more, which, by the way, may have been our particular sins. But to envelop them in two words covered them all. Whatever the sin, it has been forgiven upon confession or is forgivable.

The permanency of the pardon. "As far as the east is from the west." There are no east and west poles. What a great metaphor to describe God's erasure or blotting out of man's sin. In it, God says, "Your 'sins and iniquities will I remember no more.'" Spurgeon says, "Your old sins are buried, and they shall never have a resurrection.[631] Note. On the Day of Atonement, the priests released a goat representing the people's sins in an eastern direction, symbolizing the removal of their sins forever.

The peace of the pardon. God removes our sins from Him and their defilement and tormenting guilt "from us," enabling peace and hope to press forward. "The joy of pardon," says Spurgeon, "has a voice louder than the voice of sin. God's voice speaking peace is the sweetest music an ear can hear."[632]

"The forgiveness of sin is the great proof of God's love."[633]—J. J. Perowne.

~September 12~

Psalm 103:13

The Pity of God

"Like as a father pitieth his children, so the LORD pitieth them that fear him" (Psalm 103:13).

Who God pities. "Them that fear him." God shows tender compassion and mercy to those who revere and honor Him. Spurgeon says, "To those who truly reverence His holy name, the Lord is a father and acts as such."[634]

How God pities. "Like as a father." "He says not, as man pities man, as the rich the poor man, as the strong the feeble, as the freeman the captive, but he makes mention of that pity which a father shows to his son, which is the greatest of all."[635] Horne asserts, "God is represented as bearing towards us the fond and tender affection of a 'father,' ever ready to defend, to nourish, and to provide for us, to bear with us, to forgive us, and to receive us in the parental arms of everlasting love."[636]

Note some displays of a father's pity. A father pities his children when they are sick and comforts them; when they are falsely accused and defends them; when they do wrong and deals with them not as they deserve, but in mercy; when they suffer adversity and helps them; when they are ignorant of godly knowledge and truth and patiently instructs them until they understand; when they suffer defeat, and upholds them.

Why God pities? "For he knoweth our frame." God pities us not as we deserve but because of "the frailty of our bodies and the folly of our souls."[637] Praise God for His enduring, inexhaustible, and everlasting pity.

"The tears of Christ are the pity of God. The gentleness of Jesus is the long-suffering of God. The tenderness of Jesus is the love of God. 'He that hath seen me hath seen the Father.'"—Alexander MacLaren.

~September 13~

Psalm 104:6–9

Restraint of the Seas

"You set borders for the seas that they cannot cross" (Psalm 104:9 ICB).

Three specific lessons are stated in the text about the seas of the Earth.[638]

The freedom of the seas. If boundaries had to be set to restrict them, there was a time when they had no confines. Those times are revealed in Scripture. Water covered the earth twice—during creation and the Noahic Flood. With the first, the waters were divided into borders or bounds, providing dry land for the subsequent creation of nature, beast, and man (day two of creation).

The second covering receded to its banks when its purpose of judgment ended (Genesis 8:3).

The propensity of the seas. The natural tendency or inclination of the waters is to flow uninhibited. Without restraint, they would return to cover the earth again. Caryl said, "They would be boundless and know no limits; did not God bound and limit them."[639]

The governance of the seas. With water covering 333 million cubic miles of the Earth, or 71 percent of its surface, grave destruction and death would result if not restricted. Who sets the seas in their bounds and keeps them there? Jehovah God. Of Him, Solomon says, "He gave to the sea his decree, that the waters should not pass his commandment" (Proverbs 8:29). The psalmist says of Him, "You set borders for the seas that they cannot cross." Spurgeon said, "Jehovah's word bounds the ocean, using only a narrow belt of sand to confine it to its own limits; that apparently feeble restraint answers every purpose, for the sea is obedient as a little child to the bidding of its Maker."[640]

"Although the natural tendency of the waters is to cover the earth, yet this will not happen because God has established, by His Word, a counteracting law, and as His truth is eternal, this law must remain steadfast."[641]—John Calvin.

~September 14~

Psalm 104:13
God's Providential Care and Control

"He watereth the hills from his chambers" (Psalm 104:13).

God designed the clouds to soak up moisture only to return it to the earth as dew and rain. Solomon said, "The clouds drop down the dew" (Proverbs 3:20). Lawson says, "It is wisdom that draws up the moisture from the earth in waters, and exhales it in vapors, forming them into clouds, and again distilling them in dew, or pouring them down in the rain, that food may spring out of the earth for man and beast."[642] All living things need water to survive. Thankfully, God, in His wisdom, designed the heavens to manufacture an endless and continuous water supply.

Providing water, along with the food supply for man and animals (Psalm 104:14); shelter for birds, cony, and goats (Psalm 104:17–18); orchestration of seasons (Psalm 104:19); formation of day and night (Psalm 104:20); and the breath necessary for life (Psalm 104:29) makes God's providential care and control evident.[643] At the psalm's end, the psalmist sings praises, saying, "O LORD, how manifold are thy works! In wisdom hast thou made them all: the earth is full of thy riches" (Psalm 104:24). And to that we say amen.

"God is by no means remote from the world created long ago."[644]—L. C. Allen.

~September 15~

Psalm 104:34

The Sweetness and Profit of Meditation

"My meditation of him shall be sweet: I will be glad in the LORD" (Psalm 104:34).

Meditation is a duty of the righteous and was practiced often by David. Concisely note four aspects of it.

The focus of meditation. "My meditation of him." Meditation is to be primarily on Him—His person, instruction, works (especially in redemption), promises, and goodness. Says Spurgeon, "Meditation is the soul of religion....We ought, therefore, both for our good and for the Lord's honor to be much occupied with meditation, and that meditation should chiefly dwell upon the Lord Himself: it should be 'meditation of Him.' For want of it, much communion is lost, and much happiness is missed."

The fuel of meditation. Affection and love for the Lord prompt meditation, while the Scripture jump-starts and governs it.

The function of meditation. It is the practice of musing, mulling, and pondering scriptural teaching for its meaning and application. Müller said, "The most important thing I had to do was to read the Word of God and to meditate on it. Thus, my heart might be comforted, encouraged, warned, reproved, and instructed."

The fruit of meditation. "Shall be sweet."

1. It illuminates and instills the truth pondered.

2. It strengthens the soul.

3. It delights the heart. Spending time in God's presence is enjoyable, reflecting upon His mighty deeds, wonders, and goodness. Nothing is sweeter. Spurgeon says, "To the meditative mind, every thought of God is full of joy."[645]

4. It excites praise to God for who He is and what He has done and is doing.

5. It enhances growth in godliness.

"The finger of God is seen by us when we pursue meditation."— John Flavel.

~September 16~

Psalm 104:34

How to Meditate on God

"My meditation of him shall be sweet: I will be glad in the LORD" (Psalm 104:34).

David's meditation was "of him." How do we meditate on God exclusively?

1. Through pondering His character. Fixate upon His sovereignty, eternality, love and mercy, holiness, perfection, immensity, and attributes.

2. Through pondering His works (Psalm 77:12).

288

1) In creation. Mull over the exquisite splendor and intrinsic design of the world God made out of nothing with only a word.

2) In redemption. Mull over its divine plan, horrendous cost, and wondrous undeserved offer.

3) In providence. Mull over God's protective care and provision for the world, especially the redeemed.

3. Through musing upon His Word, its doctrines and promises.

4. Through reflection upon the believer's future estate in Heaven with Him.

"How much happier might you be if you lived near to God in the contemplation of His excellencies and in the delightful exercise of prayer and praise!"[646]—Charles Simeon.

~September 17~

Psalm 104:24

The Wonder of Creation

"O LORD, how manifold are thy works! In wisdom hast thou made them all: the earth is full of thy riches" (Psalm 104:24).

"In wisdom hast thou made them all." The Earth is just the right size—any smaller, an atmosphere would be impossible, like Mercury; any larger, its atmosphere would contain free hydrogen, like Jupiter. Earth is the only known planet to possess the right combination of gases in its atmosphere to sustain animal, plant, and human life. Earth is at the perfect distance from the sun. The planets on either side of Earth, Venus and Mars, are too close to the sun and too far from it to support life as we see it on Earth. Earth's faithful rotation on its axis enables it to be properly warmed and cooled daily.

The uniformity and stability of nature are another mirror that reveals the hand of the intelligent designer of the Earth. Nature operates by inert, unchanging laws. The Earth rotates the same distance every 24 hours, the speed of light is consistent, gravity

289

remains the same, and day and night do not cease.[647] Matthew Henry remarks, "The heavenly bodies are vast, yet there is no flaw in them; numerous, yet no disorder in them; the motion rapid, yet no wear or tear."[648] Bridges says, "Every particle of the universe glitters with infinite skill."[649]

"The earth is full of thy riches." "The Creator," asserts Spurgeon, "has filled the earth with food, and not with bare necessaries only, but with riches—dainties, luxuries, beauties, treasures. In the bowels of the earth are hidden mines of wealth, and on her surface are teeming harvests of plenty."[650]

"O Lord, my God, when I in awesome wonder
Consider all the worlds Thy Hands have made,
I see the stars; I hear the rolling thunder
Thy power throughout the universe displayed."
—Carl Boberg (1885).

~September 18~
Psalm 105:1–5
A Thanksgiving Psalm

"O give thanks unto the LORD; call upon his name: make known his deeds among the people" (Psalm 105:1).

David testifies to God's goodness, mercy, and lovingkindness toward His people in granting pardon, provision, protection, and deliverance from trouble and oppression. The psalm recounts God's goodness to Abraham, Isaac, and Jacob (Psalm 105:9–16), Joseph (Psalm 105:17–22), Israel (Psalm 105:23–24), and Moses and the Israelites (Psalm 105:26–41). God's wondrous works in history, like these, reveal His faithfulness to all generations. David states that the marvelous works of God are grounds for jubilation and thanksgiving (Psalm 105:1–3), and future obedience and faith must not be forgotten (Psalm 105:4).

David's discourse is divided into four parts, each of which is applicable to us.

1. Remember what He has done (Psalm 105:5). Remember two things. God's mighty deeds of goodness and the power and faithfulness of His word. His promises are inviolable.

2. Tell of what He has done (Psalm 105:2). Communicate the works of God, especially in salvation, at home, and 'as we go by the way' (Deuteronomy 6:7).

3. Celebrate what He has done (Psalm 105:1–2). With ecstatic joy and song, give thanks for God's bountiful blessings, notably that of salvation. Maclaren says, "A silent Christian is an anomaly, a contradiction in terms, as much as black light or dark stars. If Christ is in you, He will come out of you."[651]

4. Pursue Him for what He has done (Psalm 105:4). Continuously seek His face in praise, then His hand in provision of strength for battle and service. Spurgeon says, "We need infinite power to bear us safely to our eternal resting place; let us look to the Almighty Jehovah for it."[652]

"Jehovah is the author of all our benefits; therefore, let him have all our gratitude."[653]—C. H. Spurgeon.

~September 19~

Psalm 105:19

The Testing of Trials

"Until the time that his word came: the word of the LORD tried him" (Psalm 105:19).

Dreams of promise bring testing through trials and troubles. Had Joseph not had dreams, he would have had no trials. The troubles of intense testing are part and parcel of pursuing dreams, due to their delayed realization and the opposition they face. Joseph's dream promised his royal exaltation in the land, but it tarried in fulfillment. Until the time came for it, he was tested by embittered brothers, savage slave traders, imprisonment, and the chief butler's forgetfulness to speak of him favorably to the king. Maclaren asserts, "We might either say that the non-fulfillment of the promise tested Joseph, or that the promise, by its non-fulfillment, tested him."[654] Two years after the butler's release from jail, he recalled the promise made to Joseph and spoke of his ability to interpret dreams to the king.

Dreams of promise, forged through trials and troubles, prepare us for their fruition. The dream of the promise of royal exaltation tested, purified, and strengthened Joseph's faith in the furnace of affliction in preparation for the advancement to Pharaoh's second-in-command. "It was a discipline indispensable if *Joseph* were to fitly fill the high station for which God had designed him."[655] Maclaren says, "'The word of the LORD tried him,' and because it tried him, it purified him. If we give credence, as we ought to, to that word, it will purify *us* and test what contexture our faith is."[656]

Though difficult to bear, trials purge the dross or impurities from us so that we may become pure gold, prepared for God's assigned or promised task. "But the God of all grace, who hath called us unto his eternal glory by Christ Jesus, after that ye have suffered a while, make you perfect, stablish, strengthen, settle you" (1 Peter 5:10). "That the trial of your faith, being much more precious than of gold that perisheth, though it be tried with fire, might be found unto praise and honor and glory at the appearing of Jesus Christ" (1 Peter 1:7).

Dreams of promise, though obstructed and opposed, come to pass. Matthew Henry remarked, "God's word tried him, tried his faith and patience, and then it came in power to give command for his release [from Potiphar's jail]. There is a time set when God's word will come for the comfort of all who trust it."[657] At Joseph's release, the dream was fulfilled. He was exalted to a position of power in Pharaoh's governorship, second only to him. God will keep His promises to His children who persevere in reaching for the dream He has implanted in their hearts. "For the vision is yet for an appointed time, but at the end it shall speak, and not lie: though it tarry, wait for it; because it will surely come, it will not tarry" (Habakkuk 2:3).

"Trials come to prove and improve us."—Augustine.

~September 20~
Psalm 105:19
Though the Vision Tarries

"Until the time that his word came: the word of the LORD tried him [Joseph]" (Psalm 105:19).

What has God called you to do or accomplish that has met with trouble and trials? "Though [*the vision* tarries], wait for it; because it will surely come" (Habakkuk 2:3). Confidence or assurance that God always keeps His promises, despite the length of time from the pledge to realization, enables perseverance. The knowledge that God tests ("the LORD tried him") believers to prepare them for their promised task or plan (not necessarily because of sin; Joseph was innocent of wrong) enhances faith when such is experienced.

Joseph, knowing that God's word to him, though it lingered, would be fulfilled, fueled his willingness to endure ridicule, slavery, false accusations, and imprisonment. Faith in God's promises or words instills patience in their delay, endurance in their testing or "light affliction" (2 Corinthians 4:7), encouragement in their "setbacks," and willingness to suffer until their realization. Faith conquers doubts. Spurgeon wrote, "He [Joseph] believed the promise, but his faith was sorely exercised. A delayed blessing tests people and proves their mettle, whether their faith is of that precious kind which can endure the fire. Of many a choice promise, we may say with Daniel, 'The thing was true, but the time appointed was long.'"[658]

"If the vision tarries, it is good to wait for it with patience. There is a trying word and a delivering word, and we must bear the one till the other comes to us." [659]—C. H. Spurgeon.

~September 21~

Psalm 105:38
A Hatred for the Light

"Egypt was glad when they departed: for the fear of them fell upon them" (Psalm 105:38).

Although Pharaoh wanted to keep Israel in Egyptian bondage, the people desired their freedom and departure for several reasons. They desired Israel's exodus out of terror of what had befallen them with the plagues at the hand of Jehovah God and would happen (Psalm 105:27–37; Exodus 15:16). They desired Israel's ousting to remove their witness as "salt and light" for God and righteousness. They desired Israel's exodus out of fear for their lives. The Egyptians "were urgent upon the people, that they might send them out of the land in haste; for they said, We be all dead men (Exodus 12:33). Spurgeon suggests the Egyptians wanted Israel's departure so desperately that they paid them to go with silver and gold. Note. God can change the heart of the bitterest enemy or a hostile religion to favor His people and plan.

The world loathes the Christians' presence and wishes for their speedy removal for three primary reasons.

1. Christians are lights that expose the deeds of darkness (sin, religious heresy, injustice), revealing what Francis Schaeffer called "True Truth" (John 3:19).

2. Christians are salt that irritates and disturbs the darkness (its moral corruption and decay) through their godliness, witness, and protest. Salt rubbed into a soul's decay pains before it purifies.

3. Christians are counted as the vilest and worst of men. Paul says, "Even today, we are treated as though we were the garbage of the world—the filth of the earth" (1 Corinthians 4:13 NCV).

Unwelcome, unaccepted, scorned, and persecuted? Remember, that was the world's response to Christ. Take heart. Canaan awaits.

"We can easily forgive a child who is afraid of the dark; the real tragedy of life is when men are afraid of the light."—Plato.

~September 22~
Psalm 105:42
The Promises That Cannot Fail

"For he remembered his holy promise" (Psalm 105:42).

The promise to Abraham that his seed would gain entry to the holy land was kept. The lesson taught is that God does not forget or fail to keep His promises. They are signed with His hand and assured with an oath. He is "the faithful God, which keepeth covenant...to a thousand generations" (Deuteronomy 7:9). Pink says, "The permanence of God's character guarantees the fulfillment of his promises." Spurgeon asserts, "God has given no pledge that He will not redeem, and encouraged no hope that He will not fulfill." His promises are trustworthy and dependable (Psalm 145:13 CEB). The promises infuse the soul with strength and courage, ensuring God's help in times of need.

Thomas Brooks states, "Satan promises the best but pays with the worst. He promises honor and pays with disgrace. He promises pleasure and pays with pain. He promises profit and pays with loss. He promises life and pays with death. But God pays as He promises. All His payments are made in pure gold."

Standing on the promises that cannot fail.
When the howling storms of doubt and fear assail,
By the living Word of God, I shall prevail,
Standing on the promises of God.
~Russell Kelso Carter (1886)

Luther said, "What greater rebellion against God, what greater wickedness, what greater contempt of God is there than not believing His promise? For what is this but to make God a liar or to doubt that He is truthful."[660]

295

"The Heavenly Father will not break His Word to His own child."—C. H. Spurgeon.

~September 23~

Psalm 106:15
Leanness of Soul

"And he gave them their request; but sent leanness into their soul" (Psalm 106:15).

The Israelites insisted on flesh to eat, so God gave them quail. Within a month, the quail became loathsome and disgusting, dissatisfying to them (Numbers 11:20). Several lessons may be gleaned from Israel's experience.

1. The carnal or fleshly heart places greater faith in self-wisdom than in God's wisdom to govern life.

2. Desires granted outside God's will remain displeasing to Him and bring leanness or impoverishment to the soul. Spurgeon asserts, "How earnestly might Israel have unprayed her prayers had she known what would come with their answer!"[661] How might we have also. The possession wanted, position coveted, or friendship craved in prayer thought a must when acquired proved injurious or dissatisfying to the soul. Spurgeon continues, "We fret and fume till we have our desire, and then we have to fret still more because the attainment of it ends in bitter disappointment."[662] That was the case with the prodigal son.

3. All desires should be entrusted to God to do what is best. "Not my will, but thine be done" should be the closure of every petition. Wiersbe states, "Selfish prayers are dangerous."[663]

4. God shows mercy in withholding what is asked. "All that glitters is not gold." An ungranted healing, promotion, job, business success, friendship, or relationship is grievous at the time, but once the reason is revealed, the heart rejoices that it was withheld.

"Those that will not wait for God's counsel shall justly be given up to their own hearts' lusts, to walk in their own counsels."[664]— Matthew Henry.

~September 24~
Psalm 106:25
Murmuring Against God

"But murmured in their tents" (Psalm 106:25).

In Egyptian bondage, the Israelites murmur. In pursuit by the Egyptian soldiers in the Exodus, they murmur. In the desolation of the wilderness, they murmur, saying, "Oh, that we had died in the land of Egypt!" They murmur over the manna, the "bitter water," the giants that occupied Canaan, Moses' and Aaron's leadership, and the time it took to get to the promised land.

1. Murmuring is a sin. The Bible says, "Neither murmur ye, as some of them also murmured, and were destroyed of the destroyer" (1 Corinthians 10:10). Broadus said, "An unthankful and complaining spirit is an abiding sin against God and a cause of almost continual unhappiness. How prone we seem to be to forget the good that life knows, and remember and brood over its evil; to forget its joys, and think only of its sorrows; to forget thankfulness, and remember only to complain."[665] Do I hear you say, ouch?

2. Murmuring is unprofitable. It brings no good. The only change it causes is one's disposition; it makes it repulsive. Few things are worse than hearing Christians grumble and complain in light of all God has done and is doing for them. The chorus to "The Grumbler's Song" describes them: "Oh, they grumble on Monday, Tuesday, and Wednesday and grumble on Thursday, too. They grumble on Friday, Saturday, and Sunday and grumble the whole week through."

3. Murmuring provokes God's wrath. "And the people grumbled and deplored their hardships, which was evil in the ears of the Lord, and when the Lord heard it, His anger was kindled" (Numbers 11:1 AMPC).

4. Murmuring prompts disobedience to God. "But murmured in their tents, and hearkened not unto the voice of the LORD" (Psalm 106:25).

5. Murmuring hurts others. "Whither shall we go up? Our brethren have discouraged our heart, saying, 'The people are greater and taller than we; the cities are great and walled up to heaven, and moreover we have seen the sons of the Anakim there'" (Deuteronomy 1:28 KJ21).

"Murmuring is a great sin and not a mere weakness; it contains within itself unbelief, pride, rebellion, and a whole host of sins."[666]— C. H. Spurgeon.

~September 25~

Psalm 106:35

Worldly Conformity

"But were mingled among the heathen, and learned their works" (Psalm 106:35).

Contrary to the command of God, the Israelites mingled with the morally filthy Canaanites in fellowship, learning their abominable ways. They deserted God, served the Canaanites' idols, submitted to their rule, intermarried with them, sacrificed their children to appease the demons, and manufactured "new gods." The impact of fraternization with the wicked leads to unthinkable religious and moral corruption. Israel's decline was shocking and appalling.

Spurgeon says, "None can tell what evil has come of the folly of worldly conformity."[667] Neither can one tell what damage to God's cause, hurt to others, and ruin have come from it. Solomon says, "Hang out with fools and watch your life fall to pieces" (Proverbs 13:20 MSG). Paul admonishes, "Be ye not unequally yoked together with unbelievers: for what fellowship hath righteousness with unrighteousness? and what communion hath light with darkness?" (2 Corinthians 6:14).

The wrath of God was kindled against his people. Offended at Israel's rebellion and corruption, God "gave them into the hand of the heathen" (the Mesopotamians, the Midianites, the Philistines, the Moabites), under whose rule they were persecuted. God chastises those He loves to bring them back into fellowship with Himself and conformity with His teachings and plan (Hebrews 12:6).

"Don't change yourselves to be like the people of this world" (Romans 12:2 ERV). A preacher once came to a city to win its people to Christ. At first, the people listened to his sermons, but gradually drifted away until none heard the preacher when he spoke. One day, a traveler said to him, "Why do you go on preaching?"

The preacher replied, "In the beginning, I hoped to change these people. If I still shout, it only prevents them from changing me." We must keep "shouting" the Truth to keep the world from changing us!

"That which is rotten will sooner corrupt that which is sound than be cured or made sound by it."[668]—Matthew Henry.

~September 26~
Psalm 106:9
A Word Can Do It

"He rebuked the Red Sea also, and it was dried up" (Psalm 106:9).

A word did it. At God's word, the Red Sea dried up to permit the Israelites to escape from the Egyptian army. It's a picture of the sinner's deliverance from the tyranny of Satan and the penalty of sin at Christ's word. Upon trust in Christ and repentance, He says, "Thy faith hath saved thee; go in peace."

Delitzsch says, "He speaks, and it is done; He commands, and it stands fast."[669] The Red Sea, at God's word, provided Israel's path to freedom from cruel bondage. At His word, Calvary provided sinners with an escape from the domination of Satan and Hell. The word was effectual for Israel; they were emancipated, never again to be in Egyptian bondage. It is efficacious for the repentant sinner; he is saved from the grip and power of sin forever. With God in the equation of man's trials and sin, it only takes a Word from God to change everything—just a Word.

"Oh, the power of the word of God! He spoke, and it was done, done really, effectually, and for perpetuity."[571]—Matthew Henry.

~September 27~

Psalm 107: 2

Go Tell

"Let the redeemed of the LORD *say so, whom he hath redeemed from the hand of the enemy"* (Psalm 107:2).

The redeemed in the context of the Psalm are those rescued from captivity and exile [perhaps Babylonian]. They were to declare their deliverance wide and far to the glory of God. As the redeemed of Christ, Christians are to join them in that undertaking.

Precisely, what is it that the redeemed are to declare? They are to tell how Jesus brought their meaningless and bewildered wandering to an end, filled life with a purpose (Psalm 107:4, 7), quenched their spiritual hunger and thirst (Psalm 107:5), satisfied their longing soul (Psalm 107:9), broke the chains of their bondage and eternal death to set them free (Psalm 107:10, 14, 16); saved them out of distresses or trouble (Psalm 107:13); healed them of the terminal sickness of sin (Psalm 107:20); calmed the raging storms pounding against the vessel of their life (Psalm 107:29) and granted them an abundant life complete with material and spiritual blessings (Psalm 107:38). In capsule the redeemed are to declare His "goodness, and...wonderful works" (Psalm 107:21) and give Him praise for it.

"If the redeemed remain silent, surely God will fail of his chief glory from the earth."[670]—W. S. Plumer.

~September 28~

Psalm 107:5

The Sinner's Portrait

"Hungry and thirsty, their soul fainted in them" (Psalm 107:5).

The psalmist uses four metaphors that might be used to depict sinners and their need for salvation.

1. A wanderer in the wilderness (Psalm 107:4). The sinner searches for satisfaction, meaning, and happiness, but in all the wrong places. Only Christ "satisfieth the longing soul." "The worldling is not satisfied and cannot be."[671] Compared with the Christian's fullness of delight, the joys of the ungodly are like a water bucket to the ocean.

2. A prisoner in chains (Psalm 107:10). He is shackled with heavy chains to sin and held in cruel captivity by and slavery to Satan.

3. A sick man near death (Psalm 107:18). He is afflicted with the malady of sin, which brings guilt, misery, unhappiness, suffering, and, in the end, eternal death. He is called a fool because his transgressions and rebellion against God brought the condition upon himself.

4. A mariner at sea in a fierce storm (Psalm 107:23). Troubles, trials, and fear of destruction like the boisterous winds a sailor faces in a storm at sea drive the sinner to despair and hopelessness.

The sinner's only deliverance is in Jesus. The psalmist says, "For he satisfieth the longing soul, and filleth the hungry soul with goodness" (Psalm 107:9). "Then they cried unto the LORD in their trouble, and he delivered them out of their distresses" (Psalm 107:6).

"No man is excluded from calling upon God. The gate of salvation is set open unto all men; neither is there any other thing which keepeth us back from entering in, save only our own unbelief."— John Calvin.

301

~September 29~

Psalm 107:16
Gates of Brass and Bars of Iron

"For he hath broken the gates of brass, and cut the bars of iron in sunder" (Psalm 107:16).

God broke the gates of brass and bars of iron of the Israelites' Babylonian captivity. The text may be applied to the sinner's captivity and deliverance.

The sinner's dilemma (Psalm 107:10–12).

1. Sinners are rebellious men. "They rebelled against the words of God." All stand guilty of violating God's word, His commandments, at some point (Romans 3:23). Luther said, "The recognition of sin is the beginning of salvation."

2. They are condemned men. They "sit in…the shadow of death." The sinner sits in the shadow of eternal death (John 3:18; Romans 6:23).

3. They are shackled men. "Bound in affliction and iron." Prisoners, they are, in Satan's prison camp. Paul says, "And that they may recover themselves out of the snare of the devil, who are taken captive by him at his will" (2 Timothy 2:26).

4. They are miserable men. "He brought down their heart with labour." Sin causes misery, distress, and despair. "Many sorrows shall be to the wicked" (Psalm 32:10).

5. They are helpless men. "There was none to help." John Gill says, "When sinners see there is help in no other, they apply to Him [Christ]."

The sinner's deliverer and deliverance. "They cried unto the LORD in their trouble, and he saved them out of their distresses. He brought them out of darkness and the shadow of death, and brake their bands in sunder" (Psalm 107:13–14).

1. The deliverer of the soul taken captive by Satan is the Lord Jesus Christ. None but Him can liberate the soul from the chains of sin and Hell.

2. The deliverance is enacted by crying unto Christ for forgiveness and rescue. "For whosoever shall call upon the name of the Lord shall be saved" (Romans 10:13).

3. The deliverance will be complete and everlasting. "He brought them out of darkness and the shadow of death." Spurgeon states, "The Lord's deliverances are of the most complete and triumphant kind; He neither leaves the soul in darkness nor in bonds nor does He permit the powers of evil again to enthrall the liberated captive. What He does is done forever."[672] Hallelujah!

"When God will work deliverance, the greatest difficulties that lie in the way shall be made nothing of."[673]—Matthew Henry.

~September 30~

Psalm 107:16
John Bunyan's Salvation Text

"For he hath broken the gates of brass, and cut the bars of iron in sunder" (Psalm 107:16).

John Bunyan applied the text to Christ, breaking the gates of brass and iron of his fortified heart to save him. He wrote, "Good Lord, break it open; Lord, break these gates of brass and cut these bars of iron asunder." Bunyan's vehement resistance, induced by Satan's tug, was overcome by Christ's love and power. Spurgeon wrote, "Brass and iron are as tow before the flame of Jesus' love."[674]

Manasseh, a rebellious blasphemer who defied God and His word ardently, worshipped and sacrificed his son to Baal, consulted mediums and spiritists, practiced divination, and was counted by God to be more wicked than the Amorites, saw the brass gates and iron bars of Satan's imprisoning power and his staunch hardness to God crumble to bring about his salvation. The power that broke down Manasseh's seemingly impenetrable gate and wall can break the hardest and stubbornest heart, subdue the most rebellious will, enlighten the darkest mind to the Gospel truth, and thwart the fiercest opposition and difficulties.

Note. The text provides hope for the Christian captive to sin. Spurgeon wrote, "God is able to liberate men from every bond of sin over which they mourn. Wouldst thou be free? He will open the door. There is no habit so inveterate, there is no passion so ferocious, but God can deliver you from it. If you will but trust in Jesus Christ, the Son of God, His grace is a hammer that can break your chains."[675] Jesus said, "If the Son therefore shall make you free, ye shall be free indeed" (John 8:36).

"No man is excluded from calling upon God, the gate of salvation is set open unto all men; neither is there any other thing which keepeth us back from entering in, save only our own unbelief."— John Calvin.

~October 1~

Psalm 107:29
The Reason for Storms

"He maketh the storm a calm, so that the waves thereof are still" (Psalm 107:29).

Storms are messengers of God, enveloped in love, to either correct us, chastise us, change us (develop and mold us spiritually), or convert us.

Storms happen to correct. In response to God's call to Jonah to be a foreign missionary to Ninevah, he went in the opposite direction to Tarshish. The Bible says it was then that "the LORD hurled a powerful wind over the sea, causing a violent storm that threatened to break the ship apart" (Jonah 1:4 NLT). The storm was so horrific that seasoned sailors panicked and futilely tossed all the ship's cargo overboard and prayed to their false deities. Eventually, they realized Jonah was the reason for the storm and cast him into the sea. Immediately, the turbulent sea became a pillar of glass, and the raging winds ceased. Jonah's disobedience had caused the storm. It was a corrective storm designed to get Jonah back on the right track, which it did. We experience a correcting storm, as did Jonah, upon doing something contrary to God's Word and plan (Psalm 119:67).

Storms happen to chastise. Jeremiah said, "Look! It is a storm from the LORD! He is angry and has gone out to punish the people. Punishment will come like a storm crashing down on the evil people" (Jeremiah 30:23 NCV). Charles Stanley said, "To chastise us, to get our attention, and to get our protection lest we absolutely destroy ourselves, God does send storms into our life."

Storms happen to change. To strengthen the disciples' faith, a storm overtook them at sea (Matthew 14:24). It accomplished its purpose, for in its aftermath, they worshiped Jesus, saying, "You really are the Son of God!" (Matthew 14:33 NLT). Storms serve to build faith, trust, and utter dependence upon God.

Storms happen to convert. Trials and troubles sometimes are the loving designs of God to bring the sinner into His fold, as with the case of Manasseh (2 Chronicles 33:10–13).

He that sends the storm, designs it, controls it, and walks with us through it. Storms, once achieving their purpose, are abated. "He maketh the storm a calm."

"Sometimes the Lord rides out the storm with us, and other times He calms the restless sea around us. Most of all, He calms the storm inside us in our deepest inner soul."—Lloyd John Ogilvie.

~October 2~

Psalm 107:33
When the Watersprings Dry Up

"He turneth rivers into a wilderness, and the watersprings into dry ground" (Psalm 107:33).

Blessings can dry up "for the wickedness of them that dwell therein." A fruitful land can become barren because of its inhabitants' sins. Once a fruitful land, Canaan became infertile due to God's judgment upon Israel's rebellion (Deuteronomy 29:23). When men place God's blessings above their devotion to and dependence upon Him, abuse them, or live evilly, He can cause them to dry up. Isaac Watts wrote, "'Tis God who lifts our comforts high or sinks them in the grave. He gives, and (blessed be His name) He takes but what he gave."

He turneth the dry land into watersprings. Upon repentance, God restores what His judgment rightly took away: the water springs of bountiful and perpetual soul nourishment and refreshment. The Lord says, "I will give you back what you lost in the years when swarms of locusts ate your crops" (Joel 2:25 GNT). How does God restore the years the locusts (the judgment of God upon sin) have eaten?

1. To the nation of Israel, it meant spiritual restoration (the people's renewal and joy [Joel 2:27, 23]) and physical (their land would be replenished with good crops [Joel 2:24]).

2. Its application to saints. We deserve the severe chastisement (punishment) that accompanies our sin. Any restoration and restitution God grants in its aftermath are entirely based on His mercy, not our merit. God gives back in the same kind as he did to Job, or by giving what is akin to the likeness of what was lost.[676] Sometimes, He gives back double. "Even today do I declare that I will render double unto thee" (Zechariah 9:12). Recall that God returned to Job twice the portion of his goods so that his latter end was blessed better than the former (Job 42:12). Matthew Henry says, "In compassion, He makes restitution; as the father of the prodigal, upon his return, made up all he had lost by his sin and folly, and took him into his family, as in his former estate."[677]

"Lost years can never be restored literally. You cannot have back your time, but there is a strange and wonderful way in which God can give back to you the wasted blessings and the unripened fruits of years over which you have mourned. The fruits of wasted years may yet be yours."[678]—C. H. Spurgeon.

~October 3~
Psalm 107:43
God's Lovingkindness

"Whoso is wise, and will observe these things, even they shall understand the lovingkindness of the LORD" (Psalm 107:43).

Lovingkindness is the steadfast love, goodness, and mercy of the Lord. It is understood best upon consideration of its numerous ways of display, twelve of which are cited in the psalm. "In a thousand ways," says Spurgeon, "the lovingkindness of the Lord is shown, and if we will but prudently watch, we shall come to a better understanding of it."[679]

God satisfies the longing soul, forgives and cleanses confessed sin repeatedly, shelters in trouble, sets the captive free, heals infirmities, protects in and calms the raging storm, turns dry and withering hearts into springs of living water of health and fruitfulness, dispels darkness and ignorance, manifests goodness to the underserving, and gives a haven of rest at life's end to the righteous. Of all of the displays of God's lovingkindness, that of furnishing Heaven at life's end surfaces to the top with the redemption of our soul (Psalm 107:30). Note.

The Captain. Christ guides the saint safely to Canaan from spiritual Egypt through the wilderness of sin. We would shipwreck without His keeping and guiding hand. Pretentious captains always cause their vessels to sink.

The Carrier. "So he bringeth them." Saints are passengers aboard the old ship of Zion. It has never marooned, wandered off course, or lost a passenger. Its compass is infallible and construction invincible.

The City. For several reasons, believers look forward to their "desired haven," an eternal dwelling place in that city whose maker and builder is God.

1. King Jesus resides there.

2. Loved ones await there.

3. Joy, peace, rest, reunion, and absence of sorrow, fear, and pain abide there.

4. Praise and worship continue day and night there. Indeed, we say with Spurgeon, "Our heavenly haven shall ring with shouts of grateful joy when once we reach its blessed shore."

"God carries your picture in His wallet."—Tony Campolo.

~October 4~

Psalm 108:1

Fixation on God

"O God, my heart is fixed" (Psalm 108:1).

Tuck wrote, "What is the most striking thing in David's career is his fixity for God, the steadfastness of his purpose to live for God."[680] We all need such fixity. What constitutes a fixed heart?

1. A fixed heart is focused. It focuses on Christ, rather than the difficulty and the enemy. The French author Gustave Flaubert remarked, "The principal thing in this world is to keep one's soul aloft."[681] And that is done by constantly looking to Christ.

2. A fixed heart is firm. Alexander the Great was asked how he conquered the world, to which he replied, "By not wavering." "Therefore, my beloved brethren, be ye steadfast, unmoveable, always abounding in the work of the Lord, forasmuch as ye know that your labour is not in vain in the Lord" (1 Corinthians 15:58).

3. A fixed heart is free. It knows no fear or worries in times of trouble. An unexplainable peace envelops life in every high and low experience.

4. A fixed heart is fortified. It is protected against compromise and corruption by intimate and immense devotion to the Lord. Love for Christ restrains sin (Psalm 101:2).

A fixed heart is demonstrated in unerring trust in God, unswerving service for God, unadulterated behavior before God, undivided allegiance to God, and unending praise unto God.

"When the central axle is secure, the whole wheel is right."[682]— C. H. Spurgeon.

~October 5~

Psalm 109:6–20
David's Imprecations

"When he shall be judged, let him be condemned" (Psalm 109:7).

An imprecatory psalm, like this psalm, calls down judgment and calamity upon the enemies of God and Israel. David hated the wicked and wished for God to severely judge them based on their hatred of God and wanton, blasphemous, and rebellious conduct toward Him and His people. David said, "Do not I hate them, O LORD, that hate thee? And am not I grieved with those that rise up against thee? I hate them with perfect hatred: I count them mine enemies" (Psalm 139:21–22).

David's imprecations teach three lessons.

1. Hate the sin, not the sinner. There is a place for righteous indignation against evil and evildoers. Spurgeon asserts, "We wish well to all mankind, and for that very reason, we sometimes blaze with indignation against the inhuman wretches by whom every law which protects our fellow creatures is trampled down, and every dictate of humanity is set at naught."[683]

2. Manifest the love principles taught by Jesus in dealing with the wicked (Matthew 5:43).

3. Always leave the sinners' vengeance in God's hands. This David did. "Avenge not yourselves" (Romans 12:19). Churchill said, "Nothing is more costly, nothing is more sterile than vengeance."

"A man that studieth revenge keeps his own wounds green."—
Francis Bacon.

~October 6~

Psalm 109:1
Only a Word Did It

"Hold not thy peace" (Psalm 109:1).

David asks God to break His silence and speak to him in his
trial and hurt. It is a prayer of trustful confidence in God's ability
and readiness to help him. Says Spurgeon, "Note that he only asks
the Lord to speak; a word from God is all a believer needs."[684] The
psalmist says, "Praise him, ye heavens of heavens, and ye waters
that be above the heavens. Let them praise the name of the LORD:
for he commanded, and they were created" (Psalm 148:4–5). It only
takes one simple, powerful word from God to supply what is needed.

At God's word, the turbulent sea becomes like a pillar of glass;
the sick is raised to health; the garment of sorrow is changed to that
of praise; victory is brought out of defeat; evil is thwarted, and the
enemy overcome; sin is forgiven and cleansed; the blinded see the
truth; the impossible is made possible; and power to do mighty
works is given. God says, "In the same way, my words leave my
mouth, and they don't come back without results. My words make
the things happen that I want to happen. They succeed in doing what
I send them to do" (Isaiah 55:11 ERV). His word never returns void
or unsuccessful. Therefore, don't panic or be dismayed in life's
battles and challenges, but ask God to speak the needed word of
empowerment, provision, or deliverance.

"God's word is creative. With the utterance, the result is
achieved."[685]—G. Rawlinson.

~October 7~
Psalm 109:27
That the Wicked May Know

"That they may know that this is thy hand; that thou, LORD, hast done it" (Psalm 109:27).

David wished the punishment of the ungodly, not for fleshly satisfaction but for their acknowledgment of Jehovah's mercy to them, and as the true and faithful God.

Recall that the magicians of Egypt refuted God's hand at work in the first and second plagues. But, in the third plague, when gnats were formed from dust, they were forced to say, "This is the finger of God." Lord, do that for us that will cause the ungodly to see and acknowledge your hand of power at work as did Pharaoh's magicians, for they will dismiss YOU in the equation unless compelled by the evidence to the contrary. Note. Though the magicians recognized the hand of God at work, Pharaoh remained stubborn and resistant. Willful blindness prevents people from seeing the truth staring them in the face about God.

"Ungodly men will not see God's hand in anything if they can help it."[686]—C. H. Spurgeon.

~October 8~
Psalm 110:1
Overhearing a Heavenly Conversation

"The LORD said unto my Lord, Sit thou at my right hand, until I make thine enemies thy footstool" (Psalm 110:1).

David was privy to a heavenly conversation between God the Father and His son, referenced several times in the New Testament. Its subject is Christ's return to Heaven after winning man's salvation at Calvary and enthronement in glory and majesty.

The conversation states or implies five things about the Messiah.

1. It speaks of the Messiah's majesty. "But we see Jesus, who was made a little lower than the angels for the suffering of death, crowned with glory and honor; that he by the grace of God should taste death for every man" (Hebrews 2:9).

2. It speaks of the Messiah's ministry. "He is the one who died to cleanse us and clear our record of all sin, and then sat down in highest honor beside the great God of heaven" (Hebrews 1:3b TLB).

3. It speaks of the Messiah's message. 'Repent because the Kingdom of God is near' (Matthew 3:2).

4. It speaks of the Messiah's mediation. "He ever liveth to make intercession for them" (Hebrews 7:25).

5. It speaks of the Messiah's might. "He regulates the universe by the mighty power of his command" (Hebrews 1:3a TLB), and "He is able also to save them to the uttermost that come unto God by him" (Hebrews 7:25).

"O thou precious Lord Jesus Christ, we do adore Thee with all our hearts. Thou art Lord of all."—C. H. Spurgeon.

~October 9~

Psalm 111:10
Godly Wisdom

"The fear of the LORD is the beginning of wisdom: a good understanding have all they that do his commandments: his praise endureth forever" (Psalm 111:10).

The text resembles Proverbs 1:7 in citing or implying three facts about godly wisdom.

The foundation of wisdom. "The fear of the LORD." Wisdom is imparted to those who fear God (reverence for and obedience to Him) through biblical knowledge and the Holy Spirit (James 1:5). Plumer asserts, "There is no wisdom in men till they fear God. When they do fear God, that is the wisest thing they do.'[687]

The fruit of wisdom.

1. Based on biblical knowledge, wisdom conveys understanding or discernment to know what is right and prudent in any situation. Davies says it chooses the right end and uses the right means to obtain it.[688]

2. It helps the believer to live righteously and justly.[689]

3. Wisdom instructs in the application of the Scriptures.

4. It benefits life with happiness, success, safety, confidence, peace, contentment, and added days (Proverbs 3:16–26).

The fraud of wisdom. Trusting in one's wisdom or the world's wisdom is unwisdom.[690] Isaiah warned, "Woe unto them that are wise in their own eyes, and prudent in their own sight!" (Isaiah 5:21). William Law wrote nearly two centuries ago, "Man needs to be saved from his own wisdom as much as from his own righteousness, for they produce one and the same corruption."[691] Solomon, in Proverbs, masterfully, under divine inspiration, makes an all-out effort to rescue man from "human wisdom" by revealing its falsity, deception, corruption, and inferiority to that of God. The only source of true wisdom comes from dependence and trust in God.

"Wisdom is the right use of knowledge. To know is not to be wise. But to know how to use knowledge is to have wisdom."— C. H. Spurgeon.

~October 10~

Psalm 112:7
Don't Fear Bad News

"He is not afraid of bad news" (Psalm 112:7 ESV).

The ending thought of Psalm 111 is expanded in Psalm 112 by stating the benefits of the godly ("the man that feareth the LORD"). David includes peace in the wake of evil tidings as one of the benefits.

Evil tidings come suddenly and surprisingly in several ways.

1. The evil tidings of death. It comes when a divine messenger says to us, "Set thine house in order, for thou shalt die and not live," or news of the death of a loved one is learned.

2. The evil tidings of disease. The doctor will tell us of a terminal or debilitating sickness.

3. The evil tidings of defamation. It comes when slanderous statements about us are learned. It is believed by some scholars that David had slander in mind when writing the text.

4. The evil tidings of disaster. It comes when news of calamity and significant loss is learned. Four messengers told Job of his loss of livestock, camels, property, and the death of his servants and children. Talk about evil tidings; Job got four back-to-back!

Bad news may cause discomfort, but it fails to rattle, panic, and frighten those who trust in the Lord. Why? They say with Job, "Though he slay me, yet will I trust in him" (Job 13:15). They say confidently with Paul, "And we know that all that happens to us is working for our good if we love God and are fitting into his plans" (Romans 8:28 TLB). They say with David, "My heart is fixed, O God, my heart is fixed" (Psalm 57:7).

The heart fixed or established on the trustworthiness of God, "shall not be afraid" (Psalm 112:8). Spurgeon said, "Evil tidings may come to an heir of Heaven. He ought not to be afraid of them. The way to be prepared for them is to have the heart fixed and prepared, and the method of having the heart fixed is confident trustfulness in the Lord."[692]

Solomon says, "In the fear of the LORD is strong confidence: and his children shall have a place of refuge" (Proverbs 14:26). Horne states of the godly, "He feareth no evil report; no blast of slander and malice can touch him; no tidings of calamity and destruction can **shake his** confidence in God."[693]

"There are those whose life is full of slavish fear. But he who keeps God's Word enjoys the guardianship of his Almighty arm. 'The Lord is his confidence'; his days are spent in quietness and calmness, and 'his sleep is sweet.'"[694]—W. Clarkson.

Psalm 113:4-5

Our Incomparable God

"The LORD is high above all nations, and his glory above the heavens. Who is like unto the LORD our God, who dwelleth on high" (Psalm 113:4–5).

"Whatever men," asserts Matthew Henry, "may set in competition with Him, there is none to be compared with Him."[695]

1. None compare to God's mercifulness. The world embraces gods who will only exchange love and mercy for deeds done or a change in conduct. But Jehovah God shows love freely to all that call upon Him "without money and without cost" (Isaiah 55:1 NIV). "He," Spurgeon says, "pours forth His love in plenteous streams to undeserving, ill-deserving, Hell-deserving objects."[696]

2. None compare to God's mightiness. Watson wrote, "God hath in Himself all power to defend you, all wisdom to direct you, all mercy to pardon you, all grace to enrich you, all righteousness to clothe you, all goodness to supply you, and all happiness to crown you."

3. None compare to God's unchangeableness. "I am the LORD, I change not" (Malachi 3:6). Tozer asserts, "All that God is He has always been, and all that He has been and is He will ever be." God's purposes, promises, and plans are changeless, as is His nature.

4. None compare to God's faithfulness. He is wholly trustworthy. Pink states, "God is true. His Word of Promise is sure. In all His relations with His people, God is faithful. He may be safely relied upon. No one ever yet really trusted Him in vain."[697]

5. None compare to God's friendship. He is that friend that sticks closer than a brother and lays down his life for his friends.

The bottom line: None compares to God in any respect. And, "this God is our God forever and ever; he will be our guide even to the end" (Psalm 48:14 NIV). Hallelujah!

"In the height of His abode, none can be like Him. His throne, His whole character, His person, His being, everything about Him, is lofty and infinitely majestic so that none can be likened unto Him."[698]—C. H. Spurgeon.

~October 12~

Psalm 114:1
The Greatest of All Miracles

"When Israel went out of Egypt" (Psalm 114:1).

Israel's deliverance from bondage in Egypt is a type of the sinner's rescue from captivity to sin.

The desire for deliverance. "The Israelis groaned because of the bondage. They cried out, and their cry for deliverance from slavery ascended to God" (Exodus 2:23 ISV). Application. Salvation (deliverance) from the tyranny of sin begins with a sincere desire for it. "If any man thirst, let him come unto Me, and drink" (John 7:37).

The difficulty of deliverance. Pharaoh's iron-clad domination over the Israelites, the barren wilderness (Exodus 14:3), and the Red Sea, which would have to be transversed to escape, proved impossible. Application. The sinner cannot unshackle his chains of bondage. He is hopeless and without excuse. "When we were utterly helpless, with no way of escape, Christ came at just the right time and died for us sinners who had no use for him" (Romans 5:6 TLB).

The design for deliverance. "And Moses stretched out his hand over the sea; and the LORD caused the sea to go back by a strong east wind all that night, and made the sea dry land, and the waters were divided. And the children of Israel went into the midst of the sea upon the dry ground: and the waters were a wall unto them on their right hand, and on their left" (Exodus 14:21–22). Application. "For there is one God, and one mediator between God and men, the man Christ Jesus; who gave Himself a ransom for all" (1 Timothy 2:5–6). Christ's outstretched arms on the Cross walled the "Red Sea" up on both sides, enabling the sinner's crossing to freedom.

The delight in deliverance. "Then sang Moses and the children of Israel this song unto the LORD, and spake, saying, I will sing unto the LORD, for he hath triumphed gloriously: the horse and his rider hath he thrown into the sea" (Exodus 15:1). Application. "Yea, happy is that people, whose God is the LORD" (Psalm 144:15). The saved soul says with Doddridge, "Happy day, happy day, when Jesus washed my sins away! He taught me how to watch and pray and live rejoicing every day. Happy day, happy day, when Jesus washed my sins away!"

"The greatest of all miracles is the salvation of a soul."—C. H. Spurgeon.

~October 13~

Psalm 115:1
Boastfulness

"Not unto us, O LORD, not unto us, but unto thy name give glory, for thy mercy, and for thy truth's sake" (Psalm 115:1).

Israel renounced any right to the credit and praise God alone deserved for His mighty works in and through them. Fleshly boasting or bragging about accomplishments and works steals the glory and honor that belong to God. Jehu did this by saying to Jehonadab, "Come with me, and see my zeal for the LORD" (2 Kings 10:16). Too many, like him, say, "Come and see what I have done: the wealth I obtained, the ministry I built, the service and success I achieved" (Deuteronomy 8:17).

Boastfulness is a sin that God judges severely. He will not share His glory with any man. "I am the LORD: that is my name: and my glory will I not give to another, neither my praise to graven images" (Isaiah 42:8). Our testimonies, praises, prayers, and songs must sound the same note: "Not unto us, O LORD, not unto us, but unto thy name give glory."[699] Matthew Henry said, "All our crowns must be cast at the feet of Him that sits upon the throne, for that is the proper place for them."[700]

317

On the heels of King Henry V's overwhelming victory over Agincourt, he ordered the chaplain to read this psalm to acknowledge God's hand in it. In reading the words, "Not unto us, O LORD,...but unto thy name give glory," King Henry and the cavalry dismounted and fell to the ground, praising God for the victory.[701] In every success and accomplishment, let us be as honorable and humble to give God the credit and praise as the king and his cavalry did.

"From blade to full corn, all the harvest is of You, O Lord, and to You let it be ascribed."[702]—C. H. Spurgeon.

~October 14~

Psalm 115:12
God's Mindfulness of Man

"The LORD hath been mindful of us" (Psalm 115:12).

Without exception, God is mindful of us.

Mindful of us at the foundation of the world. In God's foreknowledge, He knew man would sin and planned his redemption through His beloved Son, Jesus.

Mindful of us before our birth. "You saw me before I was born and scheduled each day of my life before I began to breathe. Every day was recorded in your book!" (Psalm 139:16 TLB). God designed a blueprint for our lives before we were born.

Mindful of us in trouble. God is with us in trouble (Psalm 46:1), protecting us from innumerable dangers. Not a teardrop falls from our eyes, a strand of hair falls from our head, of which He is unaware or uncaring.

Mindful of us in need. Matthew Henry wrote, "He has been mindful of our case, our wants and burdens, mindful of our prayers to Him, His promises to us."[703]

Mindful of us in death. Spurgeon states that when the saint is "dying, and the cold chilly waters of Jordan are gathering about him

318

up to the neck, Jesus puts His arms around him, and cries, 'Fear not, beloved; to die is to be blessed. The waters of death have their fountainhead in Heaven.'"[704]

"All our comforts are derived from God's thoughts to usward; He has been mindful of us, though we have forgotten him."[705]— Matthew Henry.

~October 15~
Psalm 115:17
The Dead Praise Not the Lord

"The dead praise not the LORD" (Psalm 115:17).

The psalmist is not saying man's existence terminates at death, but that the ability to offer praise to God on earth ends in death. Therefore, if, as His children, we have reason to praise God, and we do, it must be done here and now. "No praises are given to God on earth by dead people."[706] Before our tongues are silenced in death, let's give God the deserving offering of praise and gratitude. Praise Him primarily for six blessings.

1. The salvation He brought and bought. "We bless the Lord with the most fervent gratitude as we realize that He has healed our disease and redeemed our life from destruction."[707]

2. The gift of life with its splendor and joys. Each day of life is a gift from God to us. How we unwrap it and use it is our gift to Him.

3. Faithful companionships that make the journey through life happier and more fulfilling. Aristotle wrote, "Without friends, no one would want to live, even if he had all other goods."

4. Good and pleasant things afforded without being deserved. Truly, "every good gift and every perfect gift is from above, coming down from the Father of lights" (James 1:17 ASV).

5. The privilege of service. Christians have been chosen to minister in His name. Jesus said, "You did not choose me; I chose you. And I gave you this work: to go and produce fruit, fruit that will last" (John 15:16 NCV). Just think, we get to preach, teach, sing, and witness for our Lord. What a blessing!

6. The Bible. Praise God for His many precious promises, precepts, and comforts.

7. The body of Christ. "LORD, I have loved the habitation of thy house, and the place where thine honor dwelleth" (Psalm 26:8). Thank God for its fellowship, worship, ministry, and unwavering stance on God's Word.

"Though the dead cannot, the wicked will not, and the careless do not praise God, yet we will shout 'Hallelujah' forever and ever."[708]—C. H. Spurgeon.

~October 16~

Psalm 115:17
Four Silenced Voices of Praise

"The dead praise not the LORD" (Psalm 115:17).

Note four silenced voices of praise, adapted from Spurgeon's sermon "Living Praise."[709]

1. The silenced voices of praise in the church. Sorely missed are the songs and words of the faithful and true who are now with the Lord. "The dead," says Spurgeon, "do not praise the Lord so far as this world is concerned. They cannot unite in the psalms and hymns and spiritual songs with which the church delights to adore her Lord. Thank God they have gone above to *swell the harmonies of the skies.*"[710]

2. The silenced voices of praise of the lost. Their hostility toward God prevents their worship and praise of Him.

3. The silenced voices of praise in Hell. None in Hell, bless and praise God. They have no access to God, the great salvation He offered on earth, or the power or desire to render Him praise (Psalm 6:5).

4. The silenced voices of our own praise. The hour will arrive when the opportunity to praise God with lips and life ends on earth. Say with the psalmist, "While I live will I praise the LORD; I will sing praises unto my God while I have any being" (Psalm 146:2 KJ21). Others cannot or will not praise God, "BUT we will bless the LORD from this time forth and for evermore" (Psalm 115:18). J. Vernon McGee said, "While we are here on earth, we are to praise the Lord—here is where it counts."[711]

"The tomb sends forth no voice."[712]—C. H. Spurgeon.

~October 17~

Psalm 116:15

Why the Death of a Saint Is Precious to God

"Precious in the sight of the LORD is the death of his saints" (Psalm 116:15).

The psalmist states that the death of the saint (a person saved by grace) is precious (honorable and valued) in the sight of God (Psalm 116:15). Thomas Spurgeon said that God rejoices in the death of a saint because it is the climax and culmination of all God's works on their behalf. Barnes asserts it's precious to God because it is "connected with His great plans," and "great purposes to be accomplished by it."

However, primarily, the death of saints is precious to God because they are His dearly beloved, prized jewels, and the redeemed of His hand. Pink wrote, "They ever were and always will be dear to Him. His saints! They were the ones on whom His love was set before the earth was formed or the Heavens made. These are they for whose sakes He left His Home on high and whom He bought with His precious blood, cheerfully laying down His life for them. These are they whose names are borne on our great High Priest's bosom and engraved on the palms of His hands. They are His Father's love-gift to Him, His children, members of His body; therefore, everything that concerns them is precious in His sight."[713]

> Most precious in our Savior's sight,
> Are all his saints' unnotic'd death!
> He bears them to eternal light,
> When they resign their mortal breath.
>
> Precious the soul by Him redeem'd,
> From threat'ning evils snatch'd away.
> Precious their dust, by Him esteem'd;
> He'll raise it at the latter day.
>
> Free from this world's unnumber'd cares,
> From Satan's rage and human spite,
> From sin's distress, and gloomy fears,
> How precious this in Jesus' sight!
>
> —James Relly (1776)

In earlier burial instructions, "Precious in the sight of the LORD is the death of his saints," along with other verses, was to be chanted. The practice is worthy of imitation.

"Those who are redeemed with precious blood are so dear to God that even their deaths are precious to Him."—C. H. Spurgeon.

~October 18~

Psalm 116:15
Why the Death of a Saint Is Precious to God

"Precious in the sight of the LORD is the death of his saints" (Psalm 116:15).

Why is the death of a saint counted as precious to God?

1. It signals the end of their sin. Death frees the believer from the power, presence, and penalty of sin. No sin plagues the believer in Heaven.

2. It signals the end of their suffering. Death ends the believer's pain and agony of illness and injury, enabling him to shout, "Free at last, free at last, Praise God Almighty, I'm free at last."

3. It signals the end of their struggle. It is said that we come into this world crying, and go out sighing. With death comes rest from trouble and trial.

4. It signals the end of their sorrow. Death brings an end to wrenching heartache and heartbreak. On the other side of death, saints dwell in a land where there is no more crying or grief (Revelation 21:4).

5. It signals the end of their separation. Presently, the saint is separated from the *physical* presence of the Lord and family and friends who preceded them to Heaven. At death, that separation ends. Hallelujah!

6. It signals the end of their shallowness. At death, ignorance of spiritual things and the acts of God will end. Paul says, "Our knowledge is incomplete and our ability to speak what God has revealed is incomplete" (1 Corinthians 13:9 GW). But at death, that which we know in part shall be known in its whole. "We'll understand it better by and by."

7. It signals the end of their sojourn. A saint's death is precious to God because it means their race is run, battle is over, and work is done. They persevered through persecution and suffering as good soldiers, standing firm, fighting courageously, and finishing well.[714]

N. Emmons asserts, "If the death of saints be precious in the sight of the Lord, then it ought to be precious and desirable in their own sight. They ought to live in hope, and not in fear of death."

"The saint's death is so precious to the Lord that He takes care to order all things respecting it for the saint's good and His own glory."—J. Walken.

~October 19~

Psalm 117:1–2
A Call to Missionary Work

"O praise the LORD, all ye nations: praise him, all ye people. For his merciful kindness is great toward us: and the truth of the LORD endureth forever. Praise ye the LORD" (Psalm 117:1–2).

It is the shortest Psalm in the Psalter and the shortest chapter in the Bible. Spurgeon states, "This Psalm, which is very little in its letter, is exceedingly large in its spirit."[715] The psalm is missionary in scope, exhorting believers to take the Gospel to all peoples of the world, bringing them to Christ so they may worship Him.

Piper states, "Missions exist because worship doesn't."[716] Pray that Psalm 117 be fulfilled so that 'all nations and peoples' will "Praise the LORD." It is then, and only then, that missionary efforts are no longer needed. Henry Martyn said, "The Spirit of Christ is the spirit of missions, and the nearer we get to Him, the more intensely missionary we must become."[717]

A South African society wrote to David Livingstone: "Have you found a good road to where you are? If so, we want to know how to send other men to join you."

Livingstone replied, "If you have men who will come only if they know there is a good road, I don't want them. I want men who will come if there is no road at all." God needs men who will go where He sends, road or no road (Luke 9:23). Will you be such a person and say, "Here am I, send me, send me?" Bonhoeffer said, "When Christ calls a man, he bids him come and die." Note. If age, sickness, or frailty prevents you from doing foreign mission work, enable others to go through praying and monetary support. "Ye also helping together by prayer for us" (2 Corinthians 1:11).

"If there be any one point in which the Christian church ought to keep its fervor at a white heat, it is concerning missions. If there is anything about which we cannot tolerate lukewarmness, it is sending the Gospel to a dying world."[718]—C. H. Spurgeon.

~October 20~

Psalm 118:8

Confidence in God, Not Man

"It is better to trust in the LORD than to put confidence in man" (Psalm 118:8).

The Bible has 31,174 verses. Psalm 118:8, fittingly, is number 15,587, making it the middle verse. Why is it better to trust God for help than man?

1. Man's help is limited in supply. The king testified from experience that the help of allies and counselors is feeble compared to that of Jehovah. It's insufficient to meet every need.

2. Man's help is limited in sphere. It is restricted to time and place, unlike the Lord's.

3. Man's help is limited in surety. It is unreliable in every circumstance and sometimes fallible in its implementation, whereas God's help is not.

4. Man's help is limited in scope. It avails not in the time of death. Only God can deliver the soul from eternal darkness and damnation to the everlasting light and glory of Heaven.

The bottom line. Man's help displays distrust in God's ability to help and provide. "It is better," says Matthew Henry, "more wise, more comfortable, and more safe, there is more reason for it, and it will speed better, to trust in the Lord, than to put confidence in man, yea, though it be in princes."[719] Spurgeon states, "Christians often look to man for help and counsel and mar the noble simplicity of their reliance upon their God. Is not God enough for thy need, or is His all-sufficiency too narrow for thy wants?"

What happens to him who trusts in man over God? Jeremiah says, "This is what the LORD says: 'Bad things will happen to those who put their trust in people. Bad things will happen to those who depend on human strength. That is because they have stopped trusting the LORD'" (Jeremiah 17:5 ERV). The psalmist is right: "It is better to trust in the LORD than to put confidence in man."

"It is better in every way to trust in the Lord because He is wiser, seeing He is more able to help than the best of men, who are only frail at best."[720]—Herbert Lockyer.

~October 21~

Psalm 118:14

What God is to the Believer

"The LORD is my strength and song, and is become my salvation" (Psalm 118:14).

When Israel was delivered from the Egyptians at the Red Sea, they sang those words. They will sing them again when gathered from the nations they are restored to their homeland. The hymn belongs to all God's children because it testifies to and praises God for all He is to them.

He is my strength. He provides enabling power to conquer the devil and temptation, stand fast in the trials of life, and render effective service in His name. Spurgeon said, "With Him for our strength, we cannot faint or fail; but, on the contrary, we shall renew our force and rise continually to something higher and better than before."[721] "Thy right hand, O LORD, is become glorious in power: thy right hand, O LORD, hath dashed in pieces the enemy" (Exodus 15:6).

He is my song. God is the fountainhead of the believer's joy and praise. He is our night song, sabbath day song, and everyday song. He provides unspeakable joy and satisfaction whatever betide.

He is my salvation. He gives grace to forgive our sins, mercy to cover them, and hope in trial, death, and the afterlife. He is our ready deliverer from harm and danger.

"It is a happy circumstance for us when we can praise God as alike our strength, song, and salvation."[722]—C. H. Spurgeon.

~October 22~

Psalm 118:22
Christ, the Cornerstone

"The stone which the builders refused is become the head stone of the corner" (Psalm 118:22).

Though rejected by those in authority, God raised David to prominence as king in Israel, making him the chief cornerstone (Psalm 118:22). However, a "greater than David" is seen here: Jesus Christ, the Messiah.

The cornerstone's design. The cornerstone is a masonry foundational stone on which the other building stones are placed. It determines the object's entire structure and durability. If the cornerstone is removed from a building, it will collapse. Jesus is the cornerstone of the Christian faith—His work (1 Peter 3:18), word (2 Timothy 3:16), and way (John 14:6). Christianity cannot stand and succeed apart from Him. He said, "Because of God's grace to me, I have laid the foundation like an expert builder. Now others are building on it. But whoever is building on this foundation must be very careful. For no one can lay any foundation other than the one we already have—Jesus Christ" (1 Corinthians 3:10–11 NLT).

The cornerstone's declaration. Cornerstones often bear an inscription citing the occasion for the structure. The church's cornerstone reads of Jesus: "He is also the head of the body, which is the church. He is the beginning, the firstborn from the dead, so that he himself might have first place in everything" (Colossians 1:18 ISV). The reception of Christ as Lord and Savior into one's life is the firm foundation on which to base saving faith. All other ground is sinking sand (Matthew 7:24–27).

The cornerstone's defiance. "The stone which the builders rejected." The builders—the rulers and the people of the Jews (Acts 4:8–11) made a fatal mistake. They rejected God's chosen one, Jesus, as the stone (promised Messiah). "He came unto his own, and his own received him not" (John 1:11). "This is the stone which was set at nought of you builders, which is become the head of the corner" (Acts 4:11).

They rejected God's choice of stone. They denied Him before Pilate (Acts 3:13), saying, "We have no king but Caesar" (John 19:15). They disdained Him before the crowd by trampling upon His position, message, and mission (Matthew 27:27–31). They plotted against Him. They crucified Him.

People still reject and despise Christ as the cornerstone of the faith (Lord and Savior of the world) without substantial cause, based on flawed theology and ideology. And of them, Spurgeon says, "Those who reject the chosen stone will stumble against him to their own hurt."[723]

The cornerstone's durability. "This is the LORD's doing." What God does "endureth forever." Let the religious builders deny and disdain God's choice as the cornerstone, Jesus Christ. Yet He "is become the head stone of the corner." Let them crucify and seal His body in a tomb with a *stone* pronouncing Him forever dead. Yet, He remains the *living stone* on which the Christian faith rests (1 Peter 2:5). "Therefore let all the house of Israel know assuredly, that God hath made the same Jesus, whom ye have crucified, both Lord and Christ" (Acts 2:36).

Matthew Henry states, "He has become the headstone of the corner; He is advanced to the highest degree both of honor and usefulness, to be above all, and all in all. He is the chief top-stone in the corner, in whom the building is completed, and who must in all things have the pre-eminence, as the author and finisher of our faith."[724]

"It is marvelous in our eyes." The works and wonders of salvation wrought by Christ, the church's cornerstone, are marvelous in our eyes. Amen.

"He is the stone in the way of eminence, without whom there can be no building, no house for God to dwell in among the children of men."[725]—Ebenezer Erskine.

Psalm 119:1–4
Traits of the Happy Man

"Blessed are the undefiled in the way, who walk in the law of the LORD. *Blessed are they that keep his testimonies, and that seek him with the whole heart. They also do no iniquity: they walk in his ways. Thou hast commanded us to keep thy precepts diligently"* (Psalm 119:1–4).

David characterizes the happy believer in four ways.

1. He consistently frames life on the commandments and instructions of God. Knowing their benefit, the righteous exert strength and force in their observance.

2. He pursues God wholeheartedly. He lives in hot pursuit of God with "all thy heart, and with all thy soul, and with all thy mind, and with all thy strength" (Mark 12:30).

3. He abstains from wickedness. Obedience to God's commandments prevents sin, enabling purity of heart (Psalm 119:11). Spurgeon says, "If it is constantly followed, no fault will arise."[726] But feet of clay occasionally will stumble in its keeping (1 John 2:1).

4. He keeps the commandments because they are God's directives. "Thou hast commanded." To base obedience to the law of God on culture, preference, or morality subjects it to compromise or disregard.

"A man who has no part in the grace of God cannot keep the commandments of God."—Martin Luther.

~October 24~

Psalm 119:5
Names Given to God's Law

"O that my ways were directed to keep thy statutes!" (Psalm 119:5).

David refers to the Word of God using ten distinct terms. Each term states what God expects and requires of us:

1. *Law.* The word occurs twenty-five times in the psalm. It is called law because it is our governing and regulatory rule and guide in righteousness.

2. *Commandments.* The Torah ("The Ten Commandments") and other "orders" or directives from the Lord. The word occurs twenty-two times.

3. *Precepts.* The word occurs twenty-one times and only appears in the Book of Psalms. It refers to the Lord's "prescribed" instructions.

4. *Word.* It refers to the communication of God, spoken or written. It is found forty-three times.

5. *Judgments.* The word is found twenty-three times. It is a judicial pronouncement of the law upon conduct.

6. *Righteousness.* The word occurs fourteen times. God's Word is holy and just, a standard or rule for righteous living.

7. *Statutes.* The word is found twenty times. It refers to the clear duties decreed by God for man.

8. *Way.* The word occurs thirteen times. It is the path (behavior; conduct) authorized by God for man's salvation and happiness.

9. *Truth.* It occurs five times. The principles of God's governing law are built on eternal truths.

10. *Testimonies.* The word occurs twenty-three times. The commandments witness God's holy and righteous nature, affirming all He has said as truth.

"The Bible in the memory is better than the Bible in the bookcase."—
C. H. Spurgeon.

Psalm 119:9
The Moral Guide for Life

"Wherewithal shall a young man cleanse his way? by taking heed thereto according to thy word" (Psalm 119:9).

There is one moral guide to governing life honorably and successfully—the word of God. It is plain, unchanging, inerrant, and applicable to all. Gill states, "The word of God is a most powerful antidote against sin, when it has a place in the heart; not only the precepts of it forbid sin, but the promises of it influence and engage to the purity of heart and life."[727]

No person can go wrong navigating life with the Bible as his guide, chart, and compass. It is the cleanest "Book" and will enable all who embrace its truth to be clean fully. "Sanctify them through thy truth: thy word is truth" (John 17:17). The man who rules his life by God's Word will be found to be honest, holy, happy, religious, reverent, and triumphant (Joshua 1:8; Psalm 1:3). Deviation from the pure and clean path to that of moral filthiness occurs when a person fails to 'take heed' to God's commandments.

"The Bible will keep you from sin, or sin will keep you from the Bible."—D. L. Moody.

Psalm 119:11
God's Word Prevents Sin

"Thy word have I hid in mine heart, that I might not sin against thee" (Psalm 119:11).

God's word, treasured in the heart, is a preventative barrier against temptation. But how does placing God's Word in the heart prevent sin?

1. By revelation. It identifies sin. Without it, the bitter may be counted as sweet and condoned.

2. By admonition. It warns of the destructive consequences of sin. "Moreover by them is thy servant warned" (Psalm 19:11).

3. By navigation. It points to the way of escape from sin. Not only does God's word detail the location of the dangerous quicksand, snares, treacherous shoals, sinkholes, and booby traps, but their way of avoidance and deliverance.

4. By fortification. It empowers restraint over sin. Gill said, "The word of God is a most powerful antidote against sin when it has a place in the heart." The Sword of the Spirit, the Word of God, is part of the believer's armor in battling evil.

God's word can enable our purity and holiness, provided it is placed in the heart and heeded.

"Heeding the Word of God leads to a godly lifestyle. Ignoring the Word of God leads to a godless rut."[728]—E. E. Hinson.

~October 27~

Psalm 119:33
Teach Me, Thy Statutes

"Teach me, O LORD, the way of thy statutes" (Psalm 119:33).

Upon asking God, like David, to instruct you in His commandments, four things will happen.

1. Teachings will be discovered. "Open thou mine eyes, that I may behold wondrous things out of thy law" (Psalm 119:18). The Divine ophthalmologist must open blinded eyes to behold the wonders of His law. And this He gladly does upon request. The naked eye is said to see only about 5,000 stars (the number varies),

but the astronomer with a powerful telescope sees millions if not billions. So, with the Bible. Its vast firmament can only be detected with the telescope of supernatural enlightenment.[729]

2. Understanding will unfold. "Give me understanding" (Psalm 119:34). The two disciples walking with Jesus on the Emmaus Road did not understand what the Word declared about the Messiah's death and resurrection. "Then opened He their understanding, that they might understand the scriptures" (Luke 24:45). Much of the scriptures are hard to understand and mystify apart from Divine illumination and enlightenment (2 Peter 3:15–16).

3. Devotion will increase. "Quicken thou me in thy way" (Psalm 119:37). As God teaches the way of His statutes, the heart is inflamed and stirred to engage in their practice.

4. Delight will intensify. "For therein do I delight" (Psalm 119:35). Spending time in the nook with the book, praying for God to unfold its teachings and understanding, enhances its desire and appetite. Soon, you will say, "Therefore I love thy commandments above gold; yea, above fine gold" (Psalm 119:127). So delightful is God's Word to him, taught by its Author, that it is 'kept to the end' (Psalm 119:33b).

"Those who are taught of God never forget their lessons."[730]— C. H. Spurgeon.

~October 28~
Psalm 119:33–36
God's Help in Keeping the Law
Part 1

"Teach me, O LORD, the way of thy statutes; and I shall keep it unto the end. Give me understanding, and I shall keep thy law; yea, I shall observe it with my whole heart. Make me to go in the path of thy commandments; for therein do I delight. Incline my heart unto thy testimonies, and not to covetousness" (Psalm 119:33–36).

David asks God to do seven things for him in the psalm. Of them, four will be reviewed today.

Teach me (Psalm 119:33). David avails himself of the right teacher (God), praying for spiritual enlightenment regarding the law (commandments) and how he might personally apply them.

Give me (Psalm 119:34). Knowledge of God's Word alone is insufficient. We must have God's wisdom to grasp its intent and profit, and His power for its adherence.

Make me (Psalm 119:35). David pleads for God's help to do what he passionately desires, not to stray from the right path. "The spirit indeed is willing, but the flesh is weak" (Matthew 26:41). Watts says, "Make me to walk in Thy commands; 'Tis a delightful road; Nor let my head, or heart, or hands, Offend against my God."

Incline me (Psalm 119:36). God must "incline" man's heart to faith, the distaste for sin and holiness of life, and the desire to obey His commandments.

"I will not trifle with my God—I will not divide my affections with the world; God shall have all."—Adam Clarke.

~October 29~

Psalm 119:37–40
God's Help in Keeping the Law
Part 2

"Turn away mine eyes from beholding vanity; and quicken thou me in thy way. Stablish thy word unto thy servant, who is devoted to thy fear. Turn away my reproach which I fear: for thy judgments are good. Behold, I have longed after thy precepts: quicken me in thy righteousness" (Psalm 119:37–40).

In addition to what was shared yesterday, David asks the Lord to do three more things for him.

Turn me (Psalm 119:37). David prays for blinders to be placed upon his eyes to that which is wrong that he might not stray, that he may pass every sort of sin without noticing it. The embryonic stage of sin is the first look.

Stablish me (Psalm 119:38). David prays, "Plant my feet solidly upon the assurance of thy promise that doubts may not jeopardize my walk." Spurgeon says, "Make me sure of thy sure Word."[731]

Quicken me (Psalm 119:37, 40). David prays for fresh or renewed strength to live a victorious life (to walk in righteousness and holiness). It is a noble, expedient prayer for all who have grown lazy, lethargic, sinfully indulgent, and complacent. "Revive me again." Thomas Watson said, "Leave not off reading the Bible till you find your hearts warmed. Let it not only inform you but inflame you."

"The Bible is the book of my life. It's the book I live with, the book I live by, the book I want to die by."—N. T. Wright.

~October 30~

Psalm 119:42–45
Promises to Make About God's Word
Part 1

"So shall I have wherewith to answer him that reproacheth me: for I trust in thy word. And take not the word of truth utterly out of my mouth; for I have hoped in thy judgments. So shall I keep thy law continually forever and ever. And I will walk at liberty: for I seek thy precepts" (Psalm 119:42–45).

Make the promises David made to God about His Word.

I will defend my belief (Psalm 119:42). The believer's faith is founded on the infallible Word of God. Therefore, its knowledge is essential to its defense (1 Peter 3:15).

I will keep thy law (Psalm 119:44). In response to God's unfailing kindness and mercies, David, in gratitude, pledges undying allegiance to the "Torah" (God's instructions and commandments on how to live righteously). Spurgeon says, "Nothing more effectually binds a man to the way of the Lord than an experience of the truth of his Word, embodied in the form of mercies and deliverances."[732]

I will walk at liberty (Psalm 119:45). The "word," instead of *shackling*, emancipates. Its adherence frees a person from the chains of sin that dominate and destroy. "Its observance is no restraint but the truest freedom."[733] Jesus affirms its liberating power: "You shall know the truth, and the truth shall set you free" (John 8:31–32 MEV). David says, "I will walk in freedom, for I have devoted myself to your commandments" (Psalm 119:45 NLT).

I will seek thy precepts (Psalm 119:45). David not only promises to walk according to the commandments that are known but "seek" them that are not. Spurgeon remarks, "Those who keep the law are sure to seek it and bestir themselves to keep it more and more."[734]

"The Bible redirects my will, cleanses my emotions, enlightens my mind, and quickens my total being."—E Stanley Jones.

~October 31~

Psalm 119:46–48
Promises to Make About God's Word
Part 2

"I will speak of thy testimonies also before kings, and will not be ashamed. And I will delight myself in thy commandments, which I have loved. My hands also will I lift up unto thy commandments, which I have loved; and I will meditate in thy statutes" (Psalm 119:46–48).

Yesterday, four promises the believer should make about God's Word based on David's pledge were cited. In this meditation, four more are considered.

I will speak of thy testimonies (Psalm 119:46). The "word" infused into David instilled confidence in the Lord, which exhibited itself in courage and bold witnessing. Trust in God's Word (promises) opens the mouth to testify without trepidation.

I will delight in thy commandments (Psalm 119:47). The statutes of God instill joy, cheerfulness, and happiness as they are absorbed and applied. J. A. Alexander wrote, "I will not obey them merely from a selfish dread of punishment or painful sense of obligation, but because I love them and derive my highest happiness from doing them."[735]

I will revere thy word (Psalm 119:48). David's reverence for God's word was expressed by worshipfully lifting his hands. McDonald asserts, "We revere the Bible in the sense that we stand in awe of its scope, its depths, its power, its treasures, and its infinity."[736]

I will meditate in thy statutes (Psalm 119:48). David pledges to ponder (as a cow chews its cud) over the Word. Matthew Henry paraphrases, "I will meditate in thy statutes, not only entertain myself with thinking of them as matters of speculation but contrive how I may observe them in the best manner."[737] "Meditation chews the cud and gets the sweetness and nutritive virtue of the Word into the heart and life; this is the way the godly bring forth much fruit."[738]

"If I were the Devil, one of my first aims would be to stop folk from digging into the Bible."—J. I. Packer.

~November 1~
Psalm 119:50
The Source of Comfort in Affliction

"This is my comfort in my affliction: for thy word hath quickened me" (Psalm 119:50).

A sure source of comfort and hope in a trial is the Holy Scripture. How does God's word quicken the troubled soul to peace?

1. It assures God's presence. The Scripture says, "He shall call upon me, and I will answer him: I will be with him in trouble; I will deliver him, and honor him" (Psalm 91:15).

2. It transmits God's power. God's word, enveloped with His sovereign power, speaks His peace and hope to the soul. Spurgeon states, "What energy a text will breathe into a man! There is more in one Divine sentence than in huge folios of human composition." The words of the most eloquent fall empty to console, but God's word brings calm and healing to the brokenhearted.

3. It attests God's promise. The promises of God are a balm of Gilead to the troubled soul. Spurgeon wrote, "Within the Scriptures, there is a balm for every wound and a salve for every sore!"[739] Whatever the hurt or hardship, grief or difficulty, anxiety or trauma, Christ provides and dispenses the needed medicine through the Holy Scriptures to comfort, console, calm, combat, cheer, and help cope victoriously. Horne says, "The promise is our 'comfort in affliction'; a comfort divine, strong, lasting; a comfort that will not, like all others, fail us when we most want it—in the day of sickness and at the hour of death."[740]

"One word of God, sealed to the heart, infuses more sensible relief than ten thousand words of man."[741]—Charles Bridges.

~November 2~
Psalm 119:63
Toxic Companions

"I am a companion of all them that fear thee, and of them that keep thy precepts" (Psalm 119:63).

David's avowal was not to associate, consort, socialize with, or take to be a friend the wicked; only those who loved God and obeyed His commandments. Toxic companions exert a destructive influence in four ways.

1. Toxic companions influence by their character. Paul states, "Do not be deceived: 'Bad company corrupts good morals'" (1 Corinthians 15:33 AMP). Goethe said, "Tell me with whom thou art found, and I will tell thee who thou art." We become like those

with whom we associate. Pure and clean water passing through a dirty pipe will become dirty. Does placing a good apple next to a rotten apple change the nature of that rotten apple? No, but the rotten apple changes the nature of the good one. Many clean and promising lives have fallen into the mire and filth of sin due to wrong associations.

2. Toxic companions influence by their counsel. The ungodly advocate for Satan, the path of corruption, and disdain of God and the commandments (Psalm 1:1). They advise the adoption of their worldly and wicked philosophy, pursuits, and plans (Proverbs 12:5). Don't allow another to be your counselor unto wickedness and ruin, as did King Ahaziah (2 Chronicles 22:3; Nahun 1:11).

3. Toxic companions influence by convictions. Mingle with the corrupt, and you will adopt their worldly ideology.

4. Toxic companions influence by their conduct. "The evil man flatters his neighbor and leads him into the way that is not good" (Proverbs 16:29 JUB). Record books attest to the multitude swayed into drug, alcohol, pornography use, lawlessness, and immorality by the behavior of another (Proverbs 4:14). "Whoever associates with fools will suffer" (Proverbs 13:20 GW). Those with whom you associate cast a long shadow of influence upon your life for good or evil.

"It is not possible wholly to avoid civil intercourse with bad men unless we go out of the world. But civility is a different thing from voluntarily making them our *companions*, our *fellows*."[742]—W. S. Plumer.

~November 3~

Psalm 119:71
The Benefits of Affliction

"It is good for me that I have been afflicted" (Psalm 119:71).

What benefits await in affliction?

1. Instruction. Spurgeon states, "Trial is our school where God teaches us on the blackboard. This schoolhouse has no windows to let in the cheerful light. It is very dark, so we cannot look out and get distracted by external objects, but God's grace shines like a candle within, and by that light, we see what else we had never seen."[654]

2. Refinement. Affliction is a crucible that purges the saint of impurities (Job 23:10). Piper says, "Suffering has a great sin-killing effect."[653]

3. Growth. Adrian Rogers testified, "I have grown the most in my own life in times of deepest despair....God stretched my life. And I'm here to tell you that I'm a better person because of it."[655]

4. Renewal. Affliction (at times) is God's grappling hook, fabricated in love, to recover the straying wanderer from grave danger in the "far country" (Luke 15:13).

5. Humility. Affliction brings arrogance to its knees.

6. Testimony. "When you are living by faith," writes Alan Redpath, "through the darkness of circumstances, other people become aware of the radiance and sweetness of your life, and they are truly blessed."[743]

7. Conformity. Spurgeon says, "The furnace of affliction is a good place for you, Christian; it benefits you; it helps you become more like Christ, and it is fitting you for Heaven."

"Sufferings are only for a moment, but the benefits of suffering are forever."[744]—William MacDonald.

~November 4~

Psalm 119:89
The Immutability of God's Word

"Forever, O LORD, thy word is settled in heaven" (Psalm 119:89).

The word is unchangeable.

1. Unchangeable means it is undebatable. What God commanded is not subject to compromise or argument. It is eternally settled in Heaven and is unalterable. Man must conform to it, not it to man. "God is not human, that he should lie, not a human being, that he should change his mind" (Numbers 23:19 NIV)

2. Unchangeable means it is unerodable. It will not deteriorate, disintegrate, or degenerate. It remains the same in its unerring teaching (inerrancy) and power.

3. Unchangeable means it is unalterable. It cannot be edited to fit man's whims and wanton ways. What was "settled" (eternally fixed) in Heaven can never be unsettled on earth. God's teachings and commandments remain immutable despite man's best attempts to undermine and alter them. Matthew 5:18 is the New Testament Psalm 119:89: "For verily I say unto you, till heaven and earth pass, one jot or one tittle shall in no wise pass from the law, till all be fulfilled." It is an anvil that has worn out the skeptic's hammers (Isaiah 40:8).

Moody remarked, "When Christ said, 'The Scriptures cannot be broken,' He meant every word He said. Devil and man and Hell have been in league for centuries to try to break the Word of God, but they cannot do it. If you get it for your footing, you have a good footing for time and eternity."[745]

"The Bible has stood the test of time because it is divinely inspired by Almighty God, written in ink that cannot be erased by any man, religion, or belief system."—Billy Graham.

~November 5~

Psalm 119:97
The Book of Books

"O how love I thy law! it is my meditation all the day" (Psalm 119:97).

What kind of book is the Bible?

It is a definitive book. "Forever, O LORD, your word is settled in heaven" (Psalm 119:89 AMP). "This Bible is a book of authority; it is an authorized book, for God has written it. Oh, tremble, tremble, lest any of you despise it; mark its authority, for it is the Word of God."[746] Trust it above the opinion of any man and religion.

It's a directional book. "Thy word is a lamp unto my feet, and a light unto my path" (Psalm 119:105). It is not within man to know how to traverse life's dark, dangerous landscape; therefore, a lamp is provided to show the way.

It's a delightful book. David testifies that the Holy Scriptures were "sweeter than honey to my mouth" (Psalm 119:103). The pleasantry of the Bible is incomparable.

It's a devotional book. The Bible supplies nourishment to the soul (Matthew 4:4).

It's a deliverance book. "He sent his word, and healed them, and delivered them from their destructions" (Psalm 107:20). Spurgeon says, "A word will do it; a word has done it thousands of times."[747]

"The Bible is alive; it speaks to me. It has feet; it runs after me. It has hands; it lays hold on me."—Martin Luther.

~November 6~

Psalm 119:105
The Function of the Light

"Thy word is a lamp unto my feet, and a light unto my path" (Psalm 119:105).

God's word is a Divine light that performs three specific functions.

It is a lamp that helps us see where to go. As a bright beacon in the darkness, it says, "This is the way, walk ye in it" (Isaiah 30:21). It clarifies what we are to do and when.

It is a lamp that helps us see how to go. Its teaching is a map and compass to navigate every circumstance and trial.

It is a lamp that helps us see where not to go. It reveals temptations, dangers, hazards, and pitfalls spread about the path to avoid.

But as with any light, for it to do its designed job, it must be taken in hand and used.

"If we take this 'lamp' in our hand it will not only point out our course in general, but also direct us in every step, and guide our 'feet' aright in the 'path' of holiness and peace."[748]—George Horne.

~November 7~
Psalm 119:105
A Light in Darkness

"Thy word is a lamp unto my feet, and a light unto my path" (Psalm 119:105).

Note six traits of the Divine light of Holy Scripture.

1. A cheering light. Its constant companionship dispels a hundred doubts, removes loneliness, ministers comfort, and infuses sunshine on the darkest day (Ecclesiastes 11:7).

2. A dependable light. No force or power can extinguish its flame "by day and night" (Exodus 13:21).

3. A bright light. Its spectrum is broad and far, making the path to travel clear and confident.

4. A user-friendly light. It is simple, easy, and void of difficulty to use.

5. A personal light. Matthew Henry says, "It is a lamp which we may set up by us and take into our hands for our own particular use."[749] Spurgeon said, "Oh, to be bathed in a text of Scripture, and to let it be sucked up in your very soul till it saturates your heart!"

343

6. A powerful light. The Holy Spirit is its power source, enabling interpretation, understanding, and application.

"Not only does the Word of God inform us of His will, but, as a light on a path in darkness, it shows us how to follow the right and avoid the wrong way."—Jamieson-Fausset-Brown Bible Commentary.

~November 8~

Psalm 119:126
It's Time for Thee to Work

"It is time for thee, LORD, to work: for they have made void thy law" (Psalm 119:126).

Grieved over man's wickedness and disdain for God's law, David pleads for God to act against them. The text may be applied to God's work in revival. Consider four aspects of revival.

Revival's signal. What necessitates it?

1. The saints relapse. "Ah, but where is the blessedness ye once spake of?" Billy Sunday said, "When is a revival needed? When carelessness and unconcern keep the people asleep."

2. The violation, rejection, and nullification of God's law. Matthew Henry said, "God's time to work is when vice has become most daring, and the measure of iniquity is full."

3. An indifference to God, the church, and holy things.

Revival's source. Whence comes it? "It is time for thee, LORD, to work." Revival is the work of God that cannot be worked up but only prayed down (Psalm 85:6). "Not by might, nor by power, but by my spirit, saith the LORD of hosts" (Zechariah 4:6). David doesn't presume to tell God how to work but to work. That's all that matters. Spurgeon said, "The Lord can work either by judgments which hurl down the ramparts of the foe or by revivals which build up the walls of his own Jerusalem."[750]

Revival's stimulus. Why have it? To stir and arouse the saints to return to their first love for Christ with new obedience and devotion, and to give Him the glory and honor due to His holy name.

Revival's splendor. Revival refreshes the saints and reaches the lost. Nothing is better than an old-fashioned revival where powerful preaching is heard, soul-stirring music is sung, saints get right with God and each other, sinners are converted, the Bible is honored, the church is set afire, passion for the lost is rekindled, prayers at the altar are answered, and excitement and joy are experienced.

I read the story of a father who took his son to the church, where he was saved years earlier through loud gospel preaching. The boy noticed a rope hanging from the ceiling inside the church and inquired about it. The father shared that the rope pulled the bell in the steeple, calling the people to church to hear the Gospel and get saved. The boy looked up at him and said, "Daddy, ring it again!" Let's ring the bell again for an old-time revival in which saints are revived, sinners are converted, and God's name is glorified.

"Oh, for another Pentecost with all its wonders, to reveal the energy of God to gainsayers and make them see that there is a God in Israel! Man's extremity, whether of need or sin, is God's opportunity."[751]—C. H. Spurgeon.

~November 9~

Psalm 119:127
Extolling God's Word

"Therefore I love thy commandments above gold; yea, above fine gold" (Psalm 119:127).

David extols God's word for three reasons.

David extols God's word for its wonder. "Thy testimonies are wonderful: therefore doth my soul keep them" (Psalm 119:129). The Bible is the book of wonders. It is a wonder in its design, uniformity, revelation, promises, doctrines, teaching, inerrancy, eternality, consolation, miracles, and understanding. It was because of the "wonder" of God's Word that David obeyed them ("therefore doth my soul keep them"). Spurgeon remarked, "Their wonderful character so impressed itself upon his mind that he kept them in his memory; their wonderful excellence so charmed his heart that he kept them in his life."[752] "Beautiful words, wonderful words, wonderful words of life."

David extols God's word for its light. "The entrance of thy words giveth light" (Psalm 119:130). Scripture is an open door that lets in knowledge, understanding, and wisdom.[753] Matthew Henry says, "As soon as the word of God enters into us, and has a place in us, it enlightens us; we find we begin to see when we begin to study the word of God."[754] Horne states, "They show us what we were, what we are, and what we shall be; they show us what God hath done for us, and what He expecteth us to do for him; they show us the adversaries we have to encounter, and how to encounter them with success; they show us the mercy and the justice of the Lord, the joys of Heaven, and the pains of Hell."[755]

David extols God's word for its delights. "Trouble and anguish have taken hold on me: yet thy commandments are my delights" (Psalm 119:143). He derived the highest happiness and pleasure in doing them, even in suffering (Psalm 119:92). Charles Bridges says, "If the Gospel separates the heart from sinful delights, it is only to make room for delights of a more elevated, satisfying, and enduring nature."[756]

"When the commandments are loved for their own sake 'above gold and exceeding precious stones,' all earthly reward compared with the commandments themselves is vile."[757]—Augustine.

~November 10~

Psalm 119:133
Navigated by God's Word

"Order my steps in thy word" (Psalm 119:133).

Pray specifically for God to govern, guard, and ground your steps in His word.

Govern my steps through Thy word. Divine guidance and supervision are needed to know where to walk and what to do. Spurgeon says, "By His grace, He enables us to put our feet step by step in the very place which His Word ordains." The word of God is a light that shows us the way to go in the darkness (Psalm 119:105).

Guard my steps in Thy word. "He will keep the feet of his saints" (1 Samuel 2:9). God's word prevents straying off course by fortifying the heart with overcoming strength. "I have refrained my feet from every evil way, that I might keep thy word" (Psalm 119:101).

Ground my steps by Thy word. "Order my steps" means to make them firm. The person grounded in the word is like a tree planted by rivers of water that cannot be moved (Psalm 1:3). He is safe, secure, and immovable by the enemy's forces.

"Lord, order my steps, not by my whims and wants, or that which is pleasing and profitable, or popular, but in Thy Word that I may do only that which is right in your sight without wavering."

"Let Thy Spirit accompany Thy word, and ingraft it within me, so that I may be guided and ruled by it."—Matthew Poole.

~November 11~
Psalm 119:136
Tears For the Ungodly

"Rivers of waters run down mine eyes, because they keep not thy law" (Psalm 119:136).

The text resembles Psalm 119:158, where David says, "I beheld the transgressors, and was grieved; because they kept not thy word." Why should we, like David, bitterly weep over man's disobedience to God's word?

1. Weep over sinners on account of their dishonor to God. David said, "Rivers of waters, plentiful and perpetual tears, witnesses of my deep sorrow for God's dishonor and displeasure."[758] Lot was vexed daily by the sins of the wicked (2 Peter 2:8). Jeremiah was brokenhearted because God's law was violated (Jeremiah 9:1). Out of love for God, His honor, and His holy word, our hearts should be broken when a person tramples His word underfoot and besmirches Him.

2. Weep over sinners on account of their hurt to themselves and others. Matthew Henry said, "The sins of sinners are the sorrows of saints."[759] The sinners inflict misery and sorrow on their souls and others by breaking God's law. "There is no peace, saith the Lord, unto the wicked" (Isaiah 48:22). It is those who keep God's word, in contrast, who know peace. David said, "Great peace have they who love Your law" (Psalm 119:165 AMPC).

3. Weep over sinners on account of their condition before God. Jesus said the sinner is "lost." What is it to be lost? To be lost is to be estranged from the presence of God. To be lost is to be condemned to eternity in Hell. To be lost is to be shortchanged of the beautiful life God planned. To be lost is to be without purpose and peace. To be lost is to be without hope of Heaven. To be lost is to live life in rebellion against God. To be lost is to be mastered and ravaged by sin. To be lost is to be under the rule of Satan.

Jesus, upon seeing a host of lost sinners, "was moved with compassion on them, because they fainted, and were scattered abroad, as sheep having no shepherd" (Matthew 9:36). We should weep for the lost, as He did.

4. Weep over sinners on account of their coming doom. Jesus said, "This is how it will be at the end of the age. The angels will come and separate the wicked from the righteous and throw them into the blazing furnace, where there will be weeping and gnashing of teeth" (Matthew 13:49–50 NIV).

Spurgeon said, "He [David] wept in sympathy with God to see the holy law despised and broken. He wept in pity for the people who were thus drawing down upon themselves the fiery wrath of

God." Hell means untold torment and suffering, but also separation from friends and family who died in the Lord forever. How can we not be brought to tears given their woeful plight?

5. Weep over sinners to keep yourself from becoming like them. Thomas Manton says, "The Lord requireth this [mourning bitterly for other men's sins] to keep our hearts the more tender and upright; it is an act God useth to make us more careful of our own souls, to be troubled at the sins of others. The soul will never agree to do that which it grieved itself to see another do."

"That man is a ripe believer who sorrows because of the sins of others."—C. H. Spurgeon.

~November 12~

Psalm 119:176
A Straying Sheep

"I have gone astray like a lost sheep; seek thy servant; for I do not forget thy commandments" (Psalm 119:176).

David's relapse. David, a redeemed sheep, acted like a lost sheep. He strayed from the commandments and counsel of God. Note. Even a man, after the heart of God, wages battle with the corruption of the flesh and occasionally stumbles (Romans 7:21).

David's remorse. With a broken heart over his straying, he confesses, "I have gone astray." That was not what he wanted to happen, and he prayed it would not happen, but sadly, it did. Unlike the unsaved, the believer moans his departure from the path of uprightness and groans for restoration.

David's remedy. A lost sheep cannot find its way home. It is a directionless, helpless, and defenseless animal who, when lost, wanders further from the fold into danger until found by the shepherd. Thus, David prays, "Seek thy servant." Erring man cannot recover himself from sin and misery; that is the work of the Good Shepherd. "O wretched man that I am! Who shall deliver me from the body of this death? I thank God through Jesus Christ our Lord" (Romans 7:24–25).

"By going astray, we lose the comfort of the green pastures and expose ourselves to a thousand mischiefs."[760]—Matthew Henry.

~November 13~

Psalm 120:1–2
Lying Lips

"In my distress I cried unto the LORD, and he heard me. Deliver my soul, O LORD, from lying lips, and from a deceitful tongue" (Psalm 120:1–2).

The liar injures others. Lying lips cause their victims misery, despair, and injury to reputation and relationships. Telling a lie is like pushing a boulder off a cliff; you never know how much harm it will do or when and where it will finally stop.[761] It's like freeing a ravenous lion from its cage. You do not know how many people it will injure or kill before it is captured.[762] It's like striking a match and dropping it in a dry forest on a windy day; it's uncontrollable and, often, unstoppable until it burns out or is extinguished at great cost to others.

The liar will be punished. He will not escape with impunity but suffer dishonor, disgrace, loss of trust, and respect from others. Solomon states, "A righteous man hateth lying: but a wicked man is loathsome, and cometh to shame" (Proverbs 13:5). Gill says the liar "makes himself to stink in the nostrils of all good men." The hurt the liar intends for another boomerangs back to him.

Second, and more severe, he will suffer the harsh judgment of God. Solomon says, "A false witness shall not be unpunished, and he that speaketh lies shall perish" (Proverbs 19:9). Hell awaits all unrepentant liars (Revelation 21:8). But Gehazi, Ananias, Sapphira and God's word testify that punishment often befalls man for lying before death (Psalm 120:4). Matthew Henry remarked, "They set God at a distance from them, but from afar His arrows can reach them."[763]

The liar will be silenced. David tells us that "the mouth of them that speak lies shall be stopped" (Psalm 63:11) and "lying lips [shall] be put to silence" (Psalm 31:18). Solomon declares that "a lying tongue is but for a moment" (Proverbs 12:19).

"Lying is Satan's work. And when we engage in lying, we let our hearts become Satan's workshop."[764]—R. Newton.

~November 14~

Psalm 121:1–2
Help Comes from the Lord

"I will lift up mine eyes unto the hills, from whence cometh my help. My help cometh from the LORD, which made heaven and earth" (Psalm 121:1–2).

The psalmist in the previous psalm looked around him in sore distress. In this psalm, he looks up in hope.[765]

My help cometh from the Lord. Help is not found in the mountains, as the superstitious Canaanites believed, but in the Creator of the mountains. The Jews did not look to the hills where the graven idols stood for help or to the people that dwelt among them for assistance, but alone unto their mighty deliverer from captivity and Holy Warrior, defender and helper, the Lord God Almighty who made the mountains. How comforting and assuring it is to know in times of trouble that He who made the mountains is our helper and defender.

I will lift up my eyes. Looking out to man, looking in to self for help, or looking down in hopeless despondency and paralyzing fear is futile. Help is found in looking up. Boice says, "The point of Psalm 121 is not that we will not have problems, but that God will keep us safe as we go through them."[766]

"Help is on the road," wrote Spurgeon, "and will not fail to reach us in due time, for he who sends it to us was never known to be too late. Jehovah, who created all things, is equal to every emergency; Heaven and earth are at the disposal of Him who made them; therefore, let us be very joyful in our infinite helper."[767]

"Mountains have a peculiar power to solemnize and to impress us all, and precisely what they bring to us is that sense of God which assures of His love, and help, and lead."[768]—R. Tuck.

~November 15~

Psalm 122:1
The Gladness of Going to Church

"I was glad when they said unto me, Let us go into the house of the LORD" (Psalm 122:1).

The reasons David found gladness in attending church are the same for every saint.

The people who gather there. "Let us go into the house of the LORD." The church is comprised of the blood-bought children of God devoted to His glory and cause.

The praise that occurs there. "To give thanks unto the name of the LORD" (Psalm 122:4). David said, "Praise waiteth for thee, O God, in Zion" (Psalm 65:1) and "I will declare thy name unto my brethren: in the midst of the congregation will I praise thee" (Psalm 22:22).

The precepts that are taught there. David said, "I will announce the good news of righteousness among those assembled for worship" (Psalm 40:9 GW). The truth of the Holy Scripture that nourishes the soul and enriches life is proclaimed within its doors.

The peace that is manifest there. The church is an oasis of tranquility, love, rest, serenity, and calm in an ocean of conflict, confusion, criticism, corruption, cruelty, and condemnation.

The power that is experienced there. In and through His church, the Lord works miracles, rescuing souls from bondage, misery, and eternal damnation.

The Person that is worshipped there. "Let us go into the house of the LORD" (Psalm 122:1). It is His "house." And we enter it primarily to worship and glorify Him. The Psalmist declared, "Then will *I go* unto the altar of God, unto God my exceeding joy: yea, upon the harp will I praise thee, O God my God" (Psalm 43:4).

"The church is so subnormal that if it ever got back to the New Testament normal, it would seem to people to be abnormal."— Vance Havner.

~November 16~

Psalm 122:6–7
Pray For Jerusalem

"Pray for the peace of Jerusalem: they shall prosper that love thee. Peace be within thy walls, and prosperity within thy palaces" (Psalm 122:6–7).

David beckons the Jews to pray for tranquility, harmony, and rest from conflict in Jerusalem, especially among her rulers, conquest over their enemies, and for the people's welfare and God's glory. The Christian yet is to pray for peace to dwell 'within her walls and palaces.'

Isaiah says, "You who call on the LORD, don't rest and don't allow God to rest until he establishes Jerusalem, and makes it the praise of the earth" (Isaiah 62:6–7 CEB). He who prays for and loves Israel is promised prosperity—the favor and blessings of God. "Pray for the peace of Jerusalem," says Spurgeon, "and thine own soul shall be refreshed."

"To open the Bible is to open a window toward Jerusalem, as Daniel did (6:10), no matter where our exile may have taken us."— N. T. Wright.

~ November 17~

Psalm 123:2

Eyes Fixated on Christ

"Behold, as the eyes of servants look unto the hand of their masters, and as the eyes of a maiden unto the hand of her mistress; so our eyes wait upon the LORD our God, until that he have mercy upon us" (Psalm 123:2).

A common practice of masters in the East was to communicate commands to their servants non-verbally through signs displayed in the movement of the eyes or hands, or a nod of the head. The form of communication required the servant's eyes to be fixated on the master constantly for compliance with his wishes. Savary, in his letters on Africa, states, "The slaves, having their hands crossed on their chest, stand silently at the end of the hall. With their eyes fastened on their master, they seek to anticipate his every wish."[769]

As servants rivet their eyes on their master to learn of and obey his every wish to please him, Christians must heartily and resolutely focus on Christ for the same (Hebrews 12:2; Psalm 32:8). Maclaren says, "They should stand where they can see Him; they should have their gaze fixed upon Him; they should look with patient trust, as well as with eager willingness to start into activity when He indicates His commands."[770]

"We must use our eyes with resolution, for they will not go upward to the Lord of themselves, but they incline to look downward, or inward, or anywhere but to the Lord."[771]—C. H. Spurgeon.

~November 18~

Psalm 124:1

Had Not God Been on Our Side

"If it had not been the LORD who was on our side" (Psalm 124:1).

David pens the psalm in the wake of Israel's deliverance at the hand of God from ruin and destruction. The "if" is the believer's eternal promise and refuge.

What "if" God had not intervened on our behalf concerning sin and its penalty? *But He did.* "There is no doubt," Spurgeon says, "as to our deliverer, we cannot ascribe our salvation to any second cause. We set every other claimant on one side and rejoice because the Lord was on our side."[544]

What "if" God had not promised us everlasting life at death? *But He did.* Paul exclaims, "'Where, O death, is your victory? Where, O death, is your sting?' The sting of death is sin, and the power of sin is the law. But thanks be to God! He gives us the victory through our Lord Jesus Christ" (1 Cor. 15:55–57 NIV).

What "if" He had not promised reunion with loved ones in Heaven? *But He did.* "We which are alive and remain shall be caught up together with them in the clouds, to meet the Lord in the air" (1 Thessalonians 4:17).

What "if" God had not intervened for us in times of sickness, bereavement, financial struggle, trouble, adversarial assault, slander, and suffering? *But He did.* Davies said, "If we had stood alone, if God had not been round about us, if unerring wisdom had not thought for us and worked for us when the calamity threatened, then had we been as the bird in the snare of the fowler; then had we been overwhelmed!"[772] Hallelujahs to the God of our many and mighty deliverances! Stop and give Him praise.

"God was on our side; He took our part, espoused our cause, and appeared for us. He was our helper and a very present help, a help on our side, nigh at hand. He was with us, not only for us, but among us, and commander-in-chief of our forces. If it had not been Jehovah himself, a God of infinite power and perfection, that had undertaken our deliverance, our enemies would have overpowered us."[773]—Matthew Henry.

~November 19~

Psalm 125:1–2
Let the Mountains Speak

"They that trust in the LORD shall be as mount Zion, which cannot be removed, but abideth forever. As the mountains are round about Jerusalem, so the LORD is round about his people from henceforth even forever" (Psalm 125:1–2).

The Jerusalem mountains symbolize the saint's stability. The redeemed are immovable in Christ Jesus. No power above, below, or on earth can remove them from His abiding presence, care, and defense (Romans 8:31–39). Page writes, "Some persons are like the sand—ever-shifting and treacherous (Matthew 7:26). Some are like the sea—restless and unsettled (Isaiah 57:20; James 1:6). Some are like the wind—uncertain and inconstant (Ephesians 4:14). Believers are like a mountain—strong, stable and secure."[774]

The Jerusalem mountains symbolize the saint's security. Jehovah's presence and protection encircle the believer, keeping him safe and secure. Luther said, "We are surrounded with divine aid. If we were surrounded by walls of steel and fire, we should feel secure and defy the Devil. But the property of faith is not to be proud of what the eye sees, but to rely on what the Word reveals."[775] And the Word states, "As the mountains are round about Jerusalem, so the LORD is round about his people from henceforth even forever."

Clarke states, "The Lord is round about His people—He is above, beneath, around them; and while they keep within it, their fortress is impregnable, and they can suffer no evil."[776] When you see a mountain next, let it remind you of your immovability, indomitability, and impregnability in Christ Jesus.

"Let not our "trust in God" be a presumptuous, ungrounded assurance; but let it be a confidence springing from faith unfeigned, out of a pure heart, a good conscience, and fervent charity. Then shall our situation, whether as a church or as individuals, resemble that of the holy mount in the beloved city, and our God will be unto us a fortress and a wall round about."[777]—George Horne.

Psalm 126:5–6
Sowers and Reapers

"They that sow in tears shall reap in joy. He that goeth forth and weepeth, bearing precious seed, shall doubtless come again with rejoicing, bringing his sheaves with him" (Psalm 126:5–6).

A spiritual application that pictures the saints as soulwinners sowing the Gospel seed with compassion in the harvest field is often made of the text. Using that adaptation reveals four aspects of soulwinning.

1. The Soulwinners' Passion. "They that sow in tears." A burden for the lost flows from Christ's concern and compassion for them to the believer who walks in close fellowship with Him.

2. The Soulwinners' Proclamation. The "precious seed." The harvest is always determined by the seed planted. The Gospel is the only seed that brings abundant and eternal life to the sinner (1 Peter 1:23).

3. The Soulwinners' Plan. "He that goeth forth." To sow, one must 'go.' *Go* is spelled GET OUT.

4. The Soulwinners' Promise. "Shall doubtless." The Gospel sown faithfully in fertile soil in the power of the Holy Spirit will produce fruit.

Soulwinning is heart work ("sow in tears"), hard work ("sow"), huge work ("goeth forth" into the entire world), happy work ("with rejoicing"), and a harvest work ("bringing his sheaves with him").

Winnie the Pooh had a donkey friend named Eeyore. Eeyore was playing too close to the water's edge, fell in, and began to drown. Unable to get to the bank, he began to float downstream on his back, anticipating the ride would be his last, for the river ended in a waterfall. As Eeyore floated underneath a bridge, he saw Winnie standing upon it, and a conversation ensued. Winnie said to Eeyore, "Seems like you've got yourself in a spot of trouble."

"Yes," Eeyore replied.

Winnie then said, "And it looks like you are going to drown."

Eeyore again answered sadly, "Yes." Then, with a pleading cry, Eeyore said to Winnie the Pooh, "If it wouldn't be too much bother, would you mind rescuing me?"[778]

About us are those floating downstream, crying out to be rescued from emptiness, meaninglessness, guilt, brokenness, and, most importantly, eternal damnation. We stand on the bridge, like Winnie the Pooh, and hear their cry, "If it wouldn't be too much bother, would you mind rescuing me?" (On my desk, I have a coffee cup with a caricature of Eeyore asking that question, which reminds me to be a rescuer, a soul winner.) How will we respond?

"Look on soul winning as a business, not an incidental matter; as work, not play; as time well spent, not wasted; as a privilege, not a boresome duty."—R. G. Lee.

~November 21~

Psalm 126:6
The Promise of Soulwinning Success

"He that goeth forth and weepeth, bearing precious seed, shall doubtless come again with rejoicing, bringing his sheaves with him" (Psalm 126:6).

The agricultural promise to Israel in their return from exile is often applied to the soulwinners' success in the labor for souls. As their exhausting labor in cultivating the soil and sowing seed would bring eventual fruit, that of the soulwinner will, too. "Faithful toil shall not fail of a reward."[779] Saith Spurgeon, *"Doubtlessly,* you will gather sheaves from your sowing. Because the Lord has written *doubtless,* heed that you do not doubt. No reason for doubt can remain after the Lord has spoken."[780]

Not only is the soulwinner promised success, but joy. *Shall reap in joy.* Israel would sow agonizing tears over the hard work and the

358

hungry, but at harvest time, they would rejoice when there would be plenty of food. Many are the causes of the soulwinners' tears.

1. The sinner's evil conduct, hardness, and rebellion against God.

2. The difficulties, heartache, hardships, and persecution faced.

3. Sin—theirs, and those of others.

4. The lukewarmness of the church.

5. Failures in the work.

But the tears will become joy and praise when a soul is saved. McDonald says, "Those who live sacrificially for the spread of the Gospel may endure present privation, but what is that compared to the joy of seeing souls saved and in Heaven worshiping the Lamb of God forever and forever?"[781] Spurgeon said, "To be a soul winner is the happiest thing in this world."

"The world is the field, and the field is the world, and henceforth that country shall be my home where I can be most used in winning souls for Christ."—Nicolaus Zinzendorf.

~November 22~

Psalm 127:3–4

Children, God's Gift

"Children are a blessing and a gift from the LORD. Having a lot of children to take care of you in your old age is like a warrior with a lot of arrows" (Psalm 127:3–4 CEV).

Solomon, who wrote most of the book of Proverbs, wrote two psalms: Psalm 72 and Psalm 127. After his fashion of pithy sayings in Proverbs, this meditation, which contrasts children to arrows, is composed.

1. Arrows (children) out of the quiver are too late to be molded.

2. Misguided, warped, or poisoned arrows, both theologically and morally, lead to wayward lives. Children, like arrows, must be fashioned from infancy with the right components—biblical values, convictions, beliefs, and discipline—to go straight (Proverbs 22:6).

3. Children born when their parents are young often grow up to be their helpers, defenders, and protectors in old age. Whatever the children can do to alleviate their parents' hardship and promote their happiness and well-being should be done.

4. Children are a treasured gift from God. Abortionists discount and doom those to whom God gives precious life.

5. Children are the next generation of crusaders. Apart from them being born and raised in the nourishment of the Lord, there will be no light for the coming ages.

6. Arrows go where the archer cannot. Children can go places and accomplish things for God that parents cannot for legitimate reasons.

7. No godly parent's hand is on the bowstring alone. God's hand is on their hand as they pull the bowstring back to release the arrow into the world. What hope and joy that thought instills.

8. Arrows sometimes miss their mark. Retrieve arrows that stray from the targeted purpose of God. The prodigal went astray but ultimately returned to the straight and narrow way.

9. Children are a treasured gift of God. "God gives children," says Spurgeon, "not as a penalty nor as a burden, but as a favor."[782]

"Children should be treated as the most sacred charge placed in the hand of man by the hand of God. No one can tell the capacities and possibilities that are folded in the form and hidden in the heart of a little child."[783]—E. Conder.

~November 23~

Psalm 128:1
Biblical Fear

"Blessed is every one that feareth the LORD; that walketh in his ways" (Psalm 128:1).

No historical setting is provided for the psalm.

The promise exclaimed. "Blessed is every one that feareth the LORD." "Happy shalt thou be, and it shall be well with thee" (Psalm 128:2). Thomas Adams said, "No man more truly loves God than he that is most fearful to offend Him."

The promise explained. The happiness promised is conditional upon the exhibition of a fear of the Lord. Fear of the Lord is twofold in its nature. First, it is a deep-seated reverence for God, the creator and sustainer of all that exists. Isaiah says, "The LORD of Hosts, him you shall regard as holy; let him be your fear, and let him be your dread" (Isaiah 8:13 RSV). The second aspect is the heart manifestation of love, honor, loyalty to Him, and obedience to His law and counsel.

1. Love and honor for God. Wardlaw asserts, "We truly fear God just in proportion as we truly love Him."[784]

2. Obedience to God. No man fears God who does not obey Him. The Bible says, "If you fear the LORD, serve him, obey him, and don't rebel against what he says" (1 Samuel 12:14 GW). Harman says, "Where true reverence towards the LORD exists, there will also be a life of obedient attention to His ways."[785] "Happy shalt thou be, and it shall be well with thee" (Psalm 128:2). Says Spurgeon, "A man's heart will be seen in his walk, and the blessing will come where heart and walk are both with God."[786]

"Heaped up happinesses in the plural belong to that man who fears the Lord. He is happy, and he shall be happy in a thousand ways."[787]—C. H. Spurgeon.

~November 24~

Psalm 128:2–3
Blessings of the Fear of the Lord

"For thou shalt eat the labor of thine hands: happy shalt thou be, and it shall be well with thee. Thy wife shall be as a fruitful vine by the sides of thine house: thy children like olive plants round about thy table" (Psalm 128:2–3).

God blesses the person who fears Him in four ways.

1. God blesses them in salvation. Their name is put in His book. They that fear the Lord will have their name written in the Book of Remembrance. "Then those who feared the LORD spoke to one another, and the LORD gave attention and heard it, and a book of remembrance was written before Him for those who fear the LORD and who esteem His name. 'They will be Mine,' says the LORD of Hosts, 'on the day when I prepare My own possession, and I will spare them as a man spares his own son who serves him'" (Malachi 3:16–17 NASB).

2. God blesses them in their work. Work is successful and provides sufficient income for household support. "He shall not live by begging, by knavery, by any unworthy means, but by God's blessing upon his honest toil."[788]

3. God blesses them in their marriage. A husband and wife find happiness, peace, comfort, and support in each other. Children, if ordained, provide cheer and joy around the table.

4. God blesses them in their walk. Matthew Henry says, "Happy shalt thou be, that is, it shall be well with thee; whatever befalls thee, good shall be brought out of it; it shall be well with thee while thou livest, better when thou diest, and best of all to eternity."[789]

"Happiness belongeth not to the rich, the powerful, and the prosperous, as such; but in every state and condition, blessed is the man that 'feareth Jehovah,' that so feareth him as to obey him, and to 'walk in his ways,' notwithstanding all the obstructions he may meet with from the world, the flesh, and the Devil."[790]—George Horne.

Psalm 129:2
Persecution

"Many a time have they afflicted me from my youth: yet they have not prevailed against me" (Psalm 129:2).

The Egyptians and Babylonians maliciously and mercilessly 'plowed upon their backs' (the Israelites) from her "youth" (birth as a people), making deep and long furrows (Psalm 129:3) and bound them with "cords" of captivity (Psalm 129:4). But God "cut asunder" the cords and delivered them (Psalm 129:4).

The saint's persecution. "Many a time have they afflicted me." Saints, like Israel, live in a cradle of conflict with and cruel persecution by the world. "Enemy-occupied territory—that is what the world is."[791] Watson said, "The saints have no charter of exemption from trials. Though they live ever so meek, merciful, and pure in heart, their piety will not shield them from suffering. The way to Heaven is by way of thorns and blood. Though it be full of roses in regard of the comforts of the Holy Spirit—yet it is full of thorns in regard of persecutions."[792] "For unto you it is given in the behalf of Christ, not only to believe on him, but also to suffer for his sake" (Philippians 1:29).

Barclay states, "When a man is called on to suffer something for his Christianity, that is always a crucial moment; it is the great occasion; it is the clash between the world and Christ; it is a moment in the drama of eternity. To have a share in such a moment is not a penalty but a glory. 'Rejoice at such a moment,' says Jesus, 'and be glad.'"[793]

The saint's perseverance. "The plowers plowed upon my back." Israel endured a long time of oppression. How long must saints persevere in suffering and ill-treatment? "To the end" (Matthew 24:13). Morris says, "To the end means not only to the end of some period of time but to the end of the trials, the persecutions. It is not good enough for the followers of Jesus to renounce His allegiance somewhere along the line. Real discipleship means perseverance through whatever trials the world throws in our way."[794]

And such trials will only cease upon the exodus to Heaven. Spurgeon's words are timely: "Like true soldiers, may we buckle on our harness and resolve that, let the battle rage as it may, through divine grace, we will not desert our colors. We prefer death to the disgrace of forsaking a cause so true, a doctrine so pure, a Savior so gracious, a Prince so noble, and so worthy of our most loyal service."[795] And to that, I say a hearty Amen.

The saint's preservation. But "they have not prevailed." Israel's enemies failed; she prevailed. Why? "The LORD is righteous" (Psalm 129:4). When the rains, winds, and floods (symbolic of persecution) beat against the house built upon the rock, it will not crumble or collapse, for God is righteous to defend His own (Matthew 7:24–25).[796] Morris says, "The power of God is such that He can and will sustain His faithful servants through whatever trials they may be called upon to endure."[797]

"Let it never surprise us if we have to endure mockery, ridicule, and false reports because we belong to Christ. The disciple is not greater than His Master, nor the servant than His Lord."—J. C. Ryle.

~November 26~

Psalm 130:3–4

Plenteous Forgiveness

"But there is forgiveness with thee, that thou mayest be feared" (Psalm 130:4).

Israel had sinned and was punished. The psalm is their song for mercy and forgiveness.

The scope of the forgiveness. "But." This is the "Whisper of Hope" for the sinner.[798] God's forgiveness encompasses all manner of sin regardless of its hideousness. Spurgeon says, "Where God draws no limit, do not you draw any."[799] None are exempt from the need or the gift of salvation.

The source of the forgiveness. Barnes remarked, "God is a Being who does pardon sin, and this is the only ground of hope."[800] Plumer wrote, "Human merits are excluded from the whole scheme of salvation."[801]

The splendor of forgiveness. It gives its recipients wondrous, unspeakable joy, hope, and peace in all circumstances and a home in Heaven at life's end.

The supply of forgiveness. "With him is plenteous redemption" (Psalm 130:7). The supply of God's mercy to grant forgiveness to sinners is equal to that at its first. It's inexhaustible.

The surety of forgiveness. "There is." Forgiveness is readily available to all who desire and request it through repentance. In this moment, there is forgiveness; in all of life's tomorrows, there is forgiveness. Says Spurgeon, "The power of pardon is permanently resident with God; He has forgiveness ready to His hand at this instant."[802]

The sign of forgiveness. A result of forgiveness is that God is feared. Alexander says, "Fear or godly reverence is here represented as one fruit and evidence of pardoned sin."[803] The person who is washed clean of sin and made right with God possesses reverence for and trust in Him and walks in keeping with His Word.

"It is our unspeakable comfort, in all our approaches to God, that there is forgiveness with Him, for that is what we need."[804]— Matthew Henry.

~November 27~

Psalm 131:1
Signs of Humility

"Lord, my heart is not haughty, nor mine eyes lofty: neither do I exercise myself in great matters, or in things too high for me" (Psalm 131:1).

David attests to his humility without losing it. Cox explains, "To claim this virtue is as a rule to forfeit it, but David contrives to claim humility with humility. His words have no taint of pride in them."[805] Humility, David says, is free from three fleshy contaminants.

1. Humility is free from superciliousness—a superiority complex. "My heart is not haughty." Aesop said, "The smaller the mind, the greater the conceit."

2. Humility is free from pompousness—an inflated ego. "Nor mine eyes lofty." An Arabic proverb says, "The nose is in the heavens; the seat is in the mire."[806]

3. Humility is free from presumptuousness—pious ambition. "Neither do I exercise myself in…things too high for me." Matthew Henry says, "It is our wisdom, and will be our praise, to keep within our sphere, and not to intrude into things which we have not seen, or meddle with that which does not belong to us."[807] Though he possesses one talent, the arrogant aspire to the same position as those with the ten.

"Pride, like the magnet, constantly points to one object—self; but, unlike the magnet, it has no attractive pole, but at all points repels."—Charles Caleb Colton.

~November 28~

Psalm 131:2
Spiritual Weaning

"Surely I have behaved and quieted myself, as a child that is weaned of his mother: my soul is even as a weaned child" (Psalm 131:2).

Weaning is necessary for a baby's growth and that of believers.

From what must the soul be weaned?

1. From the corrupt pleasures of the world (Hebrews 11:26).

2. From presumptuous sins.

3. From tolerance of evil.

4. From worldly influence.

5. From the passions and affections of the old man that remain.

Simeon says, "Our hearts must be weaned from all so as to be ready to part with everything, whenever God, in His providence, shall call for it."[808]

How is the soul weaned?

1. By discipline. By the brute force of denial of the wrong through God's power (Philippians 4:13).

2. By disappointment. Sometimes, the forbidden ceases to satisfy and is easily given up (Hosea 2:6–7).

3. By disconnection. "Neither give place to the devil" (Ephesians 4:27). An overweight person trying to wean off sweets doesn't rent an apartment above a bakery.

4. By discomfort (Hebrews 12:6). Sometimes, the Lord must wean a believer from a besetting sin with painful judgment.

What are the effects of the weaned soul? The weaned soul is happy. The weaned soul is holy. The weaned soul is healthy. The weaned soul is heedful. Paul says, "And be not conformed to this world: but be ye transformed by the renewing of your mind, that ye may prove what is that good, and acceptable, and perfect, will of God" (Romans 12:2).

When does weaning end? Weaning is an unending effort. Spurgeon observes, "When we think ourselves safely through the weaning, we sadly discover that the old appetites are rather wounded than slain, and we begin crying again for the breasts which we had given up. It is easy to begin shouting before we are out of the woods, and no doubt hundreds have sung this Psalm long before they have understood it."[809]

"The problem with too many of us is that we have grown old without growing up—we still need to be weaned."[810]—Warren Wiersbe.

~November 29~

Psalm 132:2–5

What to do with Unreachable Dreams

"How he sware unto the LORD, and vowed unto the mighty God of Jacob; Surely I will not come into the tabernacle of my house, nor go up into my bed; I will not give sleep to mine eyes, or slumber to mine eyelids, Until I find out a place for the LORD, an habitation for the mighty God of Jacob" (Psalm 132:2–5).

David rashly, but with admirable intention and passion, vowed not to sleep until he built a "habitation for the mighty God of Jacob," a place to house the ark of the Covenant. Three lessons may be gleaned from the text.

1. Intentions are good and noble, but don't always translate into achievements. "When thou vowest a vow unto God, defer not to pay it; for he hath no pleasure in fools: pay that which thou hast vowed" (Ecclesiastes 5:4). Consider the weight of a vow before you make it. Says Spurgeon, "We had better not swear to do anything before we know the Lord's mind about it, and then we shall not need to swear."[811]

2. When what you want to do for God is not permitted or possible, help another to do it. David could not fulfill the vow and dream to build the Temple but supported Solomon in its building. He provided the plans for its construction, along with the gold, silver, precious stones, bronze, and iron. Unable or not divinely permitted to fulfill a dream? Let someone else do it with your help.[812]

3. Pine for a devoted passion for God's House like David. Spurgeon wrote of David's heart for the house of God, "Alas, we have many around us who will never carry their care for the Lord's worship too far! No fear of their being indiscreet! They are housed and bedded, and as for the Lord, His people may meet in a barn, or

368

never meet at all; it will be all the same to them.…[David] could not enjoy sleep till he had done his best to provide a place for the ark."

"The Lord shows the acceptance of what we desire to do by permitting us to do something else which His infinite mind judges to be fitter for us and more honorable to Himself."[813]—C. H. Spurgeon.

~November 30~

Psalm 132:8-9
The Dedication of a Church

"Arise, O LORD, into thy rest; thou, and the ark of thy strength. Let thy priests be clothed with righteousness; and let thy saints shout for joy" (Psalm 132:8–9).

In Solomon's prayer for the dedication of the Temple, he prays for God's presence, the joy of the worshippers, and the holiness of its priests. The prayer serves as a pattern of prayer for the dedication of a new or existing church.

1. The habitation of God. "Arise, O LORD, into thy rest." Worship is vain unless the Lord meets with the people and displays the power of His holy presence. Spurgeon says, "Oh, that the Lord would indeed abide in all the churches and cause His power to be revealed in Zion."[814]

2. The holiness of the priests. "Let thy priests be clothed with righteousness." Pray for holy and consecrated ministers. Scarborough said, "Those who handle the vessels of the Lord must have pure hearts and clean hands. 'Holiness unto the LORD' must be on the skirts of God's spiritual priests today."[815] Whitefield liked to have his preaching attire scrupulously clean. He would say, "These are not trifles; a minister must be without spot, even in his garments, if he can." Based on Whitefield's words, Spurgeon said, "Purity cannot be carried too far in a minister."[816] Brooks said, "It does not take great men to do great things; it only takes consecrated men."

3. The happiness of the people. "Let thy saints shout for joy." Pray for the saints to be happy, not gloomy people. What are incitements to the saints' joy.

a. When the church has holy ministers providing holy ministry, the saints will be joyous.

b. Jubilation erupts in the presence of the King of Kings.

c. In recounting their deliverance from sin to salvation and subsequent blessings, saints cannot help but rejoice.

"I do not think the Devil cares how many churches you build if only you have lukewarm preachers and people in them."—C. H. Spurgeon.

~December 1~

Psalm 133:1
Unity of the Saints

"Behold, how good and how pleasant it is for brethren to dwell together in unity!" (Psalm 133:1).

The psalm was written either to bolster unity among the tribes of Israel or to celebrate it when it had occurred.[817]

Jesus said, 'A house divided against itself shall not stand' (Matthew 12:25). Unity among the "brethren" consists of five elements.

1. Harmony in doctrine. Believers "agree" to the sameness of truth expounded in the Word of God and its ethical, moral, and spiritual implications and applications. Ryle wrote, "Unity without the Gospel is a worthless unity; it is the very unity of Hell."[818]

2. Harmony in direction. They manifest a sameness of purpose and vision for the church's primary reason for existence, the task of global evangelism (Matthew 28:18–19).

3. Harmony in disposition. Despite differences, they mutually treat one another with love, grace, and respect.

4. Harmony in duty. They don't jockey for another's position or role or their own way but, in humility, assume the task assigned.

5. Harmony in deference. They are willing to set aside personal preferences for the spirit of unity.

Burke said, "Whatever disunites man from God also disunites man from man." Envision God seated in a chair encircled by chairs of seated saints. As the chairs draw closer to God's chair, they draw closer to each other.

"We need not all agree, but if we disagree, let us not be disagreeable in our disagreements."—M. R. DeHaan.

~December 2~

Psalm 134:1–3
Saints to Encourage Servants

"Behold, bless ye the LORD, all ye servants of the LORD, which by night stand in the house of the LORD. Lift up your hands in the sanctuary, and bless the LORD. The LORD that made heaven and earth bless thee out of Zion" (Psalm 134:1–3).

An unnamed speaker charged and encouraged the priests who ministered in and patrolled the Temple at night to 'lift up their hands in the sanctuary' and bless the Lord (praise Him and fulfill their duties to Him). Plumer says, "The sacred fire was kept burning on the altar all night, the lamps also burned all night, and songs were sung in the temple by night. Fry says: 'We know generally that there was a nightly service in the temple.'"[819]

The application. It is the task of the church member to encourage the *servants of the Lord* to maintain hearty worship ("Bless ye the LORD"), continued faithfulness to their lofty duty and the church ("which by night stand in the house of the LORD") and holiness in life ("Lift up your hands in the sanctuary"; to lift the hands both in prayer and praise toward the *Holy of Holies* ministers must be holy.)

371

Ministers need healthy doses of encouragement from the laity to stave off burnout and dropout, such as Onesiphorus gave Paul (2 Timothy 1:16–18). "Onesiphorus. This friend was true to his name; he was a real help-bringer—bringer of comfort and strength to the great warrior whose battles were nearly over. He was a helper in presence of difficulties."[820] May his tribe increase among the saints.

"He that receives a prophet shall have a prophet's reward."—Jesus.

~December 3~

Psalm 134:3
The Lord Bless Thee

"The LORD that made heaven and earth bless thee out of Zion" (Psalm 134:3).

Saints are to bless the Lord. "Bless the LORD" (Psalm 134:2b). Saints bless the Lord with their worship—adoration, exaltation, praise, and thanksgiving for His goodness, lovingkindness, and grace. "Bless the LORD, O my soul: and all that is within me, bless his holy name" (Psalm 103:1). Spurgeon states, "This is their main business."[821]

Saints are to bless others. "The LORD...bless thee" (Psalm 134:3). A blessing was to be pronounced upon the priests and Levites who had the night watch in the Temple. Blessings are authoritative when given in Jesus' name—"The LORD...bless thee." Outside of that authority, they are merely good wishes.[822] Saints bless others in His name through their biblical teaching, witness, godly demeanor, works and example, and displays of compassion, concern, and care.

The Lord blesses His people. "The LORD that made heaven and earth bless thee" (Psalm 134:3).

He, the maker of heaven and earth, can bless us with untold mercies, goodness, and favor. He can instill peace and grant joy in our hearts.[823] He, whose faithfulness is new every morning, can make us abound in all blessings. "And God is able to bless you

372

abundantly, so that in all things at all times, having all that you need, you will abound in every good work" (2 Corinthians 9:8 NIV). The channel of His blessings is the Holy Scriptures and often the church, its ministers, and its people.[824]

"You have desired us to bless the Lord, and now we pray the Lord to bless you."—C. H. Spurgeon.

~December 4~

Psalm 135:1
Reasons to Praise God

"Praise ye the LORD. *Praise ye the name of the* LORD; *praise him, O ye servants of the* LORD*"* (Psalm 135:1).

The priests and Levites in the Temple are exhorted to praise God for four reasons.

1. Praise God for His goodness. "Praise the LORD; for the LORD is good." The word *good* cannot be spelled without including God. All that is good originates with Him. James says, "Every good gift and every perfect gift is from above, and cometh down from the Father of lights" (James 1:17).

2. Praise God for His grace. "For the LORD hath chosen Jacob unto himself, and Israel for his peculiar treasure." "Jacob's race was chosen to be the Lord's own, to be the trustees of His truth, the maintainers of His worship, the mirrors of His mercy."[825] Praise God for choosing you to bestow His mercy and grace in salvation. "Ye have not chosen me, but I have chosen you" (John 15:16).

3. Praise God for His greatness. "For I know that the LORD is great, and that our Lord is above all gods." Idols are no rival to Him (Psalm 135:15–17). His mighty power and greatness are displayed in His dominion over creation and the defeat of the enemy of His people. He reigns supreme as the King of Kings and Lord of Lords. He does whatever He wants, and no nation or man can stop Him.

4. Praise God for His government. "Whatsoever the LORD pleased, that did he." He governs man's affairs and that of all creation for their good (Psalm 135:7–12; Isaiah 40:21).

"Praise the LORD." Do it again; continue to do it; do it better and more heartily; do it in growing numbers; do it at once."[826]—C. H. Spurgeon.

~December 5~

Psalm 136:1
Undeserved Mercy of God

"O give thanks unto the LORD; for he is good: for his mercy endureth forever" (Psalm 136:1).

The psalm's author is unknown, but it is known that it was sung in Solomon's Temple (2 Chronicles 7:3, 6), and by Jehoshaphat's armies in their victory in the wilderness of Tekoa (2 Chronicles 20:20–22).[827]

Twenty-six times, the phrase, *His mercy endureth forever*, is repeated in the psalm. Note five aspects of God's rich mercy.

The source of mercy. "His mercy." Mercy, God's undeserved love, goodness, kindness, and loyalty, comes freely from His hand.

The significance of mercy. It is essential. Jeremiah says, "It is of the LORD's mercies that we are not consumed, because his compassions fail not" (Lamentations 3:22). Matthew Henry wrote, "We all owe it to the sparing mercy of God that we are not consumed. Others have been consumed round about us, and we have been in the consuming, and yet we are not consumed; we are out of the grave; we are out of Hell. Had we been dealt with according to our sins, we should have been consumed long ago, but we have been dealt with according to God's mercies."[828] Philip Henry said, "If the end of one mercy were not the beginning of another, we were undone."

The sign of mercy. God's mercies are bountiful and varied. Foremost, mercy (pardoning mercy) manifests itself in God's readiness to forgive the vilest of sinners from the pain (despair, grief of sin), power (captivity to sin), and penalty of sin, and reconcile and redeem them unto Himself. "Who remembered us in our low estate....And hath redeemed us from our enemies" (Psalm 136:23–24). Mercy is also displayed through forgiveness upon request after salvation and through untold blessings that are bestowed daily. Thomas Watson said, "Every time you draw your breath, you suck in mercy."

The supply of mercy. It is everlasting and inexhaustible. "They are new every morning" (Lamentations 3:23).

The song of mercy. "I will sing of the mercies of the LORD forever, I will sing." Spurgeon wrote, "What joy that there is mercy, mercy with Jehovah, enduring mercy, mercy enduring forever. We are ever needing it, trying it, praying for it, receiving it; therefore, let us forever sing of it."[829]

"God desires to exercise mercy as much as you desire to feel it."— Thomas Manton.

~December 6~

Psalm 137:4

Singing in a Strange Land

"How shall we sing the LORD'S song in a strange land?" (Psalm 137:4).

The psalm was written while the Israelites were in Babylonian captivity and depicts their grief and sorrow under their captors' taunting. The psalmist asserts that sorrow, suffering, and sin ("a strange land") can silence the Lord's song (hymns and spiritual songs) and begs the question as to what the saint might do to maintain it under the direst of circumstances.

The songs are kept by faith. Saith Spurgeon, "The songs we warble in the night are those that show we have real faith in God."[165] In this strange land of adversity, faith declares God is the same as

He is outside it. Not one iota has changed regarding His loving guardianship and tender, compassionate care. Every promise of the Bible remains true, our forgiveness of sin and eternal life has not been altered, the defiled garments of sin are still washed clean, citizenship in Heaven is unchanged, God yet remains in sovereign control of all that happens, the Holy Spirit's ministry of comfort and help is unabated, and God's mercies are still new every morning.

The songs are kept by fortitude. Like Job of old, to keep singing in time of trial, say unwaveringly, "Though he slay me, yet will I trust in him" (Job 13:15).

The songs are kept by foresight. "For I consider that the sufferings of this present time are not worth comparing with the glory that is to be revealed to us" (Romans 8:18 ESV). Present afflictions contrasted to our coming glory (peace, freedom, wellness, joy) are incomparable. Morris says, "Troublesome as they are to us who experience them, they are of no weight when set over against the glory that awaits God's people."[830] Focusing on the glory enables singing in the gloom.

"Any man can sing when the prison doors are open, and he is set free. The Christian soul sings in prison."—G. Campbell Morgan.

~December 7~
Psalm 138:3
Prayer Works

"In the day when I cried thou answeredst me, and strengthenedst me with strength in my soul" (Psalm 138:3).

It is believed this psalm was written by David shortly after his ten years of persecution were terminated by Saul's death.[831]

The psalm reveals a prayer of David and how the Lord received it.

The prayer was heard successfully. God listened to the psalmist's prayer. "For the eyes of the Lord are over the righteous, and his ears are open unto their prayers" (1 Peter 3:12).

The prayer was answered swiftly. No more had the psalmist prayed before it was answered. Matthew Henry comments, "It was a speedy answer: 'In the day when I cried.' Note, those that trade with Heaven by prayer grow rich by quick returns."[832]

The prayer was answered sufficiently. He received sustaining strength in his soul. Says Spurgeon, "If the burden was not removed, yet strength was given wherewith to bear it, and this is an equally effective method of help. It may not be best for us that the trial should come to an end; it may be far more to our advantage that by its pressure, we should learn patience."[833]

The psalmist's experience echoes that of myriads concerning answered prayer. Joshua prayed, and Achan's sin was exposed. Hannah prayed, and Samuel was born. Daniel prayed, and the lions became closed-mouthed. Hezekiah prayed, and a hundred and eighty-five thousand Assyrians were killed. Nehemiah prayed, and the King granted him a leave of absence to help his people. Elisha prayed, and a dead child was raised. Knox prayed, and all of Scotland was shaken. Taylor prayed, and the China Inland Mission was birthed. Müller prayed, and provision was sent to feed the orphans. Luther prayed, and the Reformation occurred.

"All things and everything are dependent on the measure of men's praying. Prayer is the genius and mainspring of life."[834]—E. M. Bounds.

~December 8~

Psalm 138:5

A Singing People

"Yea, they shall sing in the ways of the LORD" (Psalm 138:5).

Christians are singing people.[835]

1. They sing out of spontaneous joy and delight because of what Christ did for them. Matthew Henry says, "Those that walk in the ways of the Lord have reason to sing in those ways, to go on in them with a great deal of cheerfulness, for they are ways of pleasantness,

and it becomes us to be pleasant in them; and, if we are so, great is the glory of the Lord."[836]

2. They sing in the way of Jesus.

In worship. "Serve the LORD with gladness: come before his presence with singing" (Psalm 100:2).

In work. "Let those refuse to sing, who never knew our God; But children of the heav'nly King shall speak their joys abroad."

3. They don't have to go to the world to find a reason to sing. Their song is not birthed in a tavern, sensual pleasures, or drugs, but in the delights of their blessed savior.

4. They sing not only in the way of the Lord but also songs of which He is the subject. Ackley wrote, "I'll ever sing of Jesus' love for me, and how He died upon Mount Calvary; I'll sing it now and thro' eternity, for that's the sweetest song I know." They sing songs about the ways of the Lord, His saving blood, amazing grace and mercy, goodness, excellent greatness, blessed consolation, sweet friendship, and heavenly Home.

"Let a man once know the ways of Jehovah, and he will find therein abundant reason for song."[837]—C. H. Spurgeon.

~December 9~

Psalm 138:5
The Points of the Saint's Song

"Yea, they shall sing in the ways of the LORD" (Psalm 138:5). Christians instinctively sing. The psalmist cites the subject of their song.

1. Sing about God's lovingkindness. "Praise thy name for thy lovingkindness" (Psalm 138:2). "I will sing of thy love forever."

2. Sing about God's truth. "And for thy truth" (Psalm 138:2). God's promises are His truth. Sing of them.

3. Sing about God's answered prayers. "In the day when I cried thou answeredst me" (Psalm 138:3).

4. Sing about God's fellowship. "Though the LORD be high, yet hath he respect unto the lowly" (Psalm 138:6). God stoops to commune with the humble.

5. Sing about God's deliverance from trouble. "Though I walk in the midst of trouble, thou wilt revive me....thy right hand shall save me" (Psalm 138:7).

6. Sing about God's mercy. "Thy mercy, O LORD, endureth forever" (Psalm 138:8). "I will sing of the mercies of the Lord forever, I will sing, I will sing."

A song birthed in my heart in the youth choir sixty years ago challenges saints to sing as they march to Zion, the wonderful city of God. "Sing! Make a joyful sound! Sing! New life in Christ is found! Now, in my heart, He lives. Sing! Sing! Sing!" And as you sing, include praises for the six things cited in this psalm.

"It is very much for the honor of God that kings should walk in His ways, and that all those who walk in them should sing in them, and so proclaim to all the world that He is a good Master and His work its own wages."[838]—Matthew Henry.

~December 10~

Psalm 139:6
Divine Attributes
Part 1

"Such knowledge is too wonderful for me; it is high, I cannot attain unto it" (Psalm 139:6).

We must confess with David that God's complete knowledge is past finding out. But that which may be known should be acquired. "Nothing will so enlarge the intellect," states Spurgeon, "nothing so magnifies the whole soul of man as a devout, earnest, continued investigation of the great subject of the Deity. I know nothing which can so comfort the soul, so calm the swelling billows of grief and sorrow, so speak peace to the winds of trial, as a devout musing upon the subject of the Godhead."[839] Several attributes of God are stated in the psalm.

Divine omniscience. "Thou compassest my path and my lying down, and art acquainted with all my ways" (Psalm 139:3). Has it ever occurred to you that nothing has ever occurred to God? God is not in the dark about anything in the past, present, and future (Hebrews 4:13). "To Him, all hearts are open, all desires known." Matthew Henry says, "Secret sins, services, and sorrows are under his eye."[840] To know that God's all-seeing eyes encompass every step taken brings consolation, confidence, cheer, and courage.

Divine omnipresence. "Whither shall I go from thy spirit? or whither shall I flee from thy presence?" (Psalm 139:7). God is ever with us. His presence is inescapable on land, in the air, and in the sea. God asked Jeremiah, "Am I a God at hand, declares the LORD, and not a God far away? Can a man hide himself in secret places so that I cannot see him? declares the LORD. Do I not fill heaven and earth? declares the LORD" (Jeremiah 23:23–24 ESV). Heartily embracing God's omnipresence—His abiding presence and care in whatever happens and wherever it occurs—provides peace and hope (Proverbs 15:3).

"What comes into our minds when we think about God is the most important thing about us."—A. W. Tozer

~December 11~

Psalm 139:6
Divine Attributes
Part 2

"Such knowledge is too wonderful for me; it is high, I cannot attain unto it" (Psalm 139:6).

Knowledge of the character of God bears wondrous benefits. God's omniscience and omnipresence were noted yesterday. Note His omnipotence and immutability today.

Divine omnipotence. "Your works are miraculous, and my soul is fully aware of this" (Psalm 139:14 GW). God's power and authority are without limit or restriction. It surpasses every hardship and hurt, conflict and concern, challenge and crisis, needs and want. Omnipotence speaks of God's sovereign, absolute control of all that happens. The "immeasurable greatness of His power" (Ephesians 1:19 ESV) provides a firm foundation to rest secure despite the circumstances that shake and rattle life.

Divine immutability. God's immutability is His unflagging and unfailing faithfulness to His people. It is His abiding constancy. "Jesus Christ the same yesterday, and today, and forever" (Hebrews 13:8). Spurgeon, in the sermon "The Immutability of God," states that God is changeless regarding His essence, attributes, promises, plans, threats, and the objects of His love. He is the unchangeable One.

David doesn't speak of this attribute in the psalm, but he does by saying God is a Rock elsewhere (Psalm 62:2). A rock is a good metaphor for immutability. Take one in hand and try to change it! Knowing that God's love and care are unchangeable provides calm, comfort, and confidence.

Packer says there are four effects of the attributes of God: "Those who know God have great energy for God....Those who know God have great thoughts of God....Those who know God show great boldness for God....Those who know God have great contentment in God. A little knowledge of God is worth more than a great deal of knowledge about Him."[841]

"The attributes of God tell us what He is and who He is."— William Ames.

~December 12~
Psalm 139:13–14
Wondrously Made

"You made all the delicate, inner parts of my body and knit them together in my mother's womb. Thank you for making me so wonderfully complex! It is amazing to think about. Your workmanship is marvelous—and how well I know it" (Psalm 139:13–14 TLB).

Spurgeon comments, "We need not go to the ends of the earth for marvels, nor even across our own threshold; they abound in our own bodies."[842]

What happens when a baby is aborted?

A life is terminated. The Bible consistently uses the same Greek word, *brephos*, to describe an unborn (Luke 1:44), born (Luke 2:12), and young child (Luke 18:15).[843] Why? Creator God sees no biological difference in a child inside or outside the womb; they both are persons.

A law is transgressed. "Thou shalt not murder." The Israelites clearly understood the sixth commandment to include murder by sword, poison, strangulation, and abortion.[844] The same punishment was to be inflicted upon a person who killed an unborn child as an adult (Exodus 21:22–25), which indicates that God sees the unborn as a person. The early church embraced the same view. "Thou shalt not slay the child by procuring abortion; nor, again, shalt thou destroy it after it is born."[845]

A liberty is trampled. Abortion tramples upon the unborn child's right to life and freedom, as stated in the Fifth Amendment of the United States Constitution and the Declaration of Independence.

"The fetus, though enclosed in the womb of its mother, is already a human being, and it is a monstrous crime to rob it of the life which it has not yet begun to enjoy."[846]—John Calvin.

Psalm 139:17
Precious Thoughts of God

"How precious also are thy thoughts unto me, O God! how great is the sum of them!" (Psalm 139:17).

In pondering God's thoughts for him, David was overwhelmed by their actuality, constancy, and splendor.

Divine thoughts. To be thought about by a President or King is a stupendous honor. But to be in God's loving thoughts is a prized and cherished treasure of grandeur and pleasure.

Precious thoughts. God's thoughts of love for our happiness, forgiveness, provision, comfort, peace, holiness, and a thousand more things are infinite.

Innumerable thoughts. "They are more in number than the sand." The loving thoughts of God for us, David states, exceed the sand found on the seashores and ocean beaches.

Constant thoughts. Never out of His sight or out of His mind. 'When I awake every morning, I am still in your loving, protective, caring thoughts.' Spurgeon says, "A God always thinking of us makes a happy world, a rich life, a heavenly hereafter."[847]

New thoughts. God's compassion for us is new every morning (Lamentations 3:23).

"They are dear to us; we must think of them with a great deal of reverence, and yet with pleasure and thankfulness."[848]—Matthew Henry.

383

~December 14~

Psalm 139:23–24
Pursuit of Holiness

"Search me, O God, and know my heart: try me, and know my thoughts: And see if there be any wicked way in me, and lead me in the way everlasting" (Psalm 139:23–24).

J. C. Ryle said, "We must be holy, because this is the only sound evidence that we have a saving faith in our Lord Jesus Christ." A four-rung ladder leads to the holiness of life.

The first rung is thirsting. Tozer says, "Every man is as holy as he really wants to be." The reason why few are holy is that they lack the intense, desperate thirst required to be holy. George McDonald asserts, "If you will not determine to be pure, you will grow more and more impure." The pursuit of holiness begins when the soul cries out in earnest with McCheyne, "O God, make me as holy as a pardoned sinner can be." And says, with David Brainerd, "All I want is to be more holy, more like my dear Lord. Oh, for sanctification."

The second rung is searching. The word search means to dig deep. For holiness to fill the life, its dirt must be dug out and emptied. The Lord made the heart and can detect its darkest secrets. To search one's heart is difficult; the Holy Spirit's help is essential.

> Nothing between my soul and the Savior,
> Naught of this world's delusive dream;
> I have renounced all sinful pleasure;
> Jesus is mine, there's nothing between.
>
> —Charles Tindley

The third rung is cleansing. The filth and dirt revealed by the divine search and examination must be confessed to and cleansed by the Lord (Psalm 24:3–5). The Bible states, "If we confess our sins, he forgives them and cleanses us from everything we've done wrong" (1 John 1:9 GW).

The fourth rung is surrendering. "And lead me in the way everlasting." "All to Jesus, I surrender. All to Him, I freely give." With the heart purged of sin, life is to be presented to God anew in submission to and guidance in the way of holiness in thought and walk (the opposite way of impurity and defilement). Andrew Murray said, "Just as a servant knows that he must first obey his master in all things, so the surrender to an implicit and unquestionable obedience must become the essential characteristic of our lives."

Matthew Henry said, "The way of godliness is an everlasting way; it is everlastingly true and good, pleasing to God and profitable to us."[849]

"It is not great talents or great learning or great preachers that God needs, but men great in holiness."—E. M. Bounds.

~December 15~

Psalm 140:8
Foolhardy Desires of the Wicked

"Grant not, O LORD, the desires of the wicked: further not his wicked device; lest they exalt themselves" (Psalm 140:8).

David wrote the Psalm when in exile, confronted by Saul and Doeg. What are the desires of the wicked?

1. To cancel God's moral law.

2. To shipwreck and discredit believers.

3. To close or handicap the influence of the church.

4. To put in high places leaders with an anti-biblical agenda.

5. To restrict the spread of the Gospel.

6. To silence their opponents.

7. To engage in a wanton lifestyle without protest or interference.

8. To avoid the judgment of God at life's end.

9. To live without the infliction of guilt over their sin.

10. To live the wicked's life but die the righteous' death.

Grant not. Pray that God will not grant the desires of the wicked for three reasons. They are harmful to themselves. They are detrimental to others. They are toxic to the cause of God.

"Thus we are to pray against the enemies of God's people, that they may not succeed in any of their enterprises."[850]—Matthew Henry.

~December 16~

Psalm 141:9

The Devil's Snares

"Keep me from the snares which they have laid for me, and the gins of the workers of iniquity" (Psalm 141:9).

David closes the psalm with a prayer for safe-keeping from the snares of his persecutors and friends.

The existence of snares. "The snares." Though unseen, the Christian life is inundated with traps that cause shipwrecks and captivity. This truth is attested by Scripture, experience, and history. Jonathan Swift wrote, "Human brutes, like other beasts, find snares and poison in the provision of life, and are allured by their appetites to their destruction." Says Spurgeon, "There is not a place beneath which a believer walks that is free from snares. Behind every tree, there is the Indian with his barbed arrow; behind every bush, there is the lion seeking to devour; under every piece of grass, there lieth the adder. Everywhere they are."[851]

The engineer of snares. "Which they have laid for me." Our archenemy, Satan, is the strategist of a snare's design, placement, and time.

The entrapment of snares. "Laid for me." A snare's fabrication is unique to its prey. The bait that allures one may not entice another. Its form may be that of alcohol, drugs, pornography, immorality, gambling, anger stimulation, pride, or something else that is a personal weakness and vulnerability. David's snare was adultery with Bathsheba. Samson's snare was a romance with Delilah. Gehazi's snare was greed with Naaman. Peter's snare was that of compromise with the damsel.

"There is one thing that all Satan's cunning and all the snares of temptation cannot take by surprise—an undivided will."—Soren Kierkegaard.

~December 17~

Psalm 141:10
Escape From Snares

"Let the wicked fall into their own nets, whilst that I withal escape" (Psalm 141:10).

The escape from snares. "Keep me" (Psalm 141:9). God can keep our feet from falling into a snare. "Now unto him that is able to keep you from falling, and to present you faultless before the presence of his glory with exceeding joy" (Jude 24). Benson says, "Keep me from being taken in it; give me to discover and evade it."[852] Matthew Henry remarked, "Be the gin [snare] placed with ever so much subtlety; God can and will secure His people from being taken in it."[853] "Amidst a thousand snares," wrote Spurgeon, "I stand. Upheld and guarded by Thy hand; that hand unseen shall hold me still and lead me to thy holy hill."[854]

But should we fall prey to a snare, God can grant deliverance. David said, "Mine eyes are ever toward the LORD; for he shall pluck my feet out of the net" (Psalm 25:15). Spurgeon wrote, "The Lord is equal to every emergency, and the most skillfully placed nets of the hunter shall never be able to hold His chosen ones."[855] Saints testify of God's power to rescue and deliver, having been in a snare, a cage of entrapment.

"Satan, who is a wonderful contriver of delusions, is constantly laying snares to entrap ignorant and heedless people."—John Calvin.

~December 18~

Psalm 142:4

The Cave of Despair

"I looked on my right hand, and beheld, but there was no man that would know me: refuge failed me; no man cared for my soul" (Psalm 142:4).

David's conflict. "My spirit was overwhelmed within me." What precipitated the despair?

1. Desertion of friends (Psalm 142:4). The sharpest dagger to the heart is betrayal, indifference, or abandonment of a friend in a time of need. "No man cared for my soul." Despite the many people David knew, none in his trouble "knew" him. Spurgeon paraphrases David: "Whether I lived or died was no concern of anybody. I was cast out as an outcast. No soul cared for my soul. I dwelt in no-man's-land, where none cared to have me, and none cared about me."

2. Persecution (Psalm 142:6). Saul, Doeg, and the Ziphites were among David's persecutors. Matthew Henry says, "Christ's followers cannot expect better treatment in the world than their Master had."

3. Dire circumstances (Psalm 142:7). The cave was, to David, a prison confinement. He was shut up within its walls of despair and loneliness without a way of escape, or so he thought.

David's confidence. "Thou shalt deal bountifully with me." David's faith prompts trust in God for deliverance. No one else may care about his trouble, but he knows that God does. With David, we are confident that God is close at hand, ready to help us, that He is more potent than our foe, and that He can break the net of our captivity to set us free. "Casting all your care upon him; for he careth for you" (1 Peter 5:7).

David's celebration. "That I may praise thy name." The deliverances of God are always the occasion for jubilation and praise to Him.

"Throw your cares, which are so cutting and distracting, which wound your souls and pierce your hearts, upon the wise and gracious providence of God; trust in Him with a firm composed mind, for He careth for you."[856]—Matthew Henry.

~December 19~

Psalm 142:4
No Man Cares for My Soul

"No man cared for my soul" (Psalm 142:4).

Its legitimacy. What circumstances justify David's accusation?

1. When a person is untold of Christ and His provision of rescue and salvation.

2. When a person is shown no sympathy or tenderness in affliction or adversity.

3. When a person is unsought in straying from the fold.

4. When a person is unprayed for in sorrow, suffering, or sickness.

5. When a person is unvisited in a convalescent home, prison, and home confinement.

How piercing is the sorrowful crying of the many who say, "No man cared for my soul."

Its indictment. The accusation is an incrimination against Christians, whom God charges with caring for the souls of all men. "I was…naked, and ye clothed me: I was sick, and ye visited me: I was in prison, and ye came unto me" (Matthew 25:35–36).

Its inexcusability. Failure to care for souls is a sin against the last command of Jesus and bears grave punishment (Ezekiel 3:17–18).

"No man cared for my soul." What David said of man cannot be spoken of God. Although Christians may not display care for souls, God forever draws them to Himself through His goodness and blessings. "Casting all your care upon him; for he careth for you" (1 Peter 5:7).

"Do you really care? Do you know how to share? With people everywhere, do you really care?"—Bill Cates (1967).

~December 20~

Psalm 142:4
Who Cares for Your Soul?

"No man cared for my soul" (Psalm 142:4).

Who cares if a person is saved from a life of degradation, meaninglessness, despair, and an eternity in Hell?

God cares; that's why He sent His only Son into the world to die upon an old, rugged Cross to make possible man's forgiveness for sin and reconciliation with Himself.

Jesus cares; that's why He willingly bore the ridicule, mockery, torture, and crucifixion at Calvary to make atonement for man's sin.

The Holy Spirit cares; that's why He convicts man of sin, draws him to Christ, orchestrates opportunities for hearing the Gospel, and shares appeals to be saved.

The Christian cares; that's why he risks rejection and persecution and expends time, treasure, and energy in sharing the Good News with men. Spurgeon said of John Bunyan that "he often felt while preaching that he could give his own salvation for the salvation of his hearers."[25] Spurgeon said, "And I pity the man who has not felt the same."[26]

The Church cares; that's why within her doors, the unadulterated gospel message of Christ crucified, buried, and raised from the dead is preached clearly and soundly, with appeals to be reconciled to

God, and outreach and mission endeavors are implemented to reach the unsaved.

The Sinner in Hell cares; that's why he begs Abraham to send Lazarus or someone else back from the dead to warn family members not to go to that place of eternal torment.

The Saint in Heaven cares; that's why there is rejoicing about the throne when a lost soul is saved from the jaws of ruination and damnation. At the last judgment, no man can say, "No man cared for my soul" (Psalm 142:4).

"From the first infant step to the last step of manhood on the sharp spike of Calvary, a journey for you—oh, how He cared for your soul!"—Talmage.

~December 21~

Psalm 143:6
How to Pray in Difficulty

"I stretch forth my hands unto thee: my soul thirsteth after thee, as a thirsty land" (Psalm 143:6).

A Psalm composed by David, perhaps on Absalom's rebellion. David's request reveals the way to help in times of trouble. Pray like David in times of difficulty for rescue and relief.

Hear me (Psalm 143:7). Exhibit trust in God by bringing the trial to Him. God is always the first resort of help.

Cause me (Psalm 143:8). Ask to hear God speak and for understanding about what you are to do. The godly ask not for the easy way to go but the right way. Knowing the way to go (and walking that way) automatically brings joy, peace, and happiness.

Deliver me (Psalm 143:9). God is the protector and strong tower of refuge against the enemy. Ask Him to hide you in the covert of His wings from persecutors and others who seek your harm. Augustine said, "I who once fled from Thee, now flee to Thee."[857]

Teach me (Psalm 143:10a). The Holy Spirit illuminates the *what* and *how* of God's will. It's expedient to seek His guidance in knowing and applying it totally to life. "It is the desire and endeavor of all God's faithful servants," says Matthew Henry, "to know and to do his will, and to stand complete in it."[858]

Lead me (Psalm 143:10b). Spurgeon says, "The way is long and steep, and he who goes without a divine leader will faint on the journey; but with Jehovah to lead, it is delightful to follow, and there is neither stumbling nor wandering."[859]

Quicken me (Psalm 143:11). Pray for God to revive your soul, bring it out of its gloom and despair for His glory and honor.

"If the Holy Spirit can take over the subconscious with our consent and cooperation, then we have almighty Power working at the basis of our lives, then we can do anything we ought to do, go anywhere we ought to go and be anything we ought to be."—E. Stanley Jones.

~December 22~

Psalm 144:3

Why God is Mindful of Man

"LORD, what is man, that thou takest knowledge of him!" (Psalm 144:3).

It is believed that David wrote the Psalm following the death of Absalom and Israel's restoration to peace.[860] David questions the reason for God's concern, compassion, and care for man, who is but a "worm." Why is God mindful of sinful man?

1. He is cognizant of man because He created him in His image. Harman states, "Man occupies a special position in creation, in that he alone of all the creatures was made in the image and likeness of God (Genesis 1:26–27; 5:1)."[861]

2. He is mindful of man because He placed everything under his dominion. Hasting asserts, "At the summit of creation, God stamped man with the Divine image, crowned him, and gave him

392

dominion over all creatures. This is the Bible doctrine of the origin of man, and it takes us to the heights."[862]

3. He is mindful of man because of His desire to save him from ruination and damnation (2 Peter 3:9).

4. He is aware of man because it is His nature to show love, compassion, and mercy to broken and bruised people.

5. He is mindful of man because He wants to bring them to repentance (Romans 2:4).

6. He is mindful of man, for He longs for those He created to reign with Him in eternity.

Man's insignificance, nothingness, unworthiness, emptiness, and transitoriness ought to cause him to seek the Lord who has demonstrated unfailing love, care, and kindness toward him so that he might have life abundantly and eternally.

"Though man is a worm, and the son of man is a worm (Job 25:6), yet God puts respect upon him and shows him an abundance of kindness; man is, above all the creatures in this lower world, the favorite and darling of Providence."[863]—Matthew Henry.

~ December 23~

Psalm 145:4
Duty of Each Generation

"One generation shall praise thy works to another, and shall declare thy mighty acts" (Psalm 145:4).

The psalm is David's final in the Psalter. It provides no historical occasion for its composition.

Each generation amasses "fresh" witnesses (testimony, insight, and knowledge) to God's glory, honor, and goodness that must be preserved for future generations. Horne states, "As one generation drops it, another should take it up and prolong the delightful strain till the sun and the moon shall withdraw their light, and the stars fall extinguished from their orbs."[381] The passing down from generation to generation the mighty doings of God (miracles, awakenings, and deliverances) is the primary mode cited in Scripture, whereby such knowledge continues unabated through the ages.[382] Pope says, "It has pleased God to make every generation a trustee for the generations to come."

Receiving the gospel truth, which was handed down to us, granting deliverance from the penalty of sin, places us under divine obligation to pass it on to the next generation. Saith Spurgeon, "Our negligent silence must not deprive our own and our father's offspring of the precious truth of God." Parents are to instill biblical truth into their children's hearts and their children's children (Deuteronomy 6:7). Politicians are to ensure the continuance of biblical values, policies, principles, and laws, as well as religious freedom. Bible colleges and seminaries are to retain and maintain biblical integrity and evangelistic fervor in the instruction and training of ministers. Religious authors must be theologically accurate in writing about God's attributes, Word, and works. Multiplied harvest workers must be raised, trained, and thrust out into the mission fields around the world (Matthew 9:37–38). All this must be done "so that the death of God's worshippers shall be no diminution of His worship, for a new generation shall rise up in their room to carry on that good work, more or less, to the end of time."[864]

"The people that live in one age shall relate them [the works of God] to their posterity, and so successively in all ages."—Matthew Poole.

~December 24~

Psalm 146:5
The Reason for Happiness and Hope

"Happy is he that hath the God of Jacob for his help, whose hope is in the LORD his God" (Psalm 146:5).

The final five Psalms (Psalm 146–150) are collectively called *Hallelujah Psalms*. No author is identified.

The titles of God stated in Psalm 146 indicate why the person who knows Him is happy and possesses hope for the present and future.

The God of Jacob is the creator. "Which made heaven, and earth." He who made something from nothing and sustains it can care for man's needs.

The God of Jacob is the righteous judge. "Which executeth judgment." God redresses the wrong done to the righteous through judgment.

The God of Jacob is the emancipator. "The LORD looseth the prisoners." No prison of bondage, moral or mental, is strong enough to keep captive the person God sets free. 'He the son sets free shall be free indeed.'

The God of Jacob is the illuminator. "The LORD openeth the eyes of the blind." God enables the spiritually blind to see their plight and need for salvation. He gives inner light to His children so they know His word and will.

The God of Jacob is the comforter. He "raiseth them that are bowed down." God consoles and supports those who are bereaved, persecuted, and cast down.

The God of Jacob is the preserver. "The LORD preserveth." God protects desolate, defenseless, and helpless people like strangers, widows, and orphans.

The God of Jacob is the everlasting King. "The LORD shall reign forever." Man's help, at best, is temporal. God's help is forevermore. "Jehovah is King," wrote Spurgeon, "and His kingdom can never end. Neither does He die, nor abdicate, nor lose His crown by force. Glory be to His name; His throne is never in jeopardy."[865]

What should be our reaction to this God who bears such wondrous titles? That of "Praise ye the LORD."

"Happy the people of such a God; happy the subjects of such a King! Rejoice, and sing, and shout aloud."[866]—George Horne.

~December 25~

Psalm 146:9
The Way of the Wicked Frustrated

"The way of the wicked he turneth upside down" (Psalm 146:9).

God's protection and preservation of the righteous mandate the frustration of the plans and goings of the wicked against them. He fills their ways with crooked paths, distortions, diversions, reverses, and failure (Proverbs 19:21). The truth is well illustrated by Joseph's brothers, Haman, and many before our very eyes. Of them, Spurgeon asserts, "That which the man aimed at he misses, and he secures that for himself which he would gladly have avoided." Plumer says, "The most dreadful disasters that have overtaken the wicked in past ages are but feeble tokens of their ruin, the utter disappointment of all their hopes, the perfect defeat of all their plans in the world to come."[867]

To have God as one's adversary is a fearful and terrible thing. "I'm against you, you arrogant one! Declares the LORD God of heavenly forces. Your day has come, your time of reckoning" (Jeremiah 50:31 CEB). "It is a fearful thing to fall into the hands of the living God" (Hebrews 10:31). But, "Happy is he that hath the God of Jacob for his help, whose hope is in the LORD his God" (Psalm 146:5) and has Him as their shield and refuge (Psalm 146:9).

Cowman said, "Very often, the enemy seems to triumph for a season, and God allows it. But then He comes in and upsets the work of the enemy, overthrows the apparent victory, and as the Bible says, 'frustrates the ways of the wicked' (Psalm 146: 9)."[868] God always gets the last word.

"It is the glory of the Messiah that he will subvert all the counsels of Hell and earth that militate against His church, so that, having Him for us, we need not fear anything that can be done against us."[869]—Matthew Henry.

~December 26~

Psalm 147:3

The Hurt and Healer

"He healeth the broken in heart, and bindeth up their wounds" (Psalm 147:3).

Israel was wounded, miserable, and brokenhearted in exile (Psalm 137:1–4), but upon restoration to her land, she was "healed."

The hurt. "The broken in heart." To be brokenhearted is to be wounded, crushed, and shattered by the shame, dishonor, and pain sin brings to God and oneself. It is to have a sick soul and a troubled spirit. David experienced a broken heart in the aftermath of adultery (Psalm 51). The Bible states it is the broken in spirit over sin who God will not despise (Psalm 51:17). The condition equally applies to those who are distressed over any disturbance to inner peace and joy—the death of a loved one, failure, betrayal, troublesomeness, abandonment of a friend, and illness (Psalm 42:7).

The healer. "He." Our God is a friend to the broken heart. A bruised reed he will not break, the smoking flax he will not quench. "The LORD is nigh unto them that are of a broken heart" (Psalm 34:18). Spurgeon says, "Come, broken hearts, come to the Physician who never fails to heal; uncover your wounds to him who so tenderly binds them up!"[870]

The Great Physician can do what people, medicine, and therapy cannot. In Luke 4:18, Jesus says, "He [God] hath sent me to heal the brokenhearted." In Matthew 11:28, He says, "Come unto me, all ye that labor and are heavy laden, and I will give you rest." The psalmist instructs, "Cast thy burden upon the LORD, and He shall sustain thee" (Psalm 55:22). In Christ, you will find an anchor that holds despite the fierceness of the storm, an antidote (certainty of His abiding presence and Heaven that gives a peace that passes all understanding) that relieves the heavy, burdened heart vexed and confused by its circumstances, and true and tried promises that will sustain. They are all awesome wind and sails to the brokenhearted. Spurgeon states, "Hope in God always crests the stormiest billow."[871]

"Few will associate with the despondent, but Jehovah chooses their company and abides with them till He has healed them by His comforts."[872]—C. H. Spurgeon.

~December 27~

Psalm 147:3
The Healing

"He healeth the broken in heart, and bindeth up their wounds" (Psalm 147:3).

Yesterday, we examined the hurt and the healer. Today, *the healing*. "Healeth." "Humpty Dumpty sat on a wall; Humpty Dumpty had a great fall. All the king's horses, all the king's men, couldn't put Humpty together again."

Regardless of the "fall" experienced—the brokenness of dreams, relationships, hope, and significance for existing—King Jesus can do what "all the king's horses, all the king's men" cannot do: put man back together again! "He healeth the broken in heart." "Ye people, pour out your heart before him: God is a refuge for us" (Psalm 62:8). Wiersbe says, "The God who numbers and names the stars knows about your broken heart and can heal it—if you give all the pieces to Him."[873]

"He knows how to speak, and the darkness becomes light. The very affliction that would drag you down lifts you up; the things that are weights become wings. That which, if you could, you would have prevented lifts you up to Heaven."[874]—A. C. Dixon.

Psalm 148:1

The Tribute of the Heavenlies

"Praise ye the LORD. Praise ye the LORD from the heavens: praise him in the heights" (Psalm 148:1).

The Psalmist calls for the "bodies celestial" (the heavenlies) to praise God for three reasons.

He is creator. "He commanded, and they were created." Let them praise God for His great power in making them. It only took a word from Him to hang the stars, moon, and sun in the majestic sky.

He is controller. "He hath made a decree." The heavenlies and all that reside therein are under God's decree to function harmoniously according to His ordained plan "forever and ever." They cannot violate that governing rule. Cataclysmic chaos and destruction would happen if they did. Let them praise God for meticulously and constantly regulating their existence and movement.

He is conservator. "He hath also stablished them forever and ever." That which God ordained for the "bodies celestial" will not fail because He is their guardian and keeper. Let them praise Him for their preservation.

For the same reasons, all of creation, especially man, should shout and thunder praise to God.

"The voice which said 'Let them be,' now saith 'Let them praise.'"[875]—C. H. Spurgeon.

Psalm 149:2b

Joy in Thy King

"Let the children of Zion be joyful in their King" (Psalm 149:2b).

Why do Christians have reason to be joyful in their King?

1. He is a Royal King. He is the eternal God, clothed with majesty and glory, who sits upon His throne in Heaven.

2. He is a Reigning King. "But the LORD is king forever; he has set up his throne for judgment." (Psalm 9:7 GNT). His rule is from everlasting to everlasting (Psalm 90:2).

3. He is a Redeeming King. He is a compassionate King who stoops to rescue man from the plight of sin.

4. He is a Rich King. He is incomparably rich. "For every beast of the forest is mine, and the cattle upon a thousand hills" (Psalm 50:10). God's richness means man's supply for every need. "But my God shall supply all your need" (Philippians 4:19). Simeon wrote, "What cause can he possibly have for discontent, who has God for his God, and an express promise that all his need shall be supplied? God has not only engaged to give His people whatever they need but, on many occasions, has interposed in a miraculous manner to fulfill his word."[876]

5. He is a Returning King. He shall come to take His children to Heaven to live with Him forever. "Oh, that the LORD would come!" exclaimed Spurgeon; "He is coming! He is on the road and traveling quickly. The sound of His approach should be as music to our hearts! Ring out, ye bells of hope!"[877]

"To speak of the Godhood of God then is to say that God is on the Throne, on the Throne as a fact and not as a say so; on a Throne that is high above all."[878]—A. W. Pink.

~December 30~

Psalm 149:4a
God Delights in His Children

"For the LORD taketh pleasure in his people." (Psalm 149:4a).

Incredible as it is, *God takes pleasure* (delight and favor) *in His children*. He takes pleasure in their likeness unto Himself. He takes pleasure in their faith. He takes pleasure in their regeneration. He takes pleasure in their fellowship. He takes pleasure in their service. He takes pleasure in their worship. He takes pleasure in their repentance. He takes pleasure in what they yet shall be. He takes pleasure in their prayers and praise.

Spurgeon says, "Jesus remembers that He died for us, the Holy Spirit remembers that He strove with us, the great Father remembers how He has preserved us, and because of all this goodness in the past, He takes pleasure in us."[879] He takes so much pleasure and delight in His children that He joys "over thee with singing" (Zephaniah 3:17).

"What condescension is this on Jehovah's part, to notice, to love, and to delight in his chosen! Surely there is nothing in our persons, or our actions, which could cause pleasure to the Ever-blessed One, were it not that he condescends to people of low estate."[880]— J. I. Packer.

~December 31~

Psalm 150:1
Give Praises to God

"Praise ye the LORD" (Psalm 150:1).

What a fitting psalm to close the psalter and this devotional.

The sphere of praise. "Praise God in his sanctuary: praise him in the firmament of his power" (Psalm 150:1). Hallelujahs should be presented in His church below and courts above.

The subject of praise. Give praise to the King of Kings and Lord of Lords, the maker and ruler of all things, and the giver of good gifts to the children of men. Spurgeon said, "Harp and lyre—the choicest, the sweetest—must be all our Lord's."

The scope of praise. "For His mighty acts." Praise God for His eminence and supreme excellence, wonders, and works in creating and governing the world and in man's redemption.

The source of praise. "Let everything that hath breath praise the LORD" (Psalm 150:6). The requirement for praise is *breathing*, not musical ability.

The style of praise. Utilize musical instruments (trumpet, psaltery, harp, stringed instruments, tambourine) with the voice to extoll Him (Psalm 150:3–5).

The span of praise. Praise is to be perpetual on earth and eternal in Heaven. Matthew Henry remarked that in Heaven, "Prayers will there be swallowed up in everlasting praises; there will be no intermission in praising God, and yet no weariness—hallelujahs forever repeated, and yet still new songs. Hallelujah is the word there; let us echo to it now, as those who hope to join in it shortly. Hallelujah, praise you, the Lord."[881]

"In serving God, we should spare no cost nor pains. That the best music in God's ears is devout and pious affections."[882]— Matthew Henry.

[1] Spurgeon, C. H. *Psalms*. (Wheaton, IL: Crossway Books, 1993), 11.

[2] Henry, M. *Matthew Henry's Commentary on the Whole Bible: Complete and Unabridged in One Volume*. (Peabody: Hendrickson, 1994), 743.

[3] Stott, John. *Favorite Psalms*. (Grand Rapids: Baker Books, 1988), 5.

[4] Simeon, C. *Horae Homileticae: Psalms, I–LXXII* (Vol. 5). (Samuel Holdsworth, 1836), 4.

[5] Exell, J. S. *The Biblical Illustrator: Second Corinthians*. (Fleming H. Revell Company, n.d.), 345.

[6] MacArthur, J., Jr. (ed.). *The MacArthur Study Bible* (electronic ed.). (Word Pub., 1997), 743.

[7] Henry, M. *Matthew Henry's Commentary on the Whole Bible: Complete and Unabridged in One Volume*. (Peabody: Hendrickson, 1994), 744.

[8] Plumer, W. S. *Studies in the Book of Psalms: Being a Critical and Expository Commentary, with Doctrinal and Practical Remarks on the Entire Psalter*. (Philadelphia; Edinburgh: J. B. Lippincott Company; A & C Black, 1872), 28.

[9] Exell, J. S. *The Biblical Illustrator: The Psalms* (Vol. 1). (Fleming H. Revell Company; Francis Griffiths, n.d.), 12.

[10] Spurgeon, C. H. *The Treasury of David: Psalms 1–26* (Vol. 1). (Marshall Brothers, n.d.), 2.

[11] Watson, Thomas. *A Christian on the Mount: On the Necessity of Meditation*, 36.

[12] Plumer, W. S. *Studies in the Book of Psalms: Being a Critical and Expository Commentary, with Doctrinal and Practical Remarks on the Entire Psalter*. (Philadelphia; Edinburgh: J. B. Lippincott Company; A & C Black, 1872), 29.

[13] Spurgeon, C. H. *The Treasury of David: Psalms 1–26* (Vol. 1). (Marshall Brothers, n.d.), 2.

[14] MacArthur, J., Jr. (ed.). *The MacArthur Study Bible* (electronic ed.). (Word Pub., 1997), 1615.

[15] Exell, J. S. *The Biblical Illustrator: The Psalms* (Vol. 1). (Fleming H. Revell Company; Francis Griffiths, n.d.), Psalm 1:3.

[16] VanGemerin, 56.

[17] Horne, G. *A Commentary on the Book of Psalms*. (New York: Robert Carter & Brothers, 1856), 39.

[18] Ibid.

[19] Spurgeon, C. H. *Morning and Evening*. (London: Passmore & Alabaster), November 10 (Evening).

[20] Cochran, Gregory C. "Christian Persecution as Explained by Jesus (Matthew 5:10–12)." SBJT-18.1-Christian-Persecution-as-explained-by-Jesus-Matthew-5-10-12.pdf, 11. Accessed March 10, 2021.

[21] Ibid.

[22] Plumer, W. S. *Studies in the Book of Psalms: Being a Critical and Expository Commentary, with Doctrinal and Practical Remarks on the Entire Psalter.* (Philadelphia; Edinburgh: J. B. Lippincott Company; A & C Black, 1872), 40.

[23] Wiersbe, W. W. *Wiersbe's Expository Outlines on the Old Testament.* (Wheaton, IL: Victor Books, 1993), Ps 2:4–6.

[24] Henry, M. *Matthew Henry's Commentary on the Whole Bible: Complete and Unabridged in One Volume.* (Peabody: Hendrickson, 1994), 745.

[25] Ibid.

[26] Spence-Jones, H. D. M. (ed.) *Psalms* (Vol. 1). (London; New York: Funk & Wagnalls Company, 1909), 20.

[27] Spurgeon, C. H. *Psalms.* (Wheaton, IL: Crossway Books, 1993), 10.

[28] Henry, M. *Matthew Henry's Commentary on the Whole Bible: Complete and Unabridged in One Volume.* (Peabody: Hendrickson, 1994), 748.

[29] Plumer, W. S. *Studies in the Book of Psalms: Being a Critical and Expository Commentary, with Doctrinal and Practical Remarks on the Entire Psalter.* (Philadelphia; Edinburgh: J. B. Lippincott Company; A & C Black, 1872), 60.

[30] Kidner, D. *Psalms 1–72: An Introduction and Commentary* (Vol. 15). (InterVarsity Press, 1973), 71.

[31] Spurgeon, C. H. *Psalms.* (Wheaton, IL: Crossway Books, 1993), 9.

[32] Selderhuis, H. J., T. George, S. M. Manetsch, & D. W. McNutt, eds. *Psalms 1–72: Old Testament* (Vol. VII). (IVP Academic, 2015), 33.

[33] Spurgeon, C. H. *The Treasury of David: Psalms 1–26* (Vol. 1). (Marshall Brothers, n.d.), 23.

[34] Henry, M. *Matthew Henry's Commentary on the Whole Bible: Complete and Unabridged in One Volume.* (Peabody: Hendrickson, 1994), 747.

[35] Chadwick, J. W. "Eternal Ruler of the Ceaseless Round." Kidner, D. *Psalms 1–72: An Introduction and Commentary* (Vol. 15). (InterVarsity Press, 1973).

[36] Craigie, P. C. *Psalms 1–50* (Vol. 19). (Dallas: Word, Incorporated, 1998), 74.

[37] Plumer, W. S. *Studies in the Book of Psalms: Being a Critical and Expository Commentary, with Doctrinal and Practical Remarks on the Entire Psalter.* (Philadelphia; Edinburgh: J. B. Lippincott Company; A & C Black, 1872), 57.

[38] Ibid.

[39] Andriote, John-Manuel. "8 Ways to Keep Sugar from Ruining Your Sleep." Updated on August 3, 2023.

[40] Spurgeon, C. H. "The Peculiar Sleep of the Beloved," March 4, 1855 (Sermon).

[41] Simeon, C. *Horae Homileticae: Psalms, I–LXXII* (Vol. 5). (Samuel Holdsworth, 1836), 14.

[42] Spurgeon, C. H. "The Sound in the Mulberry Trees." Sermon delivered May 31, 1857, New Park Street Chapel.

[43] Henry, M. *Matthew Henry's Commentary on the Whole Bible: Complete and Unabridged in One Volume.* (Peabody: Hendrickson, 1994), 749.

ENDNOTES

[44] Edwards, John. *Veritas Redux. Evangelical Truths Restored: Namely Those ...,* Volume 3. (Printed for T. Cox, at The Lamb, under the Royal Exchange, MDCCXXVI), 383.

[45] Spurgeon, C. H. *The Treasury of David: Psalms 1–26* (Vol. 1). (Marshall Brothers, n.d.), 39.

[46] Spurgeon, C. H. *Psalms.* (Wheaton, IL: Crossway Books, 1993), 14.

[47] Ibid.

[48] Maclaren, Alexander. *The Book of Psalms,* 171.

[49] *Benson Commentary,* Psalm 5:1–2.

[50] Spurgeon, C. H. *Psalms.* (Wheaton, IL: Crossway Books, 1993), 14.

[51] Plumer, W. S. *Studies in the Book of Psalms: Being a Critical and Expository Commentary, with Doctrinal and Practical Remarks on the Entire Psalter.* (Philadelphia; Edinburgh: J. B. Lippincott Company; A & C Black, 1872), 79–80).

[52] Maclaren, Alexander. *The Book of Psalms,* Psalm 5:3.

[53] Plumer, W. S. *Studies in the Book of Psalms: Being a Critical and Expository Commentary, with Doctrinal and Practical Remarks on the Entire Psalter.* (Philadelphia; Edinburgh: J. B. Lippincott Company; A & C Black, 1872), 89.

[54] Spurgeon, C. H. *The Treasury of David: Psalms 1–26* (Vol. 1). (Marshall Brothers, n.d.), 47.

[55] Boice, J. M. *Psalms 1–41: An Expositional Commentary.* (Grand Rapids, MI: Baker Books, 2005), 47.

[56] Henry, M. *Matthew Henry's Commentary on the Whole Bible: Complete and Unabridged in One Volume.* (Peabody: Hendrickson, 1994), 1233.

[57] Plumer, W. S. *Studies in the Book of Psalms: Being a Critical and Expository Commentary, with Doctrinal and Practical Remarks on the Entire Psalter.* (Philadelphia; Edinburgh: J. B. Lippincott Company; A & C Black, 1872), 82.

[58] Wiersbe, W. W. With the Word Commentary. (Nashville: Thomas Nelson, 1991), Mt. 14:1.

[59] Exell, J. S. *The Biblical Illustrator: St. John,* Vol. 2. (London: James Nisbet & Co.), 243.

[60] Harman, A. *Psalms: A Mentor Commentary* (Vol. 1–2). (Ross-shire, Great Britain: Mentor, 2011), 122.

[61] Spurgeon, C. H. *Morning and Evening.* (London: Passmore & Alabaster), December 9 (Morning).

[62] "Hom. xiv. in Phil.," Oxford transl. Spence-Jones, H. D. M. (ed.) Proverbs. (London; New York: Funk & Wagnalls Company, 1909), 503.

[63] Thackeray, William Makepeace.

[64] Craigie, P. C. *Psalms 1–50* (Vol. 19). (Dallas: Word, Incorporated, 1998), 108.

[65] Spurgeon, C. H. *The Treasury of David,* Psalm 144:3.

[66] Henry, M. *Matthew Henry's Commentary on the Whole Bible: Complete and Unabridged in One Volume.* (Peabody: Hendrickson, 1994), 754.

[67] Spurgeon, C. H. *The Treasury of David: Psalms 1–26* (Vol. 1). (Marshall Brothers, n.d.), 103.

[68] Ibid.

[69] Graham, Billy. *Peace with God.* (Waco, TX: Word, 1953), 83.

[70] Spurgeon, C. H. "Thoughts on the Last Battle," (Sermon, May 13, 1855).

[71] Interview with John Piper. "If God Never Leaves Me, Why Does He Withdraw?" https://www.desiringgod.org/interviews/if-god-never-leaves-me-why-does-he-withdraw, accessed August 4, 2024.

[72] Henry, M. *Matthew Henry's Commentary on the Whole Bible: Complete and Unabridged in One Volume.* (Peabody: Hendrickson, 1994), 756–757.

[73] Spurgeon, C. H. "An Immovable Foundation," Sermon delivered May 13, 1866, Metropolitan Tabernacle.

[74] Ibid.

[75] Boice, J. M. *Psalms 1–41: An Expositional Commentary.* (Grand Rapids, MI: Baker Books, 2005), 93.

[76] Spurgeon, C. H. *Psalms.* (Wheaton, IL: Crossway Books, 1993), 33.

[77] Exell, J. S. *The Biblical Illustrator: The Psalms* (Vol. 1). (Fleming H. Revell Company; Francis Griffiths, 1909), 189.

[78] Plumer, W. S. *Studies in the Book of Psalms: Being a Critical and Expository Commentary, with Doctrinal and Practical Remarks on the Entire Psalter.* (Philadelphia; Edinburgh: J. B. Lippincott Company; A & C Black, 1872), 178.

[79] Henry, M. *Matthew Henry's Commentary on the Whole Bible: Complete and Unabridged in One Volume.* (Peabody: Hendrickson, 1994), 760.

[80] Spurgeon, C. H. "The Bible," (sermon, March 18, 1855). http://www.spurgeon.org/sermons/0015.htm, accessed October 6, 2014.

[81] Spurgeon, C. H. "Love at Its Utmost," Sermon preached, September 11, 1887, Metropolitan Tabernacle.

[82] Henry, M. *Matthew Henry's Commentary on the Whole Bible: Complete and Unabridged in One Volume.* (Peabody: Hendrickson, 1994), 2215.

[83] Spurgeon, C. H. *The Treasury of David: Psalms 27–57* (Vol. 2). (Marshall Brothers, n.d.), 403.

[84] Spurgeon, C. H. "Free-Will—A Slave," Sermon delivered December 2, 1855, New Park Street.

[85] Spurgeon, C. H. *The Treasury of David: Psalms 1–26* (Vol. 1). (Marshall Brothers, n.d.), 177.

[86] Henry, M. *Matthew Henry's Commentary on the Whole Bible: Complete and Unabridged in One Volume.* (Peabody: Hendrickson, 1994), 762.

[87] Exell, J. S. *The Biblical Illustrator: The Psalms* (Vol. 1). (Fleming H. Revell Company; Francis Griffiths, 1909), 214.

[88] Ibid.

ENDNOTES

[89] Spurgeon, C. H. *Psalms*. (Wheaton, IL: Crossway Books, 1993), 43.

[90] Wiersbe, Warren. *Prayer, Praise, and Promises*. (Grand Rapids, MI: Baker Books, 1991), 38.

[91] Pink, A. W. "God's Jewels." https://gracegems.org/Pink, accessed January 27, 2025.

[92] Henry, M. *Matthew Henry's Commentary on the Whole Bible: Complete and Unabridged in One Volume*. (Peabody: Hendrickson, 1994), 763.

[93] Spurgeon, C. H. *The Treasury of David: Psalms 1–26* (Vol. 1). (Marshall Brothers, n.d.), 194.

[94] Criswell, W. A., P. Patterson, E. R. Clendenen, D. L. Akin, M. Chamberlin, D. K. Patterson, & J. Pogue, (eds.) *Believer's Study Bible* (electronic ed.). (1991), Ps. 17:15.

[95] Spurgeon, C. H. *The Treasury of David: Psalms 1–26* (Vol. 1). (Marshall Brothers, n.d.), 231.

[96] Ibid., 221.

[97] Henry, M. *Matthew Henry's Commentary on the Whole Bible: Complete and Unabridged in One Volume*. (Peabody: Hendrickson, 1994), 765.

[98] Spurgeon, C. H. *The Treasury of David: Psalms 1–26* (Vol. 1). (Marshall Brothers, n.d.), 236.

[99] Wiersbe, W. W. *The Bible Exposition Commentary* (Vol. 1). (Victor Books, 1996), 81.

[100] MacArthur, J. F., Jr. *Matthew* (Vol. 3). (Moody Press, 1985–1989), 339.

[101] Henry, M. *Matthew Henry's Commentary on the Whole Bible: Complete and Unabridged in One Volume*. (Peabody: Hendrickson, 1994), 1731.

[102] Ibid., 1557.

[103] Packer, J. I. *Concise Theology: A Guide to Historic Christian Beliefs*. (Tyndale House, 1993), 9.

[104] Tozer, A. W. *The Pursuit of God*.

[105] Alexander, J. A. *The Psalms Translated and Explained*. (Edinburgh: Andrew Elliot; James Thin, 1864), 91.

[106] Spurgeon, C. H. *Morning and Evening*. (London: Passmore & Alabaster), March 16 (Evening).

[107] *Barnes Notes on the Bible*, Psalm 20:7.

[108] Spurgeon, C. H. *Psalms*. (Wheaton, IL: Crossway Books, 1993), 73.

[109] Ironside, H. A. *Studies on Book One of the Psalms*. (Loizeaux Brothers, 1952), 130.

[110] Spurgeon, C. H. *Psalms*. (Wheaton, IL: Crossway Books, 1993), 74

[111] Henry, M. *Matthew Henry's Commentary on the Whole Bible: Complete and Unabridged in One Volume*. (Peabody: Hendrickson, 1994), 770.

[112] Spurgeon, C. H. *Psalms*. (Wheaton, IL: Crossway Books, 1993), 74.

[113] Henry, M. *Matthew Henry's Commentary on the Whole Bible: Complete and Unabridged in One Volume*. (Peabody: Hendrickson, 1994), 770.

[114] Spence-Jones, H. D. M., ed. *Psalms* (Vol. 1). (Funk & Wagnalls Company, 1909), 161.

[115] Henry, M. *Matthew Henry's Commentary on the Whole Bible: Complete and Unabridged in One Volume.* (Peabody: Hendrickson, 1994), 770.

[116] Spurgeon, C. H. *The Treasury of David: Psalms 1–26* (Vol. 1). (Marshall Brothers, n.d.), 325.

[117] Ibid., 338–339.

[118] Ibid., 326.

[119] Spence-Jones, H. D. M., ed. *Psalms* (Vol. 1). (Funk & Wagnalls Company, 1909), 162.

[120] Blanchard, John. *Complete Gathered Gold.*

[121] Henry, M. *Matthew Henry's Commentary on the Whole Bible: Complete and Unabridged in One Volume.* (Peabody: Hendrickson, 1994), James 4.

[122] Cowman, L. B. *Streams in the Desert.* (Grand Rapids: Zondervan, 2006), April 24.

[123] Hutson, Curtis (ed.). *Great Preaching on Comfort.* (Murfreesboro, TN: Sword of the Lord Publishers, 1990), 122.

[124] Lawson, G. *Exposition of the Book of Proverbs* (Vol. 2). (David Brown; W. Oliphant; F. Pillans; M. Ogle; Ogle, Duncan, and Co.; J. Nisbet, 1821), 321.

[125] Tozer, A.W. *Man—The Dwelling Place of God,* Chapter 21.

[126] McGee, J. V. *Thru the Bible Commentary: Poetry (Psalms 1-41)* (electronic ed., Vol. 17). (Thomas Nelson, 1991), 135.

[127] Simeon, C. *Horae Homileticae: Psalms, I–LXXII* (Vol. 5). (Samuel Holdsworth, 1836), 138.

[128] Rogers, Adrian. "The Secret of Satisfaction," posted November 1, 2022. https://www.lwf.org/sermons/audio/the-secret-of-satisfaction-1359, accessed September 22, 2024.

[129] Spurgeon, C. H. *The Treasury of David,* Psalm 23:1.

[130] Henry, M. *Matthew Henry's Commentary on the Whole Bible: Complete and Unabridged in One Volume.* (Peabody: Hendrickson, 1994), 773.

[131] Spurgeon, C. H. *The Treasury of David: Psalms 1–26* (Vol. 1). (London; Edinburgh; New York: Marshall Brothers, n.d.), 355.

[132] Henry, M. *Matthew Henry's Commentary on the Whole Bible: Complete and Unabridged in One Volume.* (Peabody: Hendrickson, 1994), 773.

[133] Parker, Joseph. *The People's Bible,* Psalm 23:4.

[134] Plumer, W. S. *Studies in the Book of Psalms: Being a Critical and Expository Commentary, with Doctrinal and Practical Remarks on the Entire Psalter.* (Philadelphia; Edinburgh: J. B. Lippincott Company; A & C Black, 1872).

[135] *Barnes Notes on the Bible,* Psalm 23:6.

[136] Dickson, D. *A Brief Explication of the Psalms* (Vol. 1). (John Dow; Waugh and Innes; R. Ogle; James Darling; Richard Baynes, 1834), 121.

[137] Brooks, Phillips. *The Spiritual Man and Other Sermons.* (London: R.D. Dickinson, 1891), 286.

[138] Augustine of Hippo, in P. Schaff (Ed.), & A. C. Coxe (Trans.). *Saint Augustin: Expositions on the Book of Psalms* (Vol. 8). (Christian Literature Company, 1888), 60.

[139] Spurgeon, C. H. *The Treasury of David: Psalms 1–26* (Vol. 1). (Marshall Brothers, n.d.), 372.

[140] Nichols, J. W. H. *Musings in the Psalms.* (Galaxie Software, 2005), 25.

[141] Spence-Jones, H. D. M., ed. *Psalms* (Vol. 1). (Funk & Wagnalls Company, 1909), 173.

[142] *Benson Commentary,* Exodus 19:10.

[143] Exell, J. S. *The Biblical Illustrator: The Psalms* (Vol. 1). (Fleming H. Revell Company; Francis Griffiths, 1909), 482.

[144] Watson, Thomas. *The Beatitudes: An Exposition of Matthew 5:1–12.*

[145] Spurgeon, C. H. *The Treasury of David: Psalms 1–26* (Vol. 1). (Marshall Brothers, n.d.), 391.

[146] Exell, J. S. *The Biblical Illustrator: The Psalms* (Vol. 1). (Fleming H. Revell Company; Francis Griffiths, 1909), 494.

[147] Henry, M. *Matthew Henry's Commentary on the Whole Bible: Complete and Unabridged in One Volume.* (Peabody: Hendrickson, 1994), 775.

[148] Ibid., 776.

[149] Spurgeon, C. H. "Contrition."

[150] Spurgeon, C. H. *The Treasury of David: Psalms 120–150* (Vol. 6). (London; Edinburgh; New York: Marshall Brothers, n.d.), 119.

[151] Hallesby, Ole. *Prayer.* (Minneapolis, Minnesota: Augsburg Publishing House, 1931), 58.

[152] Bounds, E. M. *The Necessity of Prayer.*

[153] Duewel, Wesley. *Mighty Prevailing Prayer: Experiencing the Power of Answered Prayer.* (Grand Rapids, MI: Zondervan, 1990), 17.

[154] Spurgeon, C. H. "True Prayer—True Power." Sermon Delivered August 12, 1860.

[155] Shaw, Harold. *George Muller: Delighted in God!* (1975), 310.

[156] Thomas, I. D. E. (compiler). *A Puritan Golden Treasury.* (2000), 254. By permission of Banner of Truth, Carlisle, PA.

[157] Exell, J. S. *The Biblical Illustrator: The Psalms* (Vol. 1). (Fleming H. Revell Company; Francis Griffiths, 1909), 525.

[158] Hutson, Curtis, (ed). *Great Preaching on Thanksgiving.* (Murfreesboro: Sword of the Lord Publishers, 1987), 36.

[159] Spurgeon, C. H. *The Treasury of David: Psalms 27–57* (Vol. 2). (Marshall Brothers, n.d.), 2.

[160] *Ellicott's Commentary for English Readers,* 1 Timothy 2:8.

[161] Spurgeon, C. H. *Psalms.* (Wheaton, IL: Crossway Books, 1993), 109.

[162] Alexander, J. A. *The Psalms Translated and Explained.* (Edinburgh: Andrew Elliot; James Thin, 1864), 124.

[163] Wiersbe, W. W. *With the Word Bible Commentary.* (Nashville: Thomas Nelson, 1991), Ps. 50:1.

[164] Spurgeon, C. H. *Psalms.* (Wheaton, IL: Crossway Books, 1993), 112.

[165] Spurgeon, C. H. "Joshua's Vision." Sermon delivered February 16, 1868, Metropolitan Tabernacle.

[166] Dixon, A. C. *Through Night to Morning.* (Sermon No. 1), 1913.

[167] Spurgeon, C. H. *The Treasury of David: Psalms 27–57* (Vol. 2). (Marshall Brothers, n.d.), 45.

[168] Henry, M. *Matthew Henry's Commentary on the Whole Bible: Complete and Unabridged in One Volume.* (Peabody: Hendrickson, 1994), 783.

[169] Spurgeon, C. H. "The Last Words of Christ on the Cross." Sermon delivered June 25, 1882, Metropolitan Tabernacle.

[170] Exell, J. S. *The Biblical Illustrator: The Psalms* (Vol. 2). (Fleming H. Revell Company; Francis Griffiths, 1909), 89.

[171] Spurgeon, C. H. *The Treasury of David: Psalms 27–57* (Vol. 2). (Marshall Brothers, n.d.), 63.

[172] Plumer, W. S. *Studies in the Book of Psalms: Being a Critical and Expository Commentary, with Doctrinal and Practical Remarks on the Entire Psalter.* (Philadelphia; Edinburgh: J. B. Lippincott Company; A & C Black, 1872), 395.

[173] Allen, Kerry James (ed). *Exploring the Mind and Heart of the Prince of Preachers.* (Oswego, IL: Fox River Press, 2005), 450.

[174] Rogers, Adrian. "What to Do with Your Guilt." https://www.oneplace.com/ministries/love-worth-finding/read/articles/what-to-do-with-your-guilt-9346.html, accessed May 6, 2018.

[175] Ibid.

[176] Spurgeon, Charles H. *The Complete Works of C. H. Spurgeon, Volume 46: Sermons 2603-2655.* (Delmarva Publications, Inc.)

[177] Lutzer, (ed). *Failure: The Back Door to Success.* (Moody Publishers, 1977).

[178] *The Life, Walk and Triumph of Faith.* (James Clarke and Co. Ltd., 1793).

[179] Exell, J. S. *The Biblical Illustrator: The Psalms* (Vol. 2). (Fleming H. Revell Company; Francis Griffiths, 1909), 141.

[180] The outline adapted from Adrian Rogers' sermon "Every Christian an Evangelist"

[181] Spurgeon, C. H. *The Treasury of David: Psalms 27–57* (Vol. 2). (Marshall Brothers, n.d.), 84.

[182] Perowne, J. J. S. The Book of Psalms; A New Translation, with Introductions and Notes, Explanatory and Critical (Fifth Edition, Revised, Vol. 1). (George Bell and Sons; Deighton Bell and Co., 1883), 302.

[183] Exell, J. S. *The Biblical Illustrator: The Psalms* (Vol. 2). (Fleming H. Revell Company; Francis Griffiths, 1909), 143.

[184] Henry, M. *Matthew Henry's Commentary on the Whole Bible: Complete and Unabridged in One Volume.* (Peabody: Hendrickson, 1994), 787.

[185] Spurgeon, C. H. *The Treasury of David: Psalms 27–57* (Vol. 2). (Marshall Brothers, n.d.), 107.

[186] Ibid., 122.

[187] Henry, M. *Matthew Henry's Commentary on the Whole Bible: Complete and Unabridged in One Volume.* (Peabody: Hendrickson, 1994), 788.

[188] Ibid., 421.

[189] Talmage, T. De Witt. "David Scrabbling at the Gate" (sermon) as cited in *The Biblical Illustrator,* 1 Samuel 21:13.

[190] *Keil and Delitzsch Biblical Commentary on the Old Testament,* Psalm 34:8.

[191] Spence-Jones, H. D. M., ed. *Psalms* (Vol. 1). (Funk & Wagnalls Company, 1909), 258.

[192] MacDonald, W. (A. Farstad, Ed.) *Believer's Bible Commentary: Old and New Testaments.* (Thomas Nelson, 1995), 598.

[193] Bridges, Charles, 230.

[194] Spurgeon, C. H. *The Treasury of David: Psalms 27–57* (Vol. 2). (Marshall Brothers, n.d.), 125.

[195] Ibid.

[196] Parker, Joseph. Cited in Exell, J. S. *The Biblical Illustrator: Isaiah,* Vol. 2. (New York; Chicago; Toronto; London; Edinburgh: Fleming H. Revell Company), 304.

[197] Spurgeon, C. H. *Morning and Evening.* (London: Passmore & Alabaster), May 31 (Evening).

[198] The thoughts were inspired and adapted from the sermon by A. C. Dixon, Hutson, Curtis, (ed.). *Great Preaching on Comfort.* (Murfreesboro, TN: Sword of the Lord Publishers, 1990), 88.

[199] Graham, Billy. *Hope for the Troubled Heart.* (Dallas: Word, 1991), 71.

[200] An illustration adapted from Chuck Swindoll.

[201] Owen, John. *Of the Mortification of Sin in Believers,* 1850.

[202] Ryle, J. C. *Holiness.* (Moody Publishers, 2010), 30.

[203] Henry, M. *Matthew Henry's Commentary on the Whole Bible: Complete and Unabridged in One Volume.* (Peabody: Hendrickson, 1994), 790.

[204] Spurgeon, C. H. *The Treasury of David: Psalms 27–57* (Vol. 2). (Marshall Brothers, n.d.), 141.

[205] Criswell, W. A. *Criswell Study Bible,* Psalm 35:1–8.

[206] *Encountering the Book of Psalms,* 237.

[207] Criswell, W. A. *Criswell Study Bible,* Psalm 35:1–8.

[208] Spurgeon, C. H. *The Treasury of David: Psalms 27–57* (Vol. 2). (Marshall Brothers, n.d.), 142.

[209] Henry, M. *Matthew Henry's Commentary on the Whole Bible: Complete and Unabridged in One Volume.* (Peabody: Hendrickson, 1994), 2315.

[210] https://www.viralbeliever.com/christian-quotes/christian-quotes-about-faithfulness/, accessed May 9, 2018.

[211] Spence-Jones, H. D. M. (ed.) *Psalms* (Vol. 1). (London; New York: Funk & Wagnalls Company, 1909), 284.

[212] Spurgeon, *The Treasury of David,* Psalm 91:1.

[213] Augustine of Hippo, in P. Schaff (Ed.), & A. C. Coxe (Trans.). *Saint Augustin: Expositions on the Book of Psalms* (Vol. 8). (Christian Literature Company, 1888), 250.

[214] Alexander, J. A. *The Psalms Translated and Explained.* (Edinburgh: Andrew Elliot; James Thin, 1864), 158.

[215] Simeon, C. *Horae Homileticae: Psalms, I–LXXII* (Vol. 5). (Samuel Holdsworth, 1836), 287.

[216] Henry, M. *Matthew Henry's Commentary on the Whole Bible: Complete and Unabridged in One Volume.* (Peabody: Hendrickson, 1994), 793.

[217] Spurgeon, C. H. *The Treasury of David: Psalms 27–57* (Vol. 2). (Marshall Brothers, n.d.), 170.

[218] Augustine of Hippo, in P. Schaff (Ed.), & A. C. Coxe (Trans.). *Saint Augustin: Expositions on the Book of Psalms* (Vol. 8). (Christian Literature Company, 1888), 91.

[219] Hamilton, William W. *Sermons on the Books of the Bible: Vol. 3,* 258.

[220] Spence-Jones, H. D. M., ed. *Psalms* (Vol. 1). (Funk & Wagnalls Company, 1909), 285.

[221] Ironside, H. A. *Notes on the Book of Proverbs.* (Neptune, NJ: Loizeaux Bros, 1908), 58.

[222] Adapted by the author from "Remorse Is the Last Witness to Wisdom and Her Claims."

[223] Maclaren, Alexander. *Exposition of Holy Scripture, Proverbs.* (Grand Rapids: Baker Book House, 1977), 87.

[224] Harman, A. *Psalms: A Mentor Commentary* (Vol. 1–2). (Ross-shire, Great Britain: Mentor, 2011), 314–315.

[225] Henry, M. *Matthew Henry's Commentary on the Whole Bible: Complete and Unabridged in One Volume.* (Peabody: Hendrickson, 1994), 795.

[226] Exell, J. S. *The Biblical Illustrator: The Psalms* (Vol. 2). (Fleming H. Revell Company; Francis Griffiths, 1909), 265.

[227] https://www.goodreads.com/quotes/232403-friendship-is-one-of-the-sweetest-joys-of-life-many, accessed October 19, 2017.

[228] Henry, M. *Matthew Henry's Commentary on the Whole Bible: Complete and Unabridged in One Volume.* (Peabody: Hendrickson, 1994), 797.

[229] Plumer, W. S. *Studies in the Book of Psalms: Being a Critical and Expository Commentary, with Doctrinal and Practical Remarks on the Entire Psalter.* (Philadelphia; Edinburgh: J. B. Lippincott Company; A & C Black, 1872), 586.

[230] Exell, J. S. *The Biblical Illustrator: The Psalms* (Vol. 2). (Fleming H. Revell Company; Francis Griffiths, n.d.), 290.

[231] Spurgeon, C. H. *The Treasury of David: Psalms 27–57* (Vol. 2). (Marshall Brothers, n.d.), 216.

[232] Adapted and expanded from Exell, J. S. *The Biblical Illustrator: The Psalms* (Vol. 2). (Fleming H. Revell Company; Francis Griffiths, 1909), 290.

[233] Henry, M. *Matthew Henry's Commentary on the Whole Bible: Complete and Unabridged in One Volume.* (Peabody: Hendrickson, 1994), 798–799.

[234] Spurgeon, C. H. "The New Song on Earth." Sermon delivered July 17, 1887, Metropolitan Tabernacle.

[235] Spence-Jones, H. D. M. (ed.) *Psalms* (Vol. 1). (London; New York: Funk & Wagnalls Company, 1909), 312.

[236] Plumer, W. S. *Studies in the Book of Psalms: Being a Critical and Expository Commentary, with Doctrinal and Practical Remarks on the Entire Psalter.* (Philadelphia; Edinburgh: J. B. Lippincott Company; A & C Black, 1872), 484.

[237] Henry, M. *Matthew Henry's Commentary on the Whole Bible: Complete and Unabridged in One Volume.* (Peabody: Hendrickson, 1994), 800.

[238] Spurgeon, C. H. "Wakeful and Watchful Eyes." Sermon delivered August 13, 1882, Metropolitan Tabernacle.

[239] Exell, J. S. *The Biblical Illustrator: The Psalms* (Vol. 2). (Fleming H. Revell Company; Francis Griffiths, 1909), 324.

[240] Clarke, Adam. *The Adam Clarke Commentary.* "Commentary on Psalms 41:3." https://www.studylight.org/commentaries/acc/psalms-41.html. 1832.

[241] *Barnes Notes on the Bible*, Psalm 41:3.

[242] Spurgeon, C. H. *Psalms.* (Wheaton, IL: Crossway Books, 1993), 169.

[243] Spurgeon, C. H. *The Treasury of David: Psalms 27–57* (Vol. 2). (Marshall Brothers, n.d.), 256–257.

[244] *Barnes Notes on the Bible,* Matthew 5:7.

[245] Spurgeon, C. H. "The Preacher's Last Sermon for the Season." Sermon delivered November 29, 1885, Metropolitan Tabernacle.

[246] *Barnes Notes on the Bible,* Matthew 5:7.

[247] Ibid., 109.

[248] Ibid.

[249] Morris, L. *The Gospel According to Matthew.* (W. B. Eerdmans: Inter-Varsity Press, 1992), 99.

[250] Barclay, W., ed. *The Gospel of Matthew* (Vol. 1). (The Westminster John Knox Press, 1976), 100.

[251] Henry, M. *Matthew Henry's Commentary on the Whole Bible: Complete and Unabridged in One Volume.* (Peabody: Hendrickson, 1994), 803.

[252] King, Martin Luther, Jr.

[253] Lutzer. *Cries from the Cross.* (Moody Publishers, 2002), 100.

[254] Maclaren, Alexander. *The Book of Psalms: Book II,* 48.

[255] Spurgeon, *The Treasury of David,* Psalm 42:7.

[256] Plumer, W. S. *Studies in the Book of Psalms: Being a Critical and Expository Commentary, with Doctrinal and Practical Remarks on the Entire Psalter.* (Philadelphia; Edinburgh: J. B. Lippincott Company; A & C Black, 1872), 405.

[257] Spurgeon, C. H. *Psalms.* (Wheaton, IL: Crossway Books, 1993), 182.

[258] Baxter, Lydia. (1870).

[259] *Barnes Notes on the Bible,* Psalm 121:3.

[260] Ruskin, John. *The Stones of Venice: The Fall.* (Cosimo, Inc., 2013), 105.

[261] Plumer, W. S. *Studies in the Book of Psalms: Being a Critical and Expository Commentary, with Doctrinal and Practical Remarks on the Entire Psalter.* (Philadelphia; Edinburgh: J. B. Lippincott Company; A & C Black, 1872), 516.

[262] Spurgeon, *The Treasury of David,* Psalm 45:2.

[263] *Barnes Notes on the Bible,* Psalm 45:3.

[264] Ibid.

[265] Henry, M. *Matthew Henry's Commentary on the Whole Bible: Complete and Unabridged in One Volume.* (Peabody: Hendrickson, 1994), 807.

[266] *Barnes Notes on the Bible,* Psalm 45:4.

[267] Spurgeon, C. H. *Psalms.* (Wheaton, IL: Crossway Books, 1993), 189.

[268] Smith, J. E. The Wisdom Literature and Psalms. (Joplin, MO: College Press pub. Co., 1996), Ps 45:3.

[269] Simeon, C. *Horae Homileticae: Psalms, I–LXXII* (Vol. 5). (Samuel Holdsworth, 1836), 342.

[270] Exell, J. S. *The Biblical Illustrator: The Psalms* (Vol. 2). (Fleming H. Revell Company; Francis Griffiths, 1909), 414.

[271] M'Cheyne, Robert Murray. *Letters to a Soul Seeking Christ.*

[272] Plumer, W. S. *Studies in the Book of Psalms: Being a Critical and Expository Commentary, with Doctrinal and Practical Remarks on the Entire Psalter.* (Philadelphia; Edinburgh: J. B. Lippincott Company; A & C Black, 1872), 522–523).

[273] Ibid., 526.

[274] *Clarke's Commentary,* Psalm 46:1.

[275] Cowman, L. B. *Streams in the Desert.* (Grand Rapids: Zondervan, 2006), January 29.

[276] Exell, J. S. *The Biblical Illustrator: The Psalms* (Vol. 2). (Fleming H. Revell Company; Francis Griffiths, 1909), 449.

[277] Spurgeon, C. H. *The Treasury of David: Psalms 27–57* (Vol. 2). (Marshall Brothers, n.d.), 340.

[278] Exell, J. S. *The Biblical Illustrator: The Psalms* (Vol. 2). (Fleming H. Revell Company; Francis Griffiths, 1909), 452.

[279] Spurgeon, C. H. *The Treasury of David: Psalms 27–57* (Vol. 2). (Marshall Brothers, n.d.), 340–341.

[280] *Barnes Notes on the Bible,* Psalm 46:10.

[281] Wiersbe, Warren. *Prayer, Praise, and Promises.* (Grand Rapids, MI: Baker Books, 1991), 123.

[282] Henry, M. *Matthew Henry's Commentary on the Whole Bible: Complete and Unabridged in One Volume.* (Peabody: Hendrickson, 1994), 810.

[283] The author adapted Erskine's outline in part. Exell, J. S. *The Biblical Illustrator: The Psalms* (Vol. 2). (Fleming H. Revell Company; Francis Griffiths, 1909), 472.

[284] Ironside, H. A. *Notes on the Book of Proverbs.* (Neptune, NJ: Loizeaux Bros, 1908), 437.

[285] Henry, M. *Matthew Henry's Commentary on the Whole Bible: Complete and Unabridged in One Volume.* (Peabody: Hendrickson, 1994), 2313.

[286] MacArthur, J. F., Jr. *Ephesians.* (Moody Press, 1986), 138.

[287] Exell, J. S. *The Biblical Illustrator: The Psalms* (Vol. 2). (Fleming H. Revell Company; Francis Griffiths, 1909), 472.

[288] Pink, A. W. *Exposition of the Gospel of John.* (Swengel, PA: Bible Truth Depot, 1923–1945), 759.

[289] Spurgeon, C. H. "The Ascension of Christ." Sermon delivered March 25, 1871, Metropolitan Tabernacle.

[290] Whitlock, L. G., R. C. Sproul, B. K. Waltke, and M. Silva. *The Reformation Study Bible: Bringing the Light of the Reformation to Scripture: New King James Version.* (Nashville: T. Nelson, 1995), John 14:2.

[291] Spurgeon, C. H. *The Treasury of David: Psalms 27–57* (Vol. 2). (Marshall Brothers, n.d.), 354.

[292] Bishop Atterbury cited in Exell, J. S. *The Biblical Illustrator: The Psalms* (Vol. 2). (Fleming H. Revell Company; Francis Griffiths, 1909), 510.

[293] Spurgeon, C. H. *The Treasury of David: Psalms 27–57* (Vol. 2). (Marshall Brothers, n.d.), 354.

[294] *Clarke's Commentary,* Psalm 47:8.

[295] Lindsley, Art, Ph.D. *The Holiness of God.*

[296] Spence-Jones, H. D. M., ed. *Psalms* (Vol. 2). (Funk & Wagnalls Company, 1909), 193.

[297] Spurgeon, C. H. *The Treasury of David: Psalms 27–57* (Vol. 2). (Marshall Brothers, n.d.), 355.

[298] Spurgeon, C. H. "Concerning Prayer." Sermon preached August 23, 1888, Metropolitan Tabernacle.

[299] Spurgeon, C. H. "Safe Shelter." Sermon preached in 1869, Metropolitan Tabernacle.

[300] Gallaway, J. C. Cited in Exell, J. S. *The Biblical Illustrator: The Psalms* (Vol. 2). (Fleming H. Revell Company; Francis Griffiths, 1909), Psalm 48:9.

[301] Spence-Jones, H. D. M. (ed.) *Psalms* (Vol. 1). (London; New York: Funk & Wagnalls Company, 1909), 374.

[302] Spurgeon, C. H. *The Treasury of David: Psalms 27–57* (Vol. 2). (Marshall Brothers, n.d.), 362.

[303] Spence-Jones, H. D. M., ed. *Psalms* (Vol. 1). (Funk & Wagnalls Company, 1909), 373.

[304] Spurgeon, C. H. "A Worthy Theme for Thought." Sermon delivered May 5, 1878, Metropolitan Tabernacle.

[305] Exell, J. S. *The Biblical Illustrator: The Psalms* (Vol. 2). (Fleming H. Revell Company; Francis Griffiths, n.d.), Psalm 48:9.

[306] Spence-Jones, H. D. M. (ed.) *Psalms* (Vol. 1). (London; New York: Funk & Wagnalls Company, 1909), 375.

[307] *Gill's Exposition of the Entire Bible,* Psalm 48:9.

[308] Bridges, C. *An Exposition of the Book of Proverbs.* (Robert Carter & Brothers, 1865), 112.

[309] Exell, J. S. *The Biblical Illustrator: The Psalms* (Vol. 2). (Fleming H. Revell Company; Francis Griffiths, 1909), 497.

[310] Knight, Walter B. *Knight's Master Book of New Illustrations.* (Grand Rapids: Wm. B. Eerdmans, 1956), 644.

[311] Spurgeon, C. H. "Tearful Sowing and Joyful Reaping." Sermon delivered April 25, 1869, Metropolitan Tabernacle.

[312] Henry, M. *Matthew Henry's Commentary on the Whole Bible: Complete and Unabridged in One Volume.* (Peabody: Hendrickson, 1994), 814.

[313] Spurgeon, C. H. *Psalms.* (Wheaton, IL: Crossway Books, 1993), 204.

[314] Spence-Jones, H. D. M., ed. *Psalms* (Vol. 1). (Funk & Wagnalls Company, 1909), 379.

[315] *Clarke's Commentary,* Psalm 49:15.

[316] Craigie, P. C. *Psalms 1–50* (Vol. 19). (Dallas: Word, Incorporated, 1983), 366.

[317] Spurgeon, C. H. *The Treasury of David: Psalms 27–57* (Vol. 2). (Marshall Brothers, n.d.), 388.

[318] Henry, M. *Matthew Henry's Commentary on the Whole Bible: Complete and Unabridged in One Volume.* (Peabody: Hendrickson, 1994), Ecclesiastes 5:4.

[319] Ibid., 816.

[320] Spurgeon, C. H. *The Treasury of David: Psalms 27–57* (Vol. 2). (Marshall Brothers, n.d.), 388.

[321] Spurgeon, C. H. *Faith's Checkbook,* Preface.

[322] Ironside, H. A. "Commentary on Isaiah 40:4." *Ironside's Notes on Selected Books.* https://www.studylight.org/commentaries/isn/isaiah-40.html. 1914.

[323] Spence-Jones, H. D. M., ed. *Psalms* (Vol. 1). (Funk & Wagnalls Company, 1909), 392.

[324] Hutson, Curtis, (ed.). *Great Preaching on Comfort.* (Murfreesboro, TN: Sword of the Lord Publishers, 1990), 161–164.

[325] Henry, M. *Matthew Henry's Commentary on the Whole Bible: Complete and Unabridged in One Volume.* (Peabody: Hendrickson, 1994), 816.

[326] Bonhoeffer, Dietrich. *Temptation.* (New York: Macmillan, 1953), 116–117.

[327] Watson, Thomas. *The Select Works of the Rev. Thomas Watson, Comprising His Celebrated Body of Divinity, in a Series of Lectures on the Shorter Catechism, and Various Sermons and Treatises.* (New York, NY: Robert Carter and Brothers, 1855), 14.

[328] Henry, M. *Matthew Henry's Commentary on the Whole Bible: Complete and Unabridged in One Volume.* (Peabody: Hendrickson, 1994), 2 Samuel 11:2.

[329] https://www.christianquotes.info/quotes-by-topic/quotes-about-repentance/#ixzz5FtCNO7Mr, accessed May 18, 2018.

[330] Spence-Jones, H. D. M. (ed.) *Psalms* (Vol. 1). (London; New York: Funk & Wagnalls Company, 1909), 394.

[331] Augustine of Hippo, in P. Schaff (Ed.), & A. C. Coxe (Trans.). *Saint Augustin: Expositions on the Book of Psalms* (Vol. 8). (Christian Literature Company, 1888), 191.

[332] Swindoll, Charles. *David: A Man of Passion & Destiny.* (Dallas: Word Publishing Company, 1997), 233.

[333] *Clarke's Commentary,* Psalm 51:1.

[334] *Barnes Notes on the Bible,* Psalm 51:4.

[335] Plumer, W. S. *Studies in the Book of Psalms: Being a Critical and Expository Commentary, with Doctrinal and Practical Remarks on the Entire Psalter.* (Philadelphia; Edinburgh: J. B. Lippincott Company; A & C Black, 1872), 557.

[336] Chambers, Oswald. *My Utmost for His Highest,* November 19.

[337] Exell, J. S. *The Biblical Illustrator: The Psalms* (Vol. 3). (Fleming H. Revell Company; Francis Griffiths, 1909), 15.

[338] *Barnes Notes on the Bible,* Psalm 51:3.

[339] Spurgeon, C. H. *The Treasury of David: Psalms 27–57* (Vol. 2). (Marshall Brothers, n.d.), 409.

[340] Ibid., 404.

[341] *Barnes Notes on the Bible,* Psalm 51:10.

[342] Henry, M. *Matthew Henry's Commentary on the Whole Bible: Complete and Unabridged in One Volume.* (Peabody: Hendrickson, 1994), 818.

[343] Spurgeon, C. H. *The Treasury of David: Psalms 27–57* (Vol. 2). (Marshall Brothers, n.d.), 405.

[344] Exell, J. S. *The Biblical Illustrator: The Psalms* (Vol. 3). (Fleming H. Revell Company; Francis Griffiths, 1909), 48.

[345] Lewis, C. S. *Mere Christianity.*

[346] Tate, M. E. *Psalms 51–100* (Vol. 20). (Word, Incorporated, 1998), 26.

[347] Ibid.

[348] Henry, M. *Matthew Henry's Commentary on the Whole Bible: Complete and Unabridged in One Volume.* (Peabody: Hendrickson, 1994), 818.

[349] Spurgeon, C. H., *Sermons for Evangelistic Occasions,* 19.

[350] Spurgeon, C. H. *The Treasury of David: Psalms 27–57* (Vol. 2). (Marshall Brothers, n.d.), 406.

[351] Drummond, Lewis. *The Word of the Cross.* (Nashville: Broadman Press, 1992), 337.

[352] Spurgeon, C. H. *The Treasury of David: Psalms 27–57* (Vol. 2). (Marshall Brothers, n.d.), 407.

[353] Ibid.

[354] Henry, M. *Matthew Henry's Commentary on the Whole Bible: Complete and Unabridged in One Volume.* (Peabody: Hendrickson, 1994), 2195.

[355] King James Version Study Bible (electronic ed.). (Thomas Nelson, 1997), Ro 1:20.

[356] An illustration told by Hank Hanegraaff on his radio program.

[357] *Matthew Henry's Concise Commentary,* Psalm 52:3.

[358] Ibid.

[359] Spurgeon, C. H. *The Treasury of David: Psalms 27–57* (Vol. 2). (Marshall Brothers, n.d.), 427.

[360] Spurgeon, C. H. *The Treasury of David: Psalms 27–57* (Vol. 2). (London; Edinburgh; New York: Marshall Brothers, n.d.), 214.

[361] Newton, R. Cited in Exell, J. S. *The Biblical Illustrator: The Psalms* (Vol. 3). (Fleming H. Revell Company; Francis Griffiths, 1909), Psalm 120:2 ("Lying Lips").

[362] Davis, Al.

[363] Spurgeon, C. H. *Faith's Checkbook,* November 16.

[364] Wiersbe, W. W. Wiersbe's Expository Outlines on the Old Testament. (Wheaton, IL: Victor Books, 1993), Pr 12:17–22.

[365] Henry, M. *Matthew Henry's Commentary on the Whole Bible: Complete and Unabridged in One Volume.* (Peabody: Hendrickson, 1994), 929.

[366] McGee, J. V. *Thru the Bible Commentary* (electronic ed., Vol. 3). (Nashville: Thomas Nelson, 1997), 45.

[367] Spurgeon, C. H. *The Treasury of David: Psalms 27–57* (Vol. 2). (Marshall Brothers, n.d.), 427.

[368] Exell, J. S. *The Biblical Illustrator: The Psalms* (Vol. 3). (Fleming H. Revell Company; Francis Griffiths, 1909), 66.

[369] Spurgeon, C. H. *Lectures to My Students: Addresses Delivered to the Students of the Pastors' College, Metropolitan Tabernacle, Second Series* (Vol. 2). (New York: Robert Carter and Brothers, 1889), 242.

[370] Horne, G. *A Commentary on the Book of Psalms.* (New York: Robert Carter & Brothers, 1856), 195.

[371] Lawson, George. *Exposition of the Book of Proverbs.* (Edinburgh, 1821), Proverbs 29:1.

[372] Spurgeon, C. H. *The Treasury of David: Psalms 27–57* (Vol. 2). (Marshall Brothers, n.d.), 427.

[373] Jowett, J. H. Cited in Exell, J. S. *The Biblical Illustrator: The Psalms* (Vol. 3). (Fleming H. Revell Company; Francis Griffiths, 1909), 70.

[374] Ibid.

[375] Henry, M. *Matthew Henry's Commentary on the Whole Bible: Complete and Unabridged in One Volume.* (Peabody: Hendrickson, 1994), 820.

[376] Spurgeon, C. H. *The Treasury of David: Psalms 27–57* (Vol. 2). (Marshall Brothers, n.d.), 430.

[377] Buzzell, S. S. "Proverbs." In J. F. Walvoord & R. B. Zuck (Eds.). *The Bible Knowledge Commentary: An Exposition of the Scriptures* (Vol. 1). (Wheaton, IL: Victor Books, 1985), 907–908.

[378] Spence-Jones, H. D. M. (ed.) Proverbs. (London; New York: Funk & Wagnalls Company, 1909), 268.

[379] Bridges, Charles, 230.

[380] Turner, J. Clyde. *These Things We Believe.* (Nashville: Convention Press, 1956), 16.

[381] Wiersbe, Warren. *Prayer, Praise, and Promises.* (Grand Rapids, MI: Baker Books, 1991), 37.

[382] Spurgeon, C. H. *The Treasury of David: Psalms 27–57* (Vol. 2). (Marshall Brothers, n.d.), 434.

[383] Ibid., 435.

[384] Spence-Jones, H. D. M. (ed.) Proverbs. (London; New York: Funk & Wagnalls Company, 1909), 5.

[385] Spurgeon, C. H. *The Treasury of David: Psalms 27–57* (Vol. 2). (Marshall Brothers, n.d.), 434.

[386] Hallesby, Ole. *Prayer.* (Minneapolis, Minnesota: Augsburg Publishing House, 1931), 28.

[387] Spurgeon, C. H. *Flowers from a Puritan's Garden.* (New York: Funk & Wagnalls, 1883), 249.

[388] Rogers, Adrian. "The Privilege of Prayer." Lwf.org, accessed November 30, 2011.

[389] Henry, Matthew. *Matthew Henry's Concise Bible Commentary,* Psalm 54:2.

[390] Plumer, W. S. *Studies in the Book of Psalms: Being a Critical and Expository Commentary, with Doctrinal and Practical Remarks on the Entire Psalter.* (Philadelphia; Edinburgh: J. B. Lippincott Company; A & C Black, 1872), 576–577).

[391] Chadwick, Samuel. *Path to Prayer.* (1931), Chapter 11.

[392] Hutson, Curtis, Ed. *Great Preaching on Prayer.* (Murfreesboro, TN: Sword of the Lord Publishers, 1988), 235.

[393] Spurgeon, C. H. "Boldness at the Throne." Sermon delivered September 14, 1873 at the Metropolitan Tabernacle.

[394] Tozer, A. W. *God Tells the Man Who Cares,* 3.

[395] Pierson, A. T. *From the Pulpit to the Palm-Branch: A Memorial of Spurgeon, C. H.* (London: Alabaster, Passmore and Sons, 1892), 11.

[396] Bounds, E. M. cited in *How to Live a Life of Prayer,* 112.

[397] Spurgeon, C. H. *The Treasury of David: Psalms 27–57* (Vol. 2). (Marshall Brothers, n.d.), 447.

[398] Ibid.

[399] Augustine of Hippo. *The Confessions of St. Augustine: Modern English Version.*

[400] Maclaren, Alexander. *The Book of Psalms: Book II,* 164.

[401] Spurgeon, *The Treasury of David,* Psalm 55:12.

[402] Plumer, W. S. *Studies in the Book of Psalms: Being a Critical and Expository Commentary, with Doctrinal and Practical Remarks on the Entire Psalter.* (Philadelphia; Edinburgh: J. B. Lippincott Company; A & C Black, 1872), 581.

[403] Tan, P. L. *Encyclopedia of 7700 Illustrations: Signs of the Times.* (Garland, TX: Bible Communications, Inc., 1996), 502.

[404] "Christian Quotes on Fear," dailychristianquote.com/dcqfear.html, accessed December 1, 2011.

[405] Rogers, Adrian. "Facing Your Fear." May 14, 2013. https://www.lwf.org/articles/facing-your-fear, accessed November 12, 2020.

[406] Taylor, Hudson. *The Spiritual Secret.*

[407] Rogers, Adrian. "Facing Your Fear." May 14, 2013. https://www.lwf.org/articles/facing-your-fear, accessed November 12, 2020.

[408] https://www.christianquotes.info/top-quotes/22-powerful-quotes-overcoming-fear/, accessed November 12, 2020.

[409] Tozer, A. W. *Tozer on the Almighty God: A 365 Day Devotional.*

[410] Spurgeon, C. H. *Morning and Evening.* (London: Passmore & Alabaster), June 16 (Evening).

[411] Newton, John. *The Works of the Rev. John Newton (Letters to the Reverend Mr. R-).*

[412] Spurgeon, C. H. *Morning and Evening.* (London: Passmore & Alabaster), November 3.

[413] Henry, M. *Matthew Henry's Commentary on the Whole Bible: Complete and Unabridged in One Volume.* (Peabody: Hendrickson, 1994), 824.

[414] Spurgeon, C. H. *Psalms.* (Wheaton, IL: Crossway Books, 1993), 143.

[415] https://www.goodreads.com/quotes/368087-there-is-something-you-can-t-fix-can-t-heal-or-can-t, accessed July 17, 2020.

[416] Spurgeon, C. H. *Morning and Evening.* (London: Passmore & Alabaster), January 24 (Morning).

[417] Henry, M. *Matthew Henry's Commentary on the Whole Bible: Complete and Unabridged in One Volume.* (Peabody: Hendrickson, 1994), 825.

[418] Spence-Jones, H. D. M. (ed.) *Psalms* (Vol. 2). (London; New York: Funk & Wagnalls Company, 1909), 10.

[419] Plutarch. *Plutarch's Lives.* (New York: Harper Brothers, 1872), 421.

[420] http://www.selfgovernment.us/news/james-garfield-if-congress-is-corrupt-it-is-because-we-tolerate-it, accessed May 22, 2018.

[421] Spurgeon, C. H. *The Treasury of David: Psalms 58–87* (Vol. 3). (Marshall Brothers, n.d.), 13.

[422] Maclaren, Alexander. *Expositions of Holy Scripture* (vol. 3), The Psalms, Isaiah 1–48. (Grand Rapids: Eerdmans, 1959), part 2, 61.

[423] Henry, M. *Matthew Henry's Commentary on the Whole Bible: Complete and Unabridged in One Volume.* (Peabody: Hendrickson, 1994), 828.

[424] Spurgeon, C. H. *The Treasury of David: Psalms 58–87* (Vol. 3). (Marshall Brothers, n.d.), 18.

[425] Ibid., 30.

[426] Ibid.

[427] Bounds, E. M. *The Necessity of Prayer.*

[428] Chambers, Oswald. *Our Brilliant Heritage / If You Will Be Perfect / Disciples Indeed: The Inheritance of God's Transforming Mind & Heart.* (Discovery House, 2015), 135.

[429] Spurgeon, C. H. *The Treasury of David: Psalms 58–87* (Vol. 3). (Marshall Brothers, n.d.), 40.

[430] Ibid.

[431] Henry, M. *Matthew Henry's Commentary on the Whole Bible: Complete and Unabridged in One Volume.* (Peabody: Hendrickson, 1994), 829.

[432] Spurgeon, C. H. *The Treasury of David: Psalms 58–87* (Vol. 3). (Marshall Brothers, n.d.), 40.

[433] Ibid.

[434] Bratcher, R. G., & W. D. Reyburn. *A Translator's Handbook on the Book of Psalms.* (United Bible Societies, 1991), 116.

[435] McLaren, Alexander. *Week-Day Evening Addresses.* (London: Clay, Sons and Taylor, 1877), 133.

[436] Spurgeon, C. H. *Psalms.* (Wheaton, IL: Crossway Books, 1993), 252.

[437] Exell, J. S. *The Biblical Illustrator: The Psalms,* Vol. 3. (New York; Chicago; Toronto; London; Edinburgh: Fleming H. Revell Company), 154.

[438] Simeon, C. *Horae Homileticae: Psalms, I–LXXII* (Vol. 5). (Samuel Holdsworth, 1836), 450.

[439] Henry, M. *Matthew Henry's Commentary on the Whole Bible: Complete and Unabridged in One Volume.* (Peabody: Hendrickson, 1994), 832.

[440] Bruce, F. F. *The Gospel of John: Introduction, Exposition, Notes.* (Wm. B. Eerdmans Publishing, 1994), 105.

[441] *The Spurgeon Study Bible,* 776.

[442] Plumer, W. S. *Studies in the Book of Psalms: Being a Critical and Expository Commentary, with Doctrinal and Practical Remarks on the Entire Psalter.* (Philadelphia; Edinburgh: J. B. Lippincott Company; A & C Black, 1872), 636.
[443] Spurgeon, C. H. *The Treasury of David* (Vol. 1). (Peabody, Maryland: Hendrickson Publishing, undated), 67–68.
[444] Spurgeon, C. H. *The Treasury of David: Psalms 58–87* (Vol. 3). (Marshall Brothers, n.d.), 83.
[445] Moody, D. L. *The D. L. Moody Book: A Living Daily Message from the Words of D. L. Moody.* (Fleming H. Revell Company, 1900), 205–206.
[446] Spence-Jones, H. D. M., ed. *Psalms* (Vol. 2). (Funk & Wagnalls Company, 1909), 27.
[447] Kirkpatrick, A. F. Psalm 65:2.
[448] Spurgeon, C. H. *Psalms.* (Wheaton, IL: Crossway Books, 1993), 262.
[449] *Expositor's Bible Commentary,* Psalm 65:3.
[450] Henry, M. *Matthew Henry's Commentary on the Whole Bible: Complete and Unabridged in One Volume.* (Peabody: Hendrickson, 1994), 834.
[451] Leavell, Roland Q. *Winning Others to Christ,* 39.
[452] Spurgeon, C. H. *Psalms.* (Wheaton, IL: Crossway Books, 1993), 271.
[453] Horne, G. *A Commentary on the Book of Psalms.* (New York: Robert Carter & Brothers, 1856), 226.
[454] Chambers, Oswald. *My Utmost for His Highest,* August 24.
[455] Exell, J. S. *The Biblical Illustrator: The Psalms* (Vol. 3). (Fleming H. Revell Company; Francis Griffiths, 1909), 326.
[456] Ibid., 235.
[457] https://djameskennedy.org/devotional-detail/20150225-a-checklist-for-your-prayer-life, accessed May 9, 2017.
[458] Ryle, J. C. "A Call to Prayer," www.gracegems.org, accessed May 9, 2017.
[459] https://wmpl.org/quote/, accessed May 26, 2018.
[460] Henry, M. *Matthew Henry's Commentary on the Whole Bible: Complete and Unabridged in One Volume.* (Peabody: Hendrickson, 1994), 1007.
[461] Ibid., 838.
[462] Spurgeon, C. H. *The Treasury of David: Psalms 120–150* (Vol. 6). (London; Edinburgh; New York: Marshall Brothers, n.d.), 403.
[463] Plumer, W. S. *Studies in the Book of Psalms: Being a Critical and Expository Commentary, with Doctrinal and Practical Remarks on the Entire Psalter.* (Philadelphia; Edinburgh: J. B. Lippincott Company; A & C Black, 1872), 670.
[464] Spurgeon, C. H. *The Treasury of David: Psalms 58–87* (Vol. 3). (Marshall Brothers, n.d.), 137.
[465] Exell, J. S. *The Biblical Illustrator: The Psalms* (Vol. 3). (Fleming H. Revell Company; Francis Griffiths, 1909), 243.
[466] Henry, M. *Matthew Henry's Commentary on the Whole Bible: Complete and Unabridged in One Volume.* (Peabody: Hendrickson, 1994), 838.

[467] *Gill's Exposition of the Entire Bible,* Acts 1:20.

[468] Spurgeon, C. H. "Shutting, Sealing, and Covering; or, Messiah's Glorious Work." Sermon delivered, September 24, 1882, Metropolitan Tabernacle.

[469] Spurgeon, C. H. *The Treasury of David: Psalms 58–87* (Vol. 3). (Marshall Brothers, n.d.), 203.

[470] Spurgeon, C. H. "God's Innumerable Mercies" (Sermon #3022), October 22, 1868.

[471] Spurgeon, C. H. "The Remembrance of Christ," A sermon delivered January 7, 1855. http://www.spurgeon.org/sermons/0002.php, accessed February 6, 2017.

[472] https://www.christianquotes.info/top-quotes/22-motivating-quotes-about-prayer/#axzz4XwcXBYxu, accessed February 6, 2017.

[473] https://www.christianquotes.info/top-quotes/22-motivating-quotes-about-prayer/#axzz4XwcXBYxu, accessed February 6, 2017.

[474] Criswell, W. A. "Give Me This Mountain" (sermon, January 5, 1969). http://www.wacriswell.org/PrintTranscript.cfm/SID/2632.cfm, accessed February 4, 2017.

[475] http://www.thoughts-about-god.com/quotes/quotes-aging.html, accessed February 4, 2017.

[476] Spurgeon, C. H. "God's Glorious and Everlasting Name." Sermon delivered February 15, 1891, Metropolitan Tabernalce.

[477] Packer, J. I. *Introduction in Psalms.* (Wheaton, IL: Crossway Books, 1993), 308.

[478] Spurgeon, C. H. *The Treasury of David: Psalms 58–87* (Vol. 3). (Marshall Brothers, n.d.), 231.

[479] Henry, M. *Matthew Henry's Commentary on the Whole Bible: Complete and Unabridged in One Volume.* (Peabody: Hendrickson, 1994), 847.

[480] https://wisdomquotes.com/faith-quotes/, accessed October 15, 2021.

[481] Drummond, Henry. *Natural Law, Mortification,* 190.

[482] *Gill's Exposition of the Entire Bible,* Psalm 73:2.

[483] Augustine of Hippo, in P. Schaff (Ed.), & A. C. Coxe (Trans.). *Saint Augustin: Expositions on the Book of Psalms* (Vol. 8). (Christian Literature Company, 1888), 335.

[484] Spurgeon, C. H. *Psalm*s. (Wheaton, IL: Crossway Books, 1993), 313.

[485] Spurgeon, C. H. *The Treasury of David: Psalms 58–87* (Vol. 3). (Marshall Brothers, n.d.), 273.

[486] Ibid., 275.

[487] Ibid., 276.

[488] Henry, Matthew. *Concise Commentary on the Whole Bible*, Psalm 74:11.

[489] Spurgeon, *The Treasury of David,* Psalm 75:1.

[490] Hamilton, William W. *Sermons on the Books of the Bible: Vol. 4,* 75.

[491] Plumer, W. S. *Studies in the Book of Psalms: Being a Critical and Expository Commentary, with Doctrinal and Practical Remarks on the Entire Psalter.* (Philadelphia; Edinburgh: J. B. Lippincott Company; A & C Black, 1872), 736.

[492] Ibid.

[493] Boice, J. M. *Psalms 42–106: An Expositional Commentary.* (Grand Rapids, MI: Baker Books, 2005), 715.

[494] Spurgeon, C. H. *Psalms.* (Wheaton, IL: Crossway Books, 1993), 324.

[495] Henry, Matthew. *Matthew Henry's Concise Bible Commentary,* Psalm 77:11.

[496] *Ellicott's Commentary for English Readers,* Psalm 112:4.

[497] Wiersbe, W. W. *Be Obedient.* (Wheaton, IL: Victor Books, 1991), 41.

[498] Spurgeon, C. H. *The Treasury of David: Psalms 58–87* (Vol. 3). (Marshall Brothers, n.d.), 327.

[499] Ibid., 325.

[500] Spurgeon, C. H. *Psalms.* (Wheaton, IL: Crossway Books, 1993), 328.

[501] Bridges, Jerry. *Trusting God.* (1988), 37.

[502] Exell, J. S. *The Biblical Illustrator: The Psalms* (Vol. 3). (Fleming H. Revell Company; Francis Griffiths, 1909), 392.

[503] Exell, J. S. *The Biblical Illustrator: Deuteronomy.* (Fleming H. Revell Company, n.d.), 198.

[504] Henry, M. *Matthew Henry's Commentary on the Whole Bible: Complete and Unabridged in One Volume.* (Peabody: Hendrickson, 1994), 244.

[505] Spurgeon, *The Treasury of David,* Psalm 44:1.

[506] Boice, J. M. *Psalms 42–106: An Expositional Commentary.* (Grand Rapids, MI: Baker Books, 2005), 664–647.

[507] Exell, J. S. The Biblical Illustrator: The Psalms (Vol. 3). (New York; Chicago; Toronto: Fleming H. Revell Company, n.d.), 404.

[508] Spurgeon, C. H. *Morning and Evening.* (London: Passmore & Alabaster), January 6 (Morning).

[509] Spurgeon, C. H. "Lessons from the Manna." Sermon delivered September 12, 1889, Metropolitan Tabernacle.

[510] Henry, M. *Matthew Henry's Commentary on the Whole Bible: Complete and Unabridged in One Volume.* (Peabody: Hendrickson, 1994), 1952.

[511] Ibid.

[512] Ibid., 1689.

[513] Exell, J. S. *The Biblical Illustrator: The Psalms* (Vol. 3). (Fleming H. Revell Company; Francis Griffiths, 1909), 414.

[514] Steadman, Ray. "The Scars of Sin." https://www.raystedman.org/thematic-studies/doctrinal-topics/the-scars-of-sin, accessed June 2, 2018.

[515] Exell, J. S. *The Biblical Illustrator: The Psalms* (Vol. 3). (Fleming H. Revell Company; Francis Griffiths, 1909), 422.

[516] Winslow, Octavius. *The Sympathy of Christ,* Chapter 7, "The Sensitiveness of Christ to Suffering."

[517] Augustine of Hippo, in P. Schaff (Ed.), & A. C. Coxe (Trans.). *Saint Augustin: Expositions on the Book of Psalms* (Vol. 8). (Christian Literature Company, 1888), 386.

[518] Henry, M. *Matthew Henry's Commentary on the Whole Bible: Complete and Unabridged in One Volume.* (Peabody: Hendrickson, 1994), 860.

[519] Ravenhill, Leonard. *Why Revival Tarries.* (Minneapolis, MN: Bethany House, 1987), 119.

[520] McConkey, James H. *Prayer.* (Pittsburgh: Silver Publishing Company, 1931), 69.

[521] Whittier, John Greenleaf. in *Bartlett's Familiar Quotations, 13th ed.* (Little, Brown and Company), 527.

[522] Maclaren, Alexander. *The Book of Psalms: Book III*, 428.

[523] *Expositor's Bible Commentary,* Psalm 82:5–7.

[524] Plumer, W. S. *Studies in the Book of Psalms: Being a Critical and Expository Commentary, with Doctrinal and Practical Remarks on the Entire Psalter.* (Philadelphia; Edinburgh: J. B. Lippincott Company; A & C Black, 1872), 785.

[525] Hyman, Hon. Michael B. *Bench & Bar*, June 2016, vol. 46, no. 9.

[526] Spurgeon, C. H. *Morning and Evening.* (London: Passmore & Alabaster), December 9 (Morning).

[527] https://quotes.pub/q/cast-not-away-your-confidence-because-god-defers-his-perform-602076, accessed July 13, 2020.

[528] Spurgeon, C. H. *Morning and Evening.* (London: Passmore & Alabaster), July 2 (Evening).

[529] "Waiting When God Seems Silent," February 10, 2019. https://www.desiringgod.org/articles/waiting-when-god-seems-silent, accessed November 12, 2024.

[530] "Ask Dr. Swindoll: How Do You Respond When God is Silent?" July 14, 2017. *Voice,* Dallas Theological Seminary.

[531] *Barnes Notes on the Bible,* Psalm 84:10.

[532] Henry, M. *Matthew Henry's Commentary on the Whole Bible: Complete and Unabridged in One Volume.* (Peabody: Hendrickson, 2014), 450.

[533] Spurgeon, C. H. *The Treasury of David: Psalms 58–87* (Vol. 3). (Marshall Brothers, n.d.), 447.

[534] Graham, Billy. *Hope for the Troubled Heart.* (Dallas: Word, 1991).

[535] Spence-Jones, H. D. M., ed. *Psalms* (Vol. 2). (Funk & Wagnalls Company, 1909), 193.

[536] Spurgeon, C. H. *The Treasury of David: Psalms 58–87* (Vol. 3). (London; Edinburgh; New York: Marshall Brothers, n.d.), 434.

[537] Wesley, John. *The Works John Wesley.* (1827), 117.

[538] "The 1859 Ulster Revival." *The Revival Library.* https://revival-library.org/histories/1859-the-ulster-revival/, accessed February 18, 2025.

[539] Spurgeon, *The Treasury of David,* Psalm 86:5.

[540] Ibid.

[541] Simeon, C. *Horae Homileticae: Psalms, LXXIII–CL* (Vol. 6). (Samuel Holdsworth, 1836), 91.

[542] Henry, M. *Matthew Henry's Commentary on the Whole Bible: Complete and Unabridged in One Volume.* (Peabody: Hendrickson, 1994), 868.

[543] Hutson, Curtis, (ed.). *Great Preaching on Comfort.* (Murfreesboro, TN: Sword of the Lord Publishers, 1990), 161–162.

[544] Spurgeon, C. H. *Psalms.* (Wheaton, IL: Crossway Books, 1993), 247–248.

[545] Spurgeon, C. H. "Concerning Prayer." Sermon preached August 23, 1888, Metropolitan Tabernacle.

[546] Spurgeon, C. H. *Psalms.* (Wheaton, IL: Crossway Books, 1993), 247–248.

[547] MacArthur, John, Jr., (Ed.). *The John MacArthur Study Bible* (electronic ed.). (Nashville, TN: Word Pub., 1997), 2024.

[548] Exell, J. S. The Biblical Illustrator: Revelation. (London: James Nisbet & Co., 1909), 698.

[549] *The Westminster Presbyterian Journal.* (Philadelphia, PA: The Holmes Press, December 4, 1909), 15.

[550] Criswell, W. A. and Paige Patterson. *Heaven.* (Grand Rapids: Tyndale House Publishers, 1991), 33.

[551] Ford, Herschel. *Simple Sermons on Heaven, Hell, and Judgment.* (Grand Rapids: Zondervan, 1969), 26.

[552] Plumer, W. S. *Studies in the Book of Psalms: Being a Critical and Expository Commentary, with Doctrinal and Practical Remarks on the Entire Psalter.* (Philadelphia; Edinburgh: J. B. Lippincott Company; A & C Black, 1872), 818.

[553] Spurgeon, *The Treasury of David,* Psalm 88:1.

[554] Kidner, Derek. *Psalms 73–150: A Commentary on Books III–V of the Psalms.* (Downers Grove, Ill.: InterVarsity, 1975), 316.

[555] Henry, M. *Matthew Henry's Commentary on the Whole Bible: Complete and Unabridged in One Volume.* (Peabody: Hendrickson, 1994), 873.

[556] Ibid. 872.

[557] Plumer, W. S. *Studies in the Book of Psalms: Being a Critical and Expository Commentary, with Doctrinal and Practical Remarks on the Entire Psalter.* (Philadelphia; Edinburgh: J. B. Lippincott Company; A & C Black, 1872), 828.

[558] Graham, Billy. *Peace with God.* (Waco, TX: Word, 1953), 83.

[559] Harman, A. *Psalms: A Mentor Commentary* (Vol. 1–2). (Ross-shire, Great Britain: Mentor, 2011), 669.

[560] Spurgeon, C. H. "Ask and Have." Sermon delivered October 1, 1882, Metropolitan Tabernacle.

[561] Spurgeon, C. H. *Morning and Evening.* (London: Passmore & Alabaster), January 24 (Morning).

[562] Spurgeon, C. H. "A Poor Man's Cry, and What Came of It," sermon Delivered March 8, 1891.

[563] Spurgeon, C. H. *The Treasury of David: Psalms 88–110* (Vol. 4). (Marshall Brothers, n.d.), 112.

[564] Spurgeon, C. H. *The Treasury of David,* Psalm 91:15.

[565] *Matthew Poole's Commentary,* Psalm 91:15.

[566] Exell, J. S. *The Biblical Illustrator: Hebrews* (Vol. 2). (London: James Nisbet & Co.), 613.

[567] *Gill's Exposition of the Entire Bible,* Psalm 91:15.

[568] Spurgeon, C. H. *The Treasury of David: Psalms 88–110* (Vol. 4). (Marshall Brothers, n.d.), 94.

[569] Hamilton, William W. *Sermons on the Books of the Bible: Vol. 3,* 212.

[570] Spurgeon, C. H. *The Treasury of David: Psalms 88–110* (Vol. 4). (Marshall Brothers, n.d.), 93.

[571] Henry, M. *Matthew Henry's Commentary on the Whole Bible: Complete and Unabridged in One Volume.* (Peabody: Hendrickson, 1994), 879.

[572] Exell, J. S. *The Biblical Illustrator: The Psalms* (Vol. 4). (Fleming H. Revell Company; Francis Griffiths, 1909), 112.

[573] Ryle, J. C. *Holiness.* (Moody Publishers, 2010), 50.

[574] Exell, J. S. *The Biblical Illustrator: The Psalms* (Vol. 4). (Fleming H. Revell Company; Francis Griffiths, 1909), 112.

[575] Spurgeon, C. H. "The God of the Aged" (sermon # 81). May 25, 1856, at the New Park Street Chapel, Southwark.

[576] Fuller, Thomas. cited in *A Cry from the Vineyard,* London, Vol. 2, Issue 27. July 7, 1866.

[577] Owen, John. *The Glory of Christ,* 7.

[578] Henry, M. *Matthew Henry's Commentary on the Whole Bible: Complete and Unabridged in One Volume.* (Peabody: Hendrickson, 1994), 879.

[579] Spence-Jones, H. D. M. (ed.) *Psalms* (Vol. 2). (London; New York: Funk & Wagnalls Company, 1909), 301.

[580] Henry, M. *Matthew Henry's Commentary on the Whole Bible: Complete and Unabridged in One Volume.* (Peabody: Hendrickson, 1994), 881.

[581] Scott, Adam. cited in Exell, J. S. *The Biblical Illustrator: The Psalms* (Vol. 4). (Fleming H. Revell Company; Francis Griffiths, 1909), 146.

[582] Spurgeon, C. H. *The Treasury of David: Psalms 88–110* (Vol. 4). (Marshall Brothers, n.d.), 147.

[583] National Association of Evangelicals (NAE).

[584] Exell, J. S. *The Biblical Illustrator: The Psalms* (Vol. 4). (Fleming H. Revell Company; Francis Griffiths, 1909), 164.

[585] Simeon, C. *Horae Homileticae: Psalms, LXXIII–CL* (Vol. 6). (Samuel Holdsworth, 1836), 155.

[586] *Gill's Exposition of the Entire Bible,* Psalm 96:13.

[587] Winslow. "Holiness, the Fruit of the Chastening of Love."

[588] Spurgeon, C. H. *The Treasury of David: Psalms 88–110* (Vol. 4). (Marshall Brothers, n.d.), 184.

[589] Ibid., 197.

[590] Spurgeon, *The Treasury of David,* Psalm 97:11.

[591] Plumer, W. S. *Studies in the Book of Psalms: Being a Critical and Expository Commentary, with Doctrinal and Practical Remarks on the Entire Psalter.* (Philadelphia; Edinburgh: J. B. Lippincott Company; A & C Black, 1872), 897.

[592] Spurgeon, C. H. *The Treasury of David: Psalms 88–110* (Vol. 4). (Marshall Brothers, n.d.), 224.

[593] Henry, M. *Matthew Henry's Commentary on the Whole Bible: Complete and Unabridged in One Volume.* (Peabody: Hendrickson, 1994), 886.

[594] Hallesby, Ole. *Prayer.* (London: Hodder & Stoughton, 1936).

[595] Spurgeon, C. H. "Samuel: An Example of Intercession." Sermon delivered May 9, 1880, Metropolitan Tabernacle

[596] https://www.azquotes.com › quote › 550439, accessed February 19, 2025.

[597] https://djameskennedy.org/devotional-detail/20150225-a-checklist-foryour-prayer-life, accessed February 19, 2025.

[598] The points stated are adapted from the sermon, "Unanswered Prayer" by John Linton cited in *Great Preaching on Prayer.* (Murfreesboro, TN: Sword of the Lord Publishers, 1988), 163–168.

[599] https://www.preceptaustin.org/prayer_quotes, accessed June 15, 2022.

[600] Moody, D. L. *Prevailing Prayer: What Hinders It?* (1884,) 87.

[601] https://www.preceptaustin.org/prayer_quotes, accessed June 15, 2022.

[602] *Matthew Henry's Concise Commentary,* 2 Corinthians 12:9.

[603] https://parade.com/1311380/kelseypelzer/prayer-quotes/, accessed May 30, 2022.

[604] Spurgeon, C. H. *The Treasury of David: Psalms 88–110* (Vol. 4). (Marshall Brothers, n.d.), 233.

[605] Plumer, W. S. *Studies in the Book of Psalms: Being a Critical and Expository Commentary, with Doctrinal and Practical Remarks on the Entire Psalter.* (Philadelphia; Edinburgh: J. B. Lippincott Company; A & C Black, 1872), 896.

[606] Bonar, Andrew A. *Christ and His Church in the Book of Psalms.* (1859).

[607] Henry, M. *Matthew Henry's Commentary on the Whole Bible: Complete and Unabridged in One Volume.* (Peabody: Hendrickson, 1994), 887.

[608] Spurgeon, C. H. *The Treasury of David: Psalms 88–110* (Vol. 4). (Marshall Brothers, n.d.), 235.

[609] Ibid., 240.

[610] Henry, M. *Matthew Henry's Commentary on the Whole Bible: Complete and Unabridged in One Volume.* (Peabody: Hendrickson, 1994), 887.

[611] Ibid.

[612] Spurgeon, C. H. *The Treasury of David: Psalms 88–110* (Vol. 4). (Marshall Brothers, n.d.), 241.

[613] Ironside, H. A. *Notes on the Book of Proverbs.* (Neptune, NJ: Loizeaux Bros, 1908), 415.

[614] Spurgeon, C. H. "God's Glory in the Building Up of Zion." Sermon delivered at the Metropolitan Tabernacle, published June 3, 1909.

[615] Spurgeon, C. H. "Prayer for the Church." Sermon delivered June 20, 1879, Metropolitan Tabernacle.

[616] Exell, J. S. *The Biblical Illustrator: The Psalms* (Vol. 4). (Fleming H. Revell Company; Francis Griffiths, 1909), 241.

[617] *Benson Commentary,* Psalm 102:27.

[618] Spurgeon, C. H. *The Treasury of David: Psalms 88–110* (Vol. 4). (Marshall Brothers, n.d.), 254.

[619] Melanchthon, Philip. *Dictionary of Burning Words of Brilliant Writers.* (1895), 466.

[620] Henry, M. *Matthew Henry's Commentary on the Whole Bible: Complete and Unabridged in One Volume.* (Peabody: Hendrickson, 1994), 889.

[621] Spurgeon, C. H. *The Treasury of David: Psalms 88–110* (Vol. 4). (Marshall Brothers, n.d.), 254.

[622] Hutson, Curtis, (ed). *Great Preaching on Thanksgiving.* (Murfreesboro: Sword of the Lord Publishers, 1987), 67–68.

[623] Simeon, C. *Horae Homileticae: Psalms, LXXIII–CL* (Vol. 6). (Samuel Holdsworth, 1836), 207.

[624] Spurgeon, C. H. "The First Note of My Song." Sermon delivered August 31, 1879, Metropolitan Tabernacle.

[625] Spurgeon, C. H. *The Treasury of David: Psalms 88–110* (Vol. 4). (Marshall Brothers, n.d.), 277.

[626] *Gill's Exposition of the Entire Bible,* Psalm 103:4.

[627] Henry, M. *Matthew Henry's Commentary on the Whole Bible: Complete and Unabridged in One Volume.* (Peabody: Hendrickson, 1994), 890.

[628] Spurgeon, C. H. *The Treasury of David: Psalms 88–110* (Vol. 4). (Marshall Brothers, n.d.), 277.

[629] Plumer, W. S. *Studies in the Book of Psalms: Being a Critical and Expository Commentary, with Doctrinal and Practical Remarks on the Entire Psalter.* (Philadelphia; Edinburgh: J. B. Lippincott Company; A & C Black, 1872), 917.

[630] The author borrowed three headings from C. H. Spurgeon's sermon, "Plenary Absolution," from the outline. The sermon was delivered at the Metropolitan Tabernacle.

[631] Spurgeon, C. H. "A Saviour Such as You Need." Sermon preached October 7, 1866, Metropolitan Tabernacle.

[632] Spurgeon, C. H. *Treasury of David,* Psalm 51.

[633] Perowne, J. J. S. The Book of Psalms; A New Translation, with Introductions and Notes, Explanatory and Critical (Fifth Edition, Revised, Vol. 2). (George Bell and Sons; Deighton Bell and Co., 1883), 228.

[634] Spurgeon, C. H. *The Treasury of David: Psalms 88–110* (Vol. 4). (Marshall Brothers, n.d.), 280.

[635] Ibid., 292.

[636] Horne, G. *A Commentary on the Book of Psalms.* (New York: Robert Carter & Brothers, 1856), 365.

[637] Henry, M. *Matthew Henry's Commentary on the Whole Bible: Complete and Unabridged in One Volume.* (Peabody: Hendrickson, 1994), 891.

[638] The author adapted the three headings from the sermon of Joseph Caryl on Psalm 104:9. Spurgeon, C. H. *The Treasury of David: Psalms 88–110* (Vol. 4). (Marshall Brothers, n.d.), 317.

[639] Ibid.

[640] Ibid., 304.

[641] Exell, J. S. *The Biblical Illustrator: The Psalms* (Vol. 4). (Fleming H. Revell Company; Francis Griffiths, 1909), 303.

[642] Lawson, G. *Exposition of the Book of Proverbs* (Vol. 1). (David Brown; W. Oliphant; F. Pillans; M. Ogle; Ogle, Duncan, and Co.; J. Nisbet, 1821), 62.

[643] Allen, L. C. *Psalms 101–150* (Revised) (Vol. 21). (Word, Incorporated, 2002), 46.

[644] Ibid.

[645] Spurgeon, C. H. *The Treasury of David: Psalms 88–110* (Vol. 4). (Marshall Brothers, n.d.), 311.

[646] Simeon, C. *Horae Homileticae: Psalms, LXXIII–CL* (Vol. 6). (Samuel Holdsworth, 1836), 218.

[647] Adapted. Source unknown.

[648] Henry, M. *Matthew Henry's Commentary on the Whole Bible: Complete and Unabridged in One Volume.* (Peabody: Hendrickson, 1994), 961.

[649] Bridges, Charles, 35.

[650] Spurgeon, *The Treasury of David,* Psalm 104:24.

[651] Exell, J. S. *The Biblical Illustrator: The Psalms* (Vol. 4). (Fleming H. Revell Company; Francis Griffiths, 1909), 365.

[652] Spurgeon, C. H. *The Treasury of David: Psalms 88–110* (Vol. 4). (Marshall Brothers, n.d.), 337.

[653] Ibid., 336.

[654] Maclaren, Alexander. *Maclaren's Expositions.* (GOD'S PROMISES TESTS), Psalm 105:19.

[655] Spence-Jones, H. D. M. (ed.) *Psalms* (Vol. 2). (London; New York: Funk & Wagnalls Company, 1909), 420.

[656] Maclaren, Alexander. *Maclaren's Expositions.* (GOD'S PROMISES TESTS), Psalm 105:19.

[657] Henry, M. *Matthew Henry's Commentary on the Whole Bible: Complete and Unabridged in One Volume.* (Peabody: Hendrickson, 1994), 895.

[658] Spurgeon, *The Treasury of David,* Psalm 105:19.

[659] Spurgeon, C. H. *The Treasury of David: Psalms 88–110* (Vol. 4). (Marshall Brothers, n.d.), 341.

[660] *Freedom of a Christian,* 59.

[661] Spurgeon, C. H. *The Treasury of David: Psalms 88–110* (Vol. 4). (Marshall Brothers, n.d.), 367.

[662] Ibid.

[663] Wiersbe, W. W. *Prayer, Praise & Promises,* 275.

[664] *Matthew Henry's Concise Commentary,* Psalm 106:15.

[665] "Christian Joy." https://www.reformedreader.org/rbs/broadus/broadus08.htm, accessed February 19, 2025.

[666] Spurgeon, C. H. *The Treasury of David: Psalms 88–110* (Vol. 4). (Marshall Brothers, n.d.), 370.

[667] Ibid., 373.

[668] Henry, M. *Matthew Henry's Commentary on the Whole Bible: Complete and Unabridged in One Volume.* (Peabody: Hendrickson, 1994), 898.

[669] Keil, C. F. & F. Delitzsch. Commentary on the Old Testament (Vol. 1). (Peabody, MA: Hendrickson, 1996), 30.

[670] Plumer, W. S. *Studies in the Book of Psalms: Being a Critical and Expository Commentary, with Doctrinal and Practical Remarks on the Entire Psalter.* (Philadelphia; Edinburgh: J. B. Lippincott Company; A & C Black, 1872), 960.

[671] Exell, J. S. *The Biblical Illustrator: The Psalms* (Vol. 1). (Fleming H. Revell Company; Francis Griffiths, 1909), 293.

[672] Ibid.

[673] Henry, M. *Matthew Henry's Commentary on the Whole Bible: Complete and Unabridged in One Volume.* (Peabody: Hendrickson, 1994), 899.

[674] Spurgeon, C. H. *The Treasury of David: Psalms 88–110* (Vol. 4). (Marshall Brothers, n.d.), 402.

[675] Spurgeon, C. H. "Song for the Free, and Hope for the Bound." Sermon delivered November 6, 1887, Metropolitan Tabernacle.

[676] Exell, J. S. *The Biblical Illustrator: The Minor Prophets* (Vol. 2). (Fleming H. Revell Company, n.d.), 44.

[677] Henry, M. *Matthew Henry's Commentary on the Whole Bible: Complete and Unabridged in One Volume.* (Peabody: Hendrickson, 1994), 1499.

[678] Spurgeon, C. H. "Truth Stranger Than Fiction." Sermon delivered May 30, 1886, Metropolitan Tabernacle.

[679] Spurgeon, C. H. *The Treasury of David: Psalms 88–110* (Vol. 4). (Marshall Brothers, n.d.), 408.

[680] Spence-Jones, H. D. M., ed. *Psalms* (Vol. 3). (Funk & Wagnalls Company, 1909), 17.

[681] Jones, G. C. *"1000 Illustrations for Preaching and Teaching."* (Nashville, TN: Broadman & Holman Publishers, 1986), 152.

[682] Spurgeon, C. H. *The Treasury of David: Psalms 27–57* (Vol. 2). (Marshall Brothers, n.d.), 477.

[683] Spurgeon, C. H. *The Treasury of David: Psalms 88–110* (Vol. 4). (Marshall Brothers, n.d.), 436.

[684] Ibid., 437.

[685] Spence-Jones, H. D. M., ed. *Isaiah* (Vol. 2). (Funk & Wagnalls Company, 1910), 330.

[686] Spurgeon, C. H. *The Treasury of David: Psalms 88–110* (Vol. 4). (Marshall Brothers, n.d.), 444.

[687] Plumer, W. S. *Studies in the Book of Psalms: Being a Critical and Expository Commentary, with Doctrinal and Practical Remarks on the Entire Psalter.* (Philadelphia; Edinburgh: J. B. Lippincott Company; A & C Black, 1872), 980.

[688] Davies, S. Cited in *The Biblical Illustrator,* Psalm 11:10 ("Religion the Highest Wisdom").

[689] Jeremiah, David. *The David Jeremiah Study Bible.* (Worthy Publishing (November 1, 2016), 805.

[690] Spence-Jones, H. D. M. (ed.) Proverbs. (London; New York: Funk & Wagnalls Company, 1909), 56.

[691] Bobgan, Martin and Deidre. *Psycho Heresy.* "Santa Barbara, CA: EastGate Publishers, 1987), 7.

[692] Spurgeon, C. H. "Heart's-Ease." Sermon delivered August 27, 1865, Metropolitan Tabernacle.

[693] Horne, G. *A Commentary on the Book of Psalms.* (New York: Robert Carter & Brothers, 1856), 409.

[694] Spence-Jones, H. D. M., ed. *Proverbs.* (Funk & Wagnalls Company, 1909), 81.

[695] Henry, M. *Matthew Henry's Commentary on the Whole Bible: Complete and Unabridged in One Volume.* (Peabody: Hendrickson, 1994), 1245.

[696] Spurgeon, C. H. "Grace Abounding," (Sermon delivered May 23, 1863). https://www.studylight.org/commentary/hosea/14-4.html, accessed September 1, 2021.

[697] Pink, A. W. *The Attributes of God.*

[698] Spurgeon, C. H. *The Treasury of David: Psalms 111–119* (Vol. 5). (Marshall Brothers, n.d.), 30.

[699] Henry, M. *Matthew Henry's Commentary on the Whole Bible: Complete and Unabridged in One Volume.* (Peabody: Hendrickson, 1994), 908.

[700] Ibid.

[701] Cited by T. De Witt Talmage in Exell, J. S. *The Biblical Illustrator: The Psalms* (Vol. 4). (Fleming H. Revell Company; Francis Griffiths, 1909), 466. Adapted.

[702] Spurgeon, C. H. "Crowning Blessings Ascribed to God" (Sermon # 1475), May 18, 1879. (The second sermon in commemoration of the completion of 25 years of his Ministry in the midst of the church assembling in the Tabernacle).

[703] Henry, M. *Matthew Henry's Commentary on the Whole Bible: Complete and Unabridged in One Volume.* (Peabody: Hendrickson, 1994), 909.

[704] Spurgeon, C. H. *Morning and Evening.* (London: Passmore & Alabaster), July 2 (Morning).

[705] Henry, M. *Matthew Henry's Commentary on the Whole Bible: Complete and Unabridged in One Volume.* (Peabody: Hendrickson, 1994), 909.

[706] Boice, J. M. *Psalms 107–150: An Expositional Commentary.* (Grand Rapids, MI: Baker Books, 2005), 940.

[707] Spence-Jones, H. D. M. (ed.) *Psalms* (Vol. 3). (London; New York: Funk & Wagnalls Company, 1909), 206.

[708] Spurgeon, C. H. *The Treasury of David: Psalms 111–119* (Vol. 5). (Marshall Brothers, n.d.), 57.

[709] Spurgeon, C. H. *Living Praise. My Sermon Notes—From Genesis to Proverbs.* (Funk & Wagnalls, 1891), 240.

[710] Spurgeon, *The Treasury of David,* Psalm 115:17.

[711] McGee, J. V. *Thru the Bible Commentary: Poetry (Psalms 90–150)* (electronic ed., Vol. 19). (Thomas Nelson, 1991), 82.

[712] Spurgeon, *The Treasury of David,* Psalm 115:17.

[713] Pink, A. W. *Comfort for Christians.* (Lafayette, IN: Sovereign Grace Publishers, 2007), 77.

[714] McCarthy, Jim. "Three Reasons the Saint's Death Is Precious in the Sight of The Lord," June 24, 2024. https://reformation21.org/three-reasons-the-saints-death-is-precious-in-the-sight-of-the-lord/, accessed August 3, 2025. The author borrowed only the names of the three reasons.

[715] Spurgeon, *The Treasury of David,* Psalm 117 (Introduction).

[716] Piper, John. "Everlasting Truth for the Joy of All Peoples," Psalm 117. October 26, 2003. https://www.desiringgod.org/messages/everlasting-truth-for-the-joy-of-all-peoples, accessed July 7, 2018.

[717] *The Church Missionary Review, Volume 43.* (London: Church Missionary Society, Salisbury Square, Jan. 1892), 65.

[718] Spurgeon, Charles H. *The Complete Works of C. H. Spurgeon, Volume 14: Sermons 788-847.* (Delmarva Publications, Inc.).

[719] Henry, M. *Matthew Henry's Commentary on the Whole Bible: Complete and Unabridged in One Volume.* (Peabody: Hendrickson, 1994), 912.

[720] Lockyer, Herbert, Sr. *Psalms: A Devotional Commentary.* (Grand Rapids: Kregel Publications, 1993), Psalm 118: 8.

[721] Spurgeon, C. H. "An Epistle Illustrated by a Psalm." Sermon delivered June 19, 1884, Metropolitan Tabernacle.

[722] Spurgeon, C. H. *The Treasury of David: Psalms 111–119* (Vol. 5). (Marshall Brothers, n.d.), 107.

[723] Ibid., 110.

[724] Henry, M. *Matthew Henry's Commentary on the Whole Bible: Complete and Unabridged in One Volume.* (Peabody: Hendrickson, 1994), 913.

[725] Spurgeon, C. H. *The Treasury of David: Psalms 111–119* (Vol. 5). (Marshall Brothers, n.d.), 128.

[726] Spurgeon, *The Treasury of David,* Psalm 119:3.

[727] *Gill's Exposition of the Entire Bible,* Psalm 119:11.

[728] Hindson, E. E., & Kroll, W. M., eds. *KJV Bible Commentary.* (Thomas Nelson, 1994), 1148.

[729] Exell, J. S. *The Biblical Illustrator: The Psalms* (Vol. 5). (Fleming H. Revell Company; Francis Griffiths, 1909), 23. Adapted.

[730] Spurgeon, C. H. *The Treasury of David: Psalms 111–119* (Vol. 5). (Marshall Brothers, n.d.), 208.

[731] Spurgeon, *The Treasury of David,* Psalm 119:38.

[732] Ibid., Psalm 119:44.

[733] Kirkpatrick, A. F. Psalm 119:45.

[734] Spurgeon, *The Treasury of David,* Psalm 119:45.

[735] Alexander, J. A. *The Psalms Translated and Explained.* (Edinburgh: Andrew Elliot; James Thin, 1864), 488.

[736] MacDonald, W. (A. Farstad, Ed.) *Believer's Bible Commentary: Old and New Testaments.* (Thomas Nelson, 1995), 740.

[737] Henry, M. *Matthew Henry's Commentary on the Whole Bible: Complete and Unabridged in One Volume.* (Peabody: Hendrickson, 1994), 918.

[738] *Bartholomew Ashwood's Heavenly Trade,* 1688.

[739] Spurgeon, C. H. *Morning and Evening.* (London: Passmore & Alabaster), May 31 (Evening).

[740] Horne, G. *A Commentary on the Book of Psalms.* (New York: Robert Carter & Brothers, 1856), 437–438.

[741] Bridges, C. *Exposition of Psalm 119: As Illustrative of the Character and Exercises of Christian Experience* (Seventeenth Edition). (New York: Robert Carter & Brothers, 1861), 82.

[742] Plumer, W. S. *Studies in the Book of Psalms: Being a Critical and Expository Commentary, with Doctrinal and Practical Remarks on the Entire Psalter.* (Philadelphia; Edinburgh: J. B. Lippincott Company; A & C Black, 1872), 1047.

[743] Redpath, Alan, *The Making of a Man of God: Lessons from the Life of David.* (Alan Redpath Library)

[744] MacDonald, W. (A. Farstad, Ed.) *Believer's Bible Commentary: Old and New Testaments.* (Thomas Nelson, 1995), 741.

[745] Moody, D. L. *Pleasures and Profit in Bible Study.* (Grand Rapids: Fleming Revell Publishers, 1895), 32–33.

[746] Spurgeon, C. H. "The Bible." Sermon delivered March 18, 1885, Metropolitan Tabernacle.

[747] Spurgeon, C. H. *The Treasury of David: Psalms 88–110* (Vol. 4). (Marshall Brothers, n.d.), 403.

[748] Horne, G. *A Commentary on the Book of Psalms.* (New York: Robert Carter & Brothers, 1856), 451.

[749] Henry, M. *Matthew Henry's Commentary on the Whole Bible: Complete and Unabridged in One Volume.* (Peabody: Hendrickson, 1994), 923.

[750] Spurgeon, *The Treasury of David,* Psalm 119:126.

[751] Ibid., Psalm 119:126.

[752] Ibid., Psalm 119:129.

[753] *Jamieson-Fausset-Brown Bible Commentary,* Psalm 119:130.

[754] Henry, M. *Matthew Henry's Commentary on the Whole Bible: Complete and Unabridged in One Volume.* (Peabody: Hendrickson, 1994), 925.

[755] Horne, G. *A Commentary on the Book of Psalms.* (New York: Robert Carter & Brothers, 1856), 457.

[756] Bridges, Charles. *Exposition of Psalm 119,* Psalm 119:47.

[757] Augustine of Hippo, in P. Schaff (Ed.), & A. C. Coxe (Trans.). *Saint Augustin: Expositions on the Book of Psalms* (Vol. 8). (Christian Literature Company, 1888), 581.

[758] *Matthew Poole's Commentary,* Psalm 119:136.

[759] Henry, M. *Matthew Henry's Commentary on the Whole Bible: Complete and Unabridged in One Volume.* (Peabody: Hendrickson, 1994), 925.

[760] Ibid., 928–929.

[761] Exell, J. S. *The Biblical Illustrator: The Psalms* (Vol. 4). (Fleming H. Revell Company; Francis Griffiths, 1909), 148.

[762] Ibid.

[763] Henry, M. *Matthew Henry's Commentary on the Whole Bible: Complete and Unabridged in One Volume.* (Peabody: Hendrickson, 1994), 929.

[764] Newton, R. cited in *The Biblical Illustrator,* Psalm 120:2 ("Lying Lips").

[765] Spurgeon, C. H. *The Treasury of David: Psalms 120–150* (Vol. 6). (Marshall Brothers, n.d.), 14.

[766] Boice, J. M. *Psalms 107–150: An Expositional Commentary.* (Grand Rapids, MI: Baker Books, 2005), 1079.

[767] Spurgeon, C. H. *The Treasury of David: Psalms 120–150* (Vol. 6). (Marshall Brothers, n.d.), 14.

[768] Spence-Jones, H. D. M., ed. *Psalms* (Vol. 3). (Funk & Wagnalls Company, 1909), 189.

[769] Plumer, W. S. *Studies in the Book of Psalms: Being a Critical and Expository Commentary, with Doctrinal and Practical Remarks on the Entire Psalter.* (Philadelphia; Edinburgh: J. B. Lippincott Company; A & C Black, 1872), 1103.

[770] Maclaren, Alexander. In W. Robertson Nicholl, ed. *The Expositor's Bible: The Psalms* (Vol. III: Psalms XC–CL). (London: Hodder and Stoughton, 1894), 308.

[771] Spurgeon, Charles H. *The Treasury of David: Psalms 120–150* (Vol. 6). (New York, NY: Funk & Wagnalls Company), 443.

[772] Exell, J. S. The Biblical Illustrator: The Psalms (Vol. 5). (New York; Chicago; Toronto: Fleming H. Revell Company, n.d.), 181.

[773] *Matthew Henry's Commentary on the Bible,* Psalm 124:1.

[774] Cited in Spurgeon, *The Treasury of David,* Psalm 125. "EXPLANATORY NOTES AND QUAINT SAYINGS."

[775] Plumer, W. S. *Studies in the Book of Psalms: Being a Critical and Expository Commentary, with Doctrinal and Practical Remarks on the Entire Psalter.* (Philadelphia; Edinburgh: J. B. Lippincott Company; A & C Black, 1872), 1109.

[776] *Clarke's Commentary,* Psalm 125:2.

[777] Horne, G. *A Commentary on the Book of Psalms.* (New York: Robert Carter & Brothers, 1856), 474.

[778] A. A. Milne's beloved donkey, Eeyore (a bit depressed and gloomy donkey), was first introduced on Oct. 14, 1926, in Milne's classic children's book *Winnie-the-Pooh.*

[779] Spence-Jones, H. D. M. (ed.) *Psalms* (Vol. 3). (London; New York: Funk & Wagnalls Company, 1909), 223.

[780] Spurgeon, C. H. *The Treasury of David: Psalms 120–150* (Vol. 6). (London; Edinburgh; New York: Marshall Brothers, n.d.), 70–71.

[781] MacDonald, W. (A. Farstad, Ed.) *Believer's Bible Commentary: Old and New Testaments.* (Thomas Nelson, 1995), 755.

[782] Spurgeon, C. H. *The Treasury of David: Psalms 120–150* (Vol. 6). (London; Edinburgh; New York: Marshall Brothers, n.d.), 85.

[783] Spence-Jones, H. D. M. (ed.) *Psalms* (Vol. 3). (London; New York: Funk & Wagnalls Company, 1909), 236.

[784] Spence-Jones, H. D. M. (ed.) Proverbs. (London; New York: Funk & Wagnalls Company, 1909), 5.

[785] Harman, A. *Psalms: A Mentor Commentary* (Vol. 1–2). (Ross-shire, Great Britain: Mentor, 2011), 917.

[786] Spurgeon, C. H. *The Treasury of David: Psalms 120–150* (Vol. 6). (London; Edinburgh; New York: Marshall Brothers, n.d.), 97.

[787] Ibid., 98.

[788] Spence-Jones, H. D. M., ed. *Psalms* (Vol. 3). (Funk & Wagnalls Company, 1909), 236.

[789] Henry, M. *Matthew Henry's Commentary on the Whole Bible: Complete and Unabridged in One Volume.* (Peabody: Hendrickson, 1994), 934.

[790] Horne, G. *A Commentary on the Book of Psalms.* (New York: Robert Carter & Brothers, 1856), 480.

791 Lewis, C. S. *Mere Christianity,* 51.

792 Watson, Thomas. "The Beatitudes: Concerning Persecution." https://www.gracegems.org/Watson/beatitudes9.htm, accessed April 6, 2021.

793 Barclay, W. (Ed.). *The Gospel of Matthew* (Vol. 1). (Philadelphia, PA: The Westminster John Knox Press, 1976), 116.

794 Morris, L. *The Gospel According to Matthew.* (Grand Rapids, MI; Leicester, England: W.B. Eerdmans; Inter-Varsity Press, 1992), 256.

795 Spurgeon, C. H. "A Word for the Persecuted," (Sermon delivered August 16, 1864), 1 Samuel 20:10. https://www.spurgeon.org/resource-library/sermons/a-word-for-the-persecuted/#flipbook/, accessed February 14, 2021.

796 Cochran, Gregory C. "Christian Persecution as Explained by Jesus (Matthew 5:10–12)." SBJT-18.1-Christian-Persecution-as-explained-by-Jesus-Matthew-5-10-12.pdf, 11. Accessed March 10, 2021.

797 Morris, L. *The Gospel According to Matthew.* (Grand Rapids, MI; Leicester, England: W.B. Eerdmans; Inter-Varsity Press, 1992), 601.

798 Spurgeon. "There Is Forgiveness." *The Biblical Illustrator,* Psalm 130:4.

799 Ibid.

800 *Barnes Notes on the Bible,* Psalm 130:4.

801 Plumer, W. S. *Studies in the Book of Psalms: Being a Critical and Expository Commentary, with Doctrinal and Practical Remarks on the Entire Psalter.* (Philadelphia; Edinburgh: J. B. Lippincott Company; A & C Black, 1872), 1125.

802 Spurgeon, *The Treasury of David,* Psalm 130: 4.

803 Alexander, J. A. *The Psalms Translated and Explained.* (Edinburgh: Andrew Elliot; James Thin, 1864), 521.

804 Henry, M. *Matthew Henry's Commentary on the Whole Bible: Complete and Unabridged in One Volume.* (Peabody: Hendrickson, 1994), 935.

805 Perowne, J. J. S. The Book of Psalms; A New Translation, with Introductions and Notes, Explanatory and Critical (Fifth Edition, Revised, Vol. 2). (George Bell and Sons; Deighton Bell and Co., 1883), 407.

806 McKane, William. *Proverbs.* Old Testament Library, 490, cited in *The NET Bible Notes Bible First Edition Notes.* (Biblical Studies Press, 2006), Pr 16:18.

807 Henry, M. *Matthew Henry's Commentary on the Whole Bible: Complete and Unabridged in One Volume.* (Peabody: Hendrickson, 1994), 936.

808 Simeon, C. *Horae Homileticae: Psalms, LXXIII–CL* (Vol. 6). (Samuel Holdsworth, 1836), 423.

809 Packer, J. I. *Introduction in Psalms.* (Wheaton, IL: Crossway Books, 1993), 287.

810 Wiersbe, Warren. *Prayer, Praise, and Promises.* (Grand Rapids, MI: Baker Books, 1991), 337.

811 Spurgeon, C. H. *The Treasury of David: Psalms 120–150* (Vol. 6). (London; Edinburgh; New York: Marshall Brothers, n.d.), 145.

[812] Adapted or re-worded from Warren Wiersbe. *Prayer, Praises, and Promises,* 338.

[813] Spurgeon, C. H. *The Treasury of David: Psalms 120–150* (Vol. 6). (London; Edinburgh; New York: Marshall Brothers, n.d.), 146.

[814] Ibid., 147.

[815] Scarborough, L. R. *With Christ After the Lost.* (Nashville: Broadman Press, 1952), 12–13.

[816] Spurgeon, C. H. *Lectures to My Students.* (Grand Rapids: Zondervan, 1970), 197.

[817] Horne, G. *A Commentary on the Book of Psalms.* (New York: Robert Carter & Brothers, 1856), 491.

[818] https://www.christianquotes.info/quotes-by-topic/quotes-about-unity/#ixzz5NDnmejoX, accessed August 4, 2018.

[819] Plumer, W. S. *Studies in the Book of Psalms: Being a Critical and Expository Commentary, with Doctrinal and Practical Remarks on the Entire Psalter.* (Philadelphia; Edinburgh: J. B. Lippincott Company; A & C Black, 1872), 1141–1142). See 1 Chronicles 9:33.

[820] Spence-Jones, H. D. M., ed. *2 Timothy.* (Funk & Wagnalls Company, 1909), 18.

[821] Spurgeon, C. H. *The Treasury of David: Psalms 120–150* (Vol. 6). (London; Edinburgh; New York: Marshall Brothers, n.d.), 177.

[822] Ibid.

[823] Ibid.

[824] Ibid.

[825] Ibid., 184.

[826] Ibid., 183.

[827] Ibid., 204.

[828] Henry, M. *Matthew Henry's Commentary on the Whole Bible: Complete and Unabridged in One Volume.* (Peabody: Hendrickson, 1994), 1330.

[829] Spurgeon, C. H. *The Treasury of David: Psalms 120–150* (Vol. 6). (London; Edinburgh; New York: Marshall Brothers, n.d.), 204.

[830] Morris, L. *The Epistle to the Romans.* (W. B. Eerdmans; Inter-Varsity Press, 1988), 319.

[831] Plumer, W. S. *Studies in the Book of Psalms: Being a Critical and Expository Commentary, with Doctrinal and Practical Remarks on the Entire Psalter.* (Philadelphia; Edinburgh: J. B. Lippincott Company; A & C Black, 1872), 1158.

[832] Henry, M. *Matthew Henry's Commentary on the Whole Bible: Complete and Unabridged in One Volume.* (Peabody: Hendrickson, 1994), 941.

[833] Spurgeon, C. H. *The Treasury of David: Psalms 120–150* (Vol. 6). (London; Edinburgh; New York: Marshall Brothers, n.d.), 245.

[834] Bounds, E. M. *The Weapon of Prayer.* (Radford, VA: Wilder Publications, 2008), 25.

[835] This entry was inspired by and somewhat adapted from Spurgeon's sermon, "Singing in the Ways of the Lord," Delivered August 11, 1881, Metropolitan Tabernacle.

[836] Henry, M. *Matthew Henry's Commentary on the Whole Bible: Complete and Unabridged in One Volume*. (Peabody: Hendrickson, 1994), 941.

[837] Spurgeon, C. H. *The Treasury of David: Psalms 120–150* (Vol. 6). (London; Edinburgh; New York: Marshall Brothers, n.d.), 245–246.

[838] Henry, M. *Matthew Henry's Commentary on the Whole Bible: Complete and Unabridged in One Volume*. (Peabody: Hendrickson, 1994), 941.

[839] Spurgeon, C. H. "The Immutability of God" (Sermon), January 7, 1855.

[840] Henry, M. *Matthew Henry's Commentary on the Whole Bible: Complete and Unabridged in One Volume*. (Peabody: Hendrickson, 1994), 987.

[841] Packer, J. I. *Knowing God.* (Madison, Wisconsin: Intervarsity Press, 1977).

[842] Spurgeon, C. H. *The Treasury of David: Psalms 120–150* (Vol. 6). (London; Edinburgh; New York: Marshall Brothers, n.d.), 262.

[843] "The Bible and Abortion." Heritage House Literature. www.abortionfacts.com/literature/literature_9410cv.asp, accessed October 15, 2011.

[844] Ibid.

[845] Roberts, Alexander, and James Donaldson, Ed. *The Ante-Nicene Fathers.* (New York: Charles Scribner's Sons, 1905), 148.

[846] *Commentary,* Exodus 21:22, 1563.

[847] Spurgeon, C. H. *The Treasury of David: Psalms 120–150* (Vol. 6). (London; Edinburgh; New York: Marshall Brothers, n.d.), 264.

[848] Henry, M. *Matthew Henry's Commentary on the Whole Bible: Complete and Unabridged in One Volume*. (Peabody: Hendrickson, 1994), 942.

[849] Ibid., 943.

[850] Ibid.

[851] Spurgeon, C. H. "The Snare of the Fowler." Sermon delivered March 29, 1857, New Park Street Chapel.

[852] *Benson Commentary,* Psalm 141:9.

[853] Henry, M. *Matthew Henry's Commentary on the Whole Bible: Complete and Unabridged in One Volume*. (Peabody: Hendrickson, 1994), 944.

[854] Spurgeon, C. H. *Faith's Checkbook,* November 10.

[855] Spurgeon, C. H. *Morning and Evening.* (London: Passmore & Alabaster), August 19 (Evening).

[856] Henry, M. *Matthew Henry's Commentary on the Whole Bible: Complete and Unabridged in One Volume*. (Peabody: Hendrickson, 1994), 2433.

[857] Augustine of Hippo, in P. Schaff (Ed.), & A. C. Coxe (Trans.). *Saint Augustin: Expositions on the Book of Psalms* (Vol. 8). (Christian Literature Company, 1888), 653.

[858] Henry, M. *Matthew Henry's Commentary on the Whole Bible: Complete and Unabridged in One Volume.* (Peabody: Hendrickson, 1994), 946.

[859] Spurgeon, *The Treasury of David,* Psalm 143:10.

[860] *Clarke's Commentary,* Psalm 144 (Introduction).

[861] Harman, A. *Psalms: A Mentor Commentary* (Vol. 1–2). (Ross-shire, Great Britain: Mentor, 2011), 133.

[862] Hastings, James. *Great Texts on the Bible,* 232.

[863] Henry, M. *Matthew Henry's Commentary on the Whole Bible: Complete and Unabridged in One Volume.* (Peabody: Hendrickson, 1994), 754.

[864] Ibid., 948.

[865] Spurgeon, C. H. *The Treasury of David: Psalms 120–150* (Vol. 6). (London; Edinburgh; New York: Marshall Brothers, n.d.), 403.

[866] Horne, G. *A Commentary on the Book of Psalms.* (New York: Robert Carter & Brothers, 1856), 526.

[867] Plumer, W. S. *Studies in the Book of Psalms: Being a Critical and Expository Commentary, with Doctrinal and Practical Remarks on the Entire Psalter.* (Philadelphia; Edinburgh: J. B. Lippincott Company; A & C Black, 1872), 1194.

[868] Cowman, L. B. *Streams in the Desert.* (Grand Rapids: Zondervan, 2006), January 18.

[869] Henry, M. *Matthew Henry's Commentary on the Whole Bible: Complete and Unabridged in One Volume.* (Peabody: Hendrickson, 1994), 950.

[870] Spurgeon, C. H. *The Treasury of David: Psalms 120–150* (Vol. 6). (London; Edinburgh; New York: Marshall Brothers, n.d.), 415.

[871] Spurgeon. *The Treasury of David,* Psalm 42:7.

[872] Spurgeon, C. H. *The Treasury of David: Psalms 120–150* (Vol. 6). (London; Edinburgh; New York: Marshall Brothers, n.d.), 415.

[873] Wiersbe, W. W. *With the Word Bible Commentary.* (Nashville: Thomas Nelson, 1991), Ps. 147.

[874] Dixon, A. C. "Through Night to Morning" (Sermon No. 1), 1913.

[875] Spurgeon, C. H. *The Treasury of David: Psalms 120–150* (Vol. 6). (London; Edinburgh; New York: Marshall Brothers, n.d.), 439.

[876] Simeon, C. *Horae Homileticae: Philippians to 1 Timothy* (Vol. 18). (Holdsworth and Ball, 1833), 147.

[877] Spurgeon, C. H. "He Came; He Is Coming." Sermon delivered December 25.

[878] Pink, A. W. *The Godhood of God.*

[879] Spurgeon, C. H. "Hallelujah! Hallelujah!" (Sermon #2421), June 19, 1887.

[880] Packer, J. I. *Introduction in Psalms.* (Wheaton, IL: Crossway Books, 1993), 370.

[881] Henry, M. *Matthew Henry's Commentary on the Whole Bible: Complete and Unabridged in One Volume.* (Peabody: Hendrickson, 1994), 954.

[882] Ibid.

www.ingramcontent.com/pod-product-compliance
Lightning Source LLC
Chambersburg PA
CBHW030532100426
42813CB00001B/225

·